84

4 300
80 M

LUCY STONE

LUCY STONE

Speaking Out for Equality

Andrea Moore Kerr

RUTGERS UNIVERSITY PRESS

New Brunswick, New Jersey

Library of Congress Cataloging-in-Publication Data

Kerr, Andrea Moore, 1940–
    Lucy Stone : speaking out for equality / Andrea Moore Kerr.
      p.   cm.
    Includes bibliographical references and index.
    ISBN 0-8135-1859-8 (cloth) — ISBN 0-8135-1860-1
(pbk.)
    1. Stone, Lucy, 1818–1893. 2. Feminists—United States—
Biography. 3. Suffragettes—United States—Biography.
4. Abolitionists—United States—Biography.   I. Title.
HQ1413,S73K47   1992
305.42′092—dc20
[B]   92-6159
                                   CIP

British Cataloging-in-Publication information available

For my family, with thanks

Joe,

Amelia,

Megan,

Joey,

and Steven

Contents

Acknowledgments

Anyone who has written a book of this kind knows the large debt owed to archivists and librarians, to friends and family, to fellow writers and historians. To single out a few, I am grateful first to Sarah Pritchard for her enthusiasm and bibiliographic guidance at the Library of Congress; to Jacqueline Goggin for her invaluable help in the manuscript division there; to Eva Moseley, who allowed me access to the unindexed papers of the Blackwell Family at the Schlesinger Library; and to Sylvia Buck, town librarian extraordinaire, for her interest in the project.

I wish to acknowledge as well the invaluable assistance of fellow biographers Amelia Fry, Ruth Price, and Liva Baker, reserving my most heartfelt thanks for Carolyn Karcher, whose helpful comments and encouragement kept me going. I thank other friends and fellow historians for reading and commenting on the work in progress, and I am grateful to Gail Ross, my agent, for sticking with Lucy Stone through the long writing process. My thanks go also to John Blackwell, who shared his knowledge of the Blackwells with me, and to Elinor Rice Hays and Leslie Wheeler for their early help and guidance.

I owe a large debt of gratitude to the Library of Congress, which understands the scholar-writer's need for a "room of one's own." To Victoria Hill, Suzanne Thorin, and especially to Bruce Martin, a large and heartfelt thank you.

A grant from the National Endowment for the Humanities enabled me to travel to New England and examine the collections there. Most of my support, however, came from my husband and family—who bore with Lucy Stone and me for the seven years it took to write this book. Thank you all.

Introduction

The nineteenth century gave us three great woman suffragists: Lucy Stone, Elizabeth Cady Stanton, and Susan B. Anthony. Today, few are aware of Stone's importance. In the course of research into nineteenth-century American women, I read *Morning Star,* Elinor Rice Hays's fine biography of abolitionist and suffragist Lucy Stone. Afterward, I asked myself how it was that this great woman had lost her proper place in history. Hays's view of history as territory furnishes a partial answer. Stanton and Anthony, the two great nineteenth-century workers for women's rights whose conduct precipitated the first great schism in the suffrage ranks, were also the authors of the *History of Woman Suffrage.* Their insistence upon "whittling down" Stone's share in that history is part of the story told in this book. Stone's role in that history is part of the story told in this book. Stone's political activity is another part; and the story of her marriage—a remarkable and doomed effort at an equitable union—forms still another part.

Lucy Stone was a difficult subject for a biography. I am all too aware that hagiography is poor history, and I respect biography as a historian's tool. Stone posed a challenge to credibility: she was a noble woman, selfless to a fault; she hewed to the high ground, leaving her biographer to grasp at flaws. Rather than risk the "hagiography" label, I was tempted to turn the lens of popular psychology on Stone's behavior, seeing her heroism as dysfunction, her noble silence as repression, her altruism as bordering on pathology, and her self-abnegation as a form of co-dependency. Instead, I have tried simply to present the facts, leaving judgments to the reader.

Lucy Stone was in every sense a pioneer. In 1847, she launched her public speaking career on behalf of abolition and woman's rights. A natural and charismatic orator, she held crowds of two and three thousand spellbound. Stone's fame was so widespread that in 1854, P. T. Barnum tried to hire her for a series of lectures.[1] An adroit politician,

Stone lobbied legislatures and circulated petitions on behalf of suffrage and increased legal and property rights for women. She was the first woman to speak full-time for woman's rights, first woman from the state of Massachusetts to earn a college degree, and the first woman to keep her birth name after marriage. Beginning in 1850, Stone was the prime mover in the organization and presentation of a series of national woman's rights conventions. Though she curtailed her public activity between 1857 and 1865, immediately after the Civil War, she resumed a leading role in the woman's rights movement, a role she held until her death in 1893.

Stone met her historical nemesis just after the Civil War. When the exigencies of Reconstruction made clear that only black males were to be enfranchised by the Fourteenth and Fifteenth Amendments, Stanton and Anthony led a small minority of woman suffragists in a campaign to defeat the amendments. "We are lost if we turn from the middle principle and argue for one class," Stone pleaded, urging her fellow suffragists not to stand in the way of votes for the newly emancipated slaves.

The anti–Fifteenth Amendment campaign was the first of a number of tactical issues to divide the women over the next two decades, and it furnishes an ugly chapter in the story of women's march for equality. In its time, it caused deep and costly rifts in the ranks of suffrage supporters. The political story of schisms and splinter groups, of tactical squabbles and personal resentments would be unimportant were it not for the high price Stone paid. The rift lasted for twenty years, during which time Stanton and Anthony wrote the *History of Woman Suffrage,* a multi-volume, invaluable compendium of early woman's rights activity that skips over the causes of the split and gives short shrift to the massive, lasting political contribution of Lucy Stone to the cause of woman's rights.

Stone's organizing activity was prodigious and groundbreaking; the lobbying machine she set in place eventually paved the way to suffrage. If she was single-minded to a fault and inclined at times to righteous rigidity, Stone possessed a bedrock integrity, an overarching intelligence, and an undefinable gift for touching the hearts of those who came in contact with her—whether by the thousands in the great lecture halls of the nineteenth century or in a moment's audience in a railway carriage. She was a great woman; she deserves a prominent place in history. A longtime co-worker, Harriet Winslow Sewall, wrote that "her sex can never show enough gratitude to her." She went on to write, "The only weakness I have seen in her is her inveterate dislike of Mrs. Stanton, but if she had no weakness, I am afraid she would be taken up to live with the angels."[2]

In her eulogy of fellow abolitionist Abby Kelley Foster, Stone quoted an 1851 speech in which Foster told the assembled crowd: "Sisters, bloody feet wore smooth the path by which you come up here." Stone knew all too well the price she and her coworkers in the great reform movements of the nineteenth century paid for the rights many women today take for granted. Possessing a singular courage, armed with an unshakable belief in the power of the individual, Lucy Stone spoke out— against slavery, for rights for women, for equality.

CHAPTER ONE

"EXTRA! EXTRA!
Lucy Stone Is Dead!"

The day of the funeral, October 21, was another in a string of Indian summer days that settled on Boston in the autumn of 1893. The weather prompted the grieving widower to remark in a letter to his sister on the "satire" of death occurring in the midst of such "golden stillness," when the "air is like wine."[1] Outside the Church of the Disciples, along Brookline and Warren streets, a crowd had been gathering since early morning, though the memorial service for Lucy Stone would not begin until two o'clock. The church could seat only a thousand, and many more were expected. "The death of no woman in America had ever called out so general a tribute of public respect and esteem," conceded an old opponent.[2]

Mourners stood talking quietly together while they waited for the church doors to open. They were an unusual crowd; Boston Brahmins and well-known politicians standing cheek by jowl with farmers' wives and domestic workers. Some had traveled long distances by rail; others had ridden out from downtown Boston in carriages or on the electric cars. In the weeks preceding Stone's death, the *Boston Globe* carried regular bulletins on her deteriorating health. After her death at ten forty-five on the night of October 18, the news flashed across telegraph wires. "EXTRA! EXTRA!" trumpeted the *Globe*, "Lucy Stone is Dead!"[3]

The nation's dailies reported her death the next day, and newspapers around the globe—in London, Paris, Brussels, Constantinople—picked up the story. "Lucy Stone Is Dead"; "A Great Woman Gone!" "Lucy Stone Blackwell Dies!" The *New York Times* ran a ten-paragraph obituary; the *Washington Post* printed a five-paragraph notice on its front page. Editors supplemented the lengthy obituaries; interviews with friends and colleagues and feature stories about Stone's life appeared in the days and weeks following her death. Journalists wrote enthusiastically that "the women of America would some day honor her with a national statue in the Capitol at Washington"; they predicted that history would "hail her as immortal."[4]

If those penning tributes were good eulogists, they were poor prophets. History would not immortalize Lucy Stone. While the oral tradition of her life and deeds lived in the decades following her death, women made pilgrimages to her birthplace; trustees named college scholarships and public buildings after her, and mothers named daughters for her. A Lucy Stone League of women electing to keep their birth names after marriage was founded, continuing into the 1970s. Plaques and monuments went up, proclaiming: "Lucy Stone Spoke Here"; "This marks the site of the seizure for taxes of the property of Lucy Stone"; "Lucy Stone lived in this house from 1866 to 1869"; and "Lucy Stone Was Born on This Site on August 13, 1818." In time however, the oral tradition faded, and weeds grew up around the monuments. The historical sites burned or were torn down to make room for other projects, and Lucy Stone's name all but vanished from that part of the collective narrative that is history.[5]

Those waiting outside the Boston church on that October afternoon in 1893 could not have anticipated this. When at last the doors were opened, they pressed forward, and within minutes the church was completely filled. Those who could not get seats lined the aisles and stood at the rear. Many more who could not get into the church at all stood outside throughout the long service, unable either to see or to hear the proceedings.[6]

During the hour between the opening of the doors and the start of the service, a stream of mourners filed past the plain pine casket in its bower of floral offerings. Clad in her best black silk dress and lace cap, a small bouquet of lily-of-the-valley in her clasped hands, Stone lay remote in death from the adulation she had avoided in life. In the weeks before her death, Stone had planned her funeral service, asking that it be "simple and cheerful," with nothing "lugubrious" about it. Still, Charles Ames, the pastor, would characterize it as "not like a funeral, but like a solemn celebration and a coronation." One after another, politicians, reformers, and writers rose to eulogize their friend.[7]

It was more than two hours before the last song was sung and the coffin lid was lowered. As Stone had requested, six women came forward to take their places as pallbearers, among them sculptor and poet Anne Whitney, and Laura Ormiston Chant, an English suffragist. They were joined by six men, including Thomas Wentworth Higginson, Samuel May, and two of the sons of abolitionist William Lloyd Garrison. Together, they carried Stone's body to a waiting carriage for transport to a receiving tomb at Forest Lawn cemetery. There, Stone's corpse lay for two months awaiting completion of Massachusetts's first crematory.[8]

The press tributes that appeared in the weeks after her death reflected the peculiar breadth of Stone's appeal. Working women, middle-class women, Yankees, Westerners—all claimed her as one of their own. The eastern establishment press praised her "most refined and gentle disposition." In the Midwest, it was "suggestive that a farmer's daughter should be filling the world's heart with admiration and the world's eyes with tears." In Colorado, she was a populist heroine, and they wrote of her: "Poor, obscure, advocating a forlorn cause . . . the farmer's daughter went up and down the land with naught on her side but right and justice. Against the combined power of tradition, wealth, established force, Lucy was a leader of that little handful who first dared to ask that woman might be permitted to enjoy a citizen's rights."[9]

Stone's obscure origins would lead a columnist to ask how it happened "that this particular country girl . . . left the ranks, to ride almost alone at the head of the shock troops of the feminist movement?" In answer to that question lies the story of an extraordinary woman. At least part of Stone's success lay in the singularity of purpose that governed her life. "It is something to have known, in this varied and perplexing life, one perfectly single-minded human being," Higginson would say at that afternoon's memorial service.[10]

Imbued with a belief in the rights of individuals, Lucy Stone made her way through the maelstrom of moral, technical, and social upheaval that was nineteenth-century America. "I had a right," she would say by way of explanation as she defied custom, challenged the law, and fomented domestic rebellion. She left her family's subsistence farm to speak, to write, and to lobby the political and legal systems of America in pursuit of what were to her the clear and inalienable rights of the enslaved and the disfranchised. Looking back, she had said of her life's work: "It was so hard and so difficult that if I had been put at the foot of the loftiest peak of the Rocky Mountains with a jack-knife in hand, and had been told, 'Hew your way up,' it would have been pasttime [sic] compared to my task."[11]

As the carriage carrying her body slowly moved away from the Church of the Disciples, groups of mourners remained on the pavement, reluctant to disperse. Some of them would be alive in 1930, when H. L. Mencken would read about her and ask in bewilderment: "Where is Lucy Stone's monument, reaching upward to the stars? . . . For one, I believe that it is too long delayed."[12]

Those who knew of her widespread fame might wonder with Mencken at the rapid close of history over Stone's distinguished public career. She was an adroit politician and a skilled propagandist, and the organizing campaign for woman suffrage she developed should in itself guarantee her place in the history books. Yet any account of her public deeds is incomplete without a sense of the woman behind the powerful public persona—the migraine-ridden perfectionist who struggled with depression and feelings of inadequacy. The public Stone lived a widely heralded marriage of equality, while the private woman contended with a vastly different reality. Somewhere between the idealized public figure and the repressed and conflicted inner woman, between the political and the personal Lucy Stone, is a life story that is both her own, and, in a larger sense, every woman's story.

CHAPTER TWO

"I Am Sorry It Is a Girl.
A Woman's Lot Is So Hard."

Hannah Matthews Stone lay bone weary in the downstairs sleeping chamber of the clapboard farmhouse, feeling the onset of labor pains. A drenching rainstorm that evening had sent the men out into the fields to salvage the hay crop. After settling her five young children in their beds, Hannah milked eight cows. Early the following morning, August 13, 1818, she gave birth to a daughter. "Oh dear!" she exclaimed when told the infant's sex. "I am sorry it is a girl. A woman's lot is so hard."[1]

Hannah's outburst gently violated the code of silent surrender that taught nineteenth-century women that it was their "highest duty" to "suffer and be still."[2] Still, it was in keeping with the combination of subservience and subversiveness that characterized her life in the farmhouse atop Coy's Hill. Hannah's concern for her infant daughter's future reflected the harsh realities of her own life. Her time was spent cooking, canning, churning, spinning, weaving, sewing, nursing, cleaning, grooming, laundering, ironing, serving her family at table, and tending to the family kitchen garden and the dairy. If a spare moment remained, Hannah used it to augment the family income with piecework from the local shoe factory.[3]

On the surface, little distinguished the Stone family farm, located some three miles outside the town of Brookfield, Massachusetts, from its neighbors. In its plain structures—stone spring house, house and dairy, barn out back; as well as in the tools and methods used—spindle, loom, dairy implements, wooden plow, horse and wagon, tanning materials; in the wood fires for cooking and heating; and the fish the men caught and salted in barrels, the farm hearkened back to the time of English ancestors four or five centuries before.

The social structure of the family that inhabited the farm was also little different from that of its early antecedents. Hannah Bowman Matthews, whom Francis Stone married in March of 1804, appeared submissive and pious. Francis Stone was hardworking, hard-drinking, and quick to anger—very much the master of his house. That he and Hannah would produce a daughter who would alter the course of women's—and by extension political and social—history, would seem unimaginable given their surroundings. Still, the peculiar character of Lucy Stone was not altogether anomalous. The explosive catalytic energy of early nineteenth-century America and the genetic chemistry of generations of Stones, Bowmans, and Matthewses combined in her in a way that no one could have anticipated on that distant August morning.

From one or another of her forebears, the child inherited small stature, clear gray eyes, straight brown hair, and a rosy complexion. Where she might also have come by the easy disposition of her grandfather's sisters, or the more limited intellectual capability of her father's brother, she did not. Instead, Lucy Stone was heir to a prodigious intelligence, a wide streak of rebellion, and a willful stubbornness that allowed her to persevere through physical hardship and psychological pain in lifelong defiance of custom.

On her father's side, Stone could trace her rebellious roots to Gregory Stone, who, chafing under ecclesiastical authority, left England in 1635 for the newly established Massachusetts Bay Colony. Literate, able, and ambitious, he prospered in the new land. Deacon Stone, as he came to be known, was one of four citizens chosen to present the Cambridge Petition—the first formal protest in the new land against government without representation—before the General Court, in 1664. Some years later, he again defied authority by defending a young woman accused of witchcraft. He and his wife signed a public statement that they "never knew anything in her life containing witchery."[4]

At his death, a substantial estate passed to Gregory Stone's sons. He appears to have endowed his descendants with at least one of his character traits as well, for generations later, "Of the band of sixty men who stood on Lexington Common on the morning of April 19, 1775, and offered the first armed resistance of the American Revolution, at least twenty-five (including Captain Parker himself) had in their veins the blood of Dea. Gregory Stone."[5]

The family's material holdings declined steadily. By the time Lucy Stone's great-grandfather Jonathan Stone came of age, only a small parcel of land remained to him. In October 1739, he wed Elisabeth Lamb, who brought to the marriage an illegitimate child named Aaron Woods. Woods provides a bellwether to the Stone family's social and economic decline. He became a successful businessman and severed all ties to his

humble Stone relations. After Lucy Stone's rise to international prominence, Aaron Woods's son came to call, proudly presenting himself as
her first cousin. Stone commented drily to her daughter Alice on Woods's
belated claim of kinship, telling how his father earlier had snubbed them
all.[6]

Francis Stone, born in January 1740, would not live to see his grand-
daughter Lucy but would strongly influence her nonetheless. She grew up
on tales of his exploits—how at seventeen he was the veteran of three
bloody battle campaigns in the French and Indian War, how he marched
with the Minutemen to Lexington Common; how he rose to the rank of
captain in the Revolution; and how he put life and reputation on the line
during Shays's Rebellion. One historian wrote that "Captain Francis
Stone really furnished *the brains* of the movement" and was a leader of
Shays's Rebellion.[7] Later in life, he moved with his family to Braintree,
where he operated a tannery.

Following his father's death in 1802, Francis, Jr., became partners
with brother Calvin in the family tannery. His half sisters, Sarah and
Amy, fared poorly in their father's will, Sarah receiving only "two cows
and six sheep," while Amy inherited forty dollars. With no way to support themselves, Sally went to live with Lucy Stone's family, while Amy
moved in with Calvin. Aunt Sally, "crazy, but harmless, and perfectly
happy as long as she could have plenty of knitting," spent her life with
Francis Stone and his family. Calvin had Amy declared a ward of the
town of New Braintree, and for many years, the town paid him to keep
her. After his death, Amy went to the Brookfield poorhouse, where she
eventually died.[8]

Lucy Stone's father had only a rudimentary education, though family
legend has it that he had been a popular teacher in Brookfield. Small
district schools in rural areas were often taught "by local farmers who had
advanced to the rule of three, if little beyond." That Francis Stone belonged to this category seems evident in an 1861 letter from him: "[Sister
Sarah and husband] cilled a sheepe that wighed 60 lbs they have got a pig
to cill, they will do for meet. My heath was never no better I bake my on
bread have had no bad bake my bread is the first rate, I go to bed before
dark git up after sunrise git my brakefiss slick up. . . ."[9]

On legal documents, Francis Stone added "Yeoman" after his signature, eschewing the term "Gentleman," which others, including his own
great-grandfather, preferred. Lucy Stone, like most early nineteenth-century Americans, was aware of class distinctions, characterizing herself as
a "country girl" and "not anybody in particular." She once wrote that she
"did not think herself by heredity good enough to be the mother of children," though like her mother, she did take pride in her maternal family
ties.[10]

In describing her maternal lineage, Stone explained that her mother's father's family, the Matthewses, "were illiterate as compared with the Bowmans but were people of great moral integrity." Hannah's mother was a Bowman, "regarded as on a higher level socially, better educated, with Harvard men and scholars among them." Hannah noted with pride that she "had never seen her mother shed a tear," for her mother "was a Bowman." Hannah named her first child Bowman, and following his death in infancy, she named another son William Bowman and called him Bowman. When she married Francis Stone, Hannah left the prosperous and cheerful farm of her parents and moved less than eleven miles away. She would never again find time or opportunity to travel the short distance to her childhood home. In linking herself to the tightfisted and cantankerous Francis Stone, she entered into a lifetime of what her own children would later remember as almost ceaseless toil.

Two of her nine children died in infancy, two daughters died young, and one of her sons succumbed to typhoid shortly after his thirtieth birthday. Hannah found solace in religion. She took comfort as well in the strong bond of love that grew up between her and the daughter whose appearance had prompted her cry of protest. If she was bewildered by her daughter's choices, she nonetheless took great pride in Lucy. For her part, Stone would labor throughout her lifetime to redress the grievances that had prompted Hannah's outburst. In each crusade she undertook, each injustice she brought before the public, each petition she carried to a legislature, each newspaper column she wrote, pamphlet she printed, or public address she delivered, she would carry the indelible stamp of her mother's travail. Her mother's cry against custom, made in the privacy of the birth chamber, reverberated across the decades, becoming in a sense Lucy Stone's raison d'être. In 1855, she would stand before a crowd of two thousand in Cincinnati and say:

From the first years to which my memory stretches, I have been a disappointed woman. . . . In education, in marriage, in religion, in everything, disappointment is the lot of woman. It shall be the business of my life to deepen this disappointment in every woman's heart until she bows down to it no longer.[11]

The distance between Coy's Hill and "every woman's heart" can be measured in Stone's growing-up years. Though she seldom traveled more than twenty miles from her family home in the first twenty-five years of her life, by the time Lucy Stone left home in 1843, she was a force to be reckoned with. The lessons on woman's rights provided by neighbors, the examples furnished in her own home, Hannah's subtle tutelage, Francis's abusive treatment of his family, and the gradual incursion of the world across the boundaries of Coy's Hill would forge in her a singleness of purpose that would alter the course of women's history.

CHAPTER THREE

"As Light as Thistle Down"

The meadows, pastures, and brooks of the farm on Coy's Hill offered an idyllic childhood setting. Coy's Brook bubbled along the edge of the property, and in autumn, sugar maples and oaks blazed with bright color. A grove of birches sheltered the farmhouse, and a nearby stand of fruit trees offered perches from which children could observe the comings and goings on the roads below. Stone remembered a childhood day spent in the boughs of a white plum tree, eating the ripe fruit and watching the funeral procession of old John Gleason, a neighbor.[1]

Crisscrossed by a network of small roads, relics of an era when every settler was promised "a way to get to mill and meeting," Coy's Hill also provided a vantage point from which fourteen villages could be seen. Evenings, Lucy and her sisters would climb the hill to watch the sun set, causing a neighbor to ask: "What on airth do those Stone girls find on top of that hill to pay them for tramping up there so often?" Though her life would take her far from Coy's Hill, Stone would return often for the strength, solace, and peace of mind she found there.[2]

The family's move there the year before Stone's birth was one of the rare instances when Hannah's will held sway over the iron rule of Francis Stone. "There was only one will in our home, and that was my father's," Stone would say. Still, Hannah succeeded in convincing Francis to sell his share in the tannery at North Brookfield. It had become the place where his childhood cronies gathered to drink rum and hard cider and to play dominoes. As one child after another came along, Hannah grew to resent the "bad influences" of Francis's pals. Then too, she may have hoped that away from his friends, Francis himself would drink less. Hannah's hopes of banishing the ne'er-do-wells soon faded; Francis's old friends, having to travel farther, now came "to stay at [the] house a good deal." He expected Hannah to cook for them and do their laundry. Lucy Stone resented this "imposition" on her mother, and as she grew old enough to help with the chores, she begrudged them her own efforts as well.[3]

From an early age, the children were expected to share in the work. Lucy was a precocious child, able to help her mother with the weaving long before anyone expected it. The complex task of feeding the loom (handing up the appropriate colored threads as needed for the particular design) required careful concentration and memory. Barely a toddler, Lucy took her place beneath the loom, handing the appropriate skeins up to her mother for hours at a time.[4]

When she and her brother Luther were still "very little mites" they drove the cows through a neighbor's pasture to and from a meadow "a long way off." The neighbor's cows—forty or fifty of them—would sometimes "come and make demonstrations as if to fight our cows." Stone loved telling how their dog Bogue would put all forty or fifty cattle to rout. Once, after he had run off the neighbor's bull, Bogue "trotted back showing all his teeth and laughing. He was the laughingest dog I ever saw," Stone said.[5]

One day, her brother Frank heard Lucy shout at a refractory cow, "You old strumpet!" much as she had heard her father do. "Strumpet" was "not a nice word," Frank told her, and he "wished his father would not use [it], but in any case, she ought not to."[6] Frank's consternation doubtless reflected Hannah's attempts at inculcating genteel ways in her family, despite the roughness of their surroundings. The farmhouse was spartan; it lacked curtains, and the family shared chipped and cracked "coarse ware for dishes." Among these, there was a single bowl with "fluted sides and a little yellow vine around the top," and Stone later recalled how hard she would try to get this bowl for her bread and milk. She liked pretty things, and when as a child she read of a lady who sat and read "by the soft light of an astral lamp," she remembered daydreaming about how very much she too would like to be a lady and be able to sit and read by the soft glow of an astral lamp. There were no lamps at all in the Stone home, nor were there washbasins in the bedrooms such as could be found in most nearby farmhouses. Though later in life, Stone would refer to "my poverty-stricken girlhood," she nonetheless insisted that anyone writing about the farm must be sure to say:

What an opulent home it was—barrels of meat, and my father used to drive to the Connecticut River and bring home a great wagon-load of shad, and have it salted down, and we ate it all through the year, freshened and cooked with cream; and such abundance of apples; and the very best butter; I never tasted rancid butter in my mother's house; and peaches and plums (innumerable plums) and quinces and other fruits; and every kind of berries, *fresh*. We all worked hard, but we all worked in together, and had the feeling that everything was ours—the calves, etc. We had honey, more than we could eat. . . .[7]

The family ate game that the boys hunted—squirrel, woodchuck, and occasionally skunk. There were fish, the occasional turtle, and pigeons caught by the children in horsehair traps.[8]

The reality of Stone's quotidian life was at variance with her dreams of being a lady reading by softly diffused lamplight. When she and her sisters were not busy with cooking, canning, weaving, or farm and dairy chores, they sewed "coarse shoes," doing piecework for the local shoe factory. Lucy was expected to sew nine pairs a day, more than either of her sisters. The shoes brought in four cents a pair, compensation drawn in goods from the general store. At the end of one particular year, after accounts were settled, the family was owed six cents. Despite the press of work, the children found time "to run like spiders . . . perfectly free after our chores were done."[9]

Contact with the world outside came on Sundays, when the family would hitch their two horses to the wagon and alternate riding and walking to West Brookfield's Congregational Church. A rare visit to or from a relative, the occasional neighbor's visit, and church "sociables" rounded out the extra-familial scope of Lucy Stone's young life. Early on, she began to display the superior intellectual capability that would set her apart.

At three, Lucy went to stay with Hannah's older sister, Lucy Edmunds. On the evening of her return, her brother Frank, twelve years her senior, looked on admiringly as she displayed various scraps of material she had brought back with her and chattered on about whose dresses had been made of which materials and who was getting new patterns made up.[10] The trip to her aunt occurred at about the time Hannah was giving birth to her ninth and last child, Sarah. Lucy remembered wishing she were a baby as she watched her father hold Sarah between his knees, "dancing her and singing to her." His treatment of the older children was altogether different. As early as she could remember, Stone "was afraid of him" and "knew his slaps."[11]

Once, when she was still very small, Stone awakened in the night and went in search of her mother. Unable to find her, she lay down on the kitchen hearth and sobbed. Her father found her there and threatened to "lay on the slaps" if she did not return to her bed at once. Lucy remembered the terror she felt as she quietly cried herself to sleep.[12]

During the winter, darkness settled over the farm by late afternoon, when the family would gather about the hearth. In later years, Stone described the scene for her daughter: "A small square table with a light on it stood near one end of the circle, and those who were studying or sewing sat up by it for the light, and the circle of the others extended clear around the fire." Her father built "magnificent fires" in the great open fireplace that ran nearly the length of the room.[13]

The men told stories of "bears and wolves and Indians" while the young ones listened wide-eyed. Occasionally, the children would roast apples by setting them along the edge of the hearth. They would "dive down now and then to turn them, flying back in haste because the fire was so hot." If Francis Stone was not at home, Hannah permitted the children to pop corn.[14]

Many of Stone's grown-up recollections of her childhood, begun in the rosy glow of reminiscence, ended with a bitter memory of her father's harsh or abusive behavior to her, conduct she attributed to his "keeping himself cross with cider" or "taking too much cider."[15] In the course of an evening, the children were sent "down cellar" repeatedly to fill the cider pitcher for their father and his cronies. Luther, the older brother closest in age to Lucy, "was always afraid of the dark, and hated to go down cellar alone." One night when it was his turn, he asked his father to send Lucy with him to hold the candle. She protested, but her father ordered her to go. Once outside the room, Lucy refused to go, telling Luther he could set the candle on the cellar floor just as she always did. Luther told his father that Lucy would not go, whereupon Francis Stone took Lucy, "a big girl, ten or twelve years old," across his knee and beat her "with his whole strength," ordering her to accompany her brother. Lucy accompanied Luther to the basement, where she defiantly set the candle on the floor "and let it stand there all the while the cider was being drawn." That her father's beating exceeded the bounds of custom is brought home by her brother Bowman's reaction. Years later, he would recall the brutality of the beating and his own "shame" and frustration at being unable to help her. Stone told her daughter of the beating, adding by way of explanation that "very likely [father] had been taking too much cider at the time."[16]

Sarah too remembered being beaten by her father, and how the following morning he had gotten her up before the other children "to examine the marks and see how much damage he had done."[17] Blaming the cider for her father's harsh behavior was a way of exonerating him, but Stone's ideas about the relationships of men and women, and the connection of alcohol to abuse of women, were forming in a way that would mark her adult behavior. Whether Stone suffered other kinds of abuse at the hands of her father's friends is unknown. Her adult behavior may point to some hidden trauma in her childhood. She would later experience "revulsions of feeling" about sex and display numerous other personality traits now recognized as common among abused children.[18]

Stone told how once she and Luther contrived to break one of the despised jugs of rum the men brought with them. Jim Clark "had come to the house to stay over Sunday and have a good drunk, and had left his jug standing beside the stone wall." Luther set the jug on a small boulder, which he balanced on the wall. Lucy reached up with a stick and, not looking at the jug, dislodged the boulder with a stick. The jug crashed to the ground. Clark accused the children of purposely smashing his rum jar, but when questioned, Lucy told her father with evasive precision that she "had not seen his jug."[19]

Another of Francis Stone's "terrible rages" was occasioned by Stone's asking him (at her mother's prompting) for money for a new tablecloth to use when company came. He shouted at her and at her mother that the tablecloth they had was good enough for him and thus ought to be good enough for them. In telling this story, Stone again made the excuse that "much of his talk was owing to the fact that he kept himself cross with cider." Later, she said, he "grew much more genial in his old age, after the cider was all gone."[20]

Lucy Stone's experiences with her father's "rages" may have influenced her early decision to master her own "high temper." Tales of her angry outbursts pepper family reminiscences. Aunt Ann recalled the five- or six-year-old Lucy furiously engaging in a hair-pulling contest with John Burt Gleason, a neighbor. Stone's sister Eliza and John Burt's older brothers had to pull them apart. On another occasion, Lucy told of going off to Hemlock Hill, furious with Luther for teasing her about her turned-up nose, but determined to gain control of her anger. "He had no idea of the struggle that was going on inside," she said.[21]

Once, running through the house in furious pursuit of her sister Sarah, Stone caught sight of her face in the looking glass. "That is the face of a murderer," she told herself, "and if I do not get the better of my temper, that is what I shall be. And it is a thing about which no one can help me but myself." She went outdoors and sat on a rock behind the woodshed, holding one bare foot in her hand and rocking back and forth on the stone for hours, determined to master her volatile emotions, convinced that "it was a thing that [I] must do alone; that nobody could help [me] with it." As a first step, she decided that she "must not speak" when she got angry. Instead, she would find a way to "keep from speaking and not run out into such a flow of wrathful words!"[22]

Stone's anger was matched by a streak of stubborn pride. Alice recounted a story told to her by her mother:

When Mamma was a child, if any of the children found a horseshoe or ox shoe, they always took it home. And if it was a good shoe, their father gave them six cents for it. One day . . . Mamma found under the sod two horseshoes, fastened together. She was delighted and took them to her father, and held them up to him—she was just a little thing—and told him, greatly elated, how she had found them. He looked at her and said, "Lucy, you stole those shoes." She answered, "No, I did *not*."

Francis Stone did not believe her, a fact that angered Lucy, for, as she explained, "I was not a lying child." Her father took the shoes to Lamberton the blacksmith, who said that they were probably Canadian shoes, and it was most likely that Lucy had found them exactly as she said she did.

Francis offered to pay her the twelve cents, but she told him, "No, I won't take it," and strode away, leaving him looking after her. At this point in the telling of her story, Stone corrected herself. She had not said, "I won't take it," but must have said, "I don't want it," because "We did not say 'I won't' to my father."[23]

When she was old enough to begin school, Stone attended the one-room district schoolhouse presided over by Tom Coney, a neighbor. She recalled that Coney was "a cross teacher" who struck her "the hardest blow [I] ever received except from [my] father," hitting her ears so hard with a ruler that afterward her head rang.[24]

School reading materials were scarce. The stagecoach passed by the schoolhouse, and occasionally travelers would toss out pamphlets or tracts for the children to read. Once, seeing the tracts flung from the coach, Lucy leaped from her seat and scrambled through the open window. When she tried to reenter the classroom through the open door, clutching her prize high in the air for all to see, the teacher insisted that she reenter the way she had left. She remembered having to climb back in through the window to her "great mortification."[25]

The Stone home furnished little in the way of reading materials. The family subscribed to the *Worcester Spy*, the weekly newspaper, and there were a few books, among these the Bible and Fox's *Book of Martyrs*. A scattering of didactic tracts rounded out the family's reading matter. One of these, "The Lost Soul," told of a young woman who died before joining the Congregational Church and consequently went "straight to hell." Lucy reported that she and her siblings found "the horribleness of it thrilling." Hannah believed with church ministers that novels were wicked, and despite their growing popularity, she refused to have them in the house.[26]

Nevertheless, Lucy's sister Rhoda brought home a novel. Lucy was not sure whether the book was *The Lady of the Manor* or *The Children of the Abbey*. After Rhoda had reassured her that "it was not a bad book," Lucy took the book into the western chamber of the farmhouse, locked the door, and read and read. When Sarah told her mother that Lucy was secretly reading a novel, Hannah was "much distressed," but Lucy begged to be allowed to finish. Rhoda convinced Hannah that no permanent harm would come to Lucy, though Hannah expressed her disappointment that they should give in "to the silliness of reading a novel."[27]

Novels were just one way in which the outside world had begun to pierce the isolation of the Stone household. In the immediate vicinity of the farmhouse, the hillsides echoed with the rumble of black powder blasts as laborers slowly worked their way through granite and shale to make way for the railroad, which soon would connect Brookfield with Boston to the east and Albany to the west. Travel to and from these cities, and new markets for the farm produce and factory goods, wrought significant changes in the small towns of western Massachusetts.[28]

Indeed, Stone entered adolescence in an extraordinary era, and the effect on her of the alterations taking place all around her can be seen in the imaginative leap of expectations that she experienced—an internal revolution reflecting the upheaval in the outside world. Startling developments, both in travel and in communication, and the rapid growth of a mechanized and industrialized society, touched almost every aspect of rural life. Stone would say later that she and the shoe factory in the nearby town of Ware were "of an age," both having been born in the same year.[29] Soon, the shoe factory was producing sixty-five thousand pairs of shoes a year. Textile mills also grew up all around them, and many young women of Stone's acquaintance left home to live in boardinghouses and work in factories and mills. Part of their earnings went home to pay a farm mortgage or send a brother to college; with what was left, the women bought clothes or established small savings accounts.[30]

In the middle of Stone's thirteenth summer, news came that a woman would give a series of public lectures on woman's rights in nearby Worcester. Frances Wright had already delivered her lecture series before enormous crowds in Cincinnati, Pittsburgh, and New York.[31] The announcement that she was to speak in New England spread like a brushfire through dry fields. Wright's ideas—that women were entitled to an equal education with men and that wives should have the right to control their own property after marriage—found an audience receptive to her message. Women thronged to her lectures, and a shocked clergyman wrote: [Wright] made her converts . . . not among the low and vicious alone. Females of education and refinement—females of respectable standing in society—those who had been the friends and associates of my own children—were numbered among her votaries, and advocated her sentiments.[32]

Wright publicly assailed the fact that fathers "will aid the instruction of their sons, and condemn only their daughters to ignorance," giving as their reason the fact that daughters "can never *be any thing;* in fact, they *are nothing.*" She called for equal treatment for the sexes, reasoning that "In a daughter [fathers] have in charge a human being; in a son the same." Wright also lectured on marriage, claiming that for women it was "absolute spoliation, and allows of absolute robbery, and all but murder, against the unhappy female who swears away, at one and the same moment, her person and her property."[33]

Though there is no evidence that any of the Stone family women attended Wright's Worcester lecture, and though Wright herself would fall from favor because of her radical ideas about sex and marriage, the sentiments expressed in her early lectures resonated in Lucy Stone's understanding of local events. She recalled getting "one of [my] first lessons in woman's rights" from the story of the nearby Lamberton family:

The mother was an excellent woman, the father a blacksmith who got drunk and would go away and be gone a long time. Once when he had been away for weeks, and his wife was about to have a baby, her father drove over from Ware with a team, and took her and the children and the furniture, and took her home. Mr. Lamberton got wind of it, and was waiting at the door when Mr. Eaton arrived in Ware, and forbade him to unload the team, and he had to drive them back.[34]

Hearing this, Stone asked her mother, "Can't her own father take care of her?" Hannah often had Lucy carry baskets of meat or other food to the family when Lamberton was away on a binge.

Another neighbor woman's experience also brought home to Lucy Stone the inequities of marital property laws. The woman's husband died, and the homestead was sold. The children, some of them still very young, were taken from the widow and sent to various relatives. Lucy inquired whether the same thing would have happened if the wife had died. Hannah replied, "Oh no. The father would have gone right on with the farm." When Lucy questioned her mother about the justice of such arrangements, her mother replied that it was the law, and that the laws were made by men. Stone asked, "If the law can meddle with the woman, why should not the woman meddle with the law?"[35]

The issue of property would come up in her own family in later years. Francis Stone, in drawing up his will, proposed to leave Hannah only "the use of one room, with what milk she needed, etc." Hearing this, Lucy, Sarah, and Bowman managed to convince their father of the gross inequity of his arrangement and to prevail on him to revise his will so as to leave Hannah the bulk of his estate. Though Hannah did not live to inherit any of it, "It was a comfort to her. . . . She felt the justice of it."[36]

Wright's assertion that women had a right to their earnings found a timid echo in Hannah Stone's actions, if not in her words. Though the farm grew more prosperous, Francis continued to be "very ugly" to Hannah about money. She would wait until her husband had sunk into a deep sleep, then reach carefully under his pillow and withdraw the money purse he kept there. Quickly, she would remove a coin and skillfully restore the money purse to its place under the pillow. At other times, she would sell surreptitiously one of the two hundred or so cheeses kept in the cheese room. "It seems like hooking," she explained to Lucy, "but I have a right to it."[37]

Lucy remembered collaborating in the "hooking" of cheeses. On one occasion, she had thought that her father was out of the way when she went in and removed a cheese from the dairy. As she started out of the barn leading the horse, she encountered her father. "But," she told Alice, "I was as strong as a young buck. I held the cheese, which must have weighed twenty pounds, close to me, under my arm, while I led the horse out with the other arm." Having avoided detection, she rode off to the nearby town of Ware to sell the cheese.[38]

When late in life, Stone told this story to Alice, she asked that it not be included in her biography, saying, "I will not have my father blamed. It is enough simply to say that he had the Puritan idea that women were to be governed, and that he had the right to hold the purse, and to rule his own house."[39] Stone apparently saw no conflict of interest between her mother's "right" to "hook" coins and cheeses and her father's "right" to absolute control of the family purse.

Hearing her mother's stories provoked Alice to ask if Lucy "did not care a great deal more for her mother than for her father?" Lucy answered truthfully: "I loved her more than I did him, for she was always kind to me and took a great interest in us." Thomas Wentworth Higginson described meeting Hannah after Stone had become famous as a woman's rights lecturer. He wrote that Lucy entered the room "leading a fine, hale, sturdy, stout old lady, saying with an air of love and pride, 'Mr. Higginson, this is my mother, my own mother,' and the old lady looked as happy as she did."[40]

Though Hannah was herself silent, long-suffering, and submissive, she repeatedly directed her daughter's attention to the indignities, inequities, and injustices women endured. One day, as Lucy sat reading the Bible to herself, she came across the words: "Thy desire shall be to thy husband, and he shall rule over thee." The words enraged her, and she went to her mother and asked if this was true. When Hannah answered that it was, Lucy impetuously asked her mother if she had anything for her to take with which she might kill herself rather than to ever have to submit to such a rule.

Hannah tried to calm her by explaining that it was "because of the sin of our first mother, Eve." Lucy told her mother that she could not accept such an explanation; she would go to college and learn Greek and Latin so that she could read the Bible in its original languages and find the errors in translation that had led to what she was certain must be a gross misunderstanding of God's intent. In any case, Stone resolved that she would never marry.[41]

One summer day, Stone's father teased her about her appearance, warning her that her plain face would deter suitors. In her presence, he said to her brothers: "Lucy's face is like a blacksmith's leather apron; it keeps off the sparks." The ferocity of her response surprised them all. She told them angrily that "she did not wish to be married, did not want any man, would not have a husband for anything, and that she wished she were still plainer, and that the mole on her upper lip was an inch long, so as to hang down!"[42]

Francis Stone's teasing notwithstanding, Lucy was an attractive young woman. She was not conventionally pretty, but her complexion was clear, and her rosy cheeks, clear gray eyes, and profusion of silky dark brown hair lent her a fetching air. More than one young man attempted to "spark" her, but Lucy would have none of it.[43]

Stone's family no doubt believed she would outgrow her rebellious notions about education and marriage. Though women increasingly left home for short-term employment, marriage was still the only long-term, economically viable option for a young woman of the era. As a daily reminder, Stone had before her the sad spectacle of Aunt Sally and Aunt Amy.[44] Still, she vowed that she would never marry and persisted in her dream of acquiring an education. When she told her father her intention of going to college, he turned to her mother: "Is the child crazy?" He then took Lucy aside and said to her, "Your mother learned to read and write and cipher. She can keep accord [sic] of her egg and butter money. What more does a girl need to learn?"[45]

Despite her father's disapproval, Stone joined her siblings at the private tutorials intended to prepare them for college by teaching them Latin, Greek, mathematics, and rhetoric. She remembered her father's refusal to buy her a textbook, and how she "went to the woods, with my little bare toes, and gathered chestnuts, and sold them for money enough to buy the book." She later said of the purchase, "I felt a prouder sense of triumph than I have ever known since." She picked berries and nuts to purchase other books and steadily prepared herself for college.[46]

First her brother Bowman and then Frank passed their qualifying exams and departed for college. They returned periodically, bringing news and ideas into the house. The explosive energy of the forces sweeping the nation in the Jacksonian era—populism, industrialism, religious revivalism, romanticism, expansionism, abolitionism—came more and more to pierce the isolation of the Stone household. Gradually, talk of politics and reform supplanted tales of bears and Indian raids.[47]

Even the local sewing circle, where young women gathered to sew shirts for missionaries, became a forum for new ideas. Stone told the story of the appearance there of Mary Lyon, an early champion of increased educational opportunities for women. Lyon came to speak to the group about founding a female seminary where women would receive the education hitherto denied them.[48]

Stone recalled how as she listened to Mary Lyon, her heart grew "hotter and hotter." The young man whose shirt she sewed "could earn more money toward his own education in a week, by teaching, than she could earn toward hers in a month." Furious, she put down the shirt and refused to sew another stitch, adding that she "hoped no-one would ever complete it."[49]

Indeed, the subject of women teachers' earnings struck close to home. Rhoda found steady employment first as a summer school teacher, and then as a winter term teacher as well, but she received only one-fourth of a male teacher's salary, scarcely enough to support herself; she lived at home between teaching assignments. Her return from her teaching jobs in nearby towns offered a connection to the outside world as she brought home news and gossip along with books borrowed from the families with whom Rhoda boarded during teaching terms. She urged Lucy to "get an education."[50]

However, at age sixteen, Lucy came up against her father's expectation that she too teach in a neighboring school and assist with the farm debt and with the cost of her brothers' university educations. That summer, she took her first teaching job in the small nearby town of New Braintree, boarding with her sister Eliza and Eliza's husband, Ira Barlow. The Barlow farmhouse was austere and isolated, and Eliza, ten years Lucy's senior and expecting her second child, was delighted at having her sister's company. Lucy was giving "good satisfaction" as a teacher, Eliza wrote proudly to her brother.[51]

Stone described her first teaching experience, for which she received a dollar a week. She had "a very large school . . . 17 different scholars," and was "very much hurried to get along with them." Despite her proximity to her pupils' age, Stone reported that "I have not had any great trouble yet, and I don't think that I need fear a great deal on that account." Their slowness tried her patience, however: "To-day I put out 'tract' and they spelled it 'trit,' and 'trat,' and 'trut' and every way but the right . . . and they won't remember after I have told them two or three times, and if that don't worry patience, I can't know what will. But I can see that they have learned considerable; if I could not, I should give up all hopes of ever teaching school."[52]

She was at home again in January 1837, when members of the school committee came from Paxton, a nearby town, and asked if she would take over there for the rest of the winter term. "Glad of every dollar," she readily agreed. They had neglected to tell her that she would be replacing a male schoolmaster who had been thrown from the schoolroom into a snowdrift by his obstreperous scholars. As she entered the Paxton schoolhouse the first morning, Lucy was stopped by the ringleader of the bullies, "a big boy of seventeen or eighteen," who challenged her: "Are you going to lick me?" Stone ignored him, passed into the schoolroom, and began to call the roll. Afterward, she walked around the classroom, talking pleasantly with each of the scholars, asking them about their studies and other matters. When she reached the young man, she talked quietly with him for a few minutes. In an early demonstration of the charismatic power she would later display, she "entirely won over" the truculent scholar. From then on, he volunteered to build the daily classroom fire and to do other school chores. One morning, a young student broke her wrist sliding on the ice. Lucy recalled saying, "One of you must go for the doctor," whereupon the former bully was "off at once like a shot."[53]

Stone deeply resented being paid less than male teachers. Despite his ineptitude, the "pitched" male schoolteacher she replaced had earned more than twice her salary. One winter term, when Bowman fell ill, she took over his teaching job. Though she taught every subject that he had, the school committee insisted upon giving her "only a woman's pay." Still, Stone's salary increased steadily until eventually she was earning sixteen dollars per month—considered exceptionally good pay for a woman.[54]

Most of the money Stone earned went to her father, but whenever she could, she enrolled for a term in one of the select schools springing up all around them. Her resolve to attend college had become theoretically possible, as Oberlin College opened its college degree program to women in 1837. Stone was determined that should she ever save enough to go there, she would succeed in passing the entrance examinations. To that end, she alternated studying and teaching.

As she matured, Lucy's interest in abolitionism grew. Bowman, studying to be a minister, subscribed to William Lloyd Garrison's *Liberator*. An early engraving in the magazine depicted a slave woman in chains over the caption "Am I Not A Woman and A Sister?" Garrison urged women readers to look on the picture and "weep, and speak, and act in their behalf."[55] Soon the antislavery writings of Elizabeth Chandler and Maria Weston Chapman, the lectures of Frances Maria Stewart, and the brilliant and moving "Appeal" of Lydia Maria Child appeared in the paper.[56] At the same time, two young women, daughters of a South Carolina plantation owner, liberated their slaves and went north to aid in the Anti-Slavery Movement. By 1836, Sarah and Angelina Grimké were speaking publicly as paid agents for the American Anti-Slavery Society. Ignoring the warning that their speaking would be regarded as a "Fanny Wright affair," they spoke in cities and towns throughout New York, Pennsylvania, and New England.[57] Inspired by their courage, Abby Kelley, a young schoolteacher from nearby Worcester, began to make public addresses on the subject of slavery. Stone said later that she knew the "sure day [for women's equality] came when the sisters Sarah and Angelina Grimké and Abby Kelley Foster began to speak publicly in behalf of slaves. Public speaking by women was regarded as something monstrous. . . . But they held fast. . . . Literally taking their lives in their hands, they went out to speak. . . ."⁵⁸

Stone eagerly read the *Liberator* reports that over one thousand people had gathered in the Congregational Church of Worcester to hear the Grimkés speak.⁵⁹ At the North Brookfield Quadrennial Conference, the ministers issued a pastoral letter warning all church members against permitting the use of the pulpit to antislavery speakers—and most particularly to female speakers. The wording of the proclamation, which came to be known as the "Brookfield Bull," was harsh and minatory. The ministers denounced women lecturers "who so far forget themselves as to itinerate in the character of public lecturers and teachers." The character of the woman who speaks in public "becomes unnatural. If the vine, whose strength and beauty it is to lean upon the trelliswork . . . thinks to assume the independence and the overshadowing nature of the elm, it will not only cease to bear fruit, but fall in shame and dishonor into the dust."⁶⁰

Lucy Stone sat in the balcony of the church in North Brookfield on the day the pastoral letter was read. She had been teaching at a private, or "select" school in North Brookfield, where she boarded with her cousin Dalinda Edmunds. Edmunds recalled sitting next to Stone in the packed spectators' gallery, and how afterward her entire side was "black and blue from Lucy's jabs and nudges," delivered at each offending phrase emanating from the pulpit. "I was young enough then so that my indignation blazed," Lucy said later of her furious response that day. She told her cousin Dalinda "that if ever [I] had anything to say in public, [I] would say it, and all the more because of that pastoral letter."⁶¹

The words of the Brookfield Bull catalyzed Sarah Grimké, whose *Letters on the Equality of the Sexes* began to appear in installment form in the New England *Spectator*. Grimké urged women to become conscious of their own dignity and worth, and to participate fully in all moral and reform movements. She called for equal educational rights for women, countering scriptural arguments against woman's rights by insisting that the Bible was a historical document, reflective of the patriarchal society that had produced it. Grimké likened the Brookfield Bull to Cotton Mather's pronouncements on witchcraft. She continued to accept speaking engagements in churches where pastors resisted the ban.⁶²

Sometime in 1838, Deacon Henshaw, a young Brookfield clergyman, invited Abby Kelley to give an abolitionist speech from his pulpit. The night of Kelley's speech saw nearly every resident of the Brookfield area crowded into the church. The Stone family hitched up both wagons and set off to hear her speak. As Lucy went from the church out into the moonlit summer evening, she remembered the "general sense of a spree in the air—something exciting and riotous: so extraordinary and improper was it considered for a woman to speak in public." The women murmured excitedly together, and Stone recalled hearing the sound of dogs barking. Someone (later she would identify the "someone" as her father) "coolly remarked, 'When the sluts are out, the dogs will bark!'"[63]

Following his act of disobedience, Deacon Henshaw was brought to trial in the West Brookfield church. Again, Stone was present, and after the evidence was heard, the minister called for a vote. Lucy, having become a member of the church the previous year, raised her hand to vote in favor of Deacon Henshaw. Seeing her hand, the minister instructed the man counting the votes: "Don't you count her."

"Why? Isn't she a member?" asked the man.

"Yes, she is a member, but she is not a *voting* member." As Stone would later tell Alice, this last was said scornfully, and the minister's tone caused a flash of righteous anger in Lucy. The vote had to be taken six more times, and each time, she raised her hand defiantly. Fifty years later, Stone would still summon the old indignation as she told the story. "I had an opinion; I was a member; I had a right," she insisted.[64]

That autumn, Stone was again able to attend a nearby select school, where her interest in her studies was equalled by the excitement with which she read Grimké's *Letters*. She wrote Frank of the eagerness with which she read the "pieces in our paper from Miss Grimké . . . it does us lots of good." At the graduation ceremony, she was asked to prepare and read an essay. She described reading it from a jerry-built platform below the male scholars' platform, a placement she regarded as deliberately designed "to keep women down a little lower than men." Stone's feminist consciousness was expanding rapidly.[65]

Instead of taking the offer of a winter teaching term that year, Stone asked her father for permission to continue her education at Mary Lyon's academy in South Hadley. Francis Stone agreed conditionally; he would permit her to attend if she would sign a promissory note for the amount she would otherwise have contributed to the family budget by teaching. She signed the note, and after passing oral examinations in history, geography, arithmetic, and grammar, she entered with the first class of eighty young women sometime early in 1838.[66]

If she was disappointed by the absence of Latin and Greek in the curriculum at Mary Lyon's Mount Holyoke Female Seminary, or discouraged at being required to take lessons in manners and "the amenities," Stone did not complain. She listened to the lectures of visiting professors, read Milton's *Paradise Lost* and Butler's *Analogy of Religion, Natural and Revealed,* attended classes in cube roots and arithmetical progression, and studied Whately's *Logic,* geography, and natural history.[67]

While Stone was at Holyoke, Bowman continued to send along the *Liberator.* She placed the newspapers on a table in the sitting room along with an antislavery collection box. At first, no one knew who was supplying the *Liberator* and the collection box, but when Lyon questioned her, Stone readily admitted it. She remembered Lyon's rebuke: "Now the slavery question is a very great question, and a question on which the best people are divided."[68]

Whether Stone would have continued to place the *Liberator* in the sitting room was made moot by an emergency summons to the farm. On March 17, 1838, Lucy's sister Eliza, not yet thirty years old, died. Immediately after the funeral, Lucy went to stay at the New Braintree farm of Ira Barlow to care for Eliza's two infant daughters until Ira could make other arrangements. Years later, she would remember the feeling of desolation she experienced, alone in the Barlow farmhouse with her two tiny nieces, listening to the "lonesome sound" of the March winds.[69]

Hannah was distraught, and when Lucy was able to return to the farm, she did not consider resuming her studies at Miss Lyon's school. Instead, she remained at home with her mother for the remainder of the spring. In June, she took a summer teaching post. Although she had been unable to complete her term with Miss Lyon, Lucy nevertheless repaid Francis every penny of the promissory note she had signed. In the meantime, she was again able to save enough from her teaching salary to enable her to attend another "select" school, this one taught by Alfred Bartlett, a young divinity student who boarded with the Stone family.

Bartlett taught Lucy, Luther, and William Clapp, a local scholar, arithmetic, grammar, Latin, and algebra. With his genuine interest in woman's rights and in the antislavery cause, Mr. Bartlett endeared himself to Lucy, coming closer to winning the love of the almost twenty-year-old Lucy than had any other young man of her acquaintance. He lent Lucy his copies of the collected letters of Sarah Grimké, bound now in pamphlet form and titled *The Equality of the Sexes and the Condition of Women,* as he received them. Stone read eagerly, writing to Frank:

Mr. Bartlett has S.M.G. on the rights of woman, in pamphlet form, and if you could but read them, and she says nothing but what she proves, I guess that you would not think that I was too upstropuluz.[sic] I tell you they are first rate, and they only help to confirm the resolution I had made before to call no man master. I wish very much you might have the opportunity to read them, but you are so stiff I don't suppose it would make a difference—but if I can procure them I will send them to you if you have not seen them.[70]

Bartlett's interest in Stone was evident. One Sunday morning he watched from his chamber window as Stone rounded up, bridled, and harnessed the horses to the carts that would take the family to church. He came and told her that she "would do to be a missionary and drive a team over the Rocky Mountains." On another occasion, a wild rain and sleet storm came up suddenly, and Stone went to bring in the laundry, which had been hung to dry in the garden. Bartlett came out to help, and later, Lucy Lamberton, the blacksmith's daughter, asked Lucy teasingly how she liked that sort of help. Lucy responded that she liked it "very well." Stone often mentioned Bartlett in her letters to her brothers, writing that Bartlett "is a very good man . . . and I believe a Christian if there is one."[71] According to Sarah, "Mr. Bartlett fell in love with [Lucy] and [she] was also smitten with him." Though Sarah "did not know how it was that it came to nothing," it seems likely that Stone's intransigence about marriage was a likely damper on any young romance.[72]

In November 1838, her course of study with Mr. Bartlett was interrupted by Rhoda's illness. Stone went to Paxton to take over Rhoda's teaching job. When she returned early in 1839, she and Sarah were able to attend the Quaboag Seminary at Warren, a nearby private academy. Sarah described how she and Lucy rented a room together, bringing most of their provisions from the farm. They lived on corn mush, baked beans, brown bread, and other staples. Mr. Pearl, the principal, tried to interest them in dancing lessons, but they had "conscientious scruples" and refused.[73]

Rhoda's death, on July 31, 1839, brought Lucy home again. Rhoda had been a role model for Lucy, and they enjoyed a particularly close relationship despite the four years that separated them. Hannah was all but inconsolable, and Lucy came home to do what she could to assuage her mother's grief. She turned twenty-one that summer, and it would be another full year before she could resume studying. College must have seemed to her to be as out of reach as ever in the summer and fall of 1839.

In 1840, when Hannah was able to bear her absence and Lucy had earned enough money, she enrolled at the Wilbraham Academy. There, she read about the growing dissension in the ranks of the American Anti-Slavery Society. In the resulting schism, the more conservative wing declared its opposition to women lecturers and women delegates. From Wilbraham, Stone wrote Bowman:

[The new organization's] great object seems to be (if I mistake not) to crush Garrison and the women. While it *pretends* to endeavor to remove the yoke of bondage on account of color, it is *actually* summoning all its energies to rivet more and more firmly the chains that have always been fastened upon the neck of woman. . . . If woman would "open her mouth for the dumb," she *sha'n't*. If she would let her vote speak, the cry is raised again, *It shall not be allowed*. Thus the inalienable right that

God has given is wrested from her, and the talent, or if you please, *half talent,* entrusted to her keeping for improvement, is violently taken away. . . .

I admire the calm and noble bearing of Abby K. on that occasion, and cannot but wish that there were more kindred spirits.

Only let females be educated in the same manner and with equal advantages that males have, and as everything in nature seeks its level, I would risk but we would find our "appropriate sphere."[74]

Stone's 1840 letter differs in both style and tone from her other letters of that time. Its rhythms and rhetorical invention are far more characteristic of her later speeches, giving rise to speculation as to whether at Wilbraham, Stone did not try her hand at oratory, though there is no record of her having done so.

At this time, Bowman was involved in an evangelical revival, prompting Stone to write: "My own heart is cold as clay. I often think that I have never been a Christian, for how can one who has ever known the love of God go so far away?" In place of religious fervor, Stone grew fervently interested in woman's rights. At Wilbraham, she joined the ladies' literary society, writing Bowman that it had voted by a large majority that "women ought to mingle in politics, go to Congress, etc. etc.," concluding, "What do you think of that?"[75]

After Wilbraham, Stone returned to teaching until 1842, when she again enrolled in Quaboag Seminary in nearby Warren to prepare herself for the Oberlin College entrance examinations. She is listed as a member of the classics department, where she read Virgil and Sophocles and studied Latin and Greek grammar.[76]

Finally, by August 1843, Stone had learned enough and saved enough to begin her journey to Oberlin. One of her school friends, Mary Ann Bishop, helped with the sewing of the simple wardrobe she would take with her to college. Along with the excitement of setting off at last to fulfill her dream, Stone must have felt some trepidation, though those who knew her would insist that Stone "did not know what fear was." Hannah, having already lost two grown daughters, must have been terrified. It would be weeks before she could expect word of Lucy's arrival at Oberlin, and perhaps years before she would see her again.[77]

Lucy set off in high spirits. It was early August 1843; she would be twenty-five years old in two weeks, and she had been saving for this moment since 1836. Boarding the train in Brookfield, she paid $7.50 for a ticket to Albany, New York—the first (and slowest) leg of the trip that carried her westward in pursuit of her dream.[78]

CHAPTER FOUR

"This Is Not a World
to Sit Down and Whimper In"

The train Lucy Stone boarded Monday evening moved sluggishly westward, the section of track from Brookfield to Albany a tortuous route that crossed and recrossed the same stream and its branches twenty-seven times as it made its way through the mountainous countryside. The slow passage of the train through the night, rattling across trestle bridges, climbing slowly, descending carefully, with smoke from the coal-fired engine blackening the air behind it, was no doubt intensely exciting to a young woman who had never been more than twenty miles from home before. She liked the experience; as she wrote home, "I would as soon travel alone from Maine to Georgia, and from there to the Rocky Mountains, as not."[1]

The first leg of the trip, the 120-mile stretch from Brookfield to Albany, took more than ten hours. It was dawn on Tuesday before Stone arrived in Albany, where she caught a ferry across the river and then boarded the afternoon train bound for Buffalo, New York, a two-day ride. From Albany to Utica, New York, she shared the railroad car with "a real gentleman," Francis Spinner, a prominent businessman and a general in the New York state militia. When he saw that she was studying Greek and asked why, he was startled by Stone's response—that she wished to read the Bible in its original language to find out what it *really* taught about women. Though Stone could not have known it, Oberlin would provide her with far more than exegetical tools—she would mature there socially and intellectually, gaining the necessary confidence and polish to enable her to go out and "meddle with" the world in pursuit of equal rights for women.

Spinner asked why she did not study something more practical, such as the human body, to which Stone responded that she *had* studied anatomy and knew it well. How many bones did she have in her hand? he asked. Stone's ready answer caused him to concede that it "might do for her to study Greek." When the train stopped at a station along the way, Spinner bought her an ice cream—her first—which she found "very refreshing."[2]

Disembarking in Utica, Spinner pointed out his house and made Stone promise that if ever she came through that section of New York again, she would stay there with him and his family. After Stone became famous, Spinner wrote reminding her of their meeting, and when later he was appointed Treasurer by Abraham Lincoln, he often mailed Stone copies of pending legislation.[3]

Arriving in Buffalo at five o'clock on Thursday, Stone booked a deck passage to Cleveland on the steamship *New England*. In the higher-priced staterooms below, the steamer afforded a luxurious leisure activity, where "companies of ladies and gentlemen . . . on a voyage of pleasure, with guns, fishing-tackle, harps, flutes, violins, and other music" ate, laughed, drank, and made music together. On deck, Stone found a place among the horses and the freight, secured her trunk beside another and put her carpetbag by her head. She feared going to sleep in the presence of male strangers, but an old woman offered to keep watch. Stone explored the deck before settling down to sleep on a pile of grain sacks, savoring the experience.[4] "It was all so new," she wrote, "and there was a certain largeness about it that [I] liked." She reported that she was a good sailor, "not sick at all coming over the Lake. It was a very still time, and the water was as smooth as glass, except what was disturbed by the boat. We met one steamboat, and passed about fifty schooners. They looked very grand under full sail." She described her exhilaration when her ship passed the other steamer and they "spoke" one another with their whistles. "I felt quite elated and excited and as if it were going to war when the vessels ran up their two great prows and 'howled at each other.'"[5]

From Cleveland, she caught a stagecoach to Elyria, Ohio, where she boarded the coach that would carry her the last seven miles to Oberlin along a "corduroy road which bumped amazingly." This was the frontier. Early Saturday afternoon, after five days' travel by train, ferry, steamer, and stagecoach, she had come five hundred miles from Coy's Hill to the small new western town of Oberlin. Including food, the trip from Brookfield to Oberlin had cost her exactly $16.65—more than a month's wages.

Accustomed to the lush green of Massachusetts's hills, Stone may have been dismayed by Oberlin's raw newness—the four unpaved roads and small cluster of brick buildings—all built on reclaimed swampland. "The water here is poor. . . . I would give anything for a drink from Father's well. I don't think the land here is half as good as it is at home. It is all clay," she wrote in her first letter home. She went on to reassure her mother that travel was not at all dangerous; she did not tell of the typhoid fever, cholera, pneumonia, and tuberculosis that plagued Oberlin, making it a greater hazard to health. An awareness of her own mortality crept into the letter, however. She wrote that she had gathered pretty rocks along the shore of Lake Erie which she intended to give her niece "if I live to get home."[6]

Two weeks later, Stone wrote home: "I think I shall like it very well here. The teachers are pleasant, and the young ladies too. Colored gentlemen and ladies eat at the same table with us, and there appears to be no difference. . . . In church, they [the races] are on terms of perfect equality . . . nobody cares or whines about it either."[7]

Postage was expensive, so Stone sent word that she had passed her entrance examinations by mailing home a newspaper in which she had marked selected words.[8] In her next letter, she described the Ladies' Boarding Hall and her roommate, a sixteen-year-old slaveholder's daughter from South Carolina. The young woman had strict instructions to avoid any talk of slavery at Oberlin, for were she to become abolitionist, "it would kill her mother and permanently sever her association with her father."[9]

Founded in 1833 by a group of evangelical reformers and known as a "hotbed of abolitionism," Oberlin would have seemed a strange choice for a slaveholder's daughter were it not the only coeducational college in the country. Its agenda in educating women was to spread moral "perfectionism" through the agency of enlightened wives and mothers. Marriage for its women graduates "was a given, the family the model from which women's influence would be implemented in the larger society."[10]

Stone's ideas—that women should vote, run for office, study for the learned professions, and become public speakers in the cause of reform—were wholly at odds with college policy. In a speech on "Woman's Rights and Duties," Oberlin professor James Fairchild addressed Stone's challenge, asking: "Are the learned professions as naturally open to woman as to man? Should she pursue a course of education with the view of entering these?" He went on to say that "the answer must be, No, for two general reasons: it is improper and impossible."[11]

Stone's open disagreement won respect if not agreement from her classmates.[12] She was admired for having "not only the ability but the moral courage to face the prejudices of the masses . . . and of the professors of our college as well." According to a fellow student, "Lucy Stone was the topic of conversation at the table where I boarded, and indeed in all the boarding houses in town." Opinions varied as to the propriety of her ideas, he wrote, but "all admitted that she was the most brilliant woman of her age they had ever met."[13]

Though Oberlin was a busy stop on the Underground Railroad, its antislavery position was insufficiently radical for Stone. The faculty and church hierarchy were "voting" or "political" abolitionists, willing to work within the existing system to eradicate slavery. Stone, as a Garrisonian or "Come-Outer," believed there must be "No union with slaveholders." In this, she stood all but alone: "There is not a single Liberator taken in Oberlin, nor a single Liberator man, woman or child here but me. At the table where I sit, they hate Garrison." She asked Luther to send the *Liberator* regularly.[14]

Attendance at church services was mandatory for Oberlin students, as were twice-daily prayer meetings and twice-weekly religious lectures. Presided over by the renowned hellfire-and-brimstone preacher of the Second Great Awakening, Charles Grandison Finney, church became a test of endurance for Stone, who described one of his sermons in a letter home: "Professor Finney preached last Sabbath . . . the crossest-looking man I ever saw. He said, 'Of all the reformers this side of Hell, the Come-Outers most needed reforming; forever slanging the clergy; violating the Sabbath; disturbing public assemblies, etc.' He said you might as well try to convert the Devil. . . ."[15]

She began to have severe headaches in church. To ease the pain, she removed her bonnet, an action that brought her a summons to appear before the Ladies' Board and answer the charge of disobeying the biblical injunction that women must cover their hair in church. Stone defended herself by explaining that if she were not permitted to remove her bonnet, she would be "good for nothing all the rest of the day. What account shall I give to God of my wasted Sunday afternoon?" The Ladies' Board voted to permit her to remove her bonnet on the condition that she sit in a far corner where others could not see her.[16]

Wasted afternoons were a rarity at Oberlin, where the motto "Learning and Labor" meant that all students shared in the physical work of the school—cleaning, washing dishes and clothes, cooking, mending, and tending to outside maintenance—for which they received payment of three to ten cents an hour credited to their board. The same thrifty progressiveness characterized its diet as well. Students prepared and ate a modified version of the Graham health diet then in vogue. "We have meat once a day, bread and milk for supper, pudding and milk, thin cakes, etc. for breakfast. We shall live well enough." As for the bread, she wrote that one of her fellow students challenged her to a duel "with her pistol brimfull of bullets made from Graham bread."[17]

Stone quickly settled into the routine of classroom and domestic chores. A fellow student remembers watching her dry dishes in the evening. She propped her Greek book open on a rack beside the drainboard so that she could memorize her lessons as she worked. She had hoped to supplement her savings by teaching in Oberlin's preparatory department but was initially disappointed to learn that the Oberlin faculty insisted on observing would-be teachers for a year in order to assess their "mental and moral" fitness. Bowman, who had been ordained a Congregationalist minister in 1842, interceded on her behalf, sending letters that testified to her good character and to her excellent teaching ability.[18]

Stone was hired to teach in the school for fugitive slaves and freedmen. The committee member who showed her to her classroom on the first day had not told the male students that they would be getting a female teacher. When he introduced her to the class, a rebellious murmur swept the room. One young man rose to his feet and objected that grown men should not be taught by a woman. Stone addressed them in her low, sweet voice, her arguments clear and direct. Disarmed, the students settled in for what would prove a mutual education. Stone taught them the fundamentals of literacy; they provided her with firsthand accounts of the evils of a system that held one race captive to another. "When I saw how they were *dehumanized* . . . I wondered, that in the wide universe of god, one tongue could be found, that failed to utter its indignant rebuke against all that pertains to so execrable a system," she wrote.[19]

Stone described her experience with a particularly depressed former slave named Robert, who never raised his eyes from his desk, would not answer questions, and who seemed incapable of learning his lessons. Initially, Stone was slightly frightened of him. Nevertheless, she spoke to him kindly day after day. Little by little, he responded. Soon he was meeting her as she walked to school, and as they walked, he told of his experiences in slavery and of his hopes for the future. "He became one of the warmest and truest friends I had," Stone wrote.[20]

Teaching on top of an already crammed schedule meant days that began at five (and occasionally much earlier) and ended late at night. She strained the boundaries of time, causing a classmate to comment: "Miss Stone had a wonderful memory and a constitution which could endure eighteen hours of mental labor in twenty-four." The classical course included the study of trigonometry, Greek, Latin, Hebrew, astronomy, chemistry, geology, biology, natural philosophy, logic, rhetoric, and the Bible. Stone wrote "voluminous notes" in preparation for her classes, and when time permitted, she went to the reading parlor in the Ladies Literary Society, where she read what was current in intellectual culture—Emerson, Lowell, and Harriet Martineau on political economy.[21]

Although her courses were challenging, Stone was disappointed to learn that the Oberlin faculty members had voted to exclude women from the practice of rhetoric and from participation in classroom discussions and debates. She wrote in frustration: "I hoped when I came to Oberlin that the course of study would permit such practice, but I was never in a place where women are so rigidly taught that they must not speak in public." Eventually, she found ways to obtain the training she so much wanted, but in her first term at Oberlin, she had to make do with auditing the rhetoric class.[22]

During the long winter break, students earned extra money by teaching in nearby school districts. Stone taught in the town of Wellington, Ohio, but even with winter teaching and her work in the preparatory school, she could not make ends meet. After describing her schedule in a letter home, she received a surprising offer from her father:

Lucy: the first thing you will want to know after hearing that we are all well, will be about money. When you wrote that you had to get up at two o'clock to study your lesson it made me think of the old tanyard where I had to get up at one and two o'clock I little thought then that I should have children, or a child, that would have to do the same; not the same work, but perhaps as hard. I had to work late and early I was hardly able to live; and you have been under the same inconvenience, as far as money is concerned. Let this suffice. There will be no trouble about money; you can have what you will need, without studying nights, or working for eight cents an hour.

Stretching his generosity, he added

"I pay the postage on all letters that are sent and received, so pay no more postage."
Your Father Stone[23]

Stone did not take him up on his offer, borrowing small sums from Sarah and Bowman instead. The following winter, her father wrote again: "You need not teach to get money to keep along with your studies, for you can have all you want from home." Stone wrote her sister that she was "exceedingly reluctant for various reasons to ask father for money." Only after the demands of her schedule caused her to lose so much weight that her clothes "lapped wonderfully" did she finally write and ask him to lend her enough money so that she would not have to teach in the spring of her final year.[24]

Francis Stone's offer to pay the postage was generous; postal rates were high, and Stone wrote fairly often. Hannah wrote only rarely, ashamed of her lack of proficiency with the pen. "How are your bonnets, stockings, flannel petticoats, and all your clothes?" she asked. "I want to know if your apparel compares with the rest of the students. . . . Lucy I won't write no more I make such work of it. Father may finish it." In another letter, Hannah wrote how much she missed Lucy, adding, "You will not be much pleased with my hand wrighting."[25]

Frank wrote to ask if Oberlin had changed her mind about any of her peculiar notions. Stone responded, "I have not changed my views of church, ministry, sabbath or *matrimony* in the least." He wrote again to tell her that he was to be married, asking when he could expect to hear of her own engagement. Stone's response was filled with underscorings: "I am *not[engaged] to any man.*[26]

In the spring of her second year, Stone began to write and distribute a biweekly paper dubbed *The Plain Speaker*. Its masthead read: "Let every man speak truth with his neighbor"; its tone was lighthearted. To a classmate's criticism that it was "utter nonsense" to publish a paper without the consent of the class, Stone replied: "Our texture is so *stoney* that little impression was produced. We good-naturedly announced our intention, (inasmuch as this is a free country) to continue to do as we had done, until we saw *good reasons* why we should not do so."[27]

Sometime in her second year, Stone began publishing articles and letters in various reform publications. An article on the poor condition of the English laboring classes drew a long rejoinder from a prominent Ohio reformer. Another, "The Province of Woman," warned that "woman will be recreant to her duty if she does not open her mouth for the dumb." Bowman wrote congratulating her on a letter in the *Advocate*.[28]

That summer, Sarah wrote that their father had repaid her the principle and interest on the money Lucy had borrowed "so you won't have to think about that any more. Father . . . says he is not going to have the *'poor fever'* any more, for it is of no use. . . ."[29] In the spring, Stone did not return to teach in the preparatory school. Two young men took over her class, but her former students objected and petitioned for her return. They complained to the administration that the two men were not interested in them. "We *know* that Miss Stone *loved* to teach us and we want her back again," they insisted.[30] Stone went to reason with them. When she asked Robert how he was getting along, he burst into tears and ran from the room. To Sarah, Stone wrote: "That poor outcast's heart had been melted by kindness. I thought that there was *nothing* which kindness might not do if one so hardened could be made so tender." (Stone may have misunderstood the source of Robert's tears. Soon after, she received an awkwardly written love letter from a "Robert Washington" asking if she would consent to "keep company" with him.)[31]

Moved perhaps by Robert's tears, Stone agreed to return to teaching that spring, writing home, "I think it is my duty to go. . . . I think I can be more useful there than anywhere else at present. I have acquired (I hardly know how) an almost boundless influence over them, and while I retain it, I can do them a great deal of good."[32] When later a fire broke out in the Ladies Boarding Hall, a number of her former preparatory pupils rushed to the burning building, each one asking where "Miss Lucy's trunk" was in hopes that he might be the one to carry it out for her. If such virtue brought its own reward, it also cost Stone dearly; by term's end, she was sick with headaches and tired to the point of illness.[33]

The second half of Stone's third year was a critical period for her both intellectually and psychologically. Not least among the events of that spring was the arrival at Oberlin of Antoinette Brown, the daughter of a prosperous Rochester, New York, farmer. Brown had come to Oberlin in hopes of becoming the first woman to be ordained a Congregationalist minister. She had learned of Lucy Stone on the trip out to Oberlin when she shared the stagecoach with a family friend and member of the Oberlin board of trustees who warned her to avoid Stone, "a bright student, and there is nothing against her character; but she is a young woman of strange and dangerous opinions. She is a Garrisonian, and she is planning to become a public speaker, and she is always talking about woman's rights. You had better not have anything to do with her."[34]

Brown's first glimpse of Stone was in the college dining room, where Stone was engaged in an earnest debate with two fellow students and a professor. Brown remembered thinking her "too pert and forward for so young a girl in discussion with an almost middle-aged clergyman." On learning that Stone was actually twenty-eight years old, Brown reconsidered, and despite numerous political, philosophical, and religious differences, the two women became fast friends.[35]

Brown was a devout, practicing Congregationalist, while Stone had continued to draw away from orthodox religion referring to herself in a letter to Frank as his "sinful, erring sister Lucy". Stone was a Garrisonian; Brown opposed the "Come-Outers." Antoinette was enrolled in the Ladies course, Lucy in the classical course. They disagreed even in the matter of clothing. Stone disdained female ornamentation in favor of simple calico gowns and Quaker-type bonnets; she chided Brown about the artificial flowers that decorated her hat, asking her how such a sensible young woman could "carry a flower-pot on her head? Think of the example!"[36]

Although the two young women seldom were able to agree entirely on a single issue, their friendship blossomed, cemented by an emotional bond that was to endure through a lifetime. They loved one another with a preternaturally innocent intensity. Evenings, they climbed the small hill at Oberlin together and sat watching the sunset, their arms around each other. They talked of hopes and fears, of families and teachers, of dreams and plans. On winter nights they snuggled together in one or the other's bed, talking "of everything present and future, and more or less of the past. Of our studies, and of how we could get money to carry out our plans, and also of the comfort of being cuddled up together."[37]

Separated by winter term teaching jobs, they exchanged warmly affectionate letters. Brown later would describe her feelings as the "intense admiration of a younger girl for one much more experienced and influential." Summing up their friendship in a letter, she wrote in the year following Stone's graduation: "We believed no more things in common than any other of my classmates, perhaps *not as many*, & yet I have loved you more than all the rest together." Stone expressed her fear that she would learn to love Brown only to have her go away.[38]

Despite their many differences, the two young women had many similar goals. Because she hoped eventually to study theology, Brown shared Stone's interest in gaining practice at rhetoric and public debate. Together, they went to James Thome, whose rhetoric class they were allowed to audit and who was one of the few faculty members sympathetic to the idea that a woman might be trained to speak in public. They begged him to permit them a debate. Thome agreed, and word spread quickly. A large audience gathered to witness a verbal contest afterward described as "exceptionally brilliant." For their efforts, Stone and Brown were called before the Ladies' Board and rebuked.[39]

Unable to obtain rhetorical practice, Stone and Brown organized a young women's debating society, holding meetings in the house of the mother of one of Stone's former-slave pupils. Their host later confessed to having worried at first that her house might be used for "flirtatious" purposes, but any such fears were soon put to rest. On May 6, 1846, Stone opened the first meeting with a statement of purpose: "We shall leave this college with the reputation of a thorough collegiate course, yet not one of us has received any rhetorical or elocutionary training. Not one of us could state a question or argue it in successful debate."[40] Stone was elected the association's "Critic," which entailed evaluating the compositions and speeches of fellow members.

The young women met regularly from then on to discuss, declaim, and debate. On June 5, 1846, Stone took the negative side in the first of the society's formal debates, staged before the members of the association and friends.[41] Stone soon agreed to make her first public address at the local antislavery society's anniversary celebration of the abolition of slavery in the West Indies. As she prepared her speech, Stone suffered a three-week "siege of terrible headaches." Defiance of custom exacted its toll. The struggle between "dutiful daughter" and rebellious radical brought on migraine headaches, as it would continue to do throughout Stone's life. Despite her inner turmoil, when the moment arrived, she was outwardly in command. At the anniversary celebration on August 1, 1846, she ascended the speakers' platform and spoke to the large crowd.

A reporter from the Cleveland *Leader* was present, and Stone copied part of his article and sent it to her parents: "[Miss Stone's speech] gave evidence that a mind naturally brilliant had not been dimmed, but polished rather, by classical studies and the higher mathematics. I said she is a New England girl. She is so. But she is one of those who believe that neither color nor sex should deprive of equal rights, and true to her principles, she ascended the stand and in a clear full tone read her own article." Stone added, "Now don't think that I am silly because I have copied the above. . . . I know that father used to say that his mother said, 'You can tell your mother anything.' So I can tell my father and mother anything, but they need not tell of it."[42]

Hearing of the speech, the college president's wife had asked Stone if she "did not feel out of place seated on the platform with all those men? Were you not embarrassed and frightened?" Stone answered that she had not been at all afraid. "It is not considered proper here for a woman to do anything of the kind, but I thought it *was right,* and so read. . . . I have a good reason, and I stick to."[43]

The public debates and discussions put on by the Ladies' Literary Society began to draw crowds. According to a classmate, Lucy's success at debating made her "without a peer among the men as well as among the women." An older student who had been the editor of a central Ohio newspaper challenged Stone to debate him on the suffrage question, boasting that "he was double-loaded to the muzzle with arguments to prove that it would wholly unsex women to go to the polls and vote with men."

On the appointed evening, the gentleman went first, pleading his case before a largely sympathetic audience. When he had finished, he sat down. In an account of the debate furnished by a classmate, "Lucy walked out upon the platform with a smile on her face, stated clearly and concisely the objections of the gentleman, and then in witty, logical, and eloquent language riddled his arguments."[44] At breakfast the next morning, friends asked the former editor how he had done. He replied that after delivering his prepared text, he congratulated himself on having settled once and for all the perplexing woman question, "but that little blue-eyed girl in the calico gown from Massachusetts got up, and by the time she had talked five minutes, she not only had my arguments 'unsexed' but swept them away like chaff before the wind. . . . If ever that girl reaches her fiftieth birthday, American women as well as the women of the world will owe her a debt of gratitude they can never repay."[45] Though Oberlin had closed its official rhetoric classes to her, the training Stone received through such ad hoc practice probably could not have happened anywhere else.

That spring, Stone exchanged a series of letters with Abby Kelley and her new husband, Stephen Foster, fellow Garrisonians, about the possibility of their coming to Oberlin to lecture. President Asa Mahan refused the "infidels" permission to speak. Stone argued for the Fosters, and after a month-long controversy, she wrote home in frustration,"I am sorry when the true friends of the slave disagree, for union is strength, and the poor slave suffers *suffers* by disunion."[46]

Eventually, she persuaded the local antislavery society to sponsor the Fosters' visit. Following their departure, she wrote to them that she had had a *"grand* time" and thought their talks had "set the people to thinking." She thanked them for coming, writing, "I wish I *could tell* you how much *good* I received from your visit here—my heart dances gaily at the remembrance. It will be *long* before I shall be *so cheered again*—but never mind. This is not a world to sit down and whimper in."[47]

Many changes had taken place in Stone's family in her absence. Aunt Sally had died. In 1844, Frank married a young Brookfield woman, Harriet Blake, and in 1846, they had a baby daughter. Bowman and his wife Phebe Robinson had two sons born while Lucy was at Oberlin. In July 1845, Sarah married a young schoolteacher, Henry Lawrence. Getting news of these events at Oberlin made Coy's Hill seem far away, and Stone wrote Sarah:

My heart is saddened when I think that the home of my childhood is *mine no longer*—that change has made such dreadful inroads, that even if I were there, it could not seem as formerly. *You* are gone, Aunt Sally is *dead, Francis* is married. Alas, my New England home, that hillside where my hearts warmest affections are lavished, has lost many of the *gems* that made it dear. Yet still my heart yearns toward it with an indescribable longing and *bleeds* when I think that *perhaps* I shall *never* again see it. . . .[48]

With only the slow and expensive mail to link them, Stone and her mother wrote of making "spirit" visits. Describing one of these, Hannah wrote, "I go quick, no mortal sees me while I go nor when I come back,"[49] to which Stone replied,

I believe *I know every time you come here mother,* for I have a great many spirit chats with you. I have a visit almost every night between sundown and dark, and *many* times during the day too. In dreams my fancy roams about *my own dear home*. Often I drink from the spring at the bottom of the hill, and run through the woods and the pastures, till the bell calls me back, and I wake to find myself *here*.[50]

The letters Stone exchanged with her family are intimate, open, and frank. They traded ideas, opinions, and news, frequently offering one another unsolicited advice about the most personal and private details of their lives. When Frank's wife Harriet announced that she was pregnant with her second child, due when the first was just ten months old, Stone's father wrote her that Frank seemed to be going along "at rail road speed in family line." He described their baby as "the poorest thing I ever *see*," adding, "if it lives, it won't know much." When Sarah announced that she was getting married, Hannah wrote Lucy that she thought Sarah's engagement "unwise . . . for I do not think she loves him as she ought. it is a tuff case to marry one we do love [sic]"[51]

Sarah described her new husband as "having not so much external polish as a great many," but as being a man of "real integrity of character." In looks, she wrote, he is "very much like Frederic [sic] Douglass, only not quite so dark, so if you have met Douglass, you can form a very correct idea of how Henry looks."[52]

Stone, having abjured marriage for herself, was nonetheless free with marital advice: "Sarah," she wrote, "make it a matter of conscience *never to read* until your domestic duties are *all done,* for if you wish to retain your husband's love and make your home a happy one, you must make it a well ordered one, which it cannot be if it suffers neglect. You must be *prudent in cooking."* . . . The letter went on in this vein at length, ending with a plea for details of the wedding, "especially" the wedding gift from their father.[53]

Sarah responded angrily that her father had given her twenty dollars in all. "I felt as though they were hardly dealing equally with their children." Declaring herself opposed to "the principle" and not to "the fact," she wrote: "Father said I should have it sometime if I did not now, and how much do you suppose you & I are to have? Why, sis, after father & mother are done with it, we have $200 each, and the boys the rest. What father is worth after the debts are paid will be nearly $9000, so you see there will be quite a difference between the portions of the sons and daughters. . . . The boys, you know, have had a good deal more now than we have & they keep getting every day, butter, lard, cheese, soap, potatoes. . . ." Still smarting a year later, Sarah wrote advising Lucy not to pay back the money she had borrowed. "Father don't need it, and if you pay him back, you may never get *anything.* You better keep it now you have it."[54]

As she would do so often, Stone defended her father, claiming that it was "less Father's fault than it is the fault of the time when his impressions of what is right in such cases were formed." Her father's action furnished "additional proof of the tyranny of custom, and shows the necessity of making custom right, if it must rule."[55] Though Stone was not as yet ready to divulge to her family exactly how she intended to go about the business of "making custom right," she had already written Abby Kelley Foster of her intention to become a public speaker for woman's rights. "There is a growing interest in woman's rights here," she wrote Stephen and Abby Kelley Foster.[56]

As she entered her final year at Oberlin, Stone's financial situation was more secure than it had been. The earnings from her summer teaching job and the money owed her by the college freed her from the necessity of working during the school term. She wrote home asking only for some cotton cloth with which to make chemises, adding "I don't know but you will think there is no end to my wants, but remember it is only one year more, and then I can go to work to pay up the old score."[57]

Early in Stone's senior year, a quotation from Montaigne to the effect that women were more "sunk" in marriage than men prompted her to ask in class for a clarification. Professor John Morgan "fidgeted in obvious discomfort" before explaining that "a married woman loses her maiden name for one thing; her family are not as readily traceable in history as her husband's; the law gives her property unto the husband's keeping, and she is little known to the business world." Morgan's acknowledgment only confirmed what Stone had read in Grimké's *Letters* and witnessed in the married lives of friends and neighbors in West Brookfield. "I will never lose my name," she vowed to Antoinette.[58]

That autumn, Stone raised an issue Morgan had not thought to mention. In a round-robin correspondence she initiated involving Sarah, Frank, Bowman, and Luther, Stone expressed her belief that every woman should have the right to control her own body after marriage. Men's insistence upon conjugal rights without regard either to a woman's wishes or to the health consequences of frequent pregnancies was a form of "legal adultery." In the interest of health, women should have no more than one baby every three years. Husbands should practice sexual restraint, sleeping in separate beds if necessary.[59]

Sarah responded that "Husband dont! like your idea of running away from temptation." Bowman wrote that Lucy "might be a better judge of the matter if you were married." He added that as God had joined husband and wife, "Nothing should separate them from the same bed, especially on cold winter nights."[60] Frank, equally plainspoken, wrote:

This waiting three years Sis, as you intimate, is all nonsense. Have them as fast as you can if you can take care of them, and if you cant, trust Providence and obey the command given to our first parents to multiply and replenish the earth. . . . You spoke of cohabiting only fore [sic] the sake of children . . . I would ask still further for what do you take your daily meals each day; do you eat because you are hungary, so then I suppose individuals do not cohabit fore the sake of children only, but because they want to.[sic][61]

Luther wrote condemning the "Beast-like use of . . . generative organs" while underlining the statement: *"Lucy I Think It As Great A Sin To Not Suffer These Organs To Be Used At All As To Use Them To [sic] Much."*[62]

For Stone, the argument was theoretical. She was as determined as ever not to marry. In the autumn of 1846, she broke the news to her family that following graduation she intended to become a public lecturer, speaking for the antislavery cause and for the "elevation" of women. The vehemence of Sarah's response surprised her. "I hardly know what you mean by 'laboring for the restoration and salvation of our sex.'" Except for receiving unequal pay (a condition Sarah attributed to women's unwillingness to educate themselves) she "knew of no respect in which women were oppressed." In Sarah's opinion, Lucy would "degrade" herself by public lecturing, and if she were to persist, Sarah asked that she at least go someplace far from Massachusetts.[63]

Stone responded with a long letter accusing Sarah of being so blinded by her own domestic bliss that she failed to see the "untold wrongs, mental, moral, physical and social under which the mass of women are suffering." Stone's letter affords both a psychological portrait and a foreshadowing of the rhetorical prowess she would later display. Stone began by speaking of the timeliness of the woman question. "There is scarcely a paper comes to our reading room which does not contain something which looks in that direction," she wrote, moving into the speaking rhythms of the platform.

Woman will not always be a *thing*. The signs of the times indicate a change. I *see* it in the coming events whose shadows are cast before them, and in the steady growth of those great principles which lie at the foundations of all our relations. I *hear* it in the inward march of freedom's host and *feel* it deep in my inner being.

Yes, a new and glorious era is about to dawn upon us, an era in which woman taking her place on the same platform with her equal brothers, conscious of her rights, her responsibilities, her duties, will arouse, and apply her long slumbering energies for the redemption of this sin ruined world. It will take a long time to effect that change; the evil is so deep rooted and so universal, but it *will come*. The oak grows from the acorn, and the mighty river from the little rill. . . .

when I see the pulpit, and the press combine to crush her intellect and the whole machinery of society calculated to drive us wholesale into that system of legalized adultery, to which we rush rather than starve, I say when I see these things, my blood leaps like wildfire through my veins and my whole being is pledged *anew to life-long effort.*

Stone went on to remind Sarah of the shared outrage over the Brookfield Bull, and recommended that her sister read Samuel May's pamphlet *Rights and Condition of Women.*[64]

In preparation for her career, Stone initiated a correspondence with various individuals favorable to woman's rights, "but it seems that few of them go to the root of the matter," she noted. In March, Sarah wrote again hoping to persuade her sister to change her plans. Lucy's efforts as a public lecturer would be "like the wind battling the deep rooted oak," she wrote. "I know you always had peculiar power over the minds of children, you could turn them whithersoever you would. With grown up children, I fear you will be less successful."[65]

On January 10, 1847, Francis, Sr., wrote expressing his and Hannah's dismay. Ever practical, he warned her that if she insisted upon lecturing, she would get "fit out so you can't keep school," adding "Now Miss Lucy you will hear what Mother Thinks about your Public speaking Mother says she had reather you would married Walker and had a pair of twine babies every year, she did not say how many years."[66]

He warned that if she persisted in her course, "it will make much talk in our quarter of the world." Still, he acknowledged that she must do "what seems wright in your own eyes," though he could not resist adding that she could not find a friend in the world who would agree to such a plan.[67]

Frank responded by suggesting to Lucy that it would be better if she would choose to lecture on "human" rights rather than woman's rights, concluding, "If you think you have got brass enough, and can do more good by giving public lectures than any other way, I say go to it. But Mother doesn't like the idea." Harriet appended a note to Frank's letter: "Lucy, if there should be any probability of your changing your mind, I hope you will let Mother Stone know it the first thing, for she feels dreadfully about it. Mother wants you to think carefully of it, and see if you cannot do more good teaching than by lecturing. And if you think you must lecture, she wants to know if you don't think you could do more good by going house to house, as Harlan Page did."[68]

On March 14, 1847, Stone wrote again, hoping to persuade her mother with scriptural allusions and pious diction. She wrote of being "true to my Heavenly Father," and of being "actuated by high and holy principles." She asked her mother whether "because I know that I shall suffer, shall I, for this, like Lot's wife, turn back?" As for the suggestion that she go from house to house, she questioned why she should when she could reach so many more in so much less time. Her appeal continued:

I surely would not be a public speaker if I sought a life of ease, for it will be a most laborious one; not would I do it for the sake of honor, for I know that I shall be disesteemed, nay, even hated, by some who are now my friends, or who profess to be. Neither would I do it if I sought for wealth, because I could secure it with far more ease and worldly honor by being a teacher. . . . you would not object, or think it wrong, for a man to plead the cause of the suffering and the outcast, and surely the moral character of the act is not changed because it is done by a woman. . . . I expect to plead not for the slave only, but for suffering humanity everywhere. *Especially do I mean to labor for the elevation of my sex.*[69]

Stone pleaded with her mother not to "withhold your consent from my doing anything that I think is my duty to do. You will not, will you Mother?" She also sweetened the argument in favor of lecturing by adding that if she were to teach, she would probably remain in Ohio, where the need was greatest, whereas if she were to accept the offer to lecture in

Massachusetts, she could spend summers at Coy's Hill, helping with the work.[70]

Bowman alone did not discourage her, writing, "If you violate your sense of duty to please your friends, you will lose more than you will gain."[71]

Despite almost ten years of preparation, Stone had little confidence in her ability to speak as she moved toward graduation from Oberlin. She continued the meetings in the house on the edge of the woods, and that autumn, she assumed the presidency of the Young Ladies' Association. Among the speeches she delivered was one on "Wasted Intellect" in which she argued for women's intellectual parity with men, insisting that with this capability came responsibilities. Women must labor not only "in those departments in which *custom* says we may labor" but in "*whatever* department." As for "corrupt custom," women had too long "listened to its lies until we have come to regard them as truths which have so blinded our moral vision that we have lost sight of the fact that women form an *integral* part in the fabric of human society." Stone argued that women were not blameless for being regarded as intellectually inferior, for

we have suffered our minds to be engrossed with trifles light as air. . . . while the monster slavery has made every sixth woman in the land liable to outrage and every abuse, we . . . sat in conscious security by our own fireside, stitching perforated papers or embroidering muslin. . . . We must dig ourselves out of the deep mine of ignorance and sloth . . . and looking over the broad battlefield of life choose some department to which we will apply our energies and then undaunted by difficulties— true to our *one* purpose, go steadily on brave and triumphant to the accomplishment of our object.[72]

As graduation neared, Stone was the near-unanimous choice of her fellow students for the honorific of preparing a graduation essay. The women of the Ladies Literary course, whose ceremony was separate from that of the college, and who received certificates of course completion rather than diplomas, were permitted to read their own graduation speeches, but the women of the classical course had their speeches read by Professor Thome, as it was deemed a breach of propriety to have young men and women together on the speakers' platform. Stone would have none of it, writing home: "We are trying to get the Faculty to let the ladies of our class read their own pieces when they graduate. . . . we expect to read for ourselves, or not to write."[73]

Her classmates persuaded President Mahan and Miss Adams, principal of the Female Department, to plead Stone's case before the Faculty and Ladies' Board. After two weeks' deliberation, the Board decided against it, and though many of her classmates urged her to reconsider and permit Professor Thome to read her essay, Stone refused. To do so, she argued

in words that echoed the speech she had given, would be a "public acknowledgment of the rectitude of the principle which takes away from
women their rights and denies them the privilege of being co-laborers
with men in any sphere to which their ability makes them adequate."[74]

The final struggle over the issue of her graduation essay capped a four-
year relationship with the Oberlin administration that was at once adver-
sarial and amicable. Oberlin's opposition catalyzed Stone; her acts of
rebellion—the public debates, the speech at the West Indian anniversary
celebration, the underground newspaper, the women's debating society,
and the final refusal to have her essay read—tempered her resolve as no
classroom instruction could have done. Though the price of her resistance
as measured in migraine headaches was high, Stone's charismatic charm
had sheltered her from the pain and isolation that otherwise might have
resulted. "On the whole," she wrote home in 1846, "I think they respect
me more for carrying out my principles. They think I am honest, but say
they are sorry I believe as I do."[75]

For practical advice on how to proceed in beginning her lecturing career, Stone wrote to Abby Kelley Foster. Foster answered with an invitation from Samuel May to become a lecturer for the Anti-Slavery Society.
They would pay her six dollars per week and also pay the expenses of a
traveling companion for her. At the same time, Stone received an offer
from the Western Anti-Slavery Society to travel and lecture for them in
the state of Ohio in the company of antislavery lecturer Mercy Lloyd, a
woman Stone had met and liked. The western society offered the chance
to speak more informally, but either from loyalty to the Fosters or because she missed her family, Stone decided upon the Massachusetts offer.[76]

Samuel May wanted her to begin lecturing at the end of June, but as
she was not graduating until August, Stone responded that she would
come to Massachusetts immediately after graduation and begin her course of
lectures then. Meantime, William Lloyd Garrison, Frederick Douglass,
and Stephen Foster were all coming to Ohio that summer, and Stone
looked forward to hearing those who would soon be her colleagues, an
anticipation that humbled her and triggered second thoughts. "It had been
my plan to teach a year or two and save enough to pay my debts, and
during the time lecture my scholars and thus learn how to lecture publicly," she wrote home. Despite her year of "declamation and discussion," she felt that "I need more general practice before I can do justice to
myself, or to the cause either, as a public speaker."[77]

For graduation, Stone ordered a dress length of black bombazine from
New York for her first new dress in four years. On graduation day, August 25, 1847, wearing the fine new garment she had sewn for the occasion, Stone sat silently through the men's reading of their commencement

essays. No member of her family could be present to see her step forward when her name was called and have the Bachelor of Arts degree conferred upon her. She had turned twenty-nine the previous week; one long chapter of her life was ending. She was leaving Oberlin intellectually and rhetorically armed for battle in the "*one* department to which we will apply our energies."

Graduation coincided with the arrival in Oberlin of William Lloyd Garrison, the man whose picture had adorned her room through her four years at college. He had come with Stephen Foster and Frederick Douglass for the antislavery rally. Stone attended the series of meetings that drew crowds in excess of three thousand. Her feelings on meeting her hero are not recorded, but for his part, Garrison was sufficiently impressed by Stone to write home to his wife:

Among others with whom I have become acquainted is Miss Lucy Stone, who has just graduated, and yesterday left for her home in Brookfield, Mass. She is a very superior young woman, and has a soul as free as the air, and is preparing to go forth as a lecturer, particularly in vindication of the rights of woman. Her course here has been very firm and independent, and she has caused no small uneasiness to the spirit of sectarianism in the institution.[78]

After an absence of four years, Lucy Stone, returning at last to her home and family in Massachusetts, was the first of that state's daughters to receive a college degree. Diploma in hand, she boarded the stage in Oberlin. Four days later, she would be back at Coy's Hill, ready to "speak for the women."

CHAPTER FIVE

"Whether We Like It or Not, Little Woman, God Made You an Orator"

Stone returned to Coy's Hill late in August 1847. The farm was at it most beautiful as the summer days lengthened and harvest time began. While she awaited word from the New England Anti-Slavery Society about when her speaking tour would begin, she slipped back into the pleasures and chores of farm life. Away from Coy's Hill, in cities and towns across America, the autumn of 1847 was tumultuous. Bitterness mounted between expansionists, who cheered the progress of General Zachary Taylor's troops through the narrow streets of Mexico City, and reformers, who regarded Manifest Destiny and the Mexican War as a dangerous expansion of the power and territory of slaveholders. The Mexican War was just one issue of many over which Americans found themselves sharply divided.[1]

The perilous situation of native Americans; the waves of immigrants providing a labor surplus that invited exploitation; the rising tide of nativist, anti-immigrant, and anti-Catholic activity—all stirred the passions and prejudices of the young country. Political, social, economic, and spiritual issues coalesced around the issue of slavery—a pernicious wedge that soon would sunder the nation.[2]

Stone waited in vain for the summons from the New England Anti-Slavery Society; the autumn days grew shorter, and still there was no word from Samuel May. Abby Kelley Foster, Stone's primary link to the New England organization, was temporarily retired, at home in Worcester awaiting the birth of a child.

As she waited for word, Stone got to know the new members of the family. Bo and Phebe were the parents of two young sons; Frank and

Harriet had a baby daughter; both Luther and Sarah were married. Surrounded by domesticity, Stone wrote Brown that she was resolved "more than ever" that she "must not get married."[3]

Antoinette agreed; they would "stand alone" if need be and "let [the people] see that woman can take care of herself and act independently without the encouragement and sympathy of her 'lord and master'. . . . Oh no dont let us get married."[4] Stone and Brown were not alone in their resolve; the 1840s and 1850s saw the emergence of a "cult of single blessedness" among women.[5] In Stone's case, however, her aversion to marriage seemed to transcend the ideological; she had a genuine abhorrence for the idea.

When October arrived and she still had not heard from Samuel May, Stone took a winter teaching position in North Brookfield and began searching for opportunities to practice public speaking. Coy's Hill, with its surrounding warren of small towns, offered a convenient base from which to launch a series of lectures. Later that autumn, Stone made her first public speech on the subject of woman's rights at Bowman's church in Gardner. Speaking of the symbolic importance of the founding of Mary Lyon's seminary, Stone said, "Get but a truth once uttered and 'tis like a star new-born." Though Lyon had only intended to provide educated wives for missionaries, Stone told her audience that "whatever the reason . . . it lifted a mountain load for women, [for] it shattered the idea, everywhere pervasive as the atmosphere, that women were incapable of education, and would be less womanly, less desirable every way if they had it."[6] In striking at the root of the "unsexed woman" argument, Stone defused a powerful weapon of her foes. From the time of the "bluestockings," opponents of women's rights had argued that education would "masculinize" women—that women thus empowered would be unlovable and unmarriageable. Instead, she argued, women's lives would be "ennobled by grand and glorious uses."[7]

Stone was buoyed by the enthusiastic applause that followed; she was less successful on her second outing. Called upon unexpectedly, she agreed to make an extemporaneous speech at a nearby township celebration, because as she explained later, "I believed in woman's speaking in public and didn't like to back out." She "started well enough," and then "got scared and forgot all the rest." Plainspoken and honest, Stone told her audience that she had not expected to speak—but when called on had thought of some things she would like to say. Now she had forgotten just what those things were, she said, and so would sit down again. Afterward, she visited with her friend Anna Cooey Watkins and Anna's mother. The latter, making reference to Stone's embarrassment, asked hopefully: "I suppose that discouraged you and you will give up the idea of speaking any more?" Stone was indignant. "Well, I guess not! It only showed me how much work there is for me to do."[8]

Throughout that winter and spring, she seized every opportunity to speak, polishing the skills she had gained at Oberlin, learning to modulate her voice and to project its musical tones into the farthest corners of church halls and auditoriums.

In the spring of 1848 after the close of winter term, Stone traveled to Worcester to visit Abby Kelley Foster and her newborn baby daughter. In the course of the visit, Abby asked why she had changed her mind about lecturing. Stone responded that she had not changed her mind at all; no further word had come from the society. Foster wrote that day to Samuel May, and soon after, Stone reported to Bowman that she was to begin immediately as a paid lecturer for "Mr. May's anti-slavery society," under the terms that had already been promised. Before setting off on her first speaking tour, Stone made one last attempt at winning her parents' approval. She asked Bowman if he would not intervene on her behalf and "tell [Father] that it is a good plain."[9]

Bowman's efforts were futile. Hannah and Francis were implacable; it seemed to them that no less than Lucy's immortal soul was at risk. She was disobeying the biblical injunction against women preaching, they told her; she would "disgrace the family" and would "never afterward be able to earn an honest living." Stone recorded their objections in a letter to Bo, characteristically commenting: "I however thought differently, and concluded to go."[10]

Hannah and Francis Stone may well have been concerned for her physical safety as well. Antislavery speakers could expect to be beaten, harassed by mobs of angry citizens, occasionally tarred and feathered and otherwise abused. Women lecturers were accused of being vulgar, of being "Fanny Wright" women (Frances Wright's name was often associated with atheism and free love-ism in the popular press), and charged with all manner of social crimes.[11]

From Oberlin came rare words of encouragement from Antoinette Brown: "Success to the Truth and to you, dearest Lucy. . . . I am glad you are going to lecture. . . . Be good Lucy be good and dont be afraid of any body but speak as though you had a right to."[12] Stone would not speak "as though" she had a right to; she would speak because she had the right.

Her first paid speech was in Waterford, Massachusetts, before a moderately large crowd. Good newspaper accounts heightened interest and resulted in a larger crowd at Milltown, her next stop in Massachusetts. Word of the power of her oratory spread, and soon Stone was filling churches, town halls, and schoolhouses. Weather permitting, she spoke outdoors in picnic groves. A single week's schedule, published in the *Liberator,* showed her making six speeches in five different towns.[13]

Crowds gathered to heckle and stayed to cheer. Speaking without a written text in the "golden age of American oratory," Stone soon was being compared favorably with the great orators of the era. "Eloquence was dog-cheap in those days," wrote Ralph Waldo Emerson.[14] Even so, Stone stood out. After hearing her talk, one reporter gushed, "I have never, anywhere, heard a speaker whose style of eloquence I more admired: the pride of her acquaintances, the idol of the crowd, wherever she goes, the people *en masse* turn out to hear Lucy Stone." Her appearance on the platform occasioned sustained applause, and several minutes often elapsed before she was permitted to speak.[15]

Her voice was the first thing mentioned by those who sought to explain Stone's extraordinary power over audiences. An opponent of woman's rights told of Stone's visit to his hardware store: "The moment that that woman spoke to me she had me at complete command. I would have done anything for her. . . . She has the voice of an angel, and with that voice, she can't be anything but a good woman."[16] Thomas Wentworth Higginson told a similar story about his sisters and Lucy Stone. They had been "utterly opposed" to the whole [woman's rights] movement," but went out of curiosity to hear Stone speak. Higginson reported that one of his sisters "burst out in indignation not that Lucy Stone should be so objectionable, but that being a reformer she should be so lovely . . . a sweet creature, with her winning voice . . . whose very look suggests a home and a husband and a baby."[17]

Eschewing the grand style favored by the great orators of the day, Stone used the plain prose of everyday life in her speeches, moving from the general to the particular, illustrating her theoretical points with homely and poignant stories, some of them told to her by fugitive slaves while she was at Oberlin. She told the story of an escaping slave family, of their desperate flight, of the terrors they experienced as they hid, and of the father's attempts to defend his family when they were recaptured. Having stirred her audience's emotions, Stone went on to appeal to reason, showing how slavery "cursed us spiritually, morally, and materially."[18]

By fall, Stone's name was appearing alongside Garrison's and Wendell Phillips's on posters announcing antislavery conventions. Many of the antislavery reformers became warm friends as well.[19] The chance meeting at Oberlin with William Lloyd Garrison blossomed into friendship, and Stone often stayed with the Garrisons when she was in Boston. Through Garrison, she also met Francis Jackson and Charles Hovey, wealthy philanthropists who became lifelong friends and supporters. Elizabeth Peabody, the noted educator and member of a distinguished New England family, welcomed Stone to evening salons in her home on Beacon Hill.[20]

As her fame spread, Stone found herself in a social world different from any she had known. At the home of Ann and Wendell Phillips, she made the acquaintance of the group who came to be known as the transcendentalists—Henry Thoreau, Ralph Waldo Emerson, Bronson Alcott, and others. She met foreign dignitaries and made the acquaintance of legislators. In an age marked by social flux, when climbing society's ladder was uppermost in many minds, Stone remained curiously indifferent to the social status of her friends. Catharine Sedgwick, the well-known novelist and member of a socially prominent Massachusetts family, commented after meeting Stone on her "entire self-forgetfulness and divine calmness." The singleness of purpose that ordered her life spilled over into her choice of friends. Though she was widely liked and admired, Stone had little time for those she found too frivolous; not surprisingly, her litmus test for friends and acquaintances was their stand on the twin reforms she advocated.[21]

The material comfort of Stone's visits to Boston and New York contrasted sharply with her trips through the countryside. In one letter, she described an afternoon's trip aboard an open wagon in a driving rainstorm, the journey lengthened by the numerous stops the driver made along the way to deliver wine, tobacco, and "segars" to grocers. Soaked to the skin, her bonnet hanging limply around her face, Stone jounced along in the wagon. "I comforted myself on the way by thinking that we were in a free country, and that it was a capital thing to be very independent," she wrote. Stone told of going hungry one night after the overworked woman with whom she was staying chopped her washrag into the meat while struggling to cook dinner with half a dozen children at her hem. Another night Stone lay sleepless in a bed where only a "thin partition" separated her from a noisy crowd of "drinking and carousing" young men. While it may have been the noise that disturbed her, it is also possible that her fear of sexual assault kept her awake all night.[22]

Shortly after beginning a course of lectures in Boston, Stone went to see *The Greek Slave,* Hiram Powers's statue of a young woman being auctioned by Turkish captors. She described how she trembled with emotion as she looked on it: "There it stood in the silence, with fettered hands and half-averted face—so emblematic of women. I remember how the hot tears came to my eyes at the thought of the millions of women who must be freed. . . . [it] took hold of me like Samson upon the gates of Gaza."[23]

That night Stone spoke with particular vehemence, her plea for the slave entwined in a flood of rhetoric protesting the ways in which all women were enchained. Though she was being paid to lecture against slavery, woman was ascendant that night.

Samuel May rebuked her: "The people came to hear anti-slavery, and not woman's rights; and it isn't right."

"I was a woman before I was an abolitionist," Stone responded. "I must speak for the women." She offered her resignation, telling him, "I will not lecture anymore for the Anti-Slavery Society, but will work wholly for woman's rights."

May was unwilling to lose so magnetic a speaker, and Stone was unhappy about abandoning the cause of the slave. They worked out an agreement whereby she would receive only four dollars per week for preaching antislavery on Saturdays and Sundays—the days when the largest crowds gathered. On weekdays, she would speak for woman's rights at her own expense.[24]

Though Stone was the only woman in the nation making a career of lecturing on woman's rights, the topic had been arousing considerable interest throughout the United States. Ladies' literary societies debated political rights for women; women were actively campaigning for changes in married women's property laws; others were reading and circulating Grimké's *Letters on the Equality of the Sexes.* Early in the summer of 1848, a small group of friends announced a woman's rights gathering at Seneca Falls, New York. Among the planners were Elizabeth Cady Stanton and Lucretia Mott, who had met eight years before at the World Anti-Slavery Convention in London.[25] Mott, a Quaker abolitionist and advocate of woman's rights, had kept a copy of Mary Wollstonecraft's *Vindication of the Rights of Woman* on the center table in her home for over forty years, lending it to anyone who would agree to read it.[26] The friendship forged in London between the Quaker abolitionist and the brilliant feminist theorist bore fruit in 1848 in what came to be called the Seneca Falls convention.

Mott, in western New York for a church meeting, went to call on her old friend Stanton, who convinced her that the time was right for a public meeting to discuss woman's rights. They arranged for the use of the Wesleyan Methodist Chapel in Seneca Falls and published a card in the *Seneca County Courier* calling women to a "convention to discuss the social, civil, and religious condition and rights of women."[27]

Its organizers worried that few would attend the convention scheduled for July 19 and 20. They vastly underestimated the interest in woman's rights that had been growing steadily throughout the decade. On the designated morning, farm roads and stage routes throughout the surrounding countryside were clogged with wagons bringing eager women by the score to answer the call. They crowded the church and, in the course of the next two days, listened to speeches. After agreeing upon "A Declaration of Rights and Sentiments," they voted to approve resolutions proposing legal equality and the right to vote for women.[28]

Two months after the Seneca Falls meeting, Stanton wrote her friend Amy Post about the need to keep the flame ignited there alive. Although Stanton had not yet met Lucy Stone, she was aware of Stone's fame as a woman's rights speaker: "We have declared our right to vote—what now? . . . Should we have an agent to travel over the country and lecture on the subject? Lucy Stone might be engaged for this purpose. . . . I have understood she said she wished to devote herself to the cause of woman. . . ."[29]

Stone may have received the offer, for in November, she had a letter from Brown saying, "How glad I am that you are going to lecture for the Womans Rights convention or Soc. rather." The reference is unclear. Neither Stone nor Brown makes mention of the previous summer's Seneca Falls gathering.[30] Apparently, nothing came of the planned convention or society, and Stone and Stanton did not meet for another three years.

In the meantime, Stone continued to act as her own woman's rights agent, paying for the printing of the posters and the rental of the halls by taking up collections after her lectures. Reluctant to charge admission, Stone saved what money she could by boarding in the least expensive lodgings or with friends, more than once sleeping three to a bed with the landlord's daughters.

At a financial low point early in her speaking career, Stone found herself down to fifty cents. In Salem, Massachusetts, she was scheduled to precede the Hutchinsons, a well-known family of antislavery singers.[31] John Hutchinson suggested they they combine their programs that evening. As the Hutchinsons regularly charged a small admission fee, he proposed that they divide the receipts evenly. Stone's share of the gate was sufficient to allow her to buy a replacement for the threadbare cloak she had worn for so long. Still she continued to pass the hat at each meeting's end until a Vermont suffragist unwittingly printed the notice that there would be an admission charge at Stone's lecture. When Stone saw that crowds poured in despite the fee, she regularly began to charge twelve and half cents' admission. The fee "in no wise prevented those who were interested from attending," and it kept out the "stampers and hoodlums."[32]

Returning to Boston from Syracuse one afternoon, Stone climbed the stairs to the *Liberator* office. From the landing above came a booming voice: "Whether we like it or not, little woman, God made you an orator!"[33] The voice belonged to Theodore Parker, and he was quoting from an editorial in the previous day's Syracuse *Standard*.[34]

Whatever the source of Stone's oratorical power, the crowds had grown, occasionally numbering two to three thousand. After deducting the cost of travel, hall rental, and advertising, Stone was still making a handsome living. Reform was surprisingly profitable, a fact which did not escape the notice of her detractors. One reporter, after describing how Stone "enchained" her audience with the hypnotic power of her oratory, concluded: "Her task or object, if she really has any beyond filling her purse, is a hopeless one."[35]

Stone's filled purse paid for the production and distribution of a series of woman's rights pamphlets and paid for the printing in booklet form of the proceedings of the early woman's rights conventions. In the first three years of lecturing, Stone also saved more than seven thousand dollars.[36]

The admission charge did not prevent "stampers and hoodlums" from congregating outside the halls where Stone was speaking. Once, in the middle of winter, a pane of glass was smashed and she was drenched with water from a fire hose. On another occasion, pranksters locked her audience in, bolting the doors from the outside. The *Liberator* of July 14, 1848, reported that in East Bridgewater, Massachusetts, Stone's and Parker Pillsbury's arguments were answered with a "logic" consisting of "a profusion of coppers, dried apples, smoked herring, beans, and tobacco quids." There, a man in the back suddenly stood and hurled a hymnbook as hard as he could at Lucy. It struck her from behind with such force that she was momentarily stunned. Pillsbury remarked to the audience that if the man had possessed any better argument, he would not have used that one. Stone rose to speak, her ears still ringing from the force of the blow.[37]

Occasionally, Stone turned assaults to her advantage. When an egg thrown through an open window landed on her shoulder, Stone wiped her dress with her handkerchief and said calmly, "If you could as easily remove from your minds the seeds of truth which I have sown tonight as I can this stain from my garment, I should feel that my work here had been in vain. You cannot."[38]

A man in the audience hissed at her one evening, and she stepped forward as if looking for the source of the noise. Pointing in the direction from which the hissing had come, Stone said, "Somebody hisses. I am glad of it. Hiss it again, my fat friend, for it is a shameful fact, and deserves to be hissed." The audience shouted with laughter, and the man sank lower in his seat. When she continued to point, he rose shame-facedly and left the hall. The narrator of that story told how she herself had gone to hear Stone that evening out of "curiosity." By evening's end, she confessed, Stone had "captured me, convinced me, won me" to a lifelong commitment to woman's rights.[39]

When she could, Stone disarmed her detractors in advance of her meetings. Often, she would have the opportunity to meet with the ringleaders of the "hoodlums" as she went about town nailing her handbills to hitching posts and tree trunks. Young men followed her, tearing down the posters. Stone complimented them, talked to them in friendly fashion, and asked them if they did not love their mothers. Of course they did. "And your sisters are dearer to you than to all others?" Again they nodded. She told how in the South, sons and brothers just their age were wrested from their families and sold on the auction block, never again to set eyes on mother, father, brother, or sister. She then invited them to attend the evening's lectures as her "special guests." Such street recruits proved useful allies, able to defuse other troublemakers.[40]

Occasionally, angry mobs prevented her from speaking. In Harwich, Connecticut, a "furious mob" assaulted the speakers and destroyed the platform where she had been sitting, making a ruckus that could be heard a mile away.[41] At an outdoor meeting on Cape Cod, a mob bent on violence attacked the speakers' platform. The other speakers fled, but Stone and Stephen Foster refused to go. The mob seized Foster, tore his jacket in two, and began to beat him. "You had better run, Stephen," Stone advised.

Foster, a man of extraordinary physical courage, turned and asked, "But who will take care of you?"

Stone turned to the largest of the assailants, a burly man wielding a large club. Taking his arm, she said, "This gentleman will take care of me."

The startled man found himself leading her through the inflamed mob, and as they walked, she talked steadily to him. When they reached the outer edge of the grove, the man cleared a space around a tree stump and lifted Stone up on it so that she could be heard. While she addressed the crowd, he brandished his club at those who tried to shout her down. Gradually, the crowd quieted and began to listen attentively. When she finished, there was an abashed silence. Someone in the crowd suggested that they take up a collection to replace Foster's coat, and twenty dollars was collected for this purpose.[42]

The crowds continued to pour in, even as editorialists warned that being seen in the audience at one of Stone's lectures would "sink them" politically. In warm weather, the speakers' stand was placed near an open window so that those unable to squeeze into the halls could hear her through the window. "She holds her hearers in perfect captivity," wrote one reporter; they listened "in breathless silence," said another.[43] The pattern of speaking weeknights on women's rights and weekends on the abolition of slavery continued.

Following the passage in 1850 of the Fugitive Slave Act, Stone's antislavery speeches took on a harsher tone. "God's balance is hanging in the sky," she warned; slavery must be abolished "at any cost." If the Union could only hold by maintaining slavery, then "the Union must fall. We could have a Northern Republic," she told her audiences.[44]

When the fugitive slave Anthony Burns was captured and held in a Boston jail, Stone delivered a rousing speech in which she spoke of the inevitability of war, "a war which is destined to wage hotter and to grow more intense until, in the end Liberty shall be triumphant." She reminded her audience of the irony of Burns's being held captive in the cradle of freedom, "where the instinct of Liberty is swallowed up in the deep gulf that slavery has spread." She included slave women in her appeal:

He stands there bound, in the long, dark column, with two million of his sisters and our sisters in chains, and the hapless wail of the one chimes in with the sad cry of the other. They stand there, in the long, black column, reaching from yonder court house to the farthest South . . . and there is not strength enough, in this entire country, to . . . set them on the platform that God meant they should stand on, in the simple dignity of human beings.[45]

The Missouri Compromise, which had given rise to the Fugitive Slave Act, drew particular fire. Stone told of being approached in Missouri by a slave girl whose history "I dare not tell you," a "girl of sixteen summers [who] had a little girl of a year and a half." When she thought that by the Missouri Compromise "that child-mother" and her "daughter's daughter" were all slaves, Stone confessed that "I never felt so deeply the necessity for a dissolution of this Union."[46]

Though she often wove women's disabilities into her speeches against slavery, Stone seldom mixed antislavery into her woman's rights speeches. The weeknight speeches were on the "Social and Industrial Disabilities of Women"; the "Legal and Political Disabilities of Women"; and "Moral and Religious Disabilities of Women."[47] Each of the three speeches was more than two hours long, and Stone spoke without a written text. She spoke of the inequalities in marital property laws and described the bills passed and pending in the various states. Among the "moral" disabilities of women, Stone placed the "dependent" state, which she claimed had "distorted and destroyed the marriage relation." Without adequate ways of supporting themselves, women were forced to marry for money. "There is no way of remedying this evil except by making her sphere of labor wider than it is at the present day," she told them. By presenting paid employment as an aid to virtue, Stone hoped to counter the charge that leaving the home would lead to moral ruin. She also spoke of women driven to vice by their inability to support themselves.[48]

Stone's fame continued to grow. Women sought her out after her speeches, eager to pour out their personal experiences. She had tapped a wellspring of stored resentment and pain, and the stories she heard often found their way into subsequent lectures.

In her speech on the religious disabilities of women, Stone attempted a feminist scriptural exegesis. That wives were to be subject to their husbands was not a command but "a fearful prophecy," she told her listeners, adding that "the fact that a thing is foretold does not make it right."

As for her own position on marriage, she wrote Nettie in August 1849 that "My heart aches to love somebody that shall be all its own." Lest Brown construe this as a weakening of her resolve, she hastened to add: "Dont give yourself any uneasiness on my account, for I shall not be married ever." She had not yet seen any man she would be interested in marrying, she wrote, and "if I had, it will take longer than my lifetime for the obstacles to be removed, which are in the way of a married woman having any being of her own, and though it is sad and desolate to live unmarried, it is *worse* to be a *thing.*"[49]

Stone's sense of the loneliness of single life may have been connected to her genuine love of children. Her nieces and nephews regarded Aunt Lucy's visits as times of great merriment. In summer, she played games in the orchard with them, and in winter, she tossed snowballs and frolicked with them in the snowdrifts. She was a natural storyteller, and when chores were finished, her nieces and nephews gathered around and pressed for story after story. Her niece Phoebe recalled that "Aunt Lucy's homecoming was the happiest day of the year."[50] In the homes of her fellow suffragists and antislavery workers, Stone was a great favorite of the children, holding them on her lap, telling them stories, and playing games with them.

Brown also expressed her yearning for children. She wrote that while she continued firm in her resolve never to marry, she thought that she might adopt children once she was established as a minister. Stone responded indignantly: "Nette, *dont,* DONT, D-O-N-T when you "settle as a pastor" take any *children*. It will seem just like an old clucking hen, who shows her setting propensity, without having any eggs, to the merriment of the roosters, and the shame of all the hens."[51]

Stone's antipathy toward marriage remained fierce. When she learned that Richard Cushman, husband of an Oberlin friend, had died suddenly, she wrote Nettie that "Josephine [Cushman's widow] will be as much again of a woman without him, as with him. I sympathize with her grief smitten, desolate heart—but his loss—will be her gain. . . . now she is free, she may make something."[52] Wives were institutional prisoners; single women were free.

As Stone's fame grew, so did the notoriety Hannah had feared. Following a speech in Indiana, a newspaper reported seeing Stone the following morning in the local barroom, "smoking a cigar and swearing like a trooper." Prior to her arrival, the local paper in Springfield, Massachusetts, warned her: "You she-hyena, don't you come here!"[53]

Between speaking engagements, Stone returned to Coy's Hill to rest. She wrote of the peace she experienced at the farm. "I have been very happy all by myself, and today it is so still and quiet. I almost wish it would *always* keep so. It reminds me of those early days, when I seemed to hold converse with the winds and find companions in the clouds." The reverence for creation was akin to religion for Stone, whose departure from orthodoxy made her impatient with Brown's pursuit of a career as a Congregationalist minister. She lamented Brown's adherence to "that old musty theology, which already has its grave clothes on, and is about to be buried. . . ." Stone despised the *"wall* of bible, brimstone, church and corruption which has hitherto hemmed *women* into *nothingness."*[54]

In May 1850, Stone traveled to Boston for the annual anniversary convention of the American Anti-Slavery Society. There, she and a handful of other women, among them Paulina Wright Davis and Abby Kelley Foster, decided that the time was right for calling a national convention to discuss woman's rights. She and Davis posted a notice that an organizational meeting for planning such a convention would take place at the Melodeon Theatre immediately following the closing session of the anti-slavery convention. Nine women and two men met that evening—among them Stone, Davis, Abby Kelley Foster, Dr. Harriot Hunt, Wendell Phillips, and William Lloyd Garrison. Stone was named secretary of the proposed convention, and she and Davis began the preliminary correspondence. Dora and Eliza Taft, Eliza Kenney, Abby Kelley Foster, and Harriot Hunt were named to the committee on arrangements, and they chose Worcester, Massachusetts, as the convention site.[55]

The eleven agreed that if preliminary correspondence elicited enough signatories, they would issue a call and proceed with their plans for a national convention. Garrison and Phillips helped draw up a national list of possible supporters. Stone and Davis were gratified when eighty-nine men and women responded to their preliminary letter by agreeing to sign the call. The call contained the names of thirty-six from Massachusetts, eighteen from Pennsylvania, eleven from Rhode Island, seventeen from New York, six from Ohio, and one from Maryland.[56]

The call to the first national convention, with Lucy Stone's name heading the list, was sent to all major newspapers. Stone was to spend the summer in Providence working with Davis on the details of the convention. She looked forward to the "grand opportunity to improve" which access to the reading rooms of the Providence Atheneum Library would afford her. Writing Antoinette of her summer plans, Stone pleaded with her friend to agree to come to the October convention. "We *need all the women* who are accustomed to speak in public—every stick of timber *that is sound*. I wrote to Lucretia Mott this morning, and to Elisabeth Jones of Ohio to secure their presence."[57] Only "iron necessity" could curtail her plans, she told Brown.

Iron necessity arrived in the form of a letter from Hutsonville, Illinois, where brother Luther lay gravely ill with cholera. His wife Phebe, pregnant and sick, was unable to nurse him. As the only unmarried female in the family, Lucy Stone felt obliged to go. She wrote Samuel May to cancel her speaking engagements and made her apologies to Paulina Wright Davis, who was left with the remainder of the organizational work for the convention.

From Illinois, Stone wrote Samuel May in July of her brother's death. "I have no gloomy ideas of death, but it was sad indeed, to stand alone (his wife could not be present) with strangers around his dying bed. . . . My brother's wife will not be able to travel probably for two or three months. I cannot leave her here alone. It would be cruel."[58]

By late August, Phebe Stone and Lucy were able to attempt the return journey, traveling slowly and resting often. They had gone fewer than ninety miles in three days when Phebe went into labor and gave birth to a stillborn boy. Stone grieved with her sister-in-law, who had "hoped to renew the sundered tie" through the child. After nursing her sister-in-law and arranging for the child's burial, Stone herself was stricken with a severe case of typhoid fever. She and Phebe were in a small hotel in eastern Indiana, in Lucy's words "a *very* lowly one" with broken windows and cracked doors. There, for eighteen days, Stone hovered between life and death. She wrote Samuel May of the ordeal:

During all that time [I] was destitute of care for the nights. Neither "love nor money" would purchase it. I fainted again and again, alone and in darkness, and there was no one to give me a drop of water. I thought of the wish, expressed by the Orientals when parting from their friends, viz. "May you die among your kindred." . . . the neighbors would come in and looking at me ask, "do you think you shall live?"[59]

Stone recovered slowly, and it was early October before she was able to travel to Coy's Hill. Still needing frequent rest, Stone doubted whether she would be well enough to attend the convention. "It is a grievous disappointment to me, but can't be helped," she wrote May.[60]

A week later, Stone had gained sufficient strength to attend the opening session of the first national convention ever held for the cause of woman's rights. The event took place in Worcester's Brinley Hall. Over a thousand people crowded into the hall to hear the talk of woman's rights, and many more were turned away outside.[61]

The convention opened with the reading of the call, which concluded: "The signs are encouraging; the time is opportune. Come then, to this Convention. It is your duty, if you are worthy of your age and country." Paulina Wright Davis, elected president in recognition of her great organizational effort, gave the keynote address.[62]

Five more sessions were held on October 23 and 24, and various resolutions in favor of political, legal, social, educational, and industrial rights for women were offered, among them a resolution to labor for the "right of suffrage without distinction of sex or color." The list of speakers included Lucretia Mott, the Reverend William Channing, Wendell Phillips, Harriot Hunt, Stephen and Abby Kelley Foster, Ernestine Rose, Sojourner Truth, Frederick Douglass, William Lloyd Garrison, and Antoinette Brown. Stone sat listening until the last meeting, when she was finally persuaded to speak. Woman must "take her rights as far as she can get them . . . in the name of a common humanity," she told the large gathering. She urged the women to become political activists, to lobby their state legislatures for marital property rights, to work for woman suffrage. She urged them to circulate her petitions on the *"Right of Suffrage"* and the *"Right of Married Women to hold Property,"* saying:

We want to be something more than the appendages of Society; we want that Woman should be the coequal and help-meet of Man in all the interest and perils and enjoyments of human life. We want that she should attain to the development of her nature and womanhood: we want that when she dies, it may not be written on her gravestone that she was the "relict" of somebody.[63]

The tumultuous applause that greeted this statement revealed the depth of women's dissatisfaction. Stone's words, originating in her own experience of her sister Eliza's death, struck a nerve.[64]

Press coverage of the convention was extensive. Accounts of the speeches were carried in most of the major eastern dailies as well as in reform newspapers. The *New York Herald* ridiculed the Worcester proceedings at great length, referring to them as "that motley gathering of fanatical radicals, of old grannies, male and female, of fugitive slaves and fugitive lunatics, called the Woman's Rights Convention."[65]

Horace Greeley's *New York Tribune,* the most influential newspaper of the time, covered the entire convention; five and a half full columns of the October 25, 1850, issue and five full columns on October 26 reported on the proceedings. The *Tribune* circulated worldwide. In England, Harriet Taylor (soon to be the wife of John Stuart Mill) read the reports and penned an article on the woman's rights convention for the July 1851 issue of the *Westminister Review.* Taylor lauded the "organized agitation" in "public meetings" and the "practical political action" undertaken by the women in pursuit of "enfranchisement . . . admission in law, and in fact, to equality in all rights, political, civil, social, with the male citizens of the community." Following their American sisters' example, Taylor wrote, the women of Sheffield had presented a petition to the House of Lords demanding the franchise.[66]

In Rochester, New York, a young schoolteacher and temperance worker named Susan B. Anthony read and was moved by the *Tribune* account of Stone's speech at the convention. Though almost two years elapsed before Anthony involved herself directly in the woman's rights movement, she would later credit the report of Stone's speech with bringing her to the cause.[67]

Following the convention, Stone paid to have the proceedings printed, as she would do for each of the six subsequent national conventions. She sold the booklets as woman's rights tracts at subsequent conventions and at her lectures. The task of editing and publishing the booklets added to a schedule already filled with lecture engagements and with organizational and legislative lobbying chores.

Stone took responsibility for collecting the petitions and presenting them to the state legislatures; she addressed legislative committees, and when she could she spoke before legislative assemblies. She also gave talks explaining the legislative process to women and showing them the need for action. "How busy you must be in your lectures about congressional proceedings, and how hopeful the times are," Brown wrote from Oberlin.[68]

Stone was not the first to lobby. Paulina Wright Davis and Ernestine Rose had helped secure passage in New York of the Married Woman's Property Act of 1848, a legislative landmark in the legal progress of women. Prior to passage of such acts, the legal principle of coverture held that a wife's legal identity was subsumed into her husband's at the time of her marriage, her property becoming his. Under coverture, a wife could not hold property, make contracts, retain her own earnings, or keep her name after marriage.[69]

Stone continued to lobby for married women's property rights in the months following the convention. Her efforts were curtailed when, two months after the national convention, "iron necessity" again called. Her sister Sarah, nearing term in her first pregnancy, had fallen ill, and she wrote asking if Stone would come to Gardner as nurse and housekeeper until the baby was born. She remained with Sarah for more than two months. If she regretted the interruption, it surfaced only in a note of sadness in her December 1850 letter to Antoinette.[70] On January 28, 1851, Stone helped her sister deliver a daughter, staying on to help with the new baby. It was spring before she was back on the hustings—in time for the May antislavery conventions.

As her fame spread and her sense of mission deepened, Stone experienced a contentment she had not known before. The fierce, debilitating headaches that plagued her at various stages of her life, worsening in times of psychological stress, appear to have disappeared entirely during those first happy years on the road. In 1847, when she set out to lecture, she had been prepared for scorn and rejection. When it came, she was able to take it in stride. She seemed similarly able to accommodate herself to the sudden fame that her oratorical gifts had brought her.

Despite her growing anticlericalism (she had more and more come to regard the organized church as an organ of oppression against women), Stone was nevertheless indignant upon learning of her formal expulsion from the West Brookfield Congregational Church in June 1851 on the grounds that she had "engaged in a course of life evidently inconsistent with her covenant engagement to this church." Though she had long since left the Congregational Church in spirit, Stone nonetheless took the time to respond to her expulsion. Her "course of life," she wrote, "is not only not inconsistent, but is demanded by my covenant engagements."[71]

In the autumn of 1851, Stone organized the second national convention in Worcester. Well attended, it drew widespread and comprehensive press coverage. That winter, Stone's lecture schedule took her to Indiana, Ohio, New York, New Jersey, Pennsylvania, Maine, and Missouri as well as throughout the New England states and on up into Canada, where she outdrew even the world-famed songstress Jenny Lind. The largest Toronto audience that had ever assembled gathered to hear Stone speak.[72]

In May 1852, Stone traveled to Syracuse, New York, to speak at an antislavery meeting. Later, she journeyed farther upstate to the Seneca Falls home of Elizabeth Cady Stanton, who had invited Stone, Horace Greeley, and Susan B. Anthony to assist in drawing up a charter for a proposed People's College, a radical, coeducational experiment in university education.[73] This was Stone's first meeting with Stanton and Anthony.

At Stanton's house, Stone encountered Amelia Bloomer, editor of the temperance and woman's rights paper *The Lily*. Bloomer wore the trousered garment that had created such a sensation since she had printed a pattern for it in her paper. Stone admired Bloomer's trousered dress. Women's dress in the 1850s consisted of yards and yards of heavy material over voluminous petticoats—the whole buttressed by whalebone stays that squeezed the waist. Women's skirts trailed in the mud and caught on carriage wheels, and Stone could not help but appreciate the economic and health benefits of the costume. She wrote to Anthony: "Women are in bondage; their clothes are a great hindrance to their engaging in any business which will make them pecuniarily independent, and since the soul of womanhood never can be queenly and noble so long as it must beg bread for its body, is it not better even at the expense of a vast deal of annoyance [to] give an example by which woman may more easily work out her own emancipation?"[74]

Returning from Seneca Falls, Stone arranged to have her own Bloomer dress made. Sarah tried to get her at least to put lace on the pantalettes, "but Lucy scorned it."[75] Consisting of ankle-length trousers and a full skirt ending just below the knees, the reform dress, though considerably more modest than the décolleté then in vogue, was nonetheless shocking. It drew widespread ridicule.

When Stone first appeared wearing her Bloomer dress, even the radical abolitionists were divided over whether to permit her to continue to appear in it. Leaders worried that her appearance would detract from the seriousness of purpose of the speakers. Wendell Phillips came to her defense, threatening to withdraw his name as a speaker at the upcoming antislavery convention should Stone not be permitted the dress of her choice. She was allowed to appear in her Bloomer costume.[76]

Stone also cut her hair short during this period, prompting a *New York Herald* reporter to describe her as "a little lady on the wrong side of her 'teens'" who wished "to be taken for a little rosebud of 'sweet fifteen.'"[77] Ignoring the criticism, Stone wrote Anthony that "audiences listen, and assent, just as well to one who speaks truth in a short as in a long dress." She did acknowledge its disadvantages, however, complaining that the Bloomer prevented her from seeing places of interest in the cities she visited because "a horde of boys pursue me and destroy all comfort." She confessed that she was "annoyed to death by people who recognize me by my clothes, and when I get a seat in the cars, they will get a seat by me and bore me for a whole day with the stupidest stuff in the world."[78]

Occasionally, the crowds attracted by her costume turned ugly. On one occasion, en route to the post office in New York City, Stone and Anthony were hemmed in and pushed about by a menacing crowd. An acquaintance summoned a policeman and a carriage, and "we escaped with only a little rough treatment at the last."[79]

Stone told of visiting in Philadelphia with the Motts, whose daughters "said they would not go in the street with me." She also worried lest her costume embarrass her friends. "I think it would have been a real relief to them if I had not been there," she wrote after her visit.[80]

Brown, who had finished her training for the ministry, had been appointed pastor of a church in South Butler, New York, in the spring of 1853, and she invited Stone to speak at a temperance convention. Stone declined, fearing that her bloomers might embarrass Antoinette.[81] Brown accused her friend of being "the biggest little goose and granny fuss that I ever did see." She assured Stone that her congregation was aware "that you wear bloomers and are an 'infidel.'"[82]

Both Brown and Anthony identified more with the temperance movement than did Stone, whose primary interests remained woman's rights and abolition. She did attend the May 1853 planning meeting for the World Temperance Convention held at New York's Brick Church. At that meeting, Anthony's nomination to the business committee created an uproar. A credentials committee was quickly appointed, and it voted to reject the women delegates, giving as its reason that women appointees would introduce woman's rights notions to the temperance cause. Thomas Wentworth Higginson resigned in protest, as did a number of others.[83]

The dissenters announced a protest rally to be held the following day at the Broadway Tabernacle. The New York *Tribune* reported that upon learning that Stone would speak, a crowd of more than three thousand gathered.[84] Despite the widespread sympathy manifested at the protest rally, the all-male committee went ahead with its plans. Anthony, until then more interested in temperance reform, began to regard woman's rights as the organizing principle underlying all reform.[85] A tireless and talented organizer and "a driving business woman," in the words of Antoinette Brown, Anthony quickly made her presence felt in the fledgling movement for woman's rights.[86]

Following the rally, the dissenters laid plans for an alternate temperance convention, to be known as the "Whole World's Temperance Convention" as opposed to what they dubbed the "Half-World Convention." In Boston for the New England Anti-Slavery Society anniversary meetings, Stone exhorted her listeners to "strive faithfully to know the right, and then, if the heavens fall, *do it!*"[87]

Immediately following the Boston convention, Stone went before the Massachusetts legislature to testify on behalf of a "full civil rights for women" amendment to the state constitution.[88] The *Liberator* said of Stone's speech: "The whole assembly was deeply moved and men and women alike freely shed tears."[89] Though she did not know it, the power of Stone's oratory that day moved one heart in particular in a manner that would have profound consequences for her.

Chance had placed a young man in the gallery that day; he was Henry Browne Blackwell, a brother of pioneer woman physician Elizabeth Blackwell. He had come with his sister Emily to the legislative hearing. Henry, or "Harry" as he was known to friends and family throughout his life, was a Cincinnati hardware merchant who had come East hoping to find a publisher for a collection of poems he had written and to find himself a wife. In the matter of his poems, he had little luck. Just before leaving Cincinnati, Blackwell had written with characteristic effusiveness to Theodore Parker, whom he had met on a train earlier that year. Hoping that Parker would assist him in finding a publisher, he wrote: "My whole life up to this time has been a series of blunders and weaknesses." He described the "self-contempt" that would be assuaged only by the publication of the "one memorial of my struggles—in the form of a few poems." The poems were never published.[90]

Despite a few initial setbacks, Blackwell would have more luck in his search for a wife. From Brooklyn, he wrote home to his brother Sam about calling on a wealthy young woman, a Miss Pennell, who was "too old and wanting in character," so "that romance is at an end." Leaving New York for Boston, he reported his first disappointment there—"my loved and lost Edna L. who had the brutality to marry some dog of an artist only a day or two after I had reached Boston & before I had the opp'y of seeing & remonstrating with her." All was not lost, he assured Sam; "I have now about wound up all my intended doings East—I have made two very agreeable lady acquaintances in Mrs. Clark & Miss Lucy Stone." Clark was an attractive and well-to-do widow preparing to study medicine. On May 29, Emily Blackwell echoed his optimism, writing in her journal of "Harry's double conquest by Mrs. Clark and Lucy Stone."[91]

Harry's criteria for selection accorded with his philosophy of life. He had written Emily three years before: "I see but one way to get into a position to do something—and that is to find some intelligent, go-ahead lady with a fortune to back her go-aheadativeness."[92] He described his ideal wife in another letter as "a lady with a purpose, a character and a fortune."[93] He enlisted his sisters in his search, drolly asking them to "pick out . . . an heiress for me—I can get along with almost anybody from 17 to 70 years of age if she only have the funds and will let me make a good use of them."[94]

After hearing Stone's speech before the legislature, he wrote: "I shall endeavor to see more of [Stone] before I come West if practicable, as I decidedly prefer her to any lady I have ever met, always excepting the Bloomer costume which I *dont* like practically, tho theoretically I believe in it with my whole soul—It is quite doubtful whether I shall be able to succeed in again meeting her, as she is travelling around—having been born locomotive, I believe."[95]

Searching for a means of getting to know Stone, Blackwell presented himself to his late father's antislavery colleague, William Lloyd Garrison. He asked Garrison for a letter of introduction to Stone. Garrison warned that pursuing Lucy Stone was a waste of time. Many others had tried and failed, he told the would-be suitor, most recently Samuel Brooke, head of the Ohio Anti-Slavery Society. Nevertheless, Garrison provided him with a letter of introduction to Stone's friend and neighbor, Deacon Henshaw. On June 9, 1853, Emily wrote in her journal: "Harry is wandering through Massachusetts looking for Lucy Stone." When Blackwell found his way by way of Deacon Henshaw to Coy's Hill, he found Stone in Bloomer costume, standing on a table and whitewashing the sitting-room ceiling. Presenting himself as brother to Elizabeth Blackwell and an old family friend of William Lloyd Garrison, he received a cordial welcome. With typical impetuousness, Blackwell proposed marriage to the astonished Stone within an hour of their meeting.[96]

Harry's impulsive proposal, though altogether in character for a young man likened by his sister to "a comet that has not found its centre and goes wandering wildly through space," caused Stone later to accuse him of trying to "mesmerize" her.[97] She knew little of him other than that he was the brother of a woman whose reputation she knew and admired. Blackwell would prove most difficult to understand.

Henry Browne Blackwell defies easy analysis; a nineteenth-century enigma, he embodied simultaneously many of the century's best traits—a boundless idealism, a romantic belief in natural human goodness and perfectability, a commitment to reform, a passion for politics; and at least some of the worst of the century's traits—an almost obsessive desire for wealth, a preoccupation with notions of social superiority, a periodic affliction of moral myopia when issues of conscience conflicted with material desires, and a tendency to play fast and loose with the truth in pursuit of his dream. A would-be robber baron with a passion for the downtrodden, Harry Blackwell was Don Quixote in pursuit of the City of Gold.

Born May 4, 1825, in Bristol, England, Harry was the fifth of nine children of Hannah Lane and Samuel Blackwell. Like Stone's, Harry's roots crossed social lines. His maternal grandmother was a Browne, daughter of a prosperous and genteel merchant, who disappointed her family by marrying a ne'er-do-well jeweler by the name of Lane. Lane, unfaithful to his wife, was later convicted of forgery and banished to Australia as an alternative to the gallows. Hannah remembered having been fitted as a child for a black dress to wear to her father's hanging.[98]

Hannah Lane and her children moved into the Bristol home of Hannah's Browne relations, where the children grew up. In 1815, daughter Hannah married Samuel Blackwell, the prosperous young proprietor of a Bristol sugar refinery. The Blackwell family, according to Harry's sisters, was "much inferior to the Brownes," but Samuel, Jr., was "by nature" a gentleman.[99]

Despite having been refused an education by his father, a cantakerous carpenter who treated his wife and children as "chattels," Samuel Blackwell, Jr., and his brother John prospered, John as proprietor of an iron foundry. A third brother, James, went insane, fell hopelessly into debt, and eventually was murdered.[100] Though his father would die while Harry Blackwell was still a very young man, his own character and business practices were much like his father's.

In 1831, business losses in excess of seventy thousand pounds resulted in Samuel Blackwell's selling his sugar refinery to a former employee, Sam Guppy.[101] Blackwell left England for America in 1832 accompanied by his wife Hannah (then pregnant with her ninth child), their eight children, a governess, two servants, and three of his four sisters. In New York, Blackwell took a job as clerk at the Congress Sugar Refinery, where he hoped to realize "great pecuniary profits and moral benefits."[102]

Letters to his English lawyers reveal that Samuel had "very imprudently left England without a legal discharge from my creditors," who embarrassed him by attempting to collect from him through his New York mercantile house.[103] Despite the initial financial setback, Blackwell was able to persuade Samuel Guppy to go into partnership with him in a New York refinery. Blackwell claimed to have discovered a miraculous new boiling process that would make them a fortune.[104]

Blackwell had been active in English antislavery circles, and he was soon involved in the American cause. Garrison, Gerritt Smith, and Samuel May became reform associates and frequent visitors to the Blackwell household. Unfortunately, Blackwell again accumulated business debts, exacerbated by the Panic of 1837. Sam Guppy, Sr., had remained in England, but the arrival in New York of Sam Guppy, Jr., boded ill for the partnership. An audit of the refinery's books revealed that, contrary to Blackwell's claims of turning a large profit at the Congress Refinery, he had "worked to a very heavy loss."[105] Guppy accused Blackwell of giving him "faulty and evasive accounts."[106] Unable to pay his debts, Blackwell sold his share of the refinery to his foreman, Dennis Harris. Samuel Blackwell and his family left New York in 1838 bound for Cincinnati, Ohio., where Hannah had Browne family connections. Through Browne's influence, Samuel went to work for William Ludlow, proprietor of a Cincinnati sugar refinery, who was given to believe that Blackwell possessed a "secret formula for success" in the manufacture of sugar.[107]

Within two months of their arrival in Cincinnati, Samuel Blackwell was dead of malaria. After the funeral expenses were paid, Hannah and her family were left with twenty dollars in cash and a heavy load of debts. Harry's sisters were twenty-one, twenty, and seventeen years old at the time, while Sam, Jr., was not yet fifteen, and Harry was just turning thirteen. It fell to the women to support the family. A month after the funeral, Hannah opened a school for young ladies. The British accents and continental manners of Hannah and her daughters helped attract pupils to the school, and for a while it prospered.[108]

When Silas Crane, a family friend, offered free room and board to fifteen-year-old Harry at Kemper College in St. Louis, Missouri, the family agreed to let him go, paying his tuition from the proceeds of their school. Whether a decline in the family's fortunes or Harry's disappointing academic performance caused him to leave the school is uncertain, but Harry's higher education ended after just a year. Harry maintained that his grades were "manifestly unjust" owing to "a great deal of partiality" on the part of the professors.[109]

Louisa May Alcott, who lived for a time near the Blackwells in Cincinnati, described Harry in those years as "a wild boy."[110] His diary entries for the years 1845 to 1847 (he was twenty in 1845) display a temperament that vacillated between periods of extreme excitement, in which he sometimes would go without sleep for days at a time, and periods of severe depression. Harry described wakeful nights spent "dreaming with my eyes open," while "beautiful visions passed through my head and I held long conversations with various friends." Another night found him in a "state of extreme excitement," pacing up and down his room until dawn, "haunted with images like spectres—I loathed myself." Life, he wrote, "is a profound enigma if indeed it be not mad lunatic hibub & hideous chaos of fearful darkness and frantic laughter of Devils."[111]

While the ordinary excesses of an early manhood lived in the Romantic era can account for some of the wild mood swings, in Harry they seem exaggerated by an unstable temperament. One day's journal entry begins with the lament that he is so ill from a disease he likens to "living death" that he doubts whether he "will ever recover" and ends with the words "Rode out—Home Late—didn't get to bed til past 12." He was also given to other psychosomatic illnesses, complaining at one point of "the strangest oppression in my breathing . . . and an uneasy feeling impossible to describe."[112]

Much of Harry's twenty-second year was spent in search of a "suitable" position. To establish himself as a merchant, he set off for Ohio, hoping to borrow five thousand dollars from former neighbors and classmates. From Xenia, Ohio, he wrote Sam of his progress: "I did not succeed in borrowing anything from [Silas] Crane." From Akron, "saw Cas. M'Millan—no money again—treated me very kindly." In Cleveland, a lovely time, but "no money as usual." In Wheeling, West Virginia, Harry had better luck: "borrowed $1500 from Brady—fine fellow—much pleased."[113]

Blackwell's search for investment capital led him to New York, where Dennis Harris, his father's former employee, had grown wealthy as proprietor of the Congress Sugar Refinery. He persuaded Harris to invest in a Cincinnati refinery. Despite heavy borrowing, the business foundered within a year. In his journal, Sam Blackwell wrote in February 1848 that Harry was "discouraged" about the "failure of his first experiment with his plan," feeling that "his reputation and all hangs on success."[114]

Fortunately, Harry had taken out insurance on the refinery; on April 9,

1848, the day before he faced financial ruin, the refinery burned to the ground. According to Sam Blackwell, Harris suffered heavy losses in the fire.[115] Harry was more fortunate; as Elizabeth wrote to their sister Anna, the fire was "providential" in that it "saved Harry from ruin" and "diminished the dishonor of Harry's failure."[116] Afterward, Blackwell moved to New York, where Dennis Harris hired him as a bookkeeping clerk, a position Blackwell found "narrowing" and "humiliating."[117] To a former Kemper classmate, Blackwell wrote that he regarded himself as one of "those who have been favored by God with a knowledge of Sublime Truth and a key unlocking the enigma of *Evil* & solving the problems of Human Destiny."[118]

Within three months of arriving in New York, Blackwell was involved in another scrape, which prompted his sister, Emily to write, "Dear Harry, will you never learn to be prudent? . . . it is a fault in your character that you are *not* perfectly true."[119]

When his cousin Kenyon Blackwell arrived from England in December 1848, Harry pressed him for a loan of five hundred dollars to invest in a gold-panning device that Harry was sure would make him a fortune in California. His letter "distressed me exceedingly," wrote Emily, warning him that his "reputation is now balancing on a very slender support" after he had "just withdrawn or recovered from a very doubtful enterprise in Cincinnati." If he would set his course "steady and onwards," she wrote, "the past is merely unfortunate."[120]

Emily advised her brother that if he ignored his debts and went off to California, he would be "marked for life as a rash, if not unprincipled man."[121] Sam counseled him "not to depend on "these desperate leaps for instant fortune." Sam's letter concluded, "I do hope that before long it will be in my power to offer a chance in the business here.[122]

With a five-thousand-dollar loan from Kenyon, and with loans from Dennis Harris and others, Sam and Harry were able to buy into a Cincinnati hardware business. Harry returned from New York, and on May 8, 1849, the firm of Coombs, Ryland, & Blackwell was launched. The business appears to have been in trouble from the outset. Harry wrote to Harris two months later, in July 1849, that despite the fact that his mother had sold the family home and lent him the proceeds of the sale, and despite the loan of five hundred dollars by friends, he would be unable to repay him at present.[123]

Part of the money Blackwell borrowed did not go into the hardware business—it went into speculative land purchases. Over the next three years, the hardware business steadily declined. Blackwell borrowed more and more heavily, meanwhile trying to interest his siblings in various surefire schemes for making money. He would travel to Brazil and make a fortune, working four hours each morning until he had earned enough "to adopt the children of thieves, prostitutes, and murderers and teach them the higher moral law"; he would learn to speak in public and make his fortune as a lecturer; he and his friend Ainsworth would raise fifteen thousand dollars and start a "liberal paper [which] would and must make us both a fortune"; he would write and publish a book of verses that would establish his literary reputation.[124]

When Harry wrote Parker in May 1853 of his "bitter consciousness of neglected opportunities, undeveloped powers, blighted possibilities," he hoped to change his life. Despite Stone's initial and forthright rejection of his marriage proposal, he vowed to court her with a steadfastness that thus far had eluded him in his other pursuits. He would woo and win her—however long it took.[125]

CHAPTER SIX

"Putting Lucy Stone to Death"

Courting "locomotive" Lucy in the months following their meeting meant a series of long and impassioned letters that caught up with Stone at various towns and cities. Harry Blackwell's campaign to win Lucy Stone was irresistible. If one tack failed, he tried another. He enlisted the aid of friends and family; he dismantled her arguments; he charmed her. His strongest argument was that her effectiveness as a woman's rights advocate would be enhanced by marriage. To her worries that domestic life would curtail her usefulness, he responded that he would be the wife, and that she would be less "fettered" married than she was single. It would take him two years to crumble her resolute opposition to marriage, but Blackwell was persistent. Stone, on the cusp of fame and enjoying unprecedented success as a public lecturer, had little time for the merry suitor with the mesmeric manner.

By rail and by stage, by buckboard and buggy, she toured New England, Ohio, Michigan, Illinois, even traveling to Ottawa, Canada, to address Parliament. Clad in black velvet coat and knee-length skirt worn over black silk breeches, her hair cut short and combed straight back, she appeared at antislavery conventions, addressed woman's rights meetings, and delivered her series of three lectures. "Lucy is Queen of us all!" wrote Higginson.[1]

After a brief August visit with her family, Stone was in New York City in September for a series of conventions. Her role in the controversies that surrounded the meetings would result in widespread press attention. Antoinette Brown was driven from the stage at the World Temperance Convention, and the resulting donnybrook captured the attention of the press.[2]

Anticipating a continuation of the fireworks at the Woman's Rights Convention that followed, more than three thousand people packed the Broadway Tabernacle. Troublemakers were out in force; their shouts and catcalls prevented speaker after speaker from being heard. Uniformed policemen collared the ringleaders, but the din grew to a "terrific uproar, shouting, yelling, screaming, bellowing, laughing, stamping." Urged to adjourn the meeting, Lucretia Mott refused. At this point, Stone stepped forward and began to speak. Gradually the assembly grew "quiet as a congregation of churchgoers," as Stone cleverly began by praising women's domestic virtues: "I think that any woman who stands on the throne of her own house, dispensing there the virtues of love, charity, and peace, and sends out of it into the world good men, who may help to make the world better, occupies a higher position than any crowned head."

Having thus disarmed her critics, Stone argued for women to do not less, but more. She gave examples of women who had entered professions previously closed to them, citing women physicians, shopkeepers, bank cashiers, and editors. When she told how Antoinette Brown had preached before thousands the previous Sunday, hissing began. "Some men hiss who had no mothers to teach them better." The *Tribune* noted that at the end of Stone's remarks, "it was evident that if any of the rowdies had an ant-hole in the bottom of his boot, he would inevitably have sunk through it and disappeared forever."[3]

At the final Woman's Rights session, Stone spoke "for the right of woman to the control of her own person as a moral, intelligent, accountable being."[4] Earlier that spring, she had written Stanton that "I very much wish that a wife's right to her own body should be pushed at our next convention." For her part, Stanton wished to include divorce reform, and a polite disagreement arose. Stone agreed that changes in divorce laws were necessary, "for the reason that drunkenness so depraves a man's system that he is *not fit* to be a *father*." However, Stone viewed divorce as a "human" issue, devolving equally on both men and women.[5]

"I am not one bit afraid of the censure which a discussion of this question will bring," she wrote. "If only I were sure what was the right, I can stick by it through fire and flood." Despite her protestations, Stone doubtless did wish to avoid adding more public censure to the question. She was a shrewd politician; though she broke with "the tyranny of custom" in the matter of public speaking and dress, she did so in a way calculated to disarm those who would equate her behavior with any kind of moral laxity. Again and again, she stressed the moral necessity of women's widening spheres—women would be "elevated," their purpose more lofty; even the right to control their bodies was identified with increased purity in the marriage relation. Divorce was a more sexually charged issue, and Stone would have liked to keep it separate.[6]

As Blackwell continued to woo Stone, the theoretical issues became more practical. They had not seen one another since June, and he wrote asking if she would meet him at Niagara Falls, where she was lecturing on October 2. She agreed to the need for "one good, long, frank talk" and arranged to meet him, cautioning, "Believe me Mr. Henry Blackwell when I say, (and Heaven is my witness that I *mean* what I say) that, in the circumstances, I have not the remotest desire of assuming any other relations than those I now sustain."[7]

If Stone thought to discourage him, she failed. To him, their meeting was a romantic interlude, he sitting at her feet by the whirlpool, "looking down into its dark waters with a passionate and unshared and unsatisfied *yearning* in my heart that you will never know, or understand." Stone made no mention of him in her letters home. She described the "wild" and "wonderful" falls with their "grand" and "soothing" sounds, and she told of walking across the great suspension bridge connecting America and Canada.[8]

In Cleveland, to his sisters' chagrin, Blackwell made his first woman's rights speech, a rambling, two-hour discourse on the need for marriage law reform. He pressed his suit from the lecture platform, assailing the laws that gave husbands complete control of their wives' property as "no better than legalized robbery." He decried the outrage of making the husband guardian of his wife's "person"; denounced laws that gave to fathers sole custody of children. "A true marriage," he said, "will involve no subjection . . . will not limit thoughts, nor fetter activities. It will complete, not destroy, the individuality of women." What Stone thought upon hearing him is unrecorded; the press reported that Blackwell "spoke too long. He forgot it was a Women's Convention."[9]

Stone agreed to travel with him to Walnut Hills, Blackwell's Cincinnati home, after the convention. At Blackwell's urging, she made his home her base for a lecture tour that he arranged for her, through Kentucky, Missouri, Indiana, and West Virginia. Blackwell's family charmed Stone, and the tour Blackwell set up was a surprising success for a renowned Yankee abolitionist in bloomers talking in the South about women's rights. Audiences of two and three thousand packed the halls night after night.[10]

In Louisville, George Prentice, the influential Whig editor of the *Louisville Journal*, came to call. Captivated, he came to every lecture and printed long, favorable reports of her speeches in his paper. "You will find that what I have said of you in the *Journal* has opened the door for you everywhere," he told her.[11]

The success of Stone's southern tour drew her a press rebuke from Frederick Douglass. On the front page of his paper, he accused her of being willing "to say to her anti-slavery principles, stand aside, while I deal out truth less offensive." He demanded to know how "one adopting the motto of 'no union with slaveholders,' as she does, could all at once become such a prodigious favorite of slaveholders."[12]

Stone defended herself; she stubbornly failed to see any conflict between her work on behalf of woman's rights in the South and her abolitionist activity in the rest of the country. Her southern tour was highly profitable; four lectures in St. Louis netted $700; three meetings at Louisville cleared $600. Indeed, in this period Stone was earning between $500 and $1000 dollars per week. A part of her earnings paid for printing speeches and convention proceedings as tracts. Subsidized in this way, the tracts could be "circulated very cheap, and hence, very far."[13]

Unable to do business in her own name, Stone entrusted the investment of her money to Lucretia Mott's brother-in-law, who purchased bank and railroad stocks and treasury notes in her name.[14] During her stay at the Blackwells, she made the first of many substantial loans to Harry. On November 1, 1853, she lent him over six hundred dollars. Three weeks later, she mailed him another draft for almost five hundred dollars, saying: "If your Co. want it, get a bill & send me sometime."[15]

Blackwell's business was in trouble in the autumn of 1853. Heavy real estate investments had driven him further into debt. Despite the growing burden of indebtedness, he continued to buy more and more land in late 1853 and early 1854, his feverish speculation part of a national epidemic.[16]

By rail and by coach, people flocked to the pioneer territories, drawn by the "westering" spirit and by their dreams of realizing a fortune. There was a fortune to be made in land; railroads were the alchemy by which land could become gold. The mere rumor of a proposed rail line could inflate prices wildly, for railroads made the farm products, livestock, forest timber, mineral resources, and manufactured goods of distant and mountainous areas accessible to rapidly growing markets. In 1850, fewer than nine thousand miles of railroad tract existed in the United States; by 1860, there were more than thirty thousand miles.[17]

Blackwell saw a map of a proposed northern transcontinental railroad route from Chicago up through Wisconsin and learned that the state of Wisconsin was holding thirty-year mortgages on land it sold. He was sure that a fortune awaited him, not unlike the young man in a popular song of the time who sang to his wife,

And away to Wisconsin a journey we'd go
To double our fortune as other folks do.
Oh wife, let us go. Oh, don't let us wait.
Oh, I long to be there. Oh, I long to be great!
While you some rich lady—and who knows but I
Some governor may be before that I die.[18]

Blackwell bought more than a thousand acres of Illinois and Wisconsin land in 1853, and in January 1854, he acquired 6,400 acres more. He convinced a number of friends and neighbors and Cincinnati businessmen to purchase Wisconsin lands through him, assuring them of the "perfect safety" of the venture and promising appreciation of "several hundred percent *beyond a doubt*" in "from three to five years." He described setting off in a stagecoach, its springs groaning with the weight of more than six thousand dollars in gold, all of it wrapped in cotton batting and placed inside an old-fashioned hair trunk.[19] His 10 percent commission on each purchase went to buy more land for himself. At the same time, he continued to borrow from Stone. In two months, from December 1853 to January 1854, Stone sent him more than two thousand dollars.[20]

He convinced Stone to transfer the handling of her investments from Mr. Mott to himself, arguing that he was "more expert" in financial matters. He had just refused an offer of $8 per acre for land purchased the previous year for $2.25 per acre, he boasted. "The only reason I did not suggest it to you before is that I thought you wished your money in an available shape drawing a regular and certain income," he wrote in February 1854.[21] Eventually, the railroad would be built somewhere else, and the Wisconsin lands would prove "a heavy load to carry."[22]

Stone continued to send money back to Blackwell, including the proceeds of a lecture tour that took her from Washington, D.C., to Philadelphia. Arriving on the afternoon of her first scheduled lecture, she learned that the rented auditorium, the Musical Fund Hall, might refuse to admit blacks. She went with the Motts, whose son Thomas had made the arrangements, to the owner to appeal directly. They argued for two hours to no avail. Stone had sent complimentary tickets to a black woman friend, Sarah Douglass,[23] and she worried that Douglass and her party might be denied admission, but James Mott assured her that Douglass lived at a great distance from the Hall and would most certainly not attend. At five o'clock, Stone and the Motts made the decision to go ahead with that evening's lecture, hoping that a "public protest" denouncing the owner would prove "more effective than it would have been to simply abandon the meeting."[24]

Stone went onstage and denounced the proprietor, saying that she was canceling all subsequent lectures there and calling for a public boycott of the segregated facility. Though Stone did not know it, as she spoke, Sarah Douglass and her friends were turned away at the door.

One of the members of the excluded group wrote Frederick Douglass, who responded with a front-page article accusing Stone of abandoning the cause of the slave by not canceling the lecture the moment she learned that blacks were to be excluded from the hall. Friends wrote criticizing her. Characteristically, Stone made no apology. She explained how she had gone before the audience and

> stated the facts, how the Hall had been secured in ignorance of the rule which allowed no colored people there. Said that I could never hold another meeting in it . . . that the woman who was willing to secure her rights while trampling on those of any other person, did not deserve her own. . . . I made as faithful and explicit a protest as I could make. In the morning, I published a little card in Mr. Birney's paper, briefly setting forth the facts. It may be that you will still think I did not do right. If so, I should be sorry, but I cannot blame myself.[25]

Stone's stubborn self-righteousness and Douglass's anger persisted, and it was some time before the rift between them healed.

Following the Philadelphia meetings, Stone embarked on another western tour. She had agreed to meet Blackwell in Chicago at the end of December. After their meeting, she wrote: "When I loved you less than Charles [Burleigh] and Nette, I told you so, and when I loved you more than them I told you *as frankly* . . . but all that you are to me, does not come near my ideal of what is necessary to make a marriage relation."[26]

If Stone was unwilling to tie herself by marriage to Blackwell, she was becoming inextricably fastened to him financially. She continued to send him large sums: "I sent day before yesterday to Sam by express the books and papers and drafts for $760, and yesterday I sent you $275 more," Stone wrote him from Boston.[27] She was earning more in a week than he had made cumulatively in the four preceding years, but she believed in his superior business acumen. "Rely on my judgement in such matters which is remarkably good," he wrote: "send me what money you want to invest in a Draft on N.Y. or Boston and I will at once select the land for you in person—get the Certifs made out in your name and remit them to you."[28]

For the first time in years, in early February 1854, Stone experienced a recurrence of the terrible headaches she had suffered at Oberlin. Her resolve never to marry was under fire from all quarters. Blackwell continued his paper siege with letters filled with terms of endearment, philosophical arguments, and a warning from Bronson Alcott that the "Reformer who has not obtained a home & *family*—partner & child—needs to commence the reform within himself."[29] His letters promised that theirs would be a marriage different from all others—a union of equals. Lucy's independence in no way would be compromised, he promised; her work would be enhanced by marriage, her power as a speaker vastly increased.[30]

Stone wrote James and Lucretia Mott, whose marriage she and the other suffragists regarded as ideal, asking for their views on marriage. James Mott responded:

That many are disappointed in the marriage state I have no doubt. . . . I have lived in that state for more than forty years, and it has been one of harmony and love. As age advances, our love, if anything, increases. . . . I am in favor of matrimony, and wish to see all in whom I feel interested, made happy in that way, which includes thy little self. It is the natural state of man, and when rightly entered into, an increase of happiness and comfort is the certain result.[31]

Blackwell sent along a letter from his sister Elizabeth describing an idealized portrait of marriage "such as could only be enjoyed by the noblest," adding, "Lucy Stone is capable of this grand good."[32] Stone copied the letter verbatim and sent it for safekeeping to Sarah.

Blackwell also initiated a correspondence with Sarah, telling her how "strangely attracted" he had felt to Lucy when first he saw her in his hardware store his first mention of a purported earlier meeting, how he had "purposely avoided seeing her until several years after" when he "yielded to inclination and went East on purpose to see her." Sarah advised Harry that if he wished to marry her sister, he must "leave all and follow her," to which he replied lightheartedly that his "experience is that the ladies usually manage to carry their husbands pretty much where they will."[33] The foundations of Stone's opposition to marriage began to crumble; her headaches intensified.

Debilitated, unable to lecture, Stone fled to the shelter of Coy's Hill. Blackwell's letters continued to arrive. Where Stone wrote of marriage as death, Blackwell proposed a fuller, more "natural" life; where she saw enervation, he promised vitalization. As he penetrated her theoretical defenses against marriage one by one, Stone turned to her personal objections—writing of the "revulsions of feeling which continually recur" and of "the horror of being a legal wife" with its "suffocating sense of the want of that absolute freedom which I now possess." Counterpoised to that sense of suffocation, she wrote,

I have been all my life alone. I have planned and executed, without consent, without counsel, and without control. I have shared thought, and feeling, and life, with myself alone. I have made a path . . . which . . . brings me more intense & abundant happiness by far, than comes to the life of the majority of men. And it seems to me, I cannot risk it by any change. . . . The great whole of my life is richly blest. Let it remain so.[34]

Blackwell carefully met each of her objections. "My love shall *never fetter you* one iota," he promised, and "I will never directly or indirectly impair your activity." In another letter he wrote, "I do not want you to *fetter* yourself *one particle* for my sake. I do not want you to forego *one sentiment* of independence, nor one attribute of *personality*."[35]

Stone's "revulsions of feeling" and "suffocating sense" were more difficult to address. They were complex feelings—rooted in her fear of motherhood, in her sense of marriage as a form of death, and in a sexual ideology that ascribed sexuality to men and "purity" to women. Popular culture told women that they were "morally superior," their sanctity deriving from their "capacity for motherliness." Women were not passionate, but rather a means of restraining the wild excesses of passion. On a practical level, ungoverned passions meant babies. Such artificial methods of birth control as existed were widely regarded as unnatural and immoral, and "natural" means could not be counted on.[36]

That spring, Stone's ideas about a woman's right to control her body found a clerical champion in Henry Wright, a reformer and abolitionist friend who published a book on *Marriage and Parentage*. Wright insisted that *"The wife must decide how often, and under what circumstances, the husband may enjoy this passional expression of his love* [emphasis his]. . . . Passional indulgence, *demanded as a right,* is a rape upon the person whom the husband has promised . . . to love, honor, and protect."[37]

Stone sent the book to Blackwell, who responded "rather freely for a letter, but I put two extra wafers to keep impertinent curiosity from a possibility of opening it."[38] His response, which has been lost, seemed temporarily to allay Stone's anxieties, for the issue of sex disappears from their letters for awhile.

Although Stone's health improved, family responsibilities prevented her attendance at the New York anniversary meeting of the Anti-Slavery Society. Hannah, nearing seventy, had stumbled and fallen in the dark one night and was "dreadfully stunned and bruised," and Stone stayed at home to help her mother.[39]

Blackwell worried that he was losing ground. He wrote asking Stone if he might visit her at Coy's Hill. At first she refused, saying that it would be a waste of a fifty-dollar railroad fare, as it was not likely he would "get that value in return."[40] She relented, however, and Blackwell came East. They traveled to Gardner, where they stayed with Sarah and Henry Lawrence, taking long walks in the nearby hills.

At the end of their brief visit, though Blackwell had not succeeded in winning her hand, Stone admitted that his arguments had convinced her of the possibility that she might one day marry. Should she ever decide to marry, she wrote him afterward, he would not be her choice, for she heartily disliked his business practices and his preoccupation with becoming wealthy. Furthermore, she wrote, she doubted the sincerity of his reform principles.[41]

Blackwell left Gardner for New York, where he gave Elizabeth the impression that Stone had agreed to an engagement. She wrote extending "the hand of sisterly friendship" and assuring Stone of a warm welcome into the Blackwell family circle. Having begun so graciously, Elizabeth went on to a general denunciation of woman's rights activists and their conventions. Stone responded that her becoming a member of the Blackwell family was only "possible," not even "probable." She went on to meet and counter Elizabeth's arguments, enumerating the gains for women that woman's rights conventions had helped to bring about.[42]

Elizabeth wrote Harry that she did not intend to answer Stone's letter, as she and Lucy "view life from such different sides that I thought discussion would be unavailing." She explained that so far, Stone had only come to her attention in ways she disapproved—in "the eccentricities and accidents of the American phase of the nineteenth century; in bloomerism, abolitionism, woman's rightism."[43] Elizabeth Blackwell also felt that her obstetric practice suffered as a result of "the strong prejudice against me on the part of women, which is heightened by the vulgarity of the radical movement."[44]

Emily Blackwell, also a medical school graduate, had gone to England in 1854 to investigate whether she and her sister might practice more profitably there. From England, she wrote that while she was enjoying the cultural superiority so lacking in America, she found little encouragement for their idea of an English medical practice. Englishwomen, she wrote, lumped women physicians together with American women lecturers and preachers—all of them "wild developments of an unreliable go-ahead nation."[45]

For Stone, the summer of 1854 was unusually quiet. She remained at Coy's Hill. Blackwell wrote from Wisconsin that he had succeeded in "selling" some ten or twelve of the land parcels bought the previous year. The purchasers were Norwegian farmers who had been "entered out" by Blackwell's purchases. They had plowed and built homes on the land, thinking mistakenly that they had "homesteaded" their claims. Blackwell sold them back their lands—some "at about cost," others at a "handsome profit."[46]

When word of this reached town, "several unprincipled village politicians resolved to take advantage of the universal feeling against speculators to give me trouble." The citizens of Viroqua, Wisconsin, wanted stores, shops, roads, farms, and mills, and not a group of absentee speculative landlords in possession of forty-eight thousand acres of local property. Blackwell wrote Stone of the vote taken at a town meeting to tar and feather him and ride him out of town. He described how against the advice of friends, he addressed the assembled townsmen for more than an hour, reassuring them that his ownership would benefit everyone.

Blackwell confessed in the letter to Stone that he had experienced some regrets, feeling that certain of the accusations were justified. He was resigned to being unable to "advance our interests without doing a certain injustice to others. If I am able to keep these lands a few years, they will make me rich, but meantime," he admitted, "I am certainly impeding the settlement & prosperity of the Country round me."[47]

Stone was upset by this story. Her response was six pages of "large letter sheet" detailing all the reasons why marriage for them would not work out. Her next letter said it again: "Believe me, dear Harry, we do *not* belong together as husband and wife." Blackwell must reconcile himself to their being "helpers and friends . . . the *only* relation we can truly sustain."[48]

Blackwell wrote back: "In spite of all your warnings & rejections & presentiments I cannot help loving [you] as my own soul & thinking of [you] as my *wife* that is & is to be."[49]

In September, Blackwell turned the tide in his favor. He wrote a lengthy letter recounting his dramatic rescue of an eight-year-old slave girl. He had gone to Salem, Ohio, for an antislavery convention. There a dispatch came stating that a train carrying a slave girl and her master and mistress would pass through at about six o'clock that evening. A committee was appointed "to see the conductor and ask the girl if she wanted her freedom." Though not a member of the committee, Blackwell accompanied them onto the railroad car. When the child indicated that she wished to be free, he "took the child's arm, and commenced lifting her from the seat, seeing . . . there was no time to be lost." A scuffle ensued, but the child was rescued.[50]

Stone's last defenses crumbled, and she permitted herself to acknowledge at last that she loved Blackwell deeply. She wrote that as she read his letter, "I said to myself," here is a noble deed which Harry did not do from *impulse*. . . . I felt *nearer* to you then dear Harry in all that constitutes nearness, than I ever did before, and if you had been indeed my husband, I would have gathered you to my heart of hearts."[51]

Elizabeth wrote Emily that Harry seemed "to be ruining himself through injurious influences acting on his morbid craving for distinction."[52] Many of his customers and friends condemned his action, and the owner of the child swore out a warrant for his arrest in Memphis. On September 27, he wrote that he regretted his rash action, for it had caused him "a needless loss of influence" and "obloquy."[53]

If he hoped for sympathy, Stone offered none. Instead, she wrote that "the radiance of the halo I had thrown around your action there has been *dimmed*. . . . A temporizing policy, or ideas of mere expediency affect, or create your present feelings." This lack of constancy in his behavior, she warned him, is a "really most serious defect in your character."[54]

Stung by Stone's criticism, Blackwell reminded her by return mail of a number of defects of her own—prompting her cheerful response: "I reciprocate fully your wish that I sang like Jenny Lind, and were the perfection of grace and beauty etc., and especially that I were ten years younger. But in all except the last, I expect somewhere in the ages, to find myself greatly improved. Next to the being perfect, the best thing is to *wish* to *become* so."[55] In this letter, Stone responded to Blackwell's insistence that she come to Cincinnati so that they could meet and discuss their situation face to face. Stone agreed that they needed an entire day together to try "to come to some permanent understanding." She preferred someplace other than Cincinnati with its gathering of Blackwells, she told him, as "it is *you* now I want to see." They agreed on Pittsburgh, where she hoped to get "this suspense which haunts me, sleeping & waking, over." The subject of marriage had "not been absent from my mind an hour, since you left me last June. Bewildered and fearful, I see nothing clearly, and dread lest *any* step shall be a wrong one."[56]

Hannah Stone did not want her to marry. On a mid-October visit to Coy's Hill, Lucy sat writing a letter. When Hannah learned that it was Blackwell to whom she was writing, she warned her: "Young men's vows are soon forgotten." Stone repeated her mother's warning to Harry, explaining, "Her experience, in life, and in the world, makes her distrustful as it well may."[57] Stone's "as it well may" says much about her parents' marriage.

Though she had admitted her deep love for him, Stone continued to be troubled by doubts about Blackwell. When they met in Pittsburgh, she laid her worries before him in the frank manner which was so characteristic of her. She questioned his honesty, saying that while she did not doubt his conviction, "I do not think your stand point is the highest."[58] Blackwell answered her objections. He would sell the business; he would gladly fill the role of "wife" so that her career would in no way suffer; she would have complete control of her own body. "You shall choose when, where, & how often, you shall become a mother. Neither partner shall attempt to fix the residence, employment, or habits of the other—nor shall either partner feel bound to live together any longer than is agreeable to both."[59] After a long, emotional meeting, Blackwell's sixteen-month campaign succeeded, and Stone agreed to marry him as soon as she could work a wedding into her busy lecture schedule.

Blackwell's reassurances notwithstanding, Stone anxiously began referring to herself in letters that winter as "Lucy Stone that was." Blackwell's promise that their place of residence would be a mutual decision, soon was called into doubt. He referred to their future life together, saying "Sometimes I plan to live in New York . . . sometimes I plan to live at Chicago & . . . build up a wholesale grocery business there."[60]

Stone responded tartly that they had agreed to share in the decision about where they would live, and as she would continue her career, she thought it best that they plan to live in the East, where her agents, her contacts, her organization, and her family resided. Blackwell responded by return mail that of course the choice of residence would always be a joint decision, but before they could decide, he must "get clear where I am," which would necessitate her coming West at least temporarily. As for his future, he doubted the wisdom of living East. "I have the foundation of a fortune laid in the West," he wrote. If she were to *insist* on living in the East, "I will, if necessary, sacrifice even ambition to *love*."[61]

Stone was sufficiently reassured to begin buying silver and dishes and small household furnishings. When Blackwell suggested February 10 as their wedding date, however, she put him off, writing that she was so busy with bookings for lectures that she would be unable even to see him anytime soon. She added that Garrison had given her his blessing, telling her that he liked Blackwell and believed he "would not put a shackle upon anybody's freest thought."[62]

Harry wrote his sisters about his impending marriage, and they were not pleased. Emily had written to Elizabeth from England just before receiving word of their engagement: "I hope Lucy Stone has given Harry a *second* refusal—her influence over him hitherto has been so unfavorable . . . it will be a matter of great regret to us all if we hear that Harry is engaged to Lucy Stone."[63] On hearing the news, Anna wrote from England that she deeply regretted that he was marrying beneath himself culturally and artistically. Harry sent Anna's letter to Lucy, asking her to excuse his sister's bitterness, explaining that Anna had "suffered very much in this country." Stone's response demonstrates her sense of social inadequacy:

With [Anna's] high culture and artistic life, it is the most natural thing in the world that she should desire the same excellencies in the wife of her brother. And it would be a *great deal better for him* if *it could be so*. I know the *worth* of those things, not as she does, from *possessing* them, but from the *want* of them. But I have a real desire to improve, and, doing the best I can, with you all to help me, the time may come when I shall come nearer her ideal, and my own too. I wish I had a rich and varied culture, with personal wealth and beauty, and every good—but these have been all outside the rocky path over which I have toiled. I have very little, of that which the world values, to carry you, dear Harry, but *such as I have* and *all* that I have—the *unselfish* love of an individual heart are *yours*. You will never be proud of my polished exterior, nor of my brilliant intellect, nor of my high culture. But in the circle in which you will move, you will of necessity, often feel that I am inferior to it—you will be pained, and your love of approbation will suffer, many times. . . .[64]

Stone suggested that they reconsider their decision to marry. Her "deficiencies" were ever in her mind, she explained, and she did not think they could be happy. She was not the only reluctant party. Elizabeth wrote Emily that she had tried to get Harry at least to "defer the time, but that will prove as useless as any other effort." Putting a cheerful face on things, she wrote, "We must absolutely take the brightest view we can, as it seems to be inevitable, and if Lucy will soften her heresies, it may be a very happy union." At least in the matter of Stone's cultural inferiority, Elizabeth wrote that she was encouraged to learn from Harry that Lucy Stone "feels certain deficiencies in education and polish & desires to overcome them." Only Sam approved, finding Stone a "most admirable woman," as well as a "most pleasant companion" who was "brilliant in conversation."[65]

As the time for the wedding drew near, disagreements about money continued to plague their relationship. Blackwell's earlier response to her plea that he not succumb to the "degrading influence of mammon-hunting"—that he valued money "only as *power*" and wanted it "only to become *my own master* free of the world and owner of my time" apparently failed to convince Stone.[66] When in January 1855 she learned that he was in Wisconsin continuing his land speculation, she articulated her own goals, writing, "There are plenty of people who can make money—not so many who can . . . make [life's] immortal part better—fewer still, whose life . . . leaves an example, which, by its *imperishable worth* wins followers, and so makes the world *better*. . . . I hoped that we should be able to give ourselves to the great *moral* movements of the age."[67]

Stone's January itinerary took her to Toronto, Canada, where she addressed Parliament on behalf of a proposed married woman's property law. On her return, preparatory to her impending marriage, she began making arrangements to transfer her bank stocks, railroad shares, and other investments to the trusteeship of her brother Bowman and her brother-in-law Henry Lawrence. She wrote Blackwell requesting the deeds to the Wisconsin and Illinois lands he had purchased for her. When the deeds did not arrive, she wrote again. Pressed, Blackwell wrote that he had not had time properly to enter all of her properties, and many of the deeds to her lands were in his name. Stone asked him to send her the deeds with an authorization for the transfer to her name. Blackwell urged her instead to wait until he could accompany her. "I fear my dear that you will feel *pained* at doing so *without* me," he wrote in March of 1855.[68]

Stone cut short her lecture tour and returned to Coy's Hill, afflicted with a case of "hard headaches" so severe as to make her fear that she was losing her sanity. She poured out her "sufferings and fears" and her dread of sex to Sarah. Then too she continued to be dogged by feelings of social inadequacy, feelings Blackwell exacerbated by sending on another unflattering letter from Elizabeth assailing their planned wedding protest as "vulgar," and "tasteless." Good taste, Elizabeth insisted, was "a matter of instinctive perception."[69]

Stone worried that she would embarrass Blackwell, and she wrote that she feared that even were she to agree to have a child, it would be "insufficiently fine & noble" for him. Blackwell cheerfully responded that he was "too proud & too *aristocratic* ('in a certain fine sense,' as Alcott would say) to be willing to have any but fine, noble children" and if necessary, they would "*wait till we can*. But I know some things," Blackwell wrote, "which I will not tell you till I see you, which make me hope & believe that you may become a cheerful & happy Mother by me." Blackwell suggested that the best way to deal with the decision about whether to have children, a euphemism for whether or not they would have sexual relations, was to "*postpone* that question altogether till we are married."[70]

Stone's reception of the "prospect of becoming a cheerful & happy Mother" occasioned a week of such severe illness that she was unable even to write. On March 29, she began to recover: "My head is so that I have now scarcely a fear of insanity. I feel the power of *self control,* and as long as I can do that, there is no danger. . . ." If she grew any worse, she wrote Blackwell, her family would write to him.[71]

On the same day, she wrote Nettie that she was unable to fix a day for her wedding as she was so unwell. "But when it is fixed, I will write you. . . . If the ceremony is in New York, we want you to harden your heart enough to help in so cruel an operation as putting Lucy Stone to death." She added that it was more likely that she would travel to Cincinnati "& have the ruin completed there," as Harry wanted the wedding at Walnut Hills.[72]

Characterizing her impending marriage as "putting Lucy Stone to death" was humor sharpened by the keen edge of truth. Stone's dread of the sexual aspect of marriage reappeared in her letters. She wrote again of her "revulsion," adding that she was reading a book that she hoped would quiet her fears. Blackwell responded that reading would not solve her worries, and he reassured her that "*nature* will soon teach us much more than any theory good, or bad. You surely can *trust* me . . . you shall have your own way without any attempt on my part to influence you otherwise."[73]

As for the legal "death," Blackwell wrote that he would "*renounce* all the privileges which the law confers on me, which are not strictly *mutual*." He suggested that they draw up a "protest," an "outside *contract*" which would contain his "pledge . . . to never avail myself" of the legal usurpations inherent in contemporary marriage laws. Stone prepared hers with the legal advice of her lawyer-reformer friend, Wendell Phillips.[74]

Blackwell wrote in mid-March urging Stone to come to Cincinnati at the end of April to be married there.[75] On April 8, Stone agreed to his request and made arrangements to arrive in time for a Sunday, April 29, wedding at Walnut Hills. Blackwell reconsidered, however, and wrote that he thought it would be better if they were married at the home of Lucy's parents. "I do not think that it would make any difference in the case of a lady unknown, but in *you*, to come a thousand miles *to me* might seem a violation of the customary etiquette." He also worried that as it was their intention to publish their protest with the news of their marriage, it would be best if their wedding was "strictly unexceptionable."[76] Stone appeared willing to surrender herself to Blackwell's wishes, even as her headaches intensified.

"I greatly fear that you have suffered pain in contemplation of our marriage," wrote Blackwell. He promised her that if they could be together, he would calm her fears and *"all will be right."*[77] Stone agreed, and the wedding date was set for May 1. Harry had invited his sisters Marian and Elizabeth to the wedding, but Elizabeth wrote that Marian was ill and that she herself did not wish to attend. Informed of Stone's illness, Elizabeth ascribed it to overwork, writing Harry: "I think we ought to scold a little at such clear imprudence . . . the willful abuse of sound health is a sin."[78]

Blackwell arrived at Coy's Hill, followed soon after by Higginson and his wife, Mary. Higginson had agreed to officiate when Brown wrote that she would be unable to be there. Charles Burleigh, Stone's abolitionist friend, also arrived on the day before the wedding. The evening before the wedding "passed happily away," Higginson wrote, Stone seeing to everyone's comfort, so much so "that I felt as if someone else in the family were to be married and she was the Cinderella." Higginson and his wife brought greenhouse flowers from Worcester, and Stone's friend Anna Parsons added orange blossoms, the traditional bridal flower. Higginson arranged the flowers in glasses, and Stone distributed the fallen blossoms among her brother's children. "Lucy was very sweet to them, her word seemed to be law and love together," he wrote.[79]

Earlier that year, the Boston *Post* had adapted the lyrics of a popular song to poke fun at Lucy Stone. The song ended:

Oh would that she were married
   And had a *house* to care
Will no one sacrifice himself
   To save us from despair?
A name like Curtius' shall be his,
   On fame's loud trumpet blown,
Who with a wedding kiss shuts up
   The mouth of Lucy Stone![80]

Higginson had not met Blackwell before, and he described him to his mother as "rather short and stout," and seemingly "thoroughly true and

manly, earnest, sensible, and discriminating; not inspired, but valuable."
He added, "They seemed perfectly happy together."[81] And why not? This
smallish "Curtius" with the merry blue eyes and "mesmerizing" manner
not only had vowed not to "shut up the mouth of Lucy Stone," but had
promised to give new power and authority to her voice.

In the morning, everyone rose at dawn so that ceremony and reception
could be over in time for the bridal couple to catch the 8:20 train to New
York. Outside the farmhouse, a steady, cold drizzle was falling. Before
the ceremony, Bowman, Higginson, and Charles Burleigh chatted. Bo
confided that he had been sure Blackwell's courtship would "come to
nothing," as "there had been a good many after Lucy first and last." His
sister "had made short work of them." On the other side of the room, "the
queer old father" commented with a dry chuckle on the choice of Higginson as minister, saying, "Our Lucy thought there wasn't anybody in these
parts good enough to marry her, so she had to fetch somebody from
Worcester for it, hey?"[82]

The wedding service began promptly at seven o'clock. Blackwell, in
"the proper white waistcoat," stood beside a pale and shaken Stone, "she
in a beautiful silk, ashes of roses color" dress.[83] Blackwell read aloud
their Marriage Protest:

While acknowledging our mutual affection by publicly assuming the relationship of
husband and wife, yet in justice to ourselves and a great principle, we deem it a duty
to declare that this act on our part implies no sanction of, nor promise of voluntary
obedience to such of the present laws of marriage, as refuse to recognize the wife as
an independent, rational being, while they confer upon the husband an injurious and
unnatural superiority, investing him with legal powers which no honorable man
would exercise, and which no man should possess. We protest especially the laws
which give to the husband:

1. The custody of the wife's person. [This was placed first at Stone's insistence.]
2. The exclusive control and guardianship of their children.
3. The sole ownership of her personal, and use of her real estate, unless previously
settled upon her, or placed in the hands of trustees, as in the case of minors, lunatics,
and idiots.
4. The absolute right to the product of her industry.
5. Also against laws which give to the widower so much larger and more permanent
an interest in the property of his deceased wife, than they give to the widow in that of
her deceased husband.
6. Finally, against the whole system by which "the legal existence of the wife is
suspended in marriage," so that in most states, she neither has a legal part in the
choice of her residence, nor can she make a will, nor sue or be sued in her own name,
not inherit property.

The Protest went on to state their belief that marriage is "an equal and
permanent partnership and should be so recognized by law," and concluded: "Thus reverencing law, we enter our protest against rules and

customs which are unworthy of the name, since they violate justice, the essence of all law."[84]

Following the reading of the Protest, the couple exchanged vows. Stone had wished to omit the words "love, honor, and obey," but in deference to her mother's wishes, she agreed to include the first two; she would not promise to obey. Blackwell recited his vows, and then, Higginson added, "I have to add with secret satisfaction that, after this, Lucy, the heroic Lucy, *cried,* like any village bride!"

Charles Burleigh then placed a hand on each of their heads and delivered a benediction, causing Harry to write playfully that "Higginson joined our *hands,* but Mr. Burleigh joined our *heads.*"[85] Following the ceremony, the small gathering ate breakfast and wedding cake, and Lucy and Harry said their good-byes. Higginson commented later that it was "the most beautiful bridal I ever attended."[86]

Stone's parting with her mother was poignant and tearful. She wrote to acknowledge her mother's anxiety: "I know you all felt a little badly, at our wedding, because Harry was a stranger, and you did not know what I was risking, nor what future I might be making." Stone herself did not know what the future would bring as she boarded the carriage that would take them to the railroad station. At the depot, Harry wrote a detailed description of the wedding to his good friend Ainsworth Spofford, enclosing a piece of wedding cake. His lighthearted postscripts read: "Ora Pro Nobis" and "Going—going—gone."[87]

Arriving in New York later that afternoon, the newlyweds went directly to Elizabeth's house, where they found that Elizabeth and Marian had invited a large crowd to an evening celebration. Stone, overcome by the events of the day and sickened by a fierce headache, excused herself and went upstairs to bed. Writing to her mother, Stone reported on Harry's thoughtfulness in not waking her when he finally came to bed, a code phrase, perhaps, to reassure her mother that her wish to retain control of her body was being respected.[88]

The following morning, the bridal couple left for Cincinnati, where they would live with Hannah, Sam, and Harry's sister Ellen until Harry "got clear" of the hardware business. Ellen reported to her sisters that the "Bride came with a very nice wardrobe of dresses of a very tolerable length . . . has quite a store also of silver, blankets, linen etc. in which she takes considerable satisfaction, and the sedate little housekeeper peeps out in various directions."[89]

Higginson published his account of the wedding and a copy of the Marriage Protest in the Worcester *Spy* and in the *Liberator,* and both the wedding account and the Protest were reprinted in papers throughout the country. The Washington [D.C.] *Union* reported: "We understand that

Mr. Blackwell, who last fall assaulted a southern lady and stole her slave, has lately married Miss Lucy Stone. Justice, though sometimes tardy, never fails to overtake her victim."[90]

In Cincinnati, the newlyweds had no more than moved in when word came from England via Emily that Harry's younger brother Howard, through an "utterly reckless" venture, was now threatened with "financial disgrace." The English branch of the family was anxious that news of his scrape should be kept from the newspapers. Howard had gone to England in 1849 to join his uncle, Samuel Blackwell, in business. Uncle Samuel, Emily wrote, reminded her very much of Harry, for he "acts entirely from impulse—is a man of great talent and sincere admiration for everything high and noble—utterly deficient in caution, prudence, and self-command. Consequently always in hot water."[91]

Sam and Harry were unable to lend Howard any money as they continued unsuccessfully to look for buyers for the hardware store and struggled with mounting debts. Only Stone was bringing in income, money which she shared generously with her new relations. Money was not yet an issue between herself and Harry, and any anxiety about whether Blackwell would insist upon conjugal rights was put to rest, as she indicated in a letter to Susan B. Anthony. Anthony had charged her with "defection" from the woman's rights cause, to which Stone responded: "Do not do me the injustice Susan of suspecting liabilities *now* for me which are not called for by my free will. I yet keep my own custody and *all that pertains to it,* and when I can't do that I shall go back to N.E."

Stone fully intended to work as hard as ever, she wrote, and she had agreed to speak at a Saratoga Springs convention later that summer. "When after reading your letter, I asked my husband if I might go to Saratoga, only think of it! He did not give me permission, but told me to ask Lucy Stone. I can't get him to govern me at all," she wrote lightheartedly. After reassuring Anthony that her woman's rights interest was unchanged, she signed the letter, "With the old love and good will I am now and ever, Lucy Stone (only)."[92]

In August 1855, Stone traveled alone to Saratoga. After the convention, she wrote Blackwell that she had decided to remain in the East in order to give a series of lectures. She would be home in late September, and meantime would send home her lecture earnings so that Blackwell could apply them to the mortgages and taxes due on her Wisconsin and Illinois lands.

Stone was upset to learn that while she was away, Blackwell had drawn on her earnings to finance a trip to Wisconsin. He defended himself by writing that as he intended to visit her property while there, he had "pursued a course of even and exact justice . . . so never reproach me again with *cheating you,* little one!" He added that he was "not quite sure I ought to have done it."[93]

In response to Stone's statement that she intended to lecture that autumn, he wrote: "Dear Lucy—do not let your *marriage* make you feel *less free,*" but he began a subtle campaign of pressure. "If you desire to lecture this fall, I will organize for you a little tour to Wisconsin." He named the five towns where he would arrange lectures. "This would consume nearly a month and we ought not to be separated longer. Dearest, when I become free from business, we will lecture *together.* . . . The noblest *preaching* is *incomplete without* the noble life to exemplify it." He discouraged her from making other lecture plans, warning her that a longer tour might bring on a "return of the terrible suffering of last winter." He wrote longingly of a more normal family life, with "a quiet home & children & friends," arguing that these would "exemplify" a noble life and make her more credible to her audiences. "You sometimes speak depreciatingly [sic] of our union and seem to *doubt* a little if we are *in all respects* adapted," he wrote her.[94]

Stone was too busy to contemplate "a quiet home" as she went from lecture to lecture, everywhere drawing large and enthusiastic audiences and healthy gate receipts. She sent draft after draft back to Walnut Hills, furnishing her mother-in-law with household money and lending Ellen Blackwell four hundred dollars so that she could study painting in England.[95]

In September, Stone and Susan B. Anthony traveled together to Boston. There, Stone introduced Anthony to her wide circle of friends and acquaintances. They stayed with the family of Francis Jackson, and an excited Anthony wrote home to describe the circle of Stone's friends and acquaintances they visited: "We met Caroline H. Dall, Elizabeth Peabody, Mrs. McCready, the Shakespearian reader, Caroline M. Severance, Dr. Harriot K. Hunt, Charles F. Hovey, Wendell Phillips, Sarah Pugh, and others. Having worshipped these distinguished people afar off, it was a great satisfaction to meet them face to face."[96]

After Boston, Stone stopped in Brookfield on her way home to Cincinnati in early October. The anniversary of the National Woman's Rights Convention was to be held in Cincinnati on October 17. By arranging the convention so close to home, Stone hoped to placate Harry and at the same time to capitalize on the growing western sentiment for woman's rights.

The Cincinnati convention took place in Nixon's Halls, and newspapers reported standing-room-only crowds. When a heckler interrupted the proceedings and shouted that the whole movement was the work of "a few disappointed women"—a remark intended as a jibe at the unmarriageability of feminists—Stone ascended the platform to restore order. Speaking extemporaneously, she delivered one of her greatest speeches —a rebuttal of simple eloquence and great power. Because most of her speeches were unwritten, they have been lost, but fortunately, a phonographic record made at Cincinnati that day preserved Stone's speech. Beneath the force of its rhetoric, there were dark undertones.

Stone began by conceding the point to the heckler—she was indeed a disappointed woman, she told him. "From the first years to which my memory stretches, I have been a disappointed woman. When, with my brothers, I reached forth after the sources of knowledge, I was reproved with 'It isn't fit for you; it doesn't belong to women.'"

She went on to tell of her struggle to obtain an education, only to find herself disappointed in the end "when I came to seek a profession . . . every employment was closed to me, except those of the teacher, the seamstress, and the housekeeper." She pleaded with the men in her audience: "Leave women, then, to find their sphere. And do not tell us before we are born even, that our province is to cook dinners, darn stockings, and sew on buttons. . . . We want rights. The flour merchant, the housebuilder, and the postman charge us no less on account of our sex, but when we endeavor to earn money to pay all these, then indeed, we find the difference."

Hecklers and partisans alike listened as Stone chronicled the recent gains of women—the introduction of women to the professions and to the labor force, the gradual changes in the law. She spoke of women doctors and preachers, merchants and laborers. She told of one woman "at manual labor turning out chair legs in a cabinet shop," a job that "made her hands harder and broader, it is true," but, Stone added with some satisfaction, "I think a hand with a dollar and a quarter a day in it, better than one with a crossed ninepence."

She questioned how it was that the same society that admires a man who forges a new path for himself condemns a woman who does the same, requiring her to stay at home "a dependent—working little cats on worsted, and little dogs on punctured paper. But if she goes heartily and bravely to give herself to some worthy purpose, she is out of her sphere and she loses caste."

Here a note of bitterness crept into Stone's speech: "In education, in marriage, in religion, in everything, disappointment is the lot of woman." Her voice rose: "It shall be the business of my life to deepen that disappointment in every woman's heart until she bows down to it no longer." The applause that followed was thunderous.[97]

Following the convention, Stone addressed the Ohio state legislature. Ironically, while she was away testifying on behalf of a married woman's property act, Harry directed his brother George to make a real estate purchase with Lucy's earnings. "I will join you in the purchase," he wrote on October 19. "You may buy it for me and Lucy having the deed made in William B. Stone's name as Trustee for Mrs. Lucy Stone Blackwell."[98]

Blackwell's use of Lucy Stone Blackwell despite her adamant insistence upon retaining her birth name may have had to do with legal necessity. Certainly Stone continued to sign letters "Lucy Stone (only)," and she directed a lecture agent: "Never add Blackwell to my name. If a wife have any character, her own name is enough. No husband would take his wife's name. By the Golden Rule, she should not take his."[99]

If there were problems and doubts in the first six months of her marriage, Stone was also growing to love Blackwell more and more. Their marriage still was not consummated, however, and a tone of frustration crept into Blackwell's letters. His optimism that "Nature" would prevail was replaced by a steady campaign in his letters for a more "normal" life, and an insistence that if they were going to have any credibility as reformers, they must "assume the natural relations of humanity." He cited Lucretia Mott as the best example of how a "natural" life gives more "weight" to reform. Searching for a negative example of how the celibate life detracted from reform, Blackwell pointed to the "recorded life of Christ"—in his opinion an "extremely imperfect" life in that Christ "did not show forth either the *son,* the *husband* or the *father*." Blackwell's patience was wearing thin, and he wrote: "This life of renunciation is *suicidal.* How can we speak of what we do not know?"[100]

Stone considered assuming a sexual relationship, confiding to Anthony on November 2 that "as my love for Harry grows deeper and deeper the better I know him, my heart yearns more and more to blend our lives in one who can take up the work when I lay it down. . . . To almost no other, only to Nettie and you, would I write this dear Susan," she wrote.[101]

Probably sometime early in November, after the Woman's Rights Convention and before Stone left on the Wisconsin speaking tour Blackwell had arranged for her, Stone and Blackwell consummated their marriage. With the assumption of conjugal relations came a dread of its consequences. On November 8, Stone wrote to Anthony, "For the first time in my life, I feel, day after day, completely discouraged. . . . I am going to retire from the field; and if you go to work too soon and kill yourself, the two wheelhorses will be gone and then the chariot will stop."[102] Stone's talk of retirement was linked to the prospect of pregnancy.

Stone's assumption of an active sex life coincided with a sense of lost potency on the lecture platform. When December and January came and went with no signs of pregnancy, however, Stone wrote that she had recovered her old power. It appears that Blackwell may have undermined her confidence, for a late January letter heralding the return of her old force begins: "Dear critical husband of mine," and goes on to say: "You would not have been ashamed of your wife . . . it was such an *infinite blessing* to feel again the old inspiration & *faith* in *myself,* and to see the audience swayed as the wind, the grain. I would not write this, even to you my own dearest Love, only you know how I have feared."[103]

Blackwell's response was to find fault with Stone for not having mended his leggings, a task that, he reminded her, his aged mother had been forced to do for him in Stone's absence. She was contrite, promising to be a better wife to him, writing, "Be sure I did not know they [the leggings] needed it, but I *ought* to have known." In the same letter, she told of clearing $130 above expenses. "I am *so* glad to find again the old inspiration, and it comes to me more & more," she wrote. Though buoyed by her triumphs, she missed him. "Every night, when I lie down, I do so miss the sheltering love of your arms and the near personal presence! My own dear husband we *must not* in future be separate so much. I feel a constant sense of loss."[104]

This new note of physical intimacy is repeated in subsequent letters. On February 3, 1856, she wrote: "My heart *yearns* for you now as I write, and when I lie down at night, tho' I sleep more soundly alone, yet I miss you sorely."[105] Lucy was deeply in love with Harry, and he with her. Yet the problem of where they would live had become a point of contention between them. Stone had been clear from their first meeting that her work required that she live in the East. Blackwell, who had earlier promised to move East, now temporized. "Westerners," he wrote on January 16, 1856, are "not absorbed in money-making"; in another letter written two weeks later, he asked her pointedly: "How is it that poor Bo has sores on his knees in the middle of the winter in healthy New England? Really, dear Lucy, Yankee land is not any healthier than any other place."[106]

Until Blackwell could find a buyer for the business, they had little choice but to remain in Cincinnati. Stone's disappointment was mitigated in January 1856, however, when Antoinette Brown joined the Blackwell household. Sam had been courting her for the past year, and on January 24, 1856, they were married in a simple ceremony at Nettie's parents' farm in Henrietta, New York. Stone wallpapered the room in which the bridal couple was to stay in anticipation of their arrival, though when they arrived, she was away lecturing in Illinois and Indiana. She wrote Harry about a chance meeting with an old friend, John Pierpont, in the railroad station.[107] Told of Nettie's marriage, he commented, "So she has gone down into the abyss too," a remark that intimated to Stone that Pierpont was "haunted evidently with the idea that marriage is the annihilation of a wife." She added, "We must *prove* the contrary."[108]

Returning from her lecture trip a day early, Stone described how she determined to "get and give a little fun." Instead of going in the front door at Walnut Hills, she went around to the kitchen door intending to pretend she was a beggar. Seeing that it was Lucy, Hannah Blackwell, "with an exclamation of glad surprise, gave me hearty kisses and stepped back to look and assure herself and then gave me another set of kisses."[109] Hannah wrote that Stone's early return brought "a ray of sunshine to our home. I love her very much however I may differ with her." Her differences over the propriety of public lecturing did not prevent Hannah from welcoming the income from it, and she wrote proudly that "Lucy sent home upwards of $300 whilst away."[110]

Stone returned to Cincinnati as a wild courtroom drama was beginning to unfold. Margaret Garner was being brought to trial for the murder of her three-year-old child. She and her husband and children had escaped from slavery in Kentucky. Recaptured in Ohio and determined not to return her family to slavery, the young wife killed one child and was in the act of attempting to kill another when she was arrested. Stone visited Garner in prison, asking her at one point if she had a knife should the decision go against her.[111]

During a recess in the trial, Stone addressed the crowd that had jammed the courtroom, speaking with such emotional force that the Kentucky owner, there to retrieve his "property," sat perspiring with anguish and shame. After she had finished, the owner came to Stone and promised that if the court gave him a choice in the matter, he would let the woman go free. Garner was acquitted, but the owner changed his mind, and ordered her bound and brought to the ship that would return her and her children to Kentucky. An account of the trial paid tribute to Stone, whose

moving eloquence touched a sacred chord in every heart. Would that I could pen the thoughts precisely in her own words. But even then, it would lack the fascinating power of her voice, so irresistibly sweet and powerful. Its melody has lingered around my heart ever since I first heard its tones, like a magic spell, and I only wish that it might reach the ear of the nation—when I am sure its stubborn heart would relent.[112]

The likelihood of Stone's voice reaching the ear of the nation was diminishing with each passing month. Stone's autonomy was dissolving under the steady pressure of Blackwell's disapproval and her own mounting insecurity. Blackwell was proving to be a needy man, and he apparently felt diminished by her success. Stone felt worthy only insofar as she was useful; she was what she accomplished. Outside the public sphere, she was unsure of herself. However much she might be willing to dispense with the world's approval, she had grown to need Harry's affection and to fear his criticism. Blackwell's situation was very nearly the opposite. He craved the world's respect and admiration. Against such conflicting needs, the marriage of equals, so fine a concept in the abstract, became more and more elusive in reality.

Understanding Stone's vulnerability to the kind of psychological dominance Blackwell exerted is difficult. Doubtless her parents' unhappy marriage influenced her. Then too, the sheer weight of custom, the force of law, societal definitions of womanliness, and an insufficient understanding of birth control all militated against her hopes for equality in the marriage relation. Whatever the reasons, Stone's sphere was constricting by degrees.

She had given up wearing the Bloomer costume except in private; she had begun sewing Harry's shirts and mending his leggings when he charged her with the inequity of burdening his mother with these tasks. She had yielded to his pressure to restrict her lecture activity. Each month now she looked for the "last proof of her love"—the baby she feared would at least temporarily halt her public activity.

Stone had been the primary wage earner, supporting not just Harry, but to some extent his extended family as well. She had loaned and invested more than ten thousand dollars in the hardware business and land speculations in the three years before her marriage, and in the nine months since their wedding, she had brought home more than four thousand dollars. Still, when Stone suggested that her earnings were needed, an indignant Harry responded that it was a *"permanent* natural fact that the husband must, as a general thing support his wife and children." In the same letter, he asked her to lend him some more of the money she had placed in Bowman's trusteeship prior to her marriage.[113] Blackwell's loans were overdue, and on March 19, 1856, Stone directed Bo to transfer $750 to meet an overdue loan of Harry's. A week later, she drew two thousand dollars more, taking notes secured by Blackwell's property in Illinois.[114] Harry was full of remorse and promises, writing, "I certainly never intended to involve anybody in serious difficulties on my a/c [account] . . . all I have to reproach myself with is . . . that I did not speak the *whole* truth & quite love my neighbor as myself. But, thus it always is, we follow principles in the abstract, but do not come squarely up to them them in the concrete. I am sincerely desirous to *toe the mark* henceforward!"[115]

By the end of April, Blackwell was able to sell his share in Coombs, Ryland, & Blackwell. Because the business was so heavily in debt, he received no cash in the transfer, taking instead heavily mortgaged western land certificates.[116]

When Stone realized that the sale had brought no money, she pressed

Blackwell to sell some of her Wisconsin land. She had received an invitation to lecture in England, and she wished to finance the trip with money from the land sale. Blackwell put her off, writing that they should consider it "if we have no baby to look after."[117] While he went to Wisconsin, Stone stayed in Cincinnati to help Hannah close up Walnut Hills before traveling to New York for the May anniversary meetings.

The choice of residences became a struggle of wills. Blackwell wanted Stone to come west and join him in Wisconsin after the May anniversaries. She wished to live in the East. If they had not found a place of their own in the East, she wrote, she would go to her family at Gardner as soon as the May anniversary meetings were over and spend the summer there. "I am quite sure that we shall not want to *live* West. . . . So my dear, unless you remain to sell Wisconsin land, I do not think it worth my while to go back there just to look."[118]

Blackwell wrote again asking her to come to Wisconsin "to appraise and offer our lands for sale."[119] Stone's expressed intention of lining up a series of lecture engagements in the East prompted Blackwell to bring out the big guns:

> I am not sure that it will be best for you to lecture at this season, I cannot help thinking that you had better accompany me thither . . . as my life is uncertain & you may, at any time, find my affairs suddenly thrown into your hands for settlement & as we do not want any isolations in our lives—I should like you to *understand* exactly what we are doing and wherein our interests lie. I thank God for your gift of speech dear Lucy, but infinitely more for the depths of affection and sympathy and love of Right which lie behind it. I will try not to drag down your higher aspirations nor to fetter your nobler activities. Help me to help you and all will be well.[120]

Blackwell had posed the two—the "gift of speech" versus "love of Right"—as mutually exclusive. Stone, who had permitted herself to believe his pre-nuptial promises, now came up against her cultural beliefs about the role of wife. What worked for her on the lecture platform was the reassurance that woman's rights would not be man's wrongs. The "woman" who was to be free to pursue any career, who was morally responsible for her own actions and accountable for the full exercise of her gifts, was counterpoised against the "wife," and, as she had written Sarah, the domestic role was paramount. Powerless to refute Blackwell's characterization of wifely duty as a moral imperative, beckoned to the wilderness by a husband whose fragile ego would demand ever-greater proofs of her love in the years to come, Stone bowed before custom and the melodramatic hint that Blackwell's death might be imminent. She left for Chicago, where Blackwell was to meet her, and together they set off for Wisconsin.

CHAPTER SEVEN

"Rock the Cradle Lucy
And Keep the Baby Warm!"

"Very unexpectedly," wrote Stone in June 1856, "I find myself on the way to Wisconsin."[1] Her destination, Viroqua, was pioneer territory in 1856, lying some two hundred miles and nine full days' travel northwest of Chicago. To reach it, she and Blackwell jounced across roads that often were little more than cart tracks. Accommodations were primitive; they stayed at farmhouses, once sharing a room with "six room-mates," another time sleeping on filthy sheets in a room through which "two girls and a dog kept passing."[2] What they found when at last they arrived in Viroqua was a frontier hamlet comprising some thirty shanties and a small hotel. They remained there for nearly three months, living first at the hotel, and when Stone found that too dirty and uncomfortable, boarding in a rented room. As the scope of Stone's public activity diminished, she grew more emotionally dependent on Blackwell.

Within days of their arrival, Blackwell found a prospective buyer, a local man named Grace, for one of Stone's Bad Axe land parcels. The three of them set off for Bad Axe in a buggy. Stone described their harrowing journey—a trip that may have caused her to question the security of her large-scale investments in wilderness lands—in a letter home. Twelve miles out of Viroqua, the road ended; the horse fell, and they proceeded on foot, "entirely lost in grass as high as my shoulders . . . full of sloughs, frightfully deep. . . . We travelled on through the nettles, briars, tall grass . . . bitten by mosquitos and black with wood ticks that fastened on us. . . . I was wet to my knees. . . . The sun had gone down, and the stars were thick over us, and still we toiled on."

Late at night, they arrived at the junction of two "wild and high" rivers where they were able to quench "our horrid thirst." Heavy rains had swept the log bridge away, and they shouted for help for over an hour, until at last someone heard them. Their rescuer put them up for the night in his two-room log cabin. In the morning, Grace would go no farther, having lost all interest in the trade. He and Stone returned to Viroqua, while Blackwell went on alone. On his return, Blackwell assured her that Bad Axe lands were already in such demand that they would quadruple in value if they could only hold on for another year.³

Stone settled into a domestic routine, reading, writing letters, sewing shirts for Harry, occasionally engaging one or another of her neighbors in a discussion of woman's rights. On Sundays, she gave antislavery talks in support of the bloody struggle going on in Kansas. Far from the labor she loved, she wrote her mother, "If I had not a husband here, and a good one too, I should be scampering eastward in less than no time."⁴

She wrote to Bowman of the travails of frontier wives. Women had only four days in bed following childbirth, she told him, after which their husbands insisted they resume farm chores. She told of meeting a woman whose husband forced her to sleep "in an out-house" following the birth of a daughter, because "if she will have girls, cold is good enough for *her*," adding, "And he is a very good specimen of the whole."⁵

When a town delegation came to ask if she would give a Fourth of July oration, Stone agreed, and a platform was erected in the town center. Hearing that the famed Lucy Stone was to speak, settlers from farms and towns for fifty miles around crowded into Viroqua for the holiday. Midway through her speech, the platform creaked, swayed, and collapsed. "So will this country fall unless slavery is abolished!" she was heard to say above the commotion.⁶

With no income and no immediate prospect of land sales, Stone was forced to draw on her savings to support herself and Blackwell. She sent to Bo for five hundred dollars, apologizing for giving him "so much trouble, but so long as men will make laws which do not allow women to do their own business, they must expect to be bothered."⁷ In the next three months, she drew steadily on her reserves, writing optimistically to her parents: "Property costing eight hundred last year will within a year be worth three thousand."⁸

Meanwhile, Blackwell continued to buy land. Earlier that spring, two prominent Cincinnati businessmen had entrusted him with twenty-five thousand dollars to invest in Wisconsin lands. "Be very careful my love in your investments for Messrs. Howells and Worthington to keep *every* item of expense, so exactly noted that the Argus eyes of Avarice or Justice shall find no defect," Stone had warned. "You ought to have a little book expressly for that."⁹ Blackwell was not a careful man, and difficulties had begun to surface—problems with defective titles and with lands improperly "entered." His handling of both Howells's and

Worthington's money eventually involved him in a series of costly law-suits, and it would take the last of Stone's savings to extricate him from legal tangles over the faulty titles.[10] Some of Stone's lands also proved to have deficient warrants—a circumstance Harry blamed on George's "carelessness." (George, however, claimed that both he and Harry were aware that the titles were clouded when they made the purchases at below-market prices.)[11]

Financial woes were only a part of Stone's problems that summer. Until then, she had defined herself by work; she was what she did. In domestic exile, self-doubts and depression overwhelmed her. Even the organizational work she prided herself on could not be done from Viroqua, where mail delivery was agonizingly slow. Stone wrote Anthony asking her to take over the correspondence chores for the seventh national convention, giving careful instructions about how to prepare and distribute the call. "Sign . . . Lucy Stone *only* as secretary. Leave off the Blackwell," she directed.[12]

When almost two months later, Stone read through the announcement as it appeared in the *Tribune,* she saw that it was signed "Lucy Stone Blackwell." The sight made her feel "faint and sick." She wrote Anthony immediately. "Oh, Susan! What did make you do it? . . . it was so unjust, so cruel." Such an "insult" she could have borne from an enemy or detractor, she wrote, but knowing it was done by a loved and trusted friend "has wrought a wrong in me that it will take many years to wear out. . . . Hereafter I shall work, but with a loss of hope and courage."[13]

Stone's anguished response points to her emotional state. Away from the lecture platform, physically isolated and psychologically debilitated, she could not have admitted the possibility that she had made a wrong choice in marrying Blackwell. Anguish over her name was an outlet for all the misery and doubt attendant on her present domestic life in remote Wisconsin.

Anthony denied responsibility for the mistake, and Stone apologized, but a strained note crept into her correspondence. The possibility that she might be pregnant meant that she might have to turn the work of the movement over to Anthony. Up to that point, Stone had been the organizational mainstay of the movement. "I am not at all sanguine of the success of the convention," she wrote. Whether she would be able to speak or not was also uncertain, and she confided in Anthony that "however much I hope, or try to hope, the old doubt comes back. . . ."[14]

Marriage and children had temporarily hampered the activity of three woman's rights colleagues: Antoinette Brown Blackwell was confined to Elizabeth Blackwell's home awaiting the birth of a baby; Stanton was at home nursing a new baby (her sixth); Stone was far away. In understandable frustration, Anthony wrote to chide Stone for neglecting the cause.

Stone's response was sharp and defensive: "Now that I occupy a legal position in which I can not even draw in my own name the money I have earned . . . or make any contract, but am rated with fools, minors and madmen, and can not sign a legal document . . . and even the right to my own name questioned, do you think that in the grip of *such* pincers, I am likely to grow remiss?"[15]

The indignation did not altogether conceal Stone's ambivalence. If marriage was a kind of legal and metaphorical death, pregnancy to Stone threatened both the physical and the emotional life of a woman. When Nettie wrote that she was troubled by moodiness during her pregnancy, Stone consoled her: "Don't blame yourself Nettee, if you find that all the 'original sin' seems to try and manifest itself in you, for even Margaret Fuller, with all her strength and philosophy, says she was 'never so unreasonable and desponding'—Blame the circumstances, tho may be the Furies will not haunt you as they so often do, even the very best."

Still, "furies" or no, Stone professed herself disappointed that she was not yet pregnant, confiding, "For myself, I almost despair. Will you give me one of your seven? I expect some new phases of life this summer and shall try and get the honey from each moment."[16]

Late in August, Stone was summoned home to Coy's Hill, where Luther's widow Phebe had expressed the dying wish that Stone be with her. Mail delays and the long journey made her too late. Still, Stone did not return to Wisconsin, instead staying on in New England for almost two months, first at Coy's Hill and then at Gardner with Sarah. From Gardner, Stone wrote Anthony that she was not yet ready to resume lecturing but would take over the organization of the upcoming anniversary convention, delayed until after the elections in recognition of the gravity of the situation in Kansas, where pro- and anti-slavery forces battled.[17]

The political campaign that raged through the nation was as turbulent, chaotic, and eventful as any the young republic had seen. The spring and summer had been brutal—the beating of Charles Sumner nearly to death on the Senate floor, the sacking of Lawrence, Kansas, by proslavery ruffians, and John Brown's retaliatory raid at Pottowatomie Creek had shaken the country. Sectional politics had all but paralyzed Congress that year, and political parties were crumbling. The Whig party splintered; the Democrats split, and the Republican party was formed as a loose coalition of antislavery Whigs and free soil advocates. As election rhetoric grew more heated, Kansas continued to bleed, adumbrating the deadly consequences of the issues dividing the voters that autumn.

From her New England base, Stone corresponded and visited with reform leaders, hoping to increase participation in the anniversary convention. Anthony opposed inviting men to participate, but Stone argued that men had an equal stake in the claim for equality, and both sexes were "bound to rise or fall together." She tried to convince Anthony of the need for the support of male legislators to introduce suffrage bills and vote for them. It behooved women, Stone argued, to establish as influential a support network as they could. To that end, she paid calls that fall on Ralph Waldo Emerson, Henry Ward Beecher, Horace Greeley, Thomas Wentworth Higginson, and other influential men, soliciting speakers, endorsements, and publicity for the convention scheduled for November 25 and 26 in New York.[18]

In delivering the opening address at the convention, Stone reviewed the gains of the past seven years. "It seems almost a miracle that so much has been wrought which is traceable directly to our efforts." She enumerated the legal victories, noting that "almost every Northern State has more or less modified [property] laws." In Michigan, she noted, "it has been moved that *women should have a right to their own babies*." She pointed to economic gains—to the entrance of women into "new, and more remunerative industrial pursuits," and to recent educational gains for women as well. There were now two coeducational colleges, as well as a growing number of female colleges. "The ballot is not yet yielded," she said, but "it cannot be far off."[19]

In a longer afternoon speech on women and property, Stone spoke of the necessity for legislative protection for married women's property, warning: "I have known more than one man take advantage of the law, to marry a lady who had large property, in order to get control of that property and squander it."[20] Her own fortune was fast disappearing. Without lecture income, she and Blackwell were forced to move in with Elizabeth in New York, where the "large and impecunious" Blackwell clan had gathered after leaving Walnut Hills. Sam and Nettie, their new baby, Elizabeth and Kitty Barry, her ward, sisters Marion and Ellen, mother Hannah, Lucy, and Harry all crowded into the house.[21]

Although Stone worried that she had lost the power to speak, she agreed to a series of lecture tours that autumn and winter. Blackwell meanwhile had borrowed five thousand dollars and bought into an agricultural bookselling business he hoped would earn fifteen or twenty thousand dollars a year.[22]

Stone was away all but five nights in December and January, and Blackwell was able to join her for only a few of those days. "Harry darling! A week ago today, at this hour I was close by your side in the little attic, and so happy to be there!" she wrote on January 5, 1857. "When you return," she wrote, "I will try and be in N.Y. to give you the warm welcome which now is always in my heart for you."[23] When Harry was away, she shared a room with her mother-in-law. "I shall be so glad Harry, O so glad when we are able to have our own home," she wrote.[24]

As always, work banished Stone's self-doubts. She wrote of her relief at finding that she was "every day . . . getting back more and more the old faith in myself and brave courage too, which before helped me to work out all that which made *me* better, and was good for others too."[25] Blackwell was less enthusiastic, warning her that if she was pregnant, she would be guilty of neglecting her health and that of the baby if she continued her lecture tour. Stone responded that he must not "fear that I who have hitherto cared well for myself shall neglect, or not be able to do so now."[26] Stone learned in February that she was pregnant but saw no reason to curtail her schedule, as a letter to a friend describing her spring activity shows: "I had gone as far as Providence when I received a telegraphic despatch [sic] to return to Boston and give an argument to the Legislative Committee to which our petitions for woman's right to vote had been referred." In Boston, another telegraph summoned her to Augusta, Maine, where she went before the legislative committee to plead for a similar measure. In March she was in New York for another round of meetings, having made a number of stops en route.[27]

Beneath her business-as-usual demeanor, anxiety simmered. At thirty-seven, Stone saw pregnancy as a threat to both her health and her work. She wrote Blackwell of her fears: "*If* in the hour that is before me I should go out of my body, or have it left a wreck, *this* work will be worthy work to leave as my *last*." Her fears were not unfounded; her sister Eliza had died in childbirth, and Luther's wife Phebe had nearly died. "I might be brave for a long time after, if only for one little minute I might look into your eyes," she wrote.[28]

Blackwell's response was cheerful. "My dear Lucy," he wrote her, "be happy *for my sake . . . remember that I love you* and be content to give me this *last proof of your affection*." He brushed aside her worries, writing, "Do not feel nervous, nor anxious, nor worried, but keep a brave heart and try to realize that my soul's arms surround you with an *inexpressible love*."[29]

Stone also worried about how they would support themselves when she could not lecture. Her solution was to buy a small farm on which she could raise enough food to feed herself and the baby. She found a "gothic cottage" surrounded by fruit trees on an acre of ground in Orange, New Jersey. "This we, or rather I, purchased, with my husband's counsel," she wrote to a friend. They moved in on the first of April, whereupon Blackwell left immediately on an extended western trip, leaving Stone with "carpenters, masons, housecleaners, a gardener, & c."[30]

Stone continued to lecture into the sixth month of pregnancy. "This she would not do, but for our exceeding scarcity of money—and the urgent necessity for *a well and cistern*," Blackwell wrote.[31] His salary was insufficient to cover his mortgages, taxes, and loan repayments. "Lucy has succeeded in borrowing $500 from an old lady friend which enabled me to pay up my interest note of same amount due June 1st. I can now get along comfortably until next winter when I shall be short just *One Thousand Dollars*," he wrote George.[32]

As she prepared to give her final lecture, Stone wrote, "I think that I shall deposit my money with Spofford, all except what we shall use soon, and that will be nearly all finally." She signed the letter, "Ever affectionately, Poor Lucy."[33]

Blackwell's troubles were compounded that month when the agricultural libraries he had been selling proved to be of poor quality.[34] In late July, he quit the bookselling business and took a "tedious" position as a bookkeeper in New York. He wrote George of his intention "to come to Bad Axe Co next spring and locate there for several years to come."[35]

Stone, by now eight months pregnant, wrote Anthony that she continued to do all the work of the house and the garden by herself. "Harry . . . is not well at all. He goes in to N.Y. every day, but he is not fit to. I feel troubled about him." Along with the work of house and garden, Stone had agreed to take charge of sending out the call and obtaining speakers for the October anniversary convention, but "swollen feet & hands & general discomforts are not good assistants in any work," she wrote, asking Anthony to take over.[36]

Anthony was feeling overworked, and Stone suggested transferring the convention to Providence, where Elizabeth Buffum Chace had offered to take charge. Stone was again bristling under Anthony's criticisms, writing that she had recently heard from a number of friends that Susan was going about saying "that I did not appear quite right," and telling people that in "such doting ease" Stone "should become nothing." Such criticism left her feeling "wounded, grieved, hurt, almost as I never was before." At their May meeting in New York, she continued, "I felt a mountain of ice between us. I felt that without any reason, you had lost all faith in me. And I wondered at the kiss you proffered. But I am in no state of body or mind to write about it," she concluded. "I must make the path for my own feet. I have no advice or explanation to make to *anybody*."[37]

The week before the baby was due, Blackwell wrote Stone an uncharacteristically contrite letter from New York, where he was staying, expressing regret for "the defects of my character & purpose which have thrown so many obstacles in your path & so much bitterness into your cup." He continued:

Lucy dear—*however* this great crisis may eventuate, whether it result, as I hope and believe, in *our* assumption of new duties and cares, or whether in leaving me *alone* in this strange and uncongenial world—I will try to *meet* my responsibilities *worthily and well*. . . . You have ennobled my life. I fear I have *not* ennobled *your's* But Lucy dear—I hope to be your's always and forever. I cannot at once change the habits and faults of my whole life, but henceforth you shall see me *ascend and improve*.[38]

On September 14, 1857, with Dr. Emily Blackwell in attendance, Stone gave birth to a daughter. Harry described the baby as "a brave, vigorous little girl with dark blue eyes and hair blacker than my own who immediately proceeded to manifest her identity most unmistakably and who seems to have adopted as her own Garrison's celebrated motto . . . *'I will be heard!'* "[39]

A week later, Blackwell left for Chicago to resume selling books for Augustus Moore, who had bought out the partner responsible for the shoddy books.[40] Stone remained at home with the newborn, tentatively named Sarah. They agreed that the child would bear both parents' surnames but could not agree on a first name. Although they referred to the baby as "Sarah" for the better part of a year, the name eventually settled on was Alice.

When Sarah/Alice was almost two months old, Stone hired a young woman to help with housework and baby and resumed a modified lecture schedule in and around New York. In November, the tax bill for her house arrived, addressed to her. A few women had been paying their taxes under protest for the past decade, and Stone decided to carry the protest one step further, writing the Orange, New Jersey, tax collector:

Enclosed I return my tax bill, without paying it. My reason for doing so is, that women suffer taxation, and yet have no representation, which is not only unjust to one half of the adult population, but is contrary to our theory of government. . . . we believe when the attention of men is called to the wide difference . . . between the theory of government and its practice . . . the sense of justice which is in all good men will lead them to correct it. Then we shall cheerfully pay our taxes.[41]

The town responded with a posted notice announcing that the household goods of Lucy Stone would be sold at auction. Newspapers carried notice of the sale, slated for January 22 at two in the afternoon. Although it was winter, the auction took place out of doors. The officer of the law who was delegated the task of carrying Stone's meager household furnishings out onto the small piazza on that bitter January day was dismayed. Newspapers quoted him as saying he hoped he would "never have to do such a job hereafter."[42] Reading in the *Tribune* that among the items seized and sold were engraved portraits of Salmon P. Chase and William Lloyd Garrison, Higginson wrote her: "The selection of these portraits will be so melodramatic for your biography that I suspect you of having bribed the sheriff to seize them."[43]

When Blackwell came home in late February for a brief visit, he was furious about the tax protest. Stone wrote her mother that "Harry and I had an overflowing meeting about it night before last."[44]

In his short visit home, Blackwell vied with the baby for Stone's attention. Bothered by a boil and by a bruise on his leg, he afterwards apologized for having been an "insignificant cripple that gave you so much trouble."[45] The tone of the letters exchanged immediately following the brief reunion indicates that it was not a particularly happy time for either of them.

Blackwell sharply criticized Stone for leaving the baby in the care of others in order to lecture. On his way back out west, he wrote on March 3 that she should "postpone any positive arrangements for your lectures in Jersey City and Brooklyn until you are actually *located* at *Elizabeth's*, with a girl to nurse the baby during your absences under *Mother's supervision.*"[46]

Blackwell did not want her to return to lecturing, and he continued to try to convince her of the necessity of staying at home. He sent her the March issue of the *Atlantic*, advising her to read "two stories illustrative to womanly self devotion & constancy—*both admirable* & I think *true to nature.*"[47] The stories' heroines were paragons of womanly self-abnegation. In the first story, a woman reluctantly decides to remain with her aged and ailing grandmother rather than go West with her love; in the second a woman refuses to marry because she must care for a brother paralyzed in a buggy accident. "Men is allers for themselves first, an' Devil take the hindmost; but women lives in other folks's lives, and ache, and work, and endure all sorts of stress o'weather afore they'll quit the ship that's got crew and passengers aboard," muses one of the men in the stories.[48]

Stone, with time to reflect on the substance of their quarrels and aware of the implied criticism in the stories, replied; "I *am* trying to be a good wife and mother. I have wanted to tell you how hard I am trying, but I *have* tried before, and my miserable failures hitherto make me silent now. . . . I hope to be more to you, and better—when you come to me. . . . I will try and have more time to read—and to go out with you, when I can, and not neglect Sarah."[49]

Blackwell's implied charge that her pursuit of a career neglected him and baby struck at the heart of all that Stone had stood for. Her persuasiveness had derived from the outset from her reassurance that women would be more, and not less "womanly," a phrase which in the 1850s was inextricably connected to domestic performance.

Not surprisingly, Stone's headaches returned. On March 8, she wrote that she was suffering from a constant headache and a severe case of boils. Too ill to continue writing, she laid the letter aside. Illness forced her to cancel first a lecture for the benefit of the female shirt sewers' union, and then a planned series of lectures.[50] From Janesville, Wisconsin, Blackwell sent a strangely contrite letter, one which suggests the "testing" nature of his love and his need for constant assurance:

Poor Lucy I have kept you ever since our marriage in so *unsatisfied* a condition. I have carried you off to Cincinnati and Chicago and Wisconsin and New York and New Jersey—have given you no rest or permanent home—have separated you from your mother and brothers and sisters and friends—have fettered you in your public career of usefulness and fame—have given you anxiety, pain, poverty, sickness, privations manifold—have vexed and pained you to the very heart often and have been a drag instead of a helpmate to you—and yet *you love me*—poor Lucikin! I fear it is on the principle that all men love and prize *what has cost them dear.*[51]

If Stone was initially puzzled by the letter, she soon learned the reason for his contrition. Worthington had come to inspect his properties and now threatened Blackwell with legal prosecution. Blaming George for these "deficient" warrants too, Blackwell tried to settle out of court, signing over 1,640 acres of Stone's land to Worthington. When he needed her savings as well, he wrote contritely, "I feel great regret at having to take poor Lucy's Bank stock—It is *her last cash means. . . .* I only consent to it now because my *honor* is implicated."[52]

On April 3, Stone notified him that she and Sam had completed the sale of the bank stock and that the money was on its way.[53] Within a week of paying off Worthington, Blackwell wrote that he was finding investors for a railroad charter to cross their land: "*I* H.B.B.—the mammoth capitalist—and G.W.B. of LaCrosse, the eminent young lawyer, are both among the *Incorporators* of this *great project. . . .* mark my words— Lucy—within five years *that road will be in operation.* Then we shall reap the rewards of our tedious *holding on.*"[54]

Stone wrote Blackwell to forget the railroad and to sell what remained of her land. "I mean to sell my lands at anything above the cost," she wrote. "It is hardly worth while for the sake of some possible future to starve the present. If we *can't* sell, I don't know how we can manage, but I am planting potatoes, & think we shall live."[55] Blackwell ignored her directions, and Stone wrote again, insisting that if he did not sell her land, she would be forced to rent out her New Jersey cottage for the income and move in with her sister. Blackwell, who had become friendly with their neighbors in Orange, opposed Stone's plan.

In addition to their friendship with the Rowland Johnsons, Stone and Blackwell enjoyed the company of Abby and Ludlow Patton, a couple living in nearby Roseville. Patton was a wealthy Wall Street financier, and Abby, a member of the well-known singing Hutchinson family, was an antislavery friend of Stone's. Abby Patton, eleven years Stone's junior, was described as "one of the brightest, loveliest, and most talented women of her day," having an "undefinable, magnetic power."[56]

Stone's confidence ebbed steadily. Guilt and worry vied with the urgent need for income, but even were she able to disregard Blackwell's wishes, she would have been too exhausted with the work of home and baby to consider lecturing. On April 1, she wrote Anthony to say that she would not be available to speak at the May convention, as *"I can not speak well while I nurse the baby.* You are tired with 4 months work. If you had had measles and whooping cough added to all you have done it would not be *half* as hard as the taking care of a child day and night is—*I know."*[57]

In need of funds to pay the overdue taxes on her Wisconsin lands, Stone accepted a fifty-dollar lecture engagement in New York on April 22. A neighbor agreed to keep the baby overnight. As it was too late to return by the ferry and the cars, Stone spent a restless night at Elizabeth's house. When she returned the next day, she was overcome with guilt to find that the baby had "taken a dreadful cold" in her absence.[58]

Blackwell was still away, and his mother came back from New York with Stone, having agreed to care for the baby so that Stone could attend the May conventions. Stone may have blamed herself for Blackwell's prolonged absence. Late in April, she wrote: "I so wish for you Harry! I *love* you, and am trying to make the little home pleasant for you to come to dearest—and to be myself what a wife and mother should be."[59]

From Chicago, Blackwell ignored her pleas, informing her that he wished her to arrange for him to be made one of the vice presidents at the upcoming convention. "Get good help at any price!" he wrote. "Don't economize too closely." At the same time, he reported to George that he had exhausted his six-hundred-dollar advance on salary and "henceforth must *shut down and liquidate."*[60]

When Stone learned that Blackwell had traded some of her land without consulting her, she wrote an accusatory letter, reminding him of their premarital agreement. "Surely you might reasonably delegate to me such supervision, I being here, you at N. York," he responded airily.[61]

As Stone made preparations to leave for the convention, Hannah Blackwell abruptly decided to return to New York, leaving a dispirited and ailing daughter-in-law at home with the baby. With her savings all but gone, Stone pinned all her hopes on the sale of her Wisconsin lands.[62]

Blackwell refused to sell. Instead, he traded still more of her property for land on which he continued to hope to get a railroad built. Stone wrote again reminding him of the pre-nuptial agreement, to which Blackwell responded: "I admire and respect your desire to manage your own affairs and do your own work and certainly have no wish to *crop* it *one iota*—tho I do want to help you get your affairs into a more productive shape." He warned against trying to *"compel"* her lands into money, as "this is the worst possible time to do so," reassuring her that he would get everything "square" by September, "and never get into *quite such a pinch* again." He consoled her, "dear Lucy, I have suffered more in the thought of your pinching and overworking yourself during my absence than in all else."[63]

Stone made arrangements with an agent to rent out the house and went with the baby to Coy's Hill. Unhappy that she had acted against his wishes, Blackwell sent her a letter he had received from Elizabeth in which he was advised to command her to remain in Orange. "If I were you I would plant my foot, and say, that is your *home* Lucy, consider it a settled abiding fact," Elizabeth had written. "A young family needs a settled home." Unaware of their desperate financial plight, she had added, "$500 or $600 won't pay for the destruction of a *home*."[64]

What Stone thought of Elizabeth's advice is unclear. She maintained a cordial relationship with her sister-in-law despite Elizabeth's ill-concealed antipathy. Indeed, the entire clan must have proved a burden at times. The Blackwells were never happier than when they were thoroughly involved in one another's affairs. While Elizabeth was advising Harry to put his foot down, Emily urged George to "prevent Harry from getting involved in that railway he seems so much absorbed in." Sam counseled Harry to sell his Wisconsin lands; Harry proffered advice to Marian on a land deal she was engaged in.[65]

From Massachusetts, Stone begged, "Will you come home Harry dear . . . & join me at Gardner?"[66] Her boils had grown so bad that Hannah, seriously wasted by illness, had to take over the care of the baby while Stone took to her bed. The days passed in a haze of sickness, and Stone grew more and more depressed. She faulted herself in one letter for not knowing how to enjoy life more; she berated herself in another for "my want of ability to fit well to new circumstances," promising that she would try to do better in the future. "I love you, Harry," she wrote.[67]

Blackwell had little patience with Stone's complaints: "I think you can hardly have felt this separation so keenly as I . . . because you have had little Sarah to nurse and care for." The baby was nine months old, and Blackwell had spent less than three weeks of that time at home—two weeks of it in need of full-time nursing himself. Stone appeared not to mind. She did not permit herself anger or resentment. However confident she had been as public figure, she was growing more timid and insecure in her private role. She was effectively abandoned, reminded of her shortcomings, and made to feel guilty. She wrote plaintively, "In no other absence have I ever felt your loss so much, never longed so for you, never needed you, as I have during these 4 weary months." A little of her old spirit surfaced in one letter in which she wrote that she was "much obliged for your kind wish that I should rest. But Harry no one who takes care of a baby *can* rest." She added, "I have not *felt* rested for months— you may take care of baby *one* day, and you will understand it—and if you add to that, the making [of clothing], mending, washing, ironing, & c, for her & you, there will be little time for reading or rest."[68]

When Blackwell wrote that he would return in August, Stone asked if he would come to Gardner to help her with the baby on the trip home. His answer left no uncertainty as to the relative importance of his commitments. "If I find that business will *require* my presence in Boston," he would meet her, he wrote. "If not, . . . meet me at the R.R. depot in New York."[69]

In mid-August, she and baby traveled alone to join him. They moved back into Stone's small home in Orange, and three weeks later, Blackwell set off again, this time to Ohio to sell books.[70] Determined not to repeat the humiliation of being unable to support herself, Stone looked for a property with more acreage on which she could grow crops and keep livestock. She found a small house with twenty acres on a hillside in Bloomfield, New Jersey. When Blackwell returned, he arranged the sales transaction for her, putting up nearly two thousand acres of Stone's Wisconsin lands as security to the seller. Though Stone had no knowledge of it at the time, title to these lands would also prove defective, embroiling them in a lengthy lawsuit.[71]

Stone looked forward to settling in at Bloomfield. Sam and Nettie, to whom a second daughter had been born that April, had purchased a home nearby. Sam was earning fifteen hundred dollars a year as a confidential clerk in a New York firm, and Nettie had resumed lecturing in and around New York.[72]

Both Stone and Blackwell were sick that fall, she with severe dysentery, he "prostrated" by a boil on his nose that required two weeks' nursing by his sisters in New York.[73] When Stone was sufficiently recovered, she joined him in New York. There she agreed to permit Marian Blackwell to take her shopping for a new dress, hoping perhaps to please Harry by appearing more attractive. Emily wrote Elizabeth on October 1: "Lucy has bought a new gown and bonnet, and as Marian aided in the choice she looks more like other people than I have ever seen her do."[74]

In late October, Blackwell informed her that he had decided to spend the winter in Chicago.[75] This time there was no argument; Stone and baby Alice went with him. Crossing the country with a baby was a trial. "We trotted and tossed, we sang & whistled," Stone wrote, "but *her* music was in the ascendant." In Chicago, they moved into a very expensive boarding house. "Lucy counts the days till our return," Harry wrote.[76] Stone wrote her parents of their pinched financial state. *"Seventeen dollars per week, and our washing extra,"* she wrote, clearly astonished at the price. "So *somebody* has got to earn some money."[77]

Stone hoped that with Blackwell there to share in the care of Alice, she could provide income by lecturing. She set up a schedule of lectures, but Harry was unwilling or unable to arrange his business to accommodate hers. Stone had to hire a nursemaid to care for Alice, an arrangement that proved unsatisfactory. As Blackwell later described it, while Stone was away lecturing, the nursemaid took the baby outdoors, "without proper protection against the cold. My wife, returning unexpectedly, dismissed the girl and announced her intention of giving up lecturing altogether until the child was older, a resolution which practically resulted in several years withdrawal from the lecture field. . . . Soon after we went to board with a family named Bryce in Evanston."[78]

Away from lecturing, Stone experienced the familiar self-doubt and depression, writing Nettie: "I wish I felt the old impulse & power to lecture, both for the sake of cherished principles & to help Harry with the heavy burden he has to bear—but I am afraid and dare not trust Lucy Stone." Nettie enjoyed a different kind of support from Sam, who pitched in willingly with household chores and child care. Influenced perhaps by Harry's earlier criticism of her for leaving the baby with a nursemaid without family supervision, driven as well by her own idealized ideas of motherhood, Stone wrote that "when I came home & looked in Alice's sleeping face & thought of the possible evil that might befall her if my guardian eye was turned away, I shrank like a snail into its shell, & saw that for these years I can only be a mother—no trivial thing either."[79]

The mother reigned supreme in 1850s' popular culture. Books and magazine articles on motherhood abounded. Even in the *Lily,* the feminist periodical, an 1855 editorial proclaimed that " 'home mother' is the greatest accolade a woman can ever receive."[80] Though Stone challenged the legal, political, and religious status quo, her heterodoxy did not extend to the cult of motherhood. Formerly "Queen of us all," Stone's "realm" was now two rooms in a boarding house, her only "subject" the year-old Alice.

In January, Stone had learned that she was pregnant again. A premature baby boy, born early in June, lived only briefly. She wrote to her mother of the loss, saying that she and Alice were leaving Evanston for Chicago, where a "good Quakeress" and "capital nurse" would care for them until she had recovered. Stone blamed the lack of adequate medical care in Evanston in part for the premature birth: "Indeed, I do expect, if I had [the nurse] at the very first, we need not have lost our little one. We are liable to sickness and death everywhere."[81]

Stone recovered slowly. Back East, Anthony struggled with the organization of the fall anniversary meeting, frustrated by her inability to secure speakers. Domestic entanglements prevented both Stanton and Stone from helping.[82]

When Augustus Moore sold his share of the business late that summer, Stone and Blackwell left Chicago. Having received word that her mother was ill, Stone went directly to Coy's Hill. Still weak herself, Stone was shocked to find that her mother was dying. In her mother's presence, Stone confronted the paradox at the heart of her labor on behalf of women. Stone admired and loved her mother, in part for the very "womanly" qualities that now constrained her own activity. The cult of motherhood was a silken noose, its bounds the source of love. Hannah was subservient, submissive, dependent, obedient, and loved. Stone was loved by Harry as long as she too was "womanly." As she tried simultaneously to cope with her mother's approaching death and with the loss of her career to motherhood, Stone plunged ever deeper into depression.

Returning to New Jersey, Stone and Blackwell settled into their home. Blackwell opened real estate sales offices in Orange, New Jersey, and in New York City. He made the daily hour and a half trip into New York, where he worked at selling or trading his western lands. Stone filled in for him in the Orange office and busied herself with planting a kitchen garden and tending the fruit trees, hoping to produce enough cherries and potatoes to supplement the family's income. She also resumed the organizational work of the fall convention. Her extended absence had been costly to the movement. Much of the loss of momentum, however, was unavoidable, as outside events claimed the nation's attention. The North and South, like two great overheated engines, moved inexorably toward collision.

Impassioned and inflammatory rhetoric filled the newspapers, and in late September, newspapers printed a copy of a letter alleged to have been sent to Lucy Stone over the signature "Stephen Douglass [sic]." The misspelling of Douglas's name might have alerted editors, but they nonetheless printed the copy of the letter in which Douglas regretfully declined Lucy Stone's invitation to him to speak at her Chicago convention.[83]

The idea that Stone would have invited the man Garrison called "that desperate demagogue and Iscariot traitor to liberty, Stephen Arnold Douglas of Illinois" was ridiculous.[84] Having been burned by the Philadelphia "Douglass" incident, Stone immediately printed a public disclaimer in the newspapers. "The hoax seemed to me so barefaced that I never gave it a second thought," she wrote in the *Liberator*. "It is not to *such* men that the woman's Rights cause appeals for helpers."[85]

Frederick Douglass ignored Stone's widely published exposé of the hoax and commenced an attack on her in the October issue of his *Monthly,* charging her with compromising "her anti-slavery principles by a feverish desire for prominence and popularity." His denunciation of Stone ran to three full columns.[86] Unwilling to give the appearance of feuding, Stone publicly ignored the charges, but privately, she was furious. Her anger was swallowed up in the larger emotional response to the news in mid-October of John Brown's arrest for the attack at Harper's Ferry.

Frederick Douglass, one of the financial backers of Brown's raid, fled to Canada to avoid prosecution. To her mother, Stone wrote of her sympathy for Brown: "Isn't it dreadful to think that Old Brown *could* be hung—such a man! It seems as though the times of the martyrs had come again—I imagine we shall have blood shed in Congress, and maybe the dissolution of the Union." Following the executions of Brown and his cohorts, Stone petitioned West Virginia's governor for permission to arrange for proper burials for the fugitive slaves who had fought alongside Brown.[87]

In the spring of 1860, Stone was involved in an internal struggle over the agenda of the upcoming tenth anniversary convention.[88] Stanton announced her intention of making divorce a focal point of the meetings. A written debate on the topic of divorce reform was carried on in the pages of the *Tribune* that spring between Horace Greeley and Robert Dale Owen. Owen had helped to liberalize divorce in Indiana, to which Greeley now referred as "the Paradise of free-lovers."[89] The association of liberalized divorce with "free love" was not new; the same charge had been leveled at Ernestine Rose two years before following a speech in which she advocated liberalizing divorce laws.[90]

The struggle over control of the agenda marked a new departure for Stone and the women's movement. Until now, the loose organization had borne the clear imprint of her will and wishes. When the issue of divorce on grounds of drunkenness had arisen earlier, Stone had given it qualified support, though even then she had argued that it was not strictly a "woman's rights" issue. The accusations of "free love" leveled against Rose and Owen may have influenced Stone, who struggled to keep the issue out of the convention planning. "We must not call [divorce reform] 'woman's rights' for the simple reason that it concerns men just as much," she insisted. Stanton made it clear that she would introduce a series of divorce reform resolutions at the May meeting with or without Stone's agreement.[91]

Stone did not attend the convention. The letters between herself and Anthony regarding her decision not to attend are gone, but the small rift can be inferred from Anthony's speech at the anniversary meeting in which Stone's name was conspicuous by its absence. Anthony lauded "the heroic enunciators of the great idea of woman's equality—Mary Wollstonecraft, Frances Wright, Ernestine Rose, Lucretia Mott, Elizabeth Cady Stanton."[92]

At the final session, Stanton presented twelve resolutions calling for liberalized divorce laws—some thoughtful, others sensational. Among these was a resolution that children born of "loveless marriages" were bastards, "the fruit of lust but not of love—and so, not of God, divinely descended, but from beneath, whence proceed all manner of evil and uncleanness." Another resolution spoke to the "duty" of spouses to divorce when the marriage "failed to promote or produce human happiness." The audience was shocked and voted to reject her proposals. Stanton would say later that only Anthony and Rose supported her.[93]

Antoinette Brown Blackwell, far more conservative than Stone on the subject of divorce, presented thirteen counter-resolutions affirming the indissolubility of marriage. Wendell Phillips moved to strike both sets of resolutions from the record, arguing that any discussion of divorce "unnecessarily burdened" woman's rights. "No question—Anti-Slavery, Temperance, Woman's Rights—can move forward efficiently, unless it keeps its platform separate and unmixed with extraneous issues," he warned.[94]

Newspapers gleefully seized on Stanton's proposals as proof of the free-love association with woman's rights. The press might have continued in this vein were it not for the hullabaloo attending the presidential nominating conventions that immediately followed.[95] The Democrats failed to nominate a presidential candidate after southern delegates walked out rather than accept Stephen Douglas. A subsequent meeting in Baltimore in June resulted in two Democratic candidates—Douglas and Kentucky's John Cabell Breckinridge. The Republicans fared little better that summer, finally settling on Abraham Lincoln as a compromise candidate. Stone read of the nominating conventions at Coy's Hill, where she had gone to care for her mother. On September 14, she wrote to Blackwell:

This is our one wee darling's birthday, and today at two o'clock PM my good Mother went to her other children, Peacefully, without terror, or apparent pain. . . . I long for *you* when my heart is so bruised. . . . We love and loved her for the generous self-forgetting that never was absent from her, and we respect her for the wealth of truth that was part of her soul. May we deserve as well from our children, as she does from hers.

Poor father feels it intensely. I pity him, so old, alone, and needing sympathy and help all the time. I don't know when I shall go home.[96]

It was early October before Stone returned to New Jersey. Blackwell's real estate business was failing, and with mortgages and taxes due on her properties, Stone considered returning to the lecture platform. Nettie, living nearby and awaiting the birth of her third child, encouraged her to return to work. After the child's birth late in December, Sam wrote his mother: "All very well. Nettie sends much love—and counts the weeks to her first lecture engagement," demonstrating a level of support that Stone must have envied as she arranged to return to the lecture platform herself.[97]

Leaving Alice in the care of her Blackwell aunts, Stone traveled to Ohio early in 1861. Tormented by self-doubt, conflicted by guilt, still grieving for her mother, but desperately needing the money to pay over-due taxes and mortgages, Stone reentered public life. Its tonic effect on her was immediate. From Dayton, Ohio, she wrote on January 31: "I am *so* glad to find again the old inspiration, and it comes to me more and more." Though the time between Lincoln's election and his inauguration was marked by a series of mob actions against abolitionists, Stone ignored the danger as she happily made her way through a series of northern and western towns and cities. She reported jubilantly on the success of her efforts, delighted at the warm reception accorded her speeches.[98]

For three months, Stone gloried in the return to public life. Then on the morning of April 12, 1861, Fort Sumter was fired on, and the bloody trial of the young nation began. Stone, on the cusp of her reentry, revitalized and happy, heard the news, at once curtailed her tour, and headed for home. Following the lead of the antislavery societies, she and the other woman's rights leaders agreed to cancel the May meetings.[99]

The war ended Stone's activity even as it offered Blackwell hope. He sent off letters to various officials in the new administration in Washington, hoping to secure a political appointment. He also moved away from Lucy and Alice, boarding in New York City for twenty-five dollars a week.[100] Stone tended to the cherry orchard on the grounds of her New Jersey home, hoping to supplement the family income by selling the fruit in the city. That December, she wrote Bowman asking for a loan to help her and Alice through the winter. Bowman agreed to a small loan at seven percent interest, "the legal rate in New Jersey."[101]

Their financial worries eased temporarily early in 1862 when Blackwell accepted a job with Dennis Harris. He chafed under the indignity of working as a clerk, however, and worried that his name would come up in the draft. Government workers were exempt from conscription, and Blackwell wrote his old friend Ainsworth Spofford in Washington asking him to use his influence to find him "a post of honor and responsibility near Sect'y Chase." Spofford responded that he was unable to do this, offering instead an assistant librarianship, which, while "not a post which can minister to your ambition," was still one "which hundreds of the best educated young men of the country would jump at."[102]

Blackwell did not want the job, and George Blackwell took it instead.

Shortly afterward, Harry bought a one-sixth interest in a gun patent that he was sure would earn him a fortune. The weapon *"trebles* the force of the ball," he wrote George enthusiastically, offering him "an interest or compensation" if he could get it adopted by the War Department.[103]

Blackwell's newest enthusiasm coincided with a terrible bout of migraine headaches for Stone.[104] Their separation earlier that year suggests marital troubles, and once again, Stone seemed to hold herself accountable. Determined to fulfill her domestic duties, she nursed her sister-in-law Marian through a prolonged illness, and when Hannah Blackwell fell ill, Stone cheerfully cared for her mother-in-law too.[105]

Blackwell moved back home, and in early August, he invited Ainsworth Spofford and his wife to come to visit. Elizabeth wrote George that Spofford had "made Harry and Lucy feel very uncomfortable in their present mode of life—he did not like their situation, entanglements, occupations etc., and I suppose Harry consulted him as he does everybody. It pained me to be with Harry, his health is so depressed, and he is so thoroughly uncomfortable."[106]

Elizabeth's next letter to George raises the question of whether the "entanglements" pertained to her brother's business interests, or whether other domestic problems had arisen. The "necessity" for Harry's discomfort, she wrote, rose from defects in his "imperfect character, his imprudence, his speculativeness, his restless unsatisfied aspirations," as well as in his "decidedly poor" health. She also hinted at Lucy and Harry's domestic discord, blaming her brother's unhappy situation on "his marriage which has linked two excellent but unsuitable natures together; but these things cannot be helped—he must take life as it comes to him, or as he has made it, and certainly no change to Washington would mend these things."[107]

In September, both George's and Harry's names came up in the Bloomfield draft, and they paid "$100 each to substitutes."[108] Blackwell quit Dennis Harris's firm and associated himself with the New York brokerage firm of their friend and neighbor Ludlow Patton. That autumn, Blackwell boarded in the city, directing George to send all his correspondence through Ludlow Patton's business address.[109] Stone remained at the Montclair farm, supervising the completion of a woodshed, cowshed, cistern, and barn. Later that winter, she wrote that "Harry has gone to Ohio to investigate making sugar out of beets and is not expected home before February." Following news that Lincoln intended to emancipate the slaves, Stone wrote her father that she doubted that it would work, as "so many of the officers of the army are pro-slavery, and so many of the soldiers hate the negroes."[110]

In 1863, Stone joined Harry at his boardinghouse in the city. She was able to preside over the organizing convention of the Woman's National Loyal League, formed to urge the immediate emancipation of all slaves and to support the government in its war for freedom. When some western delegates objected to identifying antislavery with woman's rights, Stone likened the sentiment to that of the founding fathers, who ignored the cry of the slave in their wish for union at any price. "They said nothing, and let the wretched monster live." Leave the women out of the cry for equality now, she warned, and "we take the same backward step that our fathers took when they left out slavery."[111]

After the convention, Stone left New York with six-year-old Alice to spend the summer at Sarah's. That autumn, she returned to Montclair, while Blackwell boarded in the city. Stone hired her sister-in-law Ellen to care for Alice and briefly resumed lecturing.[112] In December, she rented out her house and joined Blackwell, boarding with him at the home of Rebecca Palmer. The on-again, off-again nature of their marriage in this period points to a deeply troubled relationship. Money was only part of their problem, but money woes continued to plague them.[113]

Family accounts for the spring of 1864 show Harry's earnings of $125 per month, augmented by a $500 loan from Dennis Harris, with quarterly supplements of $150 from the rent on Lucy Stone's two New Jersey houses. Expenses far exceeded income. They paid Palmer $25 per week for their rooms, listed $20 to $30 per week for "family expenses," and Blackwell paid $225 pew rental at Dr. Frothingham's church.[114]

That spring, their financial shortfall was compounded when Kenyon Blackwell, the English cousin who had lent Harry and Sam $10,000 to buy the hardware store, wrote an angry letter charging Blackwell with having used the proceeds from the sale of the hardware business for land investments instead of repaying him when the store was sold. Claiming to need the money, Kenyon demanded immediate payment, suggesting that Harry sell the land.[115]

In response, Blackwell offered Kenyon the deed to Lucy Stone's New Jersey home, to be held as collateral until he and Sam could repay the loan. Stone, tired of living in a boardinghouse with a six-year-old, had taken Alice and gone to Coy's Hill. There, she agreed to Blackwell's request that she transfer the deed of her property to him. From her family home, she wrote on June 14: "I have just come back from Warren where I have relinquished my dower (free from your compulsion). . . . I hope that you will at once appropriate the money to pay something, and so, make our debts less."[116]

From Brookfield, she wrote Anthony in July, "I do all the *work,* cook, wash, iron, sweep, dust, *everything,* and teach Alice an hour a day." Despite the hard work of caring for the farm and for her father, eighty-four and nearly blind, Stone felt more sure of herself away from the turbulence of her marriage. Rather than acknowledge—even to herself—that her depression might be linked to the emotional and financial insecurity of life with Blackwell, she blamed herself and impending menopause, writing to Anthony:

I escaped the last month, with only one day's headache, and none of the mental confusion that has so tormented me before. The quiet of the farm—the old associations—the total change, are worth the world to me. And if I can only survive the inevitable change of constitution and be right side up at the end of it, I shall pray again for the return of that great impulse that drove me into the world, with words that *must* be spoken.[117]

Blackwell pressed her to return to New York, but she responded that it was *"indispensable"* that she live "in a quiet corner, free from criticism, or scrutiny." That it was Blackwell's "criticism" and his "scrutiny" seems clear; nevertheless Stone continued to blame herself, writing that she hoped to "get back, somewhere near to the state of soul & spirit in which I was when you first found me," and to find "that better self of me" with which "serene and self-respecting" she had led "a life of worthy use."[118]

Though she did not blame Harry for their problems, her letters make it clear that they had discussed the possibility of a permanent separation, for she wrote: "I don't believe I could live, shut up with Alice in a suite of rooms, all next winter. . . . I *need* to be hidden, and shielded, and comforted by the large silence of the country. And if all our future is made rich, by this separation we shall be glad, when it is past, that we braved it through, or, if not, we shall at least feel, that we tried to get safely over a bridge that, after all broke.[119]

When the time for the next draft came around, she urged him to "buy a substitute at any price—*Draw on my credit if necessary!!!!*" He should become a campaign speaker instead, she wrote him, for "we *owe* to these troubled hours, *our* contribution of the best we have to give. . . . I wish I were able to help too. Maybe I shall, by and by, for I think I am getting better here. In such beautiful and simple surroundings, one *ought* to get better of one's badness."[120]

Blackwell, who had quit working for Patton and was again at Dennis Harris's refinery, wrote that he needed to spend the summer recovering his health. He traveled with friends to Green Pond, a New Jersey resort, and spent another holiday at Lake Hopatcong. Stone wished him a "grand merry time" there, adding wistfully that while she wished he would have come to Coy's Hill, she understood his need for "something that can give you more variety, and pleasure." It is clear that Stone believed the shortcomings in their marriage were hers; she had come to see herself as a drag, a drudge, and a millstone.[121]

That summer, in the wartime inflationary boom, Blackwell succeeded at last in selling some of his and Stone's properties. Stone was delighted, writing: "You can get a rest from business now my dear, and I rejoice for your sake." The sale of his land made Blackwell financially solvent for the first time in his life. Perhaps still considering the possibility of a permanent separation, Stone wrote him in August 1864: "If you buy 10-40s [war bonds] I wish you would buy the amount of my mortgage in *my name*, and let the interest be paid to me. I will return the bond. It is more important to me than you have ever known, that I should have the income of my property. Now that there is no reason why I should not, I greatly prefer to arrange so that our properties may be separate.[122]

With income at her disposal, Stone hired Clara Barlow to care for her father and rented a small farm in Gardner so that Alice could begin school nearby. Gardner was too small and Stone's reputation too large for her independent household to escape the notice of the village gossips. She dreaded shopping for provisions in "this little ridiculous town, where petty gossip retails everything that occurs." When Blackwell sent them a barrel of supplies for the winter, she thanked him for his thoughtfulness. "We shall be *very glad* to welcome you here," she added.[123]

Blackwell announced his intention to campaign for Lincoln's reelection, and as he prepared for his first speech, Stone advised him: "First, in all your speeches, be sure your *facts* are *facts*. Don't overstate." Her advice on handling the inevitable "bore" who wished to continue the discussion after the lecture was to "Put your mouth in your muffler, and tell him you can't talk on account of your throat, which you must respect if you are to speak through the campaign."[124]

On September 30, 1864, Francis Stone died. Stone described her father's last night, telling how Sarah had been delegated the night watch, but when he father looked around so desperately after his sons left, Sarah called her brothers in.[125]

Stone grieved for her father. Following the simple funeral, she wrote of her loss: "We came back from the grave to the empty rooms, with a sense of loneliness, which only they know as have felt it. All day Sunday as the dismal rain pattered on the windows of the deserted rooms, where we were arranging & deciding various matters, the tears kept gushing."[126]

Her letter reached Blackwell as he was campaigning, an experience he was finding "very agreeable." The local paper "compliments me very highly and says I speak better than most of the men who have a *National* reputation, etc," he wrote.[127] Following Lincoln's election, Blackwell extended his lecture tour, turning from campaign issues to general political reform. His retirement from business and his devotion to reform politics convinced Stone that they could try a reunion. They would find some place where they could "read, study, think, and grow *together*," she wrote hopefully in December 1864.[128]

On December 17, Stone looked forward to their reunion. "How I longed to put my arms around you, to warm and comfort you! O! Harry darling, I love you dearly. . . . I do not wish you to hurry your visit from Washington, but take a good time there, and at N. York, for I am not selfish in my love."[129]

Blackwell wrote that he did not anticipate arriving until January, and Stone wished him a "Merry Christmas and Happy New Year." She wrote, "I think I shall go to Boston about New Years. . . . The schools will begin there and Alice must be ready."[130]

Blackwell arrived in January, and for a brief time they boarded in Boston. Stone was there for the January meeting of the New England Anti-Slavery Society. Convinced that hostilities would soon cease, she and Anthony presented a resolution that after the war, the Woman's Rights and the Anti-Slavery organizations combine efforts to secure political rights, including the ballot, to emancipated blacks and women. Wendell Phillips deferred action on the motion until the May meeting, by which time they all hoped the war would be ended.[131]

In April 1865, the Confederate armies surrendered. The conflict, which had cost 620,000 lives and permanently scarred and weakened the young nation, was over; the Union had survived. The Stone-Blackwell union had also made it through. They were together again, but the extended separation had effected a subtle shift of power in their relationship. For his part, Blackwell had "gotten clear" of business and promised to devote himself to reform, while Stone claimed to have "come out on the other side" of her personal crisis. The "linking of two unsuitable natures" would continue to bump along, albeit on an altered track. Though neither of them anticipated it, they were on a collision course in that hopeful spring of 1865.

CHAPTER EIGHT

Kansas: The Rift Widens

When the news of Lincoln's assassination reached Stone in April 1865, she and Alice were alone again in a rented house in Roseville, New Jersey. She had made clear her desire to live permanently in Boston; Blackwell favored New York. Having blamed the breakdown in their marriage on the "badness" in herself, Stone now took responsibility for making their reunion work. Her participation in the January meetings in Boston marked a return to suffrage activity, a decision made easier by the fact that Alice was eight and in school full-time. Whether Blackwell's ego could withstand her return to national prominence remained to be seen. Indeed, Stone's recuperation was fraught with domestic crises as she and Blackwell struggled to balance their opposing psychological needs—she for a sense of usefulness, he for money and power. While Reconstruction played itself out on the national stage, the private drama of the Stone-Blackwell union would see its own share of turbulence, compromises, rifts, and disloyalties in the coming years.[1]

Within a week of the move to Roseville, Blackwell had gone to Ohio, where he tried unsuccessfully to use the influence of a family friend to obtain a "high paying job" there. After settling Alice into her new school, Stone resumed suffrage work, corresponding with Anthony and others about the necessity of including woman suffrage in the press for black suffrage. The Boston meetings had given the women a taste of what lay in store. At the May anniversary meeting of the Anti-Slavery Society, Wendell Phillips delivered a stirring speech on behalf of emancipated slaves, declaring that this was the "Negro's Hour," and that the hour of woman had not yet come.[2]

Phillips's speech and the fear that woman suffrage was about to be lost in the reform shuffle moved Stone to arrange a series of lectures that autumn. She barnstormed New York and New England, distributing suffrage literature and organizing educational cadres. Though she did not claim to have recovered her power over audiences, she wrote that she was enjoying "good audiences and good pay." Stone's pay went to maintain the household as, once again, Blackwell was in financial trouble. "Better times are coming," she consoled him, "and the mere loss of money is a small matter." Perhaps fearing a new rush of financial entanglements, Stone urged Harry to consider moving to England for six months, "for the sake of *your* health and the health of *yours*."[3]

In late November, Anthony came to Roseville for three days to map their strategy for pressing women's claim. Their plans included petitioning Congress for woman suffrage and lobbying for a universal suffrage amendment in the District of Columbia. Theodore Tilton, popular editor of the *Independent,* proposed merging the Anti-Slavery Society and woman's rights organization into a National Equal Rights Society.[4]

Phillips had turned back the earlier move to merge the organizations, believing that woman suffrage would endanger the hopes for passage of civil rights measures—including suffrage—for emancipated blacks, whose political status was growing more precarious. Passage of harsh and punitive black codes and the worry that by counting emancipated, unenfranchised slaves, the South could gain fifteen Democratic seats in Congress, hastened Republican action. Black votes would ensure Republican party control of Congress. Much of the task of framing the Fourteenth Amendment fell to Charles Sumner, the eloquent Massachusetts senator and longtime champion of abolition. How the amendment was worded was all-important, for its ratification depended on northern states, where support for black suffrage was dubious.[5]

The proposed amendment did not directly enfranchise blacks. Instead, it threatened to reduce representation of states that denied its "male citizens" the right to vote. Upon learning that the word "male" was to be introduced into the Constitution, Stone went to Washington to plead with Sumner to strike the word before the measure left committee. Sumner, full of apologies, told her that he had sat up all one night trying to frame the amendment some other way but could see no other way to ensure its passage.[6]

Despite the defeats, women were on the move. They laid plans for a May Woman's Rights convention, the first to be held since before the war. Stanton and Anthony pressed forward with plans for forming an Equal Rights Association, with or without the cooperation of the existing antislavery organization. Stone, after enjoying a busy and productive fall and winter, was in the grip of a new crisis in the spring of 1866. Blackwell had resumed his business relationship with Ludlow Patton, most likely in connection with Patton's plans for a Wisconsin railroad.[7]

Directing Stone to send his mail through Patton's office, Blackwell set off to invest in still more Wisconsin land. Stone closed the Roseville house and moved to Gardner with Alice, using as her excuse fear of a local cholera epidemic. That she intended to stay in Massachusetts is apparent from her correspondence. Stone's headaches were so bad that at times she was unable to write. She did not even send a letter to be read at the May Woman's Rights meeting. Those present voted to reincorporate themselves as the American Equal Rights Association. Blackwell was elected recording secretary of the new organization, and Ludlow Patton was named treasurer.[8]

Blackwell endeavored to pacify Stone. He would "come up to my new home in Massachusetts, whereafter [sic] that may be." He was "counting the days till we meet again and have the *holy and pure* joy of feeling our unity of soul." He would swear off business and arrange a joint lecture tour of Massachusetts. He would be her "supporter and aid," he promised, and "if your head aches & you don't find the spirit move you will see that I will come up *well* to the rescue." In words suggesting that once again he had been critical of her efforts the previous winter, Blackwell told Stone that if she made mistakes, she was not to worry, for "I will follow filling up all gaps and weaving in any [illegible] you may omit."[9]

Stone instead remained in seclusion in Gardner until late summer, when she joined Blackwell for a vacation at Martha's Vineyard. They were reconciled, and once again she moved back to New York. That autumn, she was on the hustings again, concentrating her efforts in New York State, where a constitutional convention was to convene in late November. Stone presided at an A.E.R.A. convention held in Albany just prior to the opening of the legislative session.[10]

Political troubles were brewing. At the convention, Stanton praised New York Democrats for their recent support for woman suffrage. Frederick Douglass objected that the Democratic party was on record as opposing any move to give suffrage or any civil rights to blacks. Democratic support for woman suffrage was "a trick of the enemy" designed to split reformers on racial lines, he warned, and he begged suffragists to resist the ploy. Douglass's words would prove prophetic; within the year, Stanton and Anthony's alliance with a racist Democrat, George Francis Train, would split the woman's movement.[11]

At the time, however, Stone was only mildly alarmed at Stanton's flirtation with the Democrats. She was more concerned at what seemed to her the abandonment of antislavery friends. The depth of her feelings is apparent in a letter to Abby Kelley Foster in which Stone asked how it was that

you and Phillips, & Garrison, and the brave workers, who for thirty years have said, "let justice be done, if the heavens fall," now smitten by a strange blindness, believe that the nation's peril can be averted if it can be induced to accept the poor half loaf of justice for the Negro, poisoned by its lack of justice for every woman in the land. . . . A wail goes through my heart akin to that which I should feel, if I saw my little daughter drowning . . . with no power to help her.[12]

Eventually, both Foster and Stone would temper their positions, but in January 1867, feelings ran high. Stone had little time to dwell on the discord, however, for from Albany, where she, Stanton, and Anthony presented their petition to the New York legislators, the three women embarked on a tour of New England and the mid-Atlantic states. They set up A.E.R.A. adjuncts, spearheaded petition drives, and lobbied Republican legislators. Toward the end of January, the three were on board a train to New York when a blizzard stranded them for more than twenty-four hours. The snowbound train offered the suffragists a captive audience of "doctors, lawyers, and legislators." Stanton, Stone, and Anthony "separated themselves far apart and each one gathered a crowd and talked and answered questions. They had a most merry time," a fellow suffragist on board wrote, "and did a vast deal of good, I have no doubt."[13]

Though Stone continued to be troubled by the unwillingness of reform Republicans to campaign for suffrage, she was mindful of Douglass's warning. She was determined to keep both black and woman suffrage before the public eye; she would not separate the two causes. In March, Stone made an eloquent plea to the New Jersey legislature on behalf of black and woman suffrage. She began by stating her object—the submission of amendments to the state constitution striking the words "male" and "white" from the list of voter qualifications. "All political power is inherent in the people," she quoted from the New Jersey Constitution. "Under our theory of government . . . every individual capable of independent rational choice is rightfully entitled to vote." Disfranchising a person because he was black, she told them, violated this principle of "rational, individual choice." She appealed to patriotism, pointing out that two hundred thousand blacks had fought on the Union side, their blood mingled with that of their fallen white comrades, and yet they were denied the vote.

Moving to the cause of women, she continued: "So too, when a woman is disfranchised because she is a woman, the principle is violated." Women were equally capable of rational, independent choice. They too had proved themselves brave and loyal in the war, yet they too were "classed politically with madmen and fools" by being denied the vote. The vote, Stone argued, was the cornerstone of democracy and the guarantor of all other rights, including the right to a decent wage. In answer to the argument that women would be "demoralized" by going to the polls, Stone asked whether they were demoralized by going to the post office or the market.

Toward the end of her lengthy address, Stone summed up the reasons why blacks and women needed the vote. She argued for the "natural justice" of it, and for the need to repeal unjust laws. Suffrage would "enable women and negroes to share all profitable employments." She deplored the exclusion of blacks from skilled labor and from the professions, arguing that blacks were equally capable and deserved access to every employment. As for women, "only the poorest employments were open" to them. Finally, Stone argued that women and blacks "need the ballot to secure equal means of education." She pointed to the continued exclusion of black children from the public schools of New Jersey. In addition, she reminded them that "the two disfranchised classes, women and negroes, are the only ones excluded from the highest schools of the State," which meant that "the highest and widest spheres of influence are thus closed to us both."

Enfranchised women, she assured them, "will influence legislation by their tastes and character." Women would bring to politics "peace and temperance," would "repress licentiousness," and "create a religious and humane spirit in legislation." Stone reminded her listeners that in the early years of the republic, New Jersey women had voted with no ill consequences. She moved finally to the practical, political advantages of adding blacks and women to the voter rolls, and she asked her audience to consider the inconsistency of having New Jersey Congressmen voting in Washington to compel southern states to enfranchise southern freedmen when New Jersey's blacks were without the vote. Finally, Stone warned against giving suffrage only to freed men, denying justice to eight million women. "The problem of American statesmanship to-day is how to . . . guarantee the rights of every citizen." The solution was easy: "Base government on the consent of the governed, and each class will protect itself."[14]

Following the New Jersey speech, Stone returned to work at the New York office of the A.E.R.A. She was there when a letter arrived from Sam Wood, a Republican politician, asking if she and other woman suffrage workers would come to Kansas to speak at an Impartial Suffrage convention in Topeka and campaign for passage of a woman suffrage referendum. Stone and Blackwell agreed to go, unaware that they were headed for a political hornets' nest that would bring the simmering issue of racism to the fore and divide the ranks of woman suffragists for more than thirty years.

Still in the process of recovery, both from its own bloody past and from the recent war, Kansas government in 1867 was a hotbed of mistrust and malfeasance, and the dominant Republican party was riven by factionalism. Nevertheless, the Kansas legislature, meeting that spring, voted to ratify the Fourteenth Amendment. Those who had labored since 1862 for

black suffrage immediately called for a November referendum on a proposal to strike the word "white" from the list of voter qualifications,
thereby enfranchising the state's sizable black population. Conservative
Republicans, copperheads, and Democrats attempted unsuccessfully to
attach a series of unpopular riders to the proposal. At this point, Sam
Wood stepped forward with a second referendum proposal to strike the
word "male." Black leaders questioned the timing and the political wisdom of Wood's move, seeing it as a deliberate attempt to sabotage the
black suffrage amendment.[15]

Into this political minefield came Stone and Blackwell, brimming with
optimism and armed with two hundred fifty pounds of suffrage tracts.
They went first to the home of former governor Charles Robinson, a
relative of Stone's by marriage and a leader of the Kansas Republican
party. Robinson regarded Sam Wood's proposal and the calling of an
Impartial Suffrage convention as a trick, but he agreed to attend.[16] Blackwell liked Wood, writing back to the New York workers: "My judgment
of men is rarely deceived, and I pronounce S. N. Wood a great man and a
political genius."[17]

Stone addressed the Impartial Suffrage convention at Topeka "with all
her old force and fire," and Blackwell's letters were ebullient. "This is a
glorious country, Mrs. S., and a glorious people."[18] Stone, more circum-
spect, worried that Republican party opposition was growing and that
"the Democrats all over the State are preparing to take us up. They are a
small minority with nothing to lose, and utterly unscrupulous. . . . There
is no such love of principle here as I had expected to find. Each man goes
for himself, and 'the devil take the hindmost.'"[19]

Stone and Blackwell were scheduled to speak every night except Sunday in cities and towns across the state at a fee of one hundred dollars per
lecture. "There is no time to write here. We ride all day, and lecture every
night, and sometimes at noon too," Stone reported. Blackwell's letter
provided a more lively account to those in the East:

You will be glad to know that Lucy and I are going over the length and breadth of this
state speaking every day, and sometimes twice, journeying from twenty-five to forty
miles daily, sometimes in a carriage and sometimes in an open wagon, with or without springs. We climb hills and dash down ravines, ford creeks, and ferry over rivers,
rattle across limestone ledges, struggle through muddy bottoms, fight the high winds
on the high rolling upland prairies, and address the most astonishing (and astonished)
audiences in the most extraordinary places. Tonight it may be a log school house,
tomorrow a stone church; next day a store with planks for seats, and in one place, if it
had not rained, we should have held forth in an unfinished courthouse, with four
stone walls but no roof whatsoever.[20]

Their meetings were crowded, and Stone reported jubilantly, "I speak
as well as ever, thank God. The audiences move to tears or laughter, just

as in the old time." She added, "Harry makes capital speeches and gets a louder cheer . . . although I believe I move a deeper feeling."[21]

Early in May, the political situation worsened. "I can not send you a telegraphic dispatch as you wish for just now there is a plot to get the Republican party to . . . agree to canvass *only* for the word 'white,'" Stone wrote.[22]

In New York, the first anniversary of the A.E.R.A. was proceeding smoothly. At the convention, a telegram from Sam Wood was read aloud to great cheers. "With the help of God and Lucy Stone, we shall carry Kansas! The world moves!" Wood's optimism was premature, and the political rumblings grew more ominous. As Stone had feared, at the May 15 meeting, Kansas Republicans voted to campaign for black suffrage only.[23]

The Kansas political squabbles attracted national press attention. Two liberal Republican papers, Greeley's *Tribune* and Tilton's *Independent*, were circulated widely in Kansas. As Stone read the Kansas reports, her frustration mounted. "What a power to hold, and not use!" Stone wrote Anthony, "I could not sleep the other night, just thinking of it; and if I had got up and written the thought that burned my very soul, I do believe that Greeley and Tilton would have echoed the cry of the old crusaders, 'God wills it;' and rushing to our half-sustained standard, would plant it high and firm on immutable principles. They *MUST* take it up. I shall see them the first thing when I get home.[24]

Though the deteriorating political situation distressed Stone, it had not yet reached a critical point. While it is doubtful that had she remained, the outcome in Kansas would have been any different, there was no doubting the effect of her presence. One political observer wrote that Kansans were so "completely won" by Lucy Stone that had the election been held in May, "while the tide of public opinion ran so high in their favor, there is little doubt that both resolutions would have carried unanimously."[25]

Immediately after returning from Kansas, Stone went to Boston to plead with Phillips for financial support to continue the Kansas campaign. He agreed to permit her to borrow money against the Jackson fund if she would give her "personal guarantee" for reimbursement. She next went to call on Greeley at the *Tribune* offices in New York. Tears came to her eyes as she pleaded with him to increase his coverage of woman suffrage. Greeley teased her, saying, "When you have been whipped as many times as I have, you won't cry about it." (In telling this story in later years, Stone added that following Greeley's defeat in his 1872 bid for the presidency, "he not only cried about it, but he broke his heart, and died.") Greeley agreed to give Stone "a finger's length" of space in the *Tribune* to say what she pleased "as often as you like." Immediately after their meeting, he wrote a long and encouraging editorial on the progress of the woman suffrage campaign in Kansas, reporting that the "signs of the agitation" in Kansas "hardly allow a doubt that women will be ere long recognized in its laws."[26]

Greeley's support ended abruptly following a political miscalculation on the part of Stanton and Anthony. Greeley had chaired the Committee on Suffrage at the state constitutional convention. When Stanton and Anthony learned in advance that his committee report recommended against striking "male" from the list of voter qualifications, they arranged to have their woman suffrage petition presented just prior to the reading of the committee's report. George William Curtis rose before the crowded assembly and announced that he wished to represent a woman suffrage petition from "Mrs. Horace Greeley and three hundred other woman citizens of Westchester." Cheers, laughter, and catcalls rang out from the gallery.[27]

Greeley was chagrined and humiliated—not so much at what he called the "shabby" political trick—but at the public use of his wife's name. It was widely known that Mary Greeley was a highly eccentric, mentally unstable woman, and Greeley went to great lengths to shelter her from public scrutiny and protect her from ridicule. Though Mary Greeley had signed the petition, she was an impolitic choice of weapons for making her husband look ridiculous.[28]

Afterward, Greeley turned his back whenever he saw either Stanton or Anthony in public. His qualified endorsement of woman suffrage became open opposition. Later, Stanton regretted that her brief triumph in Albany cost the woman suffragists "the friendship of Horace Greeley and the support of the New York *Tribune,* heretofore our most powerful and faithful allies."[29]

Stone spent most of the summer raising funds for Kansas, but in late August, she joined Blackwell on Martha's Vineyard for a short vacation. She curtailed her vacation when Anthony wrote from Kansas asking Stone to take over the running of the A.E.R.A. office in New York from Parker Pillsbury. Both Stanton and Anthony had gone to Kansas to campaign. Arriving there, they found that Sam Wood had left the offices of the Impartial Suffrage Society; the treasury was empty, and a large bundle of suffrage tracts was being held by the printer for payment. Anthony asked Stone for emergency funds, and Stone arranged to borrow the money. For the next two months, Stone worked in the New York office, sending off money and tracts and contributing some of her own funds in response to Anthony's urgent appeals. The Kansas campaign had grown increasingly divisive.[30]

In Leavenworth, Republicans established an Anti-Woman Suffrage Committee. Stung, the suffrage workers in Kansas allowed themselves to be drawn into racial divisiveness. Newspapers reported Olympia Brown as campaigning "against placing the dirty, immoral, degraded negro before a white woman," and Sam Wood was involved in a bitter exchange of words with black leaders. The antiblack tone of some of the woman suffrage workers left even favorable Republican candidates questioning their support.[31]

"Lucy is almost heart broken at the turn of affairs in Kansas and probable failure of the suffrage question," Elizabeth Blackwell wrote at the end of September. The domestic front was also troubled. Harry was hatching new business schemes. He first contemplated "a trip to the beet sugar region of France." Unable to find backing for his trip, he turned to Kansas, persuading a group of investors to commission him to buy land there on speculation. "Oh what a Harry!" Elizabeth commented.[32]

Stone had little time or attention for Harry's latest scheme. From the New York office, she sent off money as fast as she could raise it. More than a thousand dollars went to Brown in a four-week period, and twice that amount went to Anthony in September. With Harry gone to Kansas, Stone coped with full-time work in the New York office and with domestic chores in Roseville, where the family circle had grown sometime that summer by the addition of a five-year-old orphan girl named Annie Gleason. Stone had taken the child with an eye toward providing company for Alice. Harry described the child as "an active, noisy, hasty-tempered, impulsive, rollicking affectionate young girl," who after all "did not prove a congenial companion to Alice." Stone became deeply attached to the child, and her letters of the period are peppered with references to "our children."[33]

All the Blackwells were living nearby, a situation not without its frustrations for Stone, who wrote that she dreaded the necessity of putting the painfully shy Alice in Marian Blackwell's school. Alice "*needs* to be thrown with many children, and the putting her alone with Floy [Sam and Nettie's daughter Florence] only increases her natural tendency to isolate herself," she wrote.[34]

From Kansas, Blackwell wrote that his mother was coming to live with them. He would "do my best to lighten the load," he promised from afar. Meanwhile, political news from Kansas was bad. "As it is, *we are beat*," he wrote. "It is only a question whether our vote will be large enough to give us respect & bring the case up again hereafter." He added that "Negro suffrage is in *great* danger."[35]

In the last week of October, political disaster arrived at the Leavenworth headquarters of the A.E.R.A. in the person of George Francis Train. Train, a copperhead and a flamboyant showman given to eccentric dress and self-promotion, had mounted a bizarre campaign to get himself elected president of the United States. Seeing political capital to be made from the division in the Republican ranks, he offered to campaign with the women. Stanton and Anthony accepted the offer.[36]

In New York, Stone's eye fell on a paid A.E.R.A. advertisement, complimentary to Train, announcing his entry into the Kansas campaign for woman suffrage. She was shocked and angry to see her name at the bottom of the announcement. "Of this I knew nothing until I read it in the *Tribune*," she wrote. Stone accused Anthony of using her name "without the knowledge of any of us." Stone wrote, "I felt the hurt of this action of theirs as 'tho it had been a blow to my own child."[37]

Train made his motive for entering the woman suffrage campaign clear in an October 23 letter to the Leavenworth *Commercial*: "By talking woman suffrage the Democrats 'beat the Republicans.' By stumping for woman suffrage Train 'beats the Republicans.' Copperheads know that the Republicans can carry Kansas unless they are divided." Stanton and Anthony were less interested in Train's motives than in the money and Democratic party votes he promised to deliver.[38]

Anthony set off with Train on a statewide lecture tour. On the platform, she spoke first in favor of the woman suffrage referendum. Train followed, dressed in "New York opera costume." He drew laughter and applause by saying:

The first woman I had to convert to woman suffrage was the eloquent speaker who has just addressed you, Miss Anthony. (Laughter and applause.)
She commenced the campaign four-fifths negro and one fifth woman, (laughter) now she is four-fifths woman and only one-fifth negro. (Loud laughter as Mr. Train illustrated his meaning with thumb and fingers.) Keep your nose twenty years on a negro and you will have hard work to smell a white man again. (Loud laughter.)[39]

What Anthony thought is unrecorded. Train was a genius at self-promotion and regularly supplied newspapers with his own press releases in the form of printed versions of his and Anthony's meetings. Although Train's reports made only brief mention of Anthony's speeches, they were nonetheless inflammatory: "[Anthony] denounced the 'mean, low, sneaking editors' of the Republican press of Leavenworth and laid at their door the defeat of the measure, if defeat should come. She upbraided them and the Republican party generally. . . . reformers must stand alone and on their own merits. The Republican Party is too rotten to be trusted."[40]

Train's speeches contained a torrent of racist bombast calculated to play upon the worst fears and prejudices of his audience. He warned: "Carry negro suffrage and we shall see some white woman in a case of negro rape being tried by 12 negro jurymen." Newspapers carried his "epigrams" as well:

Let your corrupt politicians dance their double clogged jig
As a bid for the suffrage of the poor Kansas Nig,
For our women will vote while the base plot thickens;
Before barbers, bootblacks, melons and chickens.[41]

Anthony, longtime friend to abolition, must have winced inwardly at the invective. Still, her fierce, partisan devotion to the cause of women allowed her to countenance Train's racist and ribald remarks. Protests poured in from suffrage workers everywhere. Only Stanton stood loyally by her friend, saying, "I take my beloved Susan's judgment against the world."[42]

Back East, Stone thought that both women had taken leave of their senses. She fired off letters to Anthony protesting the use of the A.E.R.A. name and funds for handbills announcing the Train-Anthony meetings, and for using Equal Rights funds to campaign against blacks. Stone also upbraided Anthony for using her name in the *Tribune* notice and begged her to dissociate herself and woman suffrage from Train and the Democrats. Train put those Republicans who had remained loyal to woman suffrage in an untenable position. The Kansas imbroglio was closely watched in the national press, playing into the hands of Republicans who opposed woman suffrage.[43]

Stone was heartsick, worried that twenty years of hard work were being undone. Train had "made the cause a laughingstock everywhere," she wrote, labeling him "a lunatic, wild and ranting," and lamenting that "his presence as an advocate of woman suffrage [is] enough to condemn it in the minds of all persons not already convinced." Blackwell, who only weeks before had been carrying on his own "negotiations" with Democrats in Kansas, warned Anthony that she was doing "irreparable harm to the cause of votes for women *and* blacks."[44]

There was small consolation in the knowledge that Train had entered the campaign only in its last two weeks and soon would be gone. These hopes evaporated, however, with the news that Train intended to continue his campaign with the women throughout the Midwest and East. He would campaign for the presidency, they for woman suffrage. He also offered to finance a woman suffrage newspaper. Train named the paper *The Revolution* and adapted an earlier epigram he had used in a campaign to build a subway in New York for the masthead. "New York, its rights and nothing more" became "Men, their rights and nothing more; women, their rights, and nothing less."[45]

The final votes in Kansas were counted; both woman suffrage and black suffrage proposals had been defeated. Stanton and Anthony publicly credited Train with delivering the 9,070 votes cast for woman suffrage, ignoring the clear evidence that the votes came from heavily Republican counties, while Democratic counties had handily rejected both measures.[46]

In the postelection analysis, Republican party leaders used the woman suffrage issue as a political scapegoat for the failure of black suffrage. Typical of the postelection commentary was the editorial in the Emporia, Kansas, *News*: "We believe that had the 'side issue' been out of the way, and had the Republican party been united . . . it would have carried the state."[47]

Privately, Stone and many other suffragists held the Train alliance accountable for the loss of votes. Stone wrote to Olympia Brown: "I believe if Susan had done differently we should have had a much larger vote. I am utterly disgusted and vexed with her present course. . . . our grand cause is dragged in [Train's] bad name—all without my knowledge." Charles Robinson wrote Brown in the same vein: "I believe that Train and Miss Anthony lost us more votes by the disgust they created than they gained." He added regretfully, "Their campaign through Eastern cities has turned the whole movement into a farce."[48]

Stone and the others looked on helplessly as the press gleefully pursued Train and the two women suffragists in their tour of cities from Kansas eastward. Garrison spoke for most of the suffrage workers when he wrote a friend that Stanton and Anthony "seem to have taken leave of their senses." He wrote that he was "mortified and astonished beyond measure in seeing Elizabeth Cady Stanton and Susan B. Anthony travelling about the country with that harlequin and semi-lunatic George Francis Train . . . denouncing Republicanism and lauding Copperheadism."[49] Garrison, Stone, and the others pleaded with Stanton and Anthony to cut short their speaking tour and repudiate Train, but this protest was unavailing.[50] At the end of December, Stanton and Anthony returned to New York to begin publication of the *Revolution*.

An emergency meeting of the Executive Committee of the A.E.R.A. was called, and Anthony was asked why she had used the name of the organization in connection with Train without its knowledge or consent. She replied, "I AM the Equal Rights Association. Not one of you amounts to shucks except for me." Anthony then turned to Stone and said, "I know what is the matter with you. It is envy, and spleen, and hate, because I have a paper and you have not."[51]

Stone's response was to try to widen the distance between the Stanton-Anthony-Train alliance and the mainstream movement. Just prior to the appearance of the first issue of the *Revolution,* Stone wrote to Olympia Brown: "We are in the midst of a serious quarrel with Miss Anthony and Mrs. Stanton and the Train admixture from which we are trying to shield our association. We want *them* to have all the credit of the new alliance. Susan said at an executive meeting the other day that we were moved by 'envy, spleen, and hate' & etc. At all events we must try and keep the office of our association and her paper separate."[52]

Stone delivered speeches, corresponded with legislators, raised money, filled mail orders for tracts and leaflets, and continued to direct the organization of woman suffrage educational groups throughout New Jersey. She also cared for Alice and Annie and nursed her mother-in-law, who had moved in with them in November.

On the first day of 1868, Anthony confided to her diary: "All the old friends, with scarce an exception, are sure we are wrong."[53] Neither she nor Stanton appeared to consider the possibility that perhaps "all the old friends" were right and that linking themselves to a racist demagogue might damage the woman suffrage movement. They were a formidable pair—Anthony fearless, resolute, all but indefatigable; Stanton brilliant and caustic. Political *enfants terribles,* they tried to compel the cart of ideology to pull the horse of politics. The appearance of the first issues of their newspaper confirmed the worst fears of the other suffrage workers.

Prepared on the fifth floor of the *New York World* building, the *Revolution* bore the heavy stamp of Train and his campaign for the presidency on every page. The masthead of the first issue declared that the *Revolution* was "The Organ of the National Party of New America." Woman suffrage per se was nowhere among the causes listed in the lengthy masthead. Instead, the paper promised to advocate "Educated Suffrage" along with "Equal Pay for Equal Work," the "Abolition of Standing Armies and Party Despotism," paper money, the Credit Mobilier, and a host of other causes unrelated to woman suffrage, among these the prohibition of all foreign manufactures.[54]

Eventually, the *Revolution* would become a strong voice for woman's rights, but its initial issues drew widespread ridicule. The *New York Times* wrote that those fond of logic would find that "it would be as mad for anyone to enter the arena of argument as that of vituperation with the revolutionary advocates of woman's rights." The *Times* accused the *Revolution*'s editors of being unprincipled.[55]

Train's lengthy and rambling articles occupied more than half the column inches of the front section of the early issues, drawing anguished protests from other suffrage workers. William Lloyd Garrison wrote Anthony privately, praising her for all the good she had done and expressing his regret that she had "departed so far from true self respect, as to be travelling companions and associate lecturers with that crack-brained harlequin and semi-lunatic, George Francis Train! . . . The colored people and their advocates have not a more abusive assailant than this same Train; especially when he . . . delights to ring the charges upon the 'nigger,' 'nigger,' 'nigger,' *ad nauseum.*" He warned that Train "is as destitute of principle as he is of sense, and is fast gravitating toward a lunatic asylum, . . . he may be of use in drawing an audience; but so would a kangaroo, a gorilla, or a hippopotamus."[56]

Stanton and Anthony printed Garrison's private letter in the *Revolution* followed by a lengthy, scathing personal attack on him which concluded defiantly: "So long as Mr. Train speaks nobly for the woman, why should we repudiate his services, even if he does ring the charges 'nigger, nigger, nigger'?"[57]

To Olympia Brown, Stanton wrote: "All there is about [Train] is that he has made it possible for us to establish a paper. If the Devil himself had come up and said ladies I will help you establish a paper I should have said Amen!"[58]

Whether influenced by Train or out of lingering hostility about Republican defections, Stanton adopted an increasingly antiblack tone in the *Revolution*. Blacks ought not to have the vote, she wrote, for they wouldn't "know a ballot from an order for a mule." She also printed "news" stories of white women who had been raped by black men.[59]

As Stone worked to widen the distance between the two organizations, she faced yet another domestic crisis. Blackwell's new investment scheme was foundering, and his continued association with Patton continued to distress her. She plunged into a depression, accompanied by a long siege of headaches. By April, she was better, writing to Blackwell of the need to remain in New England: "[M]y shadows have fled. Only I have headaches all the time, and did yesterday, tho' it did not spoil my speech. But with this bright clear sky, and sweet ocean air, and more than all, the presence of these old friends who have real sympathy with me, and my ideas, I *must* get better."[60]

She remained in Massachusetts, giving speeches and assisting in the fund-raising efforts of the New England A.E.R.A. On April 11, she wrote, "My blues are gone. I wish they may never return to trouble me or you."[61] Returning to New Jersey, she went to work on arrangements for the May meeting of the A.E.R.A., a meeting which promised to be explosive.

On opening day, all went fairly well until the evening session, when Olympia Brown made a speech critical of the Republican party. Frederick Douglass rose to defend the Republicans, whom he characterized as "largely in favor of enfranchising woman." He challenged Brown: "Where is the Democrat who favors woman suffrage?"

When a voice in the audience shouted "Train!" an angry Douglass brought to the surface the issue troubling them all. "Yes, he hates the negro, and that is what stimulates him to substitute the cry of emancipation for women." Douglass went on to plead for suffrage for both blacks and women, but he claimed for black men an especial urgency, insisting that their suffrage was necessary to protect life and property.

Stone objected to Douglass's statement that women were not persecuted for endeavoring to obtain their rights. She charged the Republican party with being false to principle if it refused to protect women as well as black men in the exercise of their right to vote.[62] When the applause had died down, Anthony took her place at the podium. She introduced a surprise resolution urging women to oppose ratification of the Fourteenth Amendment and to resolve to work only for woman suffrage. Her resolution was overwhelmingly defeated, and those present went on to pass resolutions favorable to granting suffrage to both blacks and women; still, a wedge had been formally driven into the organization.

Frustrated, Anthony notified friends privately that she was organizing a new society in keeping with her aims. The organizational meeting of the Woman Suffrage Society was held at the office of the *Revolution*. Stanton was elected president, while Anthony became chairman of the executive committee.[63]

Hoping to convince Anthony of the folly of looking to the Democrats for support, the executive committee of the A.E.R.A. passed a resolution challenging Anthony to attend the national Democratic convention and try to get a woman suffrage plank put in the party platform. Anthony accepted the challenge, and attended the convention as delegate from the "Woman Suffrage Association of America." The woman suffrage plank she carried bore the indelible stamp of David Melliss and George Francis Train. Along with woman suffrage, Anthony's plank called for "State Rights," for abolishing the "Freedman's Bureau replacing them with Universal Amnesty and Universal Suffrage," and seven more unrelated items, among these the call for the immediate release of Americans in British jails, and the exchange of greenbacks for dollars. Anthony's attempt to introduce her plank met with "yells and shrieks and demoniac, deafening howls."[64]

In an effort to head off further racial division and to distance themselves from Stanton and Anthony and the Woman Suffrage Association, various state branches of the A.E.R.A. formally repudiated the policies of the *Revolution*. First Brooklyn, then New Jersey, and finally New England associations of the A.E.R.A. declared their opposition to *Revolution* policies, causing Anthony to write Olympia Brown in disgust: "Oh dear a me Olympia—I get so *soul sick* of the *icy faces* of Boston. . . . every one of them so far as I can learn, most heartily wishes the Revolution *dead— dead—dead* and would murder it at any minute had they the power."[65]

Anthony defensively persisted in thinking of the split as a personal issue, convinced that hatred and spite motivated those who disagreed with her. To think otherwise would have been to question the choices that she and Stanton were making. In their alliance with Train and in the ever more racist tone of their campaign, they had stepped into a political quagmire. Faced with the prospect of backing out or going forward, they chose to slog through the mud, aiming for the high ground that they hoped to find on the other side. Meanwhile, the mainstream movement flowed around them.

If Stone could not "kill" the *Revolution,* she could and did intensify her efforts to establish a separate, efficient power base of local A.E.R.A. organizations. Annie had gone to stay with a childhood friend of Stone's in Massachusetts, and Alice was left in the care of her Blackwell aunts and her grandmother, while Stone stumped cities and towns throughout New York, New Jersey, Ohio, and New England.[66] Following her speeches, she established education committees, arranged for the distribution of suffrage literature, planned meetings and conventions. Back in New Jersey in time for the elections, Stone urged all A.E.R.A. women to go to the polls and cast their votes on Election Day. On November 3, she and her mother-in-law went to the polls. Stone offered her ballot to the election inspector. He "received it respectfully, but declined to let it be deposited in the box." Stone made a speech to the crowd that, doubtless having received ample advance notice, gathered to watch her attempt.[67]

Two weeks later, Stone and Blackwell were in Boston for the organizing convention of the New England Suffrage Association. Its planners invited Stanton and Anthony and offered to pay their expenses. The New York women declined, recognizing that the new organization was intended to supplant their own. Socialite Julia Ward Howe, the widely esteemed author of the "Battle Hymn of the Republic," was elected president at the Boston convention.[68]

Following the Boston meetings, Stone was off to Grand Rapids, Michigan, where she launched a woman suffrage society. She returned by way of Washington, D.C. There she met with George Julian to lobby for the inclusion of women in the pending black suffrage amendment. After extracting Julian's promise of support, Stone returned briefly to Roseville. From there, she traveled to Vineland, New Jersey, for a December 10 convention to help in forming the New Jersey Woman Suffrage Association. Although generally Stone preferred the less ceremonial but more substantive work of the executive committee—corresponding, organizing, publishing, fund raising—she accepted the presidency of the New Jersey Woman Suffrage Association.

From cities and towns all along the way, Stone dispatched warm, intimate, and affectionate letters to Alice. From Ohio, she wrote describing the up-to-date comforts of a friend's home: "The house is large and warmed all over, and yesterday morning I had a most delicious bath. I had two great streams of hot and cold water, each pouring in to the long trough. I laid down on my back. I plunged my head under and scrubbed and rubbed, and felt very much like a duck, and wished I had you in with me. . . . we must have a bath tub too."[69]

Her letters were filled with directions and advice. From Michigan she wrote that she had sent by the day's mail a book of sign language for

Alice to learn, purchased on the train from a deaf-mute woman with three small children. "You know, my dear, I expect a great deal of you," she wrote. She described the orphan serving girl who came in the morning to build her fire, adding, "when her small hands opened my door, so early, I was glad you did not need to do the same."[70]

Many of Stone's letters were filled with a punctilious attention to household details—an attempt perhaps to soothe her own guilt and worry, though it did little to pacify her Blackwell in-laws, who disapproved of her peripatetic ways. From Ohio, she wrote:

I hope the nice plants papa carried home got all set right yesterday, and that they will get watered enough. I will give you the fine carnation pink if you will take care of it. Did you get measured for shoes Sat? You will need to attend to it so as to have them ready for Christmas. Don't go to school without a sacque and cloak and leggins, which last you must be sure to wear when you play. It is too cold to go without them—and I shall be happier if I know that you will wear them and be snug and warm.

I should like to know that the new girl does well, and that you are all comfortable. I think Phebe had better put some new wicks into the lamps in the dining room, so that they will be ready for Christmas, and if she thinks they make a smell, they may be carried to the storeroom. . . . I think if you have *one* pair of new stockings, it will do till I get home. You may buy a pair of new gloves like those of Nelly if you wish too. Papa will give you the money.[71]

With access to their joint funds, Blackwell was again investing, advising a business associate that he could "draw on us through Ludlow Patton."[72] Major trouble was brewing on the domestic horizon, but Stone, working frenetically to establish a strong separate organization, at first paid little heed. She returned for Christmas as she had promised, but on the first of January, she was off to Washington to lobby for a universal suffrage amendment.

In Washington, she met with a number of legislators, among them George Julian, the man responsible for drafting the amendment. Her meeting with Charles Sumner was disheartening. Hitherto friendly to woman suffrage, Sumner was discouraged by a recent series of close legislative defeats. "I don't want to be in this fight," he told her.[73] Her work on behalf of a universal suffrage amendment earned Stone the editorial scorn of the *Revolution*. Ironically, its editors accused Stone of trying to "create an antagonism between the rival parties struggling for enfranchisement, and raise all the latent prejudice in woman's soul against the negro."[74] Later that month, Stanton and Anthony held a convention in Washington to repudiate the Fourteenth Amendment, and to "measure their logic against Republicans, Abolitionists, and colored men."[75]

George Julian's amendment would have guaranteed the right of suffrage "without any distinction or discrimination whatever founded on race, color, or sex." He had intended it as an alternative to the proposed Fifteenth Amendment. His effort failed, and on February 27, 1869, the proposed Fifteenth Amendment guaranteeing suffrage to black men passed. Julian immediately proposed adding a Sixteenth Amendment enfranchising women. The woman suffrage proposal, presented in a joint resolution on March 15, 1869, was referred to committee.[76]

Once the Sixteenth Amendment had been introduced, Stone initiated a letter-writing campaign, urging women to continue to establish educational committees and local associations to support the amendment and to write letters and circulate petitions on its behalf. She also continued the organizational push, setting up suffrage societies in a series of conventions held throughout the eastern states.

With passage of the Fifteenth Amendment, Stanton and Anthony published a steady stream of anti–Fifteenth Amendment editorials in the *Revolution* in hopes of preventing its ratification. In March, they left the *Revolution* in the editorial care of Parker Pillsbury and set off on a two-month tour of the West. Their anti–Fifteenth Amendment campaign and the Train connection did not win them many friends. From Bloomington, Indiana, Stanton sent back to the *Revolution* a report of an encounter with an influential woman suffrage supporter who "advised me to strangle Train, gibbet the financial editor, snub the proprietor, and to say no more in the paper on the questions of political economy, until we had one and all studied the subject." Though she maintained a lighthearted tone, Stanton was worried. In a private postscript to Pillsbury, she added "*Sub rosa*, . . . we must try and circumvent Train, and fill the paper ourselves."[77] When Stanton and Anthony returned, they printed Train's valedictory article in the *Revolution* and moved the editorial offices of the paper out of the *World* building and into office space provided by a wealthy woman's rights benefactor.[78]

If Stone was mollified by the improvements, she did not let on. The public Lucy Stone was back in harness, her frenzied pace concealing the private anguish of a new *de facto* separation from Blackwell. Blackwell was infatuated with another woman. By summer, the entire Blackwell family would be buzzing about "Harry's affair with Mrs. P."

Blackwell's explanation for the separation—Stone's desire to "escape the troubles of housekeeping" and to be near sympathetic Boston friends —at first drew sympathy from his sisters. "But what will you do Harry!" wrote Marian from Paris. "I hope you will not have to lead a lonely bachelor's life—deprived of wife and child."[79]

Sam, whose house was a five-minute walk from Blackwell's Roseville home, wrote him through Ludlow Patton's office in early March, beginning with an uncharacteristic "Dear Henry." The letter, stiff and formal, asked whether what Sam had heard was true regarding Harry's intentions of going to Florida, where Ludlow and Abby Patton were spending the spring.[80] Blackwell did indeed go to Florida, and Emily wrote him care of the New York office, complaining that she did not have his Florida address nor any idea of how long he would be staying. "Lucy is supposed to be doing very well," she wrote, "but of course you hear from her direct. Alice is flourishing and enjoys Kitty [Elizabeth's ward] greatly but thinks her rights in her papa and mamma are not sufficiently regarded."[81]

Alice was being cared for by her grandmother, who had been living in the Stone-Blackwell house for two years. Ellen wrote accusingly to Harry that their mother ought not to be alone. Taking matters into her own hands, Ellen left Emily's home, where she had been acting as housekeeper, and moved in with her mother and niece. From Florida, Blackwell wrote reproaching Ellen for moving in uninvited. Ellen responded with a bill for two years' tuition for tutoring Alice.[82] Stone lost herself in work, intensifying her already frenetic pace, expanding her base of support prior to the May convention.

Flooded with news releases of the success of Stone's organizing campaign and increasingly isolated by suffragists who refused to join them in denouncing the Fifteenth Amendment, Anthony attempted a preconvention coup. Although Stone chaired the executive committee of the A.E.R.A., Anthony called an emergency meeting of the committee in mid-April while Stone was at a convention in Springfield. At the meeting, she tried and failed to pass resolutions opposed to ratification of the Fifteenth Amendment.[83]

Less than two weeks before the convention, Stanton published a conciliatory editorial calling on old friends to ignore the past and "sink all petty considerations in the one united effort to secure woman suffrage." She insisted that despite the "unkind acts and words" they had suffered, and which they had "returned with sarcasm and ridicule," they harbored "only kind feelings in our souls for all the noble men and women who have fought for freedom during the last thirty years." Stanton praised the Sixteenth Amendment, calling for all women to "urge Congress to its speedy adoption."[84]

Stone adapted a "wait-and-see" attitude. If Stanton and Anthony were willing to abandon their outspoken opposition to the Fifteenth Amendment, rapprochement was possible. Stone looked to the May meetings to resolve the public issues, meantime suppressing her private shame and anxiety over Harry's defection.

CHAPTER NINE

"Out of the Terrible Pit"

Reformers arriving for the anniversary meetings found New York City gripped by excitement, word having just arrived of the hammering-in of the golden spike linking the nation—ocean to ocean—by rail. The *New York Times* described the "booming of cannon and chiming of bells," the fire sirens, prayer services, and flag-waving that greeted the news. The festivities surrounding the completion of the railroad had barely subsided when a new fever gripped the city. Steinway Hall was besieged by throngs hoping for tickets to the anticipated showdown at the A.E.R.A. meetings. "It is a pity that the cause of 'Equal Rights' should have been so disgraced by such a lawless scrabble for entrance tickets as occurred in the vestibule of the Hall last evening," said the Brooklyn *Daily Union,* with "men and women remorselessly crushing and tearing one another, and suffocating the solitary policeman who had the matter in charge."[1] At the May anniversaries and in the months that followed, Stone would undergo a series of personal and political trials that would succeed in purging whatever country innocence remained in her. She would emerge more politically savvy, socially conservative, and emotionally hardened.

In the weeks leading up to the anniversaries, Stone, Stanton, and Anthony had attempted through intermediaries to come to some agreement regarding a joint future course of action.[2] As part of their reconciliation efforts, the three leaders had agreed to work together on correspondence preparatory to forming a national woman suffrage association in the fall. Stanton's conciliatory gestures in the *Revolution* and Train's statement of withdrawal signaled a willingness to make concessions. Stone hoped that the antislavery old guard could be brought around. At the Anti-Slavery Society meeting that preceded the A.E.R.A. convention, she spoke forcefully to the need for speedy ratification of the Fifteenth Amendment, reassuring those who had begun to see women's rights as inimical to the interests of the freedmen.

Stone's speech showed that she was mindful of the precarious position

1. Coy's Hill, Brookfield, birthplace of Lucy Stone (*Library of Congress*)

2. Lucy Stone as a young woman (*Library of Congress*)

3. (*top right*) Lucy Stone at the time of her marriage (*Library of Congress*)

4. (*right*) Henry Blackwell as a young man (*Library of Congress*)

5. Lucy Stone with daughter Alice, 1858 (*Library of Congress*)

6. Pope's Hill, Dorchester home of Lucy Stone and Henry Blackwell (*Library of Congress*)

7. Lucy Stone as an antislavery lecturer (*Sophia Smith Collection, Smith College*)

8. Lucy Stone in 1893 (*Sophia Smith Collection, Smith College*)

9. Gathering at Pope's Hill of the antislavery veterans: Front, l-r: Samuel May, William Lloyd Garrison, Jr., Harriet W. Sewall, Samuel Sewall, Wendell P. Garrison, Henry B. Blackwell, Theodore D. Weld. Rear, l-r: Elizabeth B. Chace, Francis J. Garrison, Sarah H. Southwick, Alla Foster, Abby Kelley Foster, Lucy Stone, George T. Garrison, Zilpha Spooner (*Sophia Smith Collection, Smith College*)

of the nation's blacks as they faced growing southern oppression. "It is still true to-day over almost this entire country that no black man or woman finds the same sort of recognition either in public or in private that the white man or woman finds," she said, arguing the necessity for a Sixteenth Amendment as well as the only means of permanently banishing intolerance and eliminating prejudice.[3]

If Stone hoped that Stanton's conciliatory gestures and her own speech would placate the old guard, she was disappointed. Stephen Foster and Frederick Douglass came to the following morning's opening session of the A.E.R.A. ready for a fight. Following a brief speech of welcome, Stanton turned the meeting over to committee reports. When the nominating committee put Stanton's name forward for the vice presidency, Stephen Foster fired the opening salvo: "I admire our talented president [Stanton] with all my heart," he began, "and love the woman. But I believe she has publicly repudiated the principles of the society."[4] Pressed by Stanton for particulars, Foster responded: "What are these principles? The equality of men—universal suffrage. These ladies stand at the head of a paper which has adopted as its motto Educated Suffrage. . . . *The Revolution* lately had an article headed "That Infamous Fifteenth Amendment." . . . I am not willing to take George Francis Train on this platform with his ridicule of the negro and opposition to enfranchisement."[5]

At this point, Mary Livermore chided Foster for bringing up Train after the announcement of his retirement from the *Revolution,* to which Foster objected that Train had withdrawn voluntarily and not because the *Revolution*'s editors had repudiated him. Anthony retorted: "Of course it does not." Train, she told them, was "*almost* sent by God to furnish funds for the *Revolution.*" This was too much for Foster, who said: "If you choose to put officers here that ridicule the negro and pronounce the Amendment infamous, why I must retire." He announced that the Massachusetts branch of the A.E.R.A. would go with him.[6]

Blackwell tried to pour oil on the waters by reminding the disputants that unanimity of opinion was not a requirement for sharing a platform, and that both Stanton and Anthony "believe in the right of the negro to vote." At this, Frederick Douglass came forward and denounced Stanton's insistence on characterizing blacks as "Sambo" and "bootblacks" in the *Revolution.* He begged her to cease her anti–Fifteenth Amendment campaign, arguing that suffrage for freed slaves was "a question of life or death."

A furious Anthony laid a match to any oil that remained on the troubled waters. If the "entire people" could not have suffrage, she said, then it must go first "to the most intelligent," for if "intelligence, justice, and morality, are to have precedence in the Government, let the question of woman be brought up first and that of the negro last." She then introduced resolutions opposing ratification of the Fifteenth Amendment and in favor of educated suffrage.[7]

Anthony's voice disappeared in a pandemonium of shouts and catcalls. The next speaker was forced from the stage by the shouting, stamping, and crowd disorder. At this point, newspaper reports noted that Stone came forward on the stage and appealed for order, "and her first appearance caused the most respectful silence." Stone asked the audience to consider that perhaps both sides were right in placing their claim first, for without the consent of the governed, there could be no authority. She urged withdrawal of the offending resolutions, arguing:

If one has a right to say that you can not read and therefore can not vote, then it may be said that you are a woman and therefore can not vote. We are lost if we turn away from the middle principle and argue for one class. . . . Woman has an ocean of wrongs too deep for any plummet, and the negro too has an ocean of wrongs that cannot be fathomed. There are two great oceans; in the one is the black man, and in the other is the woman. But I thank God for the Fifteenth Amendment, and hope that it will be adopted in every State. I will be thankful in my soul if *any* body can get out of the terrible pit.[8]

Stanton objected, saying that she "did not believe in allowing ignorant negroes and foreigners to make laws for her to obey." Anthony then stated her intention to continue her work to defeat the Fifteenth Amendment "because it wasn't Equal Rights" and because it "put two million more men in position of tyrants." Ernestine Rose and Paulina Wright Davis took Anthony's side in the public debate, opposing the Fifteenth Amendment, but the four women were generally without support.[9] Put to the vote, the anti–Fifteenth Amendment and Educated Suffrage resolutions were defeated, while resolutions favoring ratification and calling for adoption of the Sixteenth Amendment were passed by the overwhelming majority. A resolution calling for the establishment of a network of state and local suffrage associations passed as well.

Rebuffed, Stanton and Anthony laid plans to form their own "national" association.[10] Like many of the suffragists, Stone and Blackwell had remained in the city for the Friday meetings of the Brooklyn A.E.R.A. Blackwell had heard a rumor that Stanton and Anthony were inviting certain parties still in the city to come to the Woman's Bureau on Saturday evening to aid in forming a National Woman Suffrage Society. He went to Stanton, who assured him that no such plans were afoot, reminding him that they had agreed jointly to work toward a national society.[11]

On Saturday morning, Mary Livermore asked Anthony if there were immediate plans for forming a national organization, saying that if there were, she would remain in the city. Anthony said they "had no purpose of doing anything of the kind." Stone, Blackwell, and Mary Livermore then left the city.[12]

At the Saturday evening gathering at the Woman's Bureau, a Cincinnati suffragist, Margaret Longley, asked: "Where is Mr. Blackwell and Lucy Stone and Mrs. Livermore?" Stanton looked all around her, and with a show of surprise said she "did not see them" and thought "they must have gone out of the city." Longley commented afterward that the whole manner of forming the Society seemed strange and unbusinesslike to her.[13]

The following week's *Revolution* carried a brief notice that a "National" woman suffrage association had been formed, telling its readers that when the constitution and list of officers were "fully completed," it would give more details.[14] Though Stanton and Anthony represented but a small minority of suffragists, their claim to be a "national" organization continued to antagonize former allies.[15]

Ignoring the domestic crisis in her own house, Stone turned her attention to the greater political anxiety. Taking Alice with her, she left for Boston and the NEWSA convention. Before the general membership meeting, members of the executive committee drafted a circular letter which began: "Without depreciating the value of the Associations already existing it is yet deemed that an organization at once more comprehensive and more widely representative . . . is urgently called for. . . ." Stone sent a copy of the circular letter to Stanton along with a gracious personal note.[16]

Following a vote by the general membership, the letter went out to reformers, literary friends, newspaper editors, and leaders of state and local A.E.R.A. and other woman suffrage groups across the country. Stone and the others enclosed private notes with the circular urging the necessity of a new organization. Her letter to Elizabeth Buffum Chace, president of the Rhode Island Woman Suffrage Association, summed up Stone's rationale:

I think it is a great pity to try and create or give currency to the idea that the Woman's Movement is opposed to the 15th Amendment.

At every convention, even the last New York anniversary, we have adopted resolutions heartily endorsing the 15th amendment. . . . It is not true that our movement is opposed to the negro. But it will be very easy to make it so, to the mutual harm of both causes. . . . I feel dreadfully hurt by this new load we have to carry, and there is no need of it.[17]

Paulina Wright Davis called on Chace in an effort to persuade her to throw the backing of the Rhode Island Suffrage Association to Stanton and Anthony by arguing that passage of the Fifteenth Amendment would be injurious to the cause of women. Chace, caught between conflicting loyalties, "wavered" for a few days, finally aligning her organization with the New England association.[18]

From Kennebunkport, Maine, where she and Blackwell were vacationing with the Spoffords, Stone sent off letter after letter—to association officers, civic leaders, authors, and clergymen. The battle for hearts and minds was on. Chace received a number of letters, as did Margaret Whipple, the Connecticut suffrage leader. Stone asked Whipple to use her influence to win over Isabella Beecher Hooker, head of the Connecticut Woman Suffrage Association and a member of the influential Beecher family. She suggested that Whipple provide Hooker with a copy of Train's *Great Epigram Campaign* so as to "clear her vision."[19]

Though presentist analyses ascribe the split to "personalities," or to a liberal–conservative polarity, or to the political need to break free of old antislavery allies, the immediate cause of the split was clear to those involved. Stone's letters and Stanton's editorials establish that support for or opposition to the Fifteenth Amendment and for or against "educated suffrage" were the immediate causes. "I think we need two National Associations for the Woman Suffrage so that those who do not oppose the 15th Amendment nor take the tone of the *Revolution* may yet have an organization," Stone wrote to one old ally; to another, she described the need for a new association that "will not weaken our claim by opposition to the 15th Amendment."[20]

Stone intensified her fund-raising efforts on behalf of an alternative woman suffrage newspaper. Her belief in the power of the press to mold public opinion is evident in a letter written that summer in which she worried, "Just arouse Mrs. Stanton's ire, and with her paper circulating largely in the doubtful Western States, she can defeat the 15th Amendment."[21]

In the months following the convention, the *Revolution* stepped up its antiblack rhetoric, making frequent references to the "barbarism," "brute force," and "tyranny" of black men. It also intensified its push to defeat black suffrage. "All Wise Women Will Oppose the Fifteenth Amendment," wrote Stanton.[22]

Shuttling back and forth between Boston and the state associations, Stone addressed legislatures, wrote articles, visited newspaper offices, arranged meetings, organized new societies, laid plans for the new national organization, and raised funds for a newspaper. Her frenetic pace that summer and fall could neither stem the tide of public criticism nor mask the private pain caused by Harry's affair. By openly pursuing another woman, Blackwell forced Stone to contend not just with personal humiliation and rejection, but also with a challenge to her belief system.

From her earliest speeches, Stone's credibility had hinged on her belief that giving rights to women would enhance "womanliness." Independent women would be loved for themselves alone, she had insisted. Virtuous women would elevate the realm of politics. Women able to support themselves would end licentious behavior. Again and again, those who listened and met with Stone went away remarking on her "womanliness," on her sweetness. Now, she watched helplessly as her husband rejected her in favor of a married woman. As she had done so often before, Stone would take responsibility, seeing Harry's choice of another as a consequence of her neglect. She did not have to look far for corroboration; her Blackwell sisters-in-law were all too ready to blame Harry's wandering on Lucy's devotion to woman's rights.

Marian blamed Harry's "unhappiness" on the fact that "Lucy proposes to be away for months lecturing." Emily also blamed Stone in part, writing, "I get so angry with Harry, and about their family and woman's rights doings. I get so angry with Lucy that I have no satisfaction with either."[23] Blackwell's conduct became the object of a family round-robin. Letters between Emily in New York and Elizabeth in England were filled with a running commentary on the "great domestic anxiety" caused by Harry's "running after Mrs. P. at Roseville."[24]

Blackwell was forty-four that summer. If not conventionally handsome, he possessed great personal charm. He was fun-loving, mercurial, as much a "butterfly" in his dazzling bursts of enthusiasm as in his inconstancy in all things. His "love of approbation" had gone unsatisfied for too long. For almost two years, he had devoted himself to reform. His labors for Lincoln had not brought him a coveted Washington appointment; his efforts on behalf of woman suffrage were consistently overshadowed by Stone's charismatic power. Earlier that year, following their joint appearance before a Washington audience of members of Congress and other dignitaries, newspapers furnished lengthy, glowing reports of Stone's speech, noting only that "her husband" spoke too—never giving Blackwell's name. It was not surprising that he looked elsewhere for approbation.[25]

Blackwell's frail ego could not withstand being "husband of Lucy Stone." Winning her hand in marriage had been a coup for a failed hardware merchant, but from the first, Blackwell had shown himself unwilling to relinquish the traditional "masculine" role in their marriage. He needed to feel that he possessed superior judgment and knowledge in politics, in oratory, in his judgment of character, and in his business decisions. He believed that he should be the primary wage earner. Though Stone had earlier deferred to his judgments, more and more she acted on her own counsel. However much she blamed herself for their marital problems, she was no longer willing to accede to Harry's whims and fancies.

Despite his dismal record as a businessman, commerce was one capacity in which Blackwell did not feel overshadowed by Stone. So, too, in his relationship with Ludlow and Abby Patton, he was central to their business and social relations. Ludlow Patton was a stockbroker and a self-made man. His wife, Abby Hutchinson Patton, was musical, pretty, eleven years younger than Stone, charming, poetic, and wealthy. Abby Patton had been on the campaign trail with Blackwell in 1864, when Stone had withdrawn to Gardner. Though the evidence is largely circumstantial, it points to Abby Patton as the mysterious "Mrs. P." with whom Blackwell had an affair in 1869.[26]

Whether Blackwell's "affair with Mrs. P" included sexual infidelity is unclear. Theirs may have been an unconsummated passion, a nineteenth-century romantic folly. Abby Patton later wrote a poem about a "grand" and secret love whose name she carried "deep in my heart." Blackwell's sisters saw nothing grand about their brother's involvement with another woman. From England, where she had gone to set up an obstetric practice, Elizabeth wrote, "I can say nothing about Harry—the thing grieves and disgusts me—poor fellow!" Across the bottom of the letter, she scrawled, "Burn this at once!"[27]

For the next year, Blackwell would waver between Boston and New York; between Lucy Stone and "Mrs. P."; between remorseful spurts of supportive suffrage activity intended to reconcile him to Stone, and pursuit of Mrs. P. in New York and Roseville. Although it is unlikely that there was widespread knowledge of the affair outside the family, certainly some others were aware of it, as a letter of Emily's makes clear. She wrote that she was "glad to learn indirectly" through a third party late in the summer of 1869 that "Mrs. P." wished to terminate her "relations" with Harry. "I hope that Harry has made up his mind to break off his relations with Mrs. P.," she wrote, concluding doubtfully, "I shall not feel sure . . . how their good resolutions hold out, but I think things are more hopeful than they were, nor do I know what the result will be between H & L for I have not seen them."[28]

Blackwell had agreed to accompany Stone on a tour of the western states that autumn, a gesture that the family interpreted hopefully as pointing toward reconciliation. Stone and Blackwell spent the first three weeks of September traveling together through the West, laying the organizational groundwork for the formation of the national association. Stone would later describe the psychological pain of that summer and autumn, but in public, she was altogether focused on the western organizing campaign. She and Anthony often shared the stage at meetings and conventions, their public semblance of amity an ironic and painful counterpart to the public display of conjugal unity she and Blackwell presented that fall.[29]

On their return East, Stone presented Blackwell with an ultimatum. She was moving permanently to Boston; he could choose to follow or not, but she would not live any longer in Roseville. As her excuse, she cited her need to work closely with the New England organization headquartered in Boston. She then enrolled twelve-year-old Alice in a progressive boarding school in Newburyport, Massachusetts. As for healing their differences, she would travel less, speak less, and try to provide him the domestic refuge he craved. As she prepared to leave Roseville, Stone wrote:

I feel crushed, and torn, and homeless.
But I shall make myself very busy. Harry will join me at Newburyport, and we shall set to raise the $10,000 to start a paper. . . . I shall try and work through the paper, for the future, and quit this lecturing field altogether. It is not consistent with any home life, or any proper care of my family. I feel it more and more, and shall certainly not continue my mode of work—tho it is my natural way.[30]

By devoting herself to newspaper work, "what I think in some shape not so effective for me perhaps, but on the whole better under the circumstances," Stone would try to rebuild the bridge.[31] The "circumstances" continued to be troublesome. Emily reported that "Harry goes into [Boston] reluctantly, against his judgments and inclination." Then too, Blackwell was not willing to sever his relationship with Mrs. P. entirely. "The relation with Mrs. P. is dying out," Emily wrote in October, "but he injuriously and foolishly keeps up Lucy's [discomfort?] and distress by refusing utterly to terminate it."[32]

After only two weeks in Boston, Blackwell returned to New York. "He left Lucy hard at work trying to raise funds for their paper," Emily wrote. "She will probably spend at least till Christmas in Boston, perhaps the whole winter." Emily described Harry's internal struggle: "He VOWS he won't go into the paper but will come back to Roseville and go into business but in the next breath he discusses the possibility of his taking up the paper, and I rather incline to think he will be drawn into it."[33]

In Boston, Stone saw to last-minute details of the Cleveland convention. She mailed a copy of the call to the *Revolution* along with a warm personal letter to Stanton. "I wish I could have had a quiet hour with you, to talk about it," she wrote. "I *hope* that you will see it as I do, that with two societies, each in harmony with itself, . . . we shall secure the hearty active cooperation of *all* the friends of the cause better than either could do alone." She went on to assure Stanton that "So far as I have influence, this soc. shall never be an enemy or antagonist of yours in any way. . . . Your little girls and mine will reap the easy harvest which it costs so much to sow." Stone ended the letter, "With sincere good will, Truly your friend, Lucy Stone."[34]

Stanton responded publicly, accusing the "Boston malcontents" of hypocrisy in their wish not to "depreciate" existing societies. "Yet the contrary is well known to every worker in the movement," she wrote in the *Revolution*. "The names of persons are appended to that circular letter who have been sedulously and malignantly working for two years to undermine certain officers in the Nat'l Assn., and their journal in the minds of all who affiliate with them."[35]

In this, Stanton was correct. Stone indeed was working "sedulously" to undermine the credibility of the New York organization, though whether her efforts were "malignant" is left to historians to judge. In her voluminous correspondence that summer and fall, Stone avoided any personal attack on the two suffrage leaders. Upon learning that Higginson had invited Stanton and Anthony to Cleveland, Stone wrote privately to Antoinette Brown Blackwell that she hoped they would not come, for "it will be so dreadful an incubus to take them up again!"[36]

Harry Blackwell was in New York, ostensibly getting endorsements prior to the convention. "I am going to see Tilton tomorrow to try to make him see how necessary it is to influence Mrs. S. & Susan to *stay away from Cleveland* & not to fight us either," he wrote.[37]

Delegates from across the country gathered in Cleveland, and an Associated Press wire service reporter dispatched news of the convention's daily proceedings to papers across the land. The American Woman Suffrage Association (AWSA), the national organization formed at the convention, pledged itself to organize for suffrage state by state, to publish and distribute tracts and documents at below cost, to "prepare and circulate petitions to State Legislatures, to Congress, or to constitutional conventions in behalf of the legal and political equality of women," and "to employ lecturers and agents" for that purpose.[38]

Stone made a very proper appearance, "her hair combed in the old-fashioned, smooth, simple style. She wore a plain black dress, with a black basque, open in front, much like a gentleman's vest, and edged with white ruffling passing around the neck. No jewelry was displayed except a delicate breast-pin."[39]

Stanton did not go, but Anthony went to Cleveland hoping to effect a coup by getting Stanton elected President.[40] Her hopes faded on the second day with the announcement of the arrival of a telegram from the renowned and highly esteemed clergyman Henry Ward Beecher announcing his willingness to accept the presidency of the new association. Reverend Beecher would answer those who charged woman's rights with "free-loveism." Those at the convention had no way of knowing that, a few years hence, Beecher would be charged with "free-loveism" himself.[41]

When Anthony supporters called for a speech, Stone invited her to the podium. Anthony delivered a highly emotional peroration, saying that though the new association should "nullify and crush out the organization of which I am a member, and tread its heel on *The Revolution,* for which I have struggled for the past two years as no woman ever struggled before," she would "bless God" for the work it would do in Washington.[42]

Exhausted by her efforts to keep the *Revolution* afloat without the capital of Train and Melliss, Anthony's bitterness deepened when at the last evening's proceedings, Stone announced that Mary Livermore's *Agitator* was transferring its offices to Boston where it would merge with a new woman suffrage organ, the *Woman's Journal.*[43]

The *New York Tribune* headlined an article on the Cleveland meetings: "Woman Suffrage—Organization of a National Association." Greeley's editorial expressed hope that the new paper would "not mistake rashness for courage, folly for smartness, cunning for sagacity, badinage for wit, unscrupulousness for fidelity. . . ."[44] The *New York Times* congratulated the organizers of the Cleveland convention, praising them for the dignity and seriousness of the proceedings: "If the leaders in this agitation wish to have their demands seriously discussed, let them first be serious themselves."[45]

The media response was gratifying. Stone's campaign to present a counterimage of woman suffragists as serious, thoughtful, and respectable appeared to be succeeding. The next step was to increase the size of the new organization, and she took the lecture-circuit route home. From Cleveland to Boston, she zigzagged across the countryside, stopping at cities and towns, meeting with editors and women's groups. She showed the women how to organize, conduct meetings, arrange publicity, advertise meetings, and how to obtain and distribute propaganda materials. Where suffrage societies were already in place, she worked at persuading them to become auxiliaries of the new AWSA.

From stops all along the way, Stone sent letters to Alice, who was having a difficult time adjusting to boarding-school life at Miss Andrews' school in Newburyport. Stone's letters were affectionate, encouraging, and richly descriptive. Though Stone consistently belittled her writing skills, always thinking of herself as primarily an orator, her descriptive prose had about it a homely honesty and spare grace, as when she wrote: "Yesterday morning I woke up in Toledo, Ohio, and found the beautiful Sandusky River rolling not a stone's throw below my window; and this morning, a whole day's ride beyond, I woke and found the Grand River, with its swift rapids, just as near my window, while the hills above are crowned with oak, now leafless. A cold wintry sky hangs over all. Snow squalls have come and gone all day."[46]

She urged Alice to try to "make the best of your small room and bed, and crowded arrangements. Keep your shoulders up. . . . I am very well and shall be glad to get back. Then we must make a home." Stone promised to visit Alice soon, and "if it is convenient for Miss Andrews, I should like ever so much, to sleep with you, *my dear little cub*—we will have a grand cuddle."[47]

In the first flush of postconvention euphoria, the "great domestic anxiety" seemed to be abating. Emily reported to Elizabeth in early December that Lucy and Harry "are now on good and kindly terms together—Lucy being delighted at H's coming in to help—and I hope Mrs. P's affair is dying away." As much as the Blackwell sisters disliked woman's rights activity, Emily conceded that "I am not sorry to have H occupied and away from N.Y. although he gets sick to death of the work and the turmoil, but anything is better than idle drifting."[48]

On December 20, Emily continued optimistic, writing Elizabeth that Lucy and Harry "are working more harmoniously and the great domestic anxiety is dying out. It will end I think by Harry's following Lucy's lead. . . . On the whole, I believe it is practically his best course—it is better than to do nothing, and it ensures his domestic peace. I have realized so keenly this summer the truth that 'Satan finds some mischief & c.' that I accept as a relief the prospect of their joint work."[49]

That Christmas, Stone remained in Boston while Blackwell went with Alice to Roseville to celebrate Christmas with his family. Ostensibly, Stone needed to prepare the first issue of the *Woman's Journal* for publication, although it is doubtful that she would have consented to a return to Roseville until Blackwell had made clear his final intentions. Seeing the first issue of the *Journal* into print—from capitalization to page layouts—was an ambitious undertaking. The *Woman's Journal* was a joint stock company. Six prominent Boston businessmen had been persuaded to purchase ten shares apiece at two hundred dollars a share. Stone and Blackwell held twenty; Julia Ward Howe and Caroline Severance each held five shares, as did Alice Stone Blackwell. William Lloyd Garrison and other antislavery stalwarts, among them Sarah Grimké, Angelina Grimké Weld, Samuel May, Stephen Foster, held two shares apiece. Mary Livermore received a salary of fifteen hundred dollars per year as editor in chief, and Thomas Wentworth Higginson became a contributing editor at an annual salary of fifty dollars. From the outset, female typographers set the type and printed the paper.[50]

Five thousand copies of the first issue of the *Woman's Journal* appeared on January 8, 1870. Though suffrage was to be its "especial" focus, it promised to devote itself to "the interests of Woman, to her educational, industrial, legal and political Equality." Support for the Sixteenth Amendment, news of the granting of suffrage to women in the territory of Wyoming, as well as of woman suffrage doings in Iowa, Colorado, California, and New Hampshire—a letter from Berlin, news of Rosa Bonheur's success as a sculptor, and a description of the Cleveland convention filled the pages of the first issues.

Living above the offices of the *Journal,* Stone was wholly occupied in January 1870 with getting the newspaper established. From the start, she assumed the larger share of the work—obtaining subscribers, gathering suffrage news, seeing to it that accounts were kept and salaries paid, raising funds, obtaining letters of endorsement, finding advertisers, getting the paper laid out and to the printers each week, and then seeing to its mailing and distribution.

The first printing of five thousand copies was insufficient; a second issue of seven thousand sold out by the second day. Subscriptions poured in. With the paper running smoothly, Stone made arrangements with lecture agent Charles Mumford to deliver a series of lectures at fifty dollars per speech plus expenses.[51] She lectured in early February in Pennsylvania and Vermont, writing to Alice and Antoinette of the beauty of the mountains and the countryside. In Towanda, Pennsylvania, on St. Valentine's Day, Stone received a valentine picturing a "bouncing woman, driving an omnibus." She put it in the fire immediately, afterward regretting that she had not saved it to show her old friend, who "would have laughed well at sight of *such* woman's rights."[52]

Blackwell assisted Livermore with the paper in Stone's absence, but on her return, he left almost immediately for New York. George wrote of Harry's unexpected arrival, reporting to Elizabeth that although "he looks well," he nonetheless "misses a certain alertness and snap that he finds among his business acquaintances in New York. Boston seems to him dull and provincial—and he doesn't seem tempted much to buy and settle there. He says Alice is doing well at school. Lucy pretty well."[53]

Through the spring of 1870, Blackwell continued to vacillate between Boston and New York, between Stone and "Mrs. P." He also wavered between reform and business. "As usual [Harry] feels a leaning towards the 'sugar business,'" George wrote, "and also a fancy to pre-empt half St. Domingo, round about the Bay of Samana where Brother Jonathan [England] is insinuating his great toe. Funny Harry. I don't [know] how the butterfly streak comes into his composition—through the lighter hearted Lanes I guess rather than the sombre b's."[54]

Blackwell cut short his flirtation with the 'sugar business' in order to return to Boston and take over the paper following an urgent appeal from Stone. Annie Gleason, their adopted child, lay perilously ill in West Brookfield, and Stone went immediately to care for her. For three weeks, she kept a round-the-clock vigil at the child's bedside. "Lucy is in great tribulation about Annie," Emily wrote on March 15, 1870. "The physician can make nothing of her state but thinks she must die. Lucy watches her day and night, and I fear will have a fit of illness or be otherwise seriously affected by such fresh and mental trouble and worry."[55]

In Boston, Blackwell chafed at having to look after the paper. "I am sure I don't know why *I* am working hard here without even a salary and for no earthly reason but to try to make Lucy happy," he wrote. "It is a queer world and (I think) a muddle."[56]

If Blackwell was unhappy at having to be in Boston, his sisters were relieved to have him there. Emily wrote, "Although Harry rebels and abuses Boston, I think he is better off there and busy than unoccupied and running after Mrs. P at Roseville. I favor the move, for it seems to me the only chance of settling him in a home and an occupation."[57]

On March 15, Annie, not yet eleven years old, died in Lucy's arms. After arranging the child's funeral and burial, Stone returned to Boston, deeply grieving. "Aunt Lucy looks well but is in great trouble," wrote Kitty Barry at the end of March.[58] Fresh troubles, both domestic and political, were in store.

In early April, Stone was in New York for an executive committee meeting of the A.E.R.A. At that meeting, a motion to dissolve the organization was deferred until May 14. The committee also voted to approve a proposal put forward by Theodore Tilton to explore uniting the two woman suffrage associations in a single "Union" organization. Although Stone did not favor the plan, she agreed to a preliminary meeting, and on April 6, 1870, Stone, Higginson, and George William Curtis met with representatives of the New York association at a Fifth Avenue hotel. Parker Pillsbury, Charlotte Wilbour, and Josephine Griffing represented the National association. Lucretia Mott and Theodore Tilton came in the role of mediators. Tilton presented his plan of reconciliation with its proposed constitution for the Union organization—a plan and constitution identical to those of the Stanton/Anthony organization, with the added stipulation that all annual meetings of the Union society would be held in New York City.[59]

Stone, Higginson, and Curtis objected that the proposed constitution provided neither for a delegated society nor for the function within the organization of state societies. When more than four hours of discussion failed to produce any agreement, Mott pleaded with the two sides to make "mutual concessions."[60] However, the American wing would neither concede its delegate structure of organization nor agree to hold all annual meetings in New York. The National wing refused to modify its constitution, and the meeting foundered. When it was clear that there would be no joint association, Tilton thundered, "I will form a new society. I will lift up the suffrage banner over all your heads, and take the wind out of all your sails. I can carry it, for I have a paper [the *Independent*], I have the platform, and I have a pen. I can carry it."[61]

The notice in the *Woman's Journal* of the failed reconciliation attempt was brief. It included the full text of the proposed Union constitution, followed by a statement of the AWSA's unwillingness to form a society except on a delegate basis.[62] Tilton soon announced the formation of the Union Suffrage Society, with himself as president. The *Revolution* announced that the "proposed union, so far as the National Association was concerned, was formed . . . under the name of the Union Woman Suffrage Society."[63]

The major dailies paid little attention to the change, nor to the paid notice on April 9 that a female stockbroker named Victoria Woodhull had declared herself a candidate for president of the United States.[64] Stone returned to Boston no doubt relieved at avoiding the merger, altogether unaware that Tilton and Woodhull would prove an "incubus" more burdensome than anything the woman suffrage movement had yet encountered.

Blackwell remained in New York, unbeknownst to Emily, who wrote in apparent relief that "[Boston] seems likely to be their centre for the present—the move had had a good effect in breaking up external troubles and keeping Harry too busy for him to drift in every direction. Though I regret his absence, I think it has been a good thing in its entirety." She added, "It very much diminishes our circle."[65] Thus, Emily was surprised to receive a hastily scribbled entreaty from Stone begging her to use her influence to bring Harry to his senses:

Today Mrs. Livermore received a business letter from Harry
dated at the office of Ludlow Patton—
It is not good for him to go there to renew or take up the
old snare—
I wish you would say to him in a friendly way which a sister
may, you hope he does not make headquarters at Mr. Patton's
for it is not good to do so—He will take it kindly, and it
is all that can be done—I shall *never ever* try, to go
through such another time as that of last summer—
He is yet too near the old toils to escape if he lets him
self come within their reach—
I wish he would be kept away—
But what will be will be.[66]

Stone's uncharacteristic words to her sister-in-law, her revelation of the pain of the previous summer, and her fatalistic attitude toward the future have about them the ring of emotional exhaustion. Whether Emily's counsel succeeded, or whether either Blackwell or "Mrs. P." decided finally to end things, neither "Mrs. P." or Ludlow Patton appear after this time in family letters. Stone sold the major portion of her Roseville property in order to purchase a home in Boston, signaling her intent to stay in New England. Blackwell spent a few more weeks in Roseville before returning to Boston, thereby prolonging Stone's distress.

The bridge had withstood a second battering. As time for the May meetings drew nigh, Stone could take stock. It had been a grievous and humiliating year with the death of Annie, separation from Alice, the pain of Blackwell's public pursuit of "Mrs. P.," and the public debacle of the schism in May. Still, Blackwell was now at home; "Mrs. P." was presumably out of the picture. The new American organization was gaining auxiliaries throughout the country, and many of the outstanding orators and leading lights of the reform community had agreed to speak at the May convention in New York. Recently, Stone had found a piece of property she hoped to buy on Dorchester Heights, just outside Boston. The newspaper's circulation was expanding rapidly, and the Sixteenth Amendment was again before Congress, this time proposed by George Julian in a joint congressional resolution. The mood was upbeat. Assessing the political gains of the past four months, the *Woman's Journal* noted that "Woman Suffrage has made astonishing progress," having been "established in Wyoming, adopted in Utah, and submitted to the vote . . . in Vermont," while "Minnesota has passed a bill to submit it to the concurrent votes of men and women."[67] The article enumerated other states where woman suffrage was under consideration. In New York, however, fresh trouble was brewing.

Once again the charge of "free-loveism" was being flung at the suffragists, following a speech by Stanton warning that "with the education and elevation of women we shall have a mighty sundering of unholy ties that hold men and women together who loathe and despise one another."[68] For her part, Stone continued to insist that divorce *per se* was not a woman's rights concern. Her resolve to salvage her marriage by working closer to home wavered under the intense organizing effort preceding the AWSA convention, scheduled for May 11 and 12 at New York's Steinway Hall. Late April found her in Vermont, speaking twice daily on behalf of the woman suffrage amendment then before the state legislature. After each speech, she would encourage local women to form a suffrage association and to lobby and petition on behalf of the amendment.[69] She returned briefly to see to the *Woman's Journal* and then left for the May meetings, taking a circuitous route through New Jersey and upstate New York, working the small towns and cities all along the way.[70]

Despite "lowering clouds and driving rain," people crowded into Steinway Hall, eager to see and hear the Who's Who of orators and public figures Stone had begged and cajoled into speaking: Henry Ward Beecher, George William Curtis, James Freeman Clarke, Julia Ward Howe, Senator George Julian, Thomas Wentworth Higginson, Aaron Powell, Oliver Johnson—a parade of luminaries intended to semaphore "Respectability" to friends and foes. The speeches were grand; the halls were filled; newspapers complimented the American Association on the "dignity" and decorum maintained throughout. Resolutions passed handily pledging the association to work for passage of a woman suffrage bill in the District of Columbia and to continue state organization pending the adoption of the Sixteenth Amendment.[71]

Across town, "Miss Anthony's society," as the *New York Times* insisted upon calling the Union organization, was sparsely attended. The *Nation* congratulated the American wing on monopolizing "not only nearly all the talent, but all the honors of the occasion," while across town, "Mr. Tilton's small mountain guns" were aimed at much smaller audiences. At the Union meeting, Stanton pointed to the difference in methods as the "essential issue" dividing the two associations. The American society wished to "carry the measure stop by step, year by year through the states" thereby forcing "educated refined women . . . to kneel at the feet of paupers, knaves, and drunkards." Stanton made clear her scorn for this approach, saying that "those who have the stomach for such work" could "canvass every state from Maine to California, and humbly ask Tom, Dick, and Harry, Patrick, Hans, Yung-Tung and Sambo, to recognize such women as Lucretia Mott, Ernestine Rose, Susan B. Anthony and Anna Dickinson as *their* political equals."[72] The Union approach promised to avoid the "rabble" by working through Washington legislators for suffrage by federal amendment.

Stone remained in New York for the May 14 meeting of the old A.E.R.A. committee, unaware that the Union suffrage association had been busy. An Ohio suffragist described being invited to dine at Tiltons, where she was "entertained [by Tilton] with a boastful account of how they had tricked Lucy Stone by turning over several of the Equal Rights Clubs, with the names of their members to the National; doing it before the Blackwells could reach the meetings where this was done; and all this was represented as a conspiracy between Mrs. Stanton, Susan, and himself, . . . and they laughed over it as the best joke possible."[73]

Stanton corroborated this, writing a friend, "We have had grand times in getting the National and the Equal Rights both merged with the Union movement. Boston is *awful* sore."[74] At the May 14 meeting, Tilton moved to merge the A.E.R.A. with the Union society. When the Bostonians objected and called for a vote, a group of nonmembers who had accompanied Tilton each "threw in a dime" to become members "and then voted for the merger."[75]

Shortly after this meeting, Stone left New York. Thus, she was not in New York for the crowded meeting Stanton staged on May 19 to protest the verdict reached in the McFarland-Richardson trial. Over three thousand women came, outraged at the "Not guilty by reason of insanity" decision, which freed Daniel McFarland. The crowd was further inflamed by the judge's subsequent decision to award the "insane" father custody of the child. The trial had elements of melodrama—a beautiful actress, Abby Sage McFarland, whose allegedly abusive and alcoholic former husband Daniel shot Albert Richardson, a well-known journalist and Abby's paramour, in the offices of the *New York Tribune*. Henry Ward Beecher officiated at their deathbed wedding. Abby's testimony at the trial that she had turned to Richardson to protect her from McFarland's drunken rages won her widespread sympathy and heightened interest in freer divorce laws. Still, the protesters were not ready for Stanton's insistence that "Divorces should be granted at the will of the parties."[76]

"'Woman's Right' to Divorce," trumpeted the front-page headline of the following day's *New York Times*. The woman suffrage movement was charged with "hostility to the marriage relation." Learning of the new sensation, Stone could take scant consolation in the editorialist who noted that "Mrs. Stone saw the rock on which the New Yorkers were foundering, and in her honest zeal for the reform, broke with them." The editorial advised that if woman suffragists were to have any chance of succeeding, "they must keep free love from their platform."[77]

Disgusted at the entrance of still another "side issue," Stone planned a three-week speaking and organizing tour of Indiana and Ohio. When she was back in Boston and Alice had returned from Miss Andrews, the family traveled together to Martha's Vineyard for a vacation. In August, Blackwell's sisters summoned him to Long Island, where his mother lay dying. Hannah Lane Blackwell died on August 21, 1870, at the age of seventy-seven. Back home after the funeral, Blackwell published an eloquent tribute to his mother in the *Woman's Journal*. "For many years she made her husband and children happy in the most affectionate and trustful domestic relations," he wrote. "As wife and widow, she was the presiding genius of a beautiful home."[78] How far his own home situation departed from this description is clear from Alice's depiction of their own living arrangements in a letter to her cousin Kitty that September: "We have not very roomy quarters here, one room and a cupboard. I also have the run of the staircases, the office and the back office, and two parlors belonging to the club, I believe. Papa and Mama are out or busy a good deal, so I prowl about the house, read newspapers, and scribble."[79]

Alice did not return to Newburyport that fall; Instead, she was enrolled in a nearby coeducational school. That autumn, Stone pressed forward with her plans to purchase the Dorchester property she had seen and liked earlier that year.[80]

September was marked by a brief but intense flurry of political activity. Earlier that year, Stone had helped to organize a Massachusetts Woman Suffrage Association. Meeting in late September, the association considered the question of whether to form an independent political party, a move Stone opposed. After much discussion, the vote was carried to make woman suffrage and not party affiliation the first test of a candidate's suitability.[81] Though the suffrage organization was unaffiliated, both Stone and Livermore succeeded that fall in being elected delegates to the Massachusetts Republican nominating convention—their attendance providing a "first" in the history of Massachusetts politics. Stone addressed the convention, her plea for party backing an extended metaphor in which she likened woman suffrage to a "heavy freight train" poised before a steep grade with "an engine too weak to take it up." The train was bravely holding its own while it waited for a stronger engine. "Soon we heard the gay, triumphant whistle of a huge engine without an ounce of freight. In a moment it attached itself to the overburdened train, which at once moved up the grade. Safe on level ground, it needed no help. Gentlemen," she beseeched, "be our locomotive."[82]

The resolution in favor of a woman suffrage plank went down to defeat by a vote of 196 to 139. In the wake of the defeat, the *Woman's Journal* published the results of a candidates' poll conducted by the Woman Suffrage State Central Committee. The replies of the various candidates were printed in the October 22, 1870, issue along with a list of all the candidates from all four parties whom they knew to be supporters of woman suffrage, urging its readers to choose from among them. "Scratch remorselessly from your tickets every hostile or doubtful name."[83]

The emphasis on organization, the formation of committees, the growing political sophistication that included the use of straw polls, and the strength of the woman suffrage showing at the convention marked a new phase of woman suffrage activity. The antebellum reform movement had focused on moral suasion; in the postwar years, Stone would move her organization steadily in the direction of political activism.[84]

This strategic shift was intense and focused—the AWSA was committed to lobbying for every form of suffrage, up to and including the Sixteenth Amendment. In those years, though defeats far outnumbered victories, the constant agitation of the question and the slow but steady trickle of states and towns granting school suffrage, municipal suffrage, and, in some instances, full suffrage kept suffrage workers' hopes alive. Stone's political strategy in hewing to the suffrage line and avoiding what she called "side issues" came more and more to distinguish the American from the Union society. Stanton had moved away from suffrage, declaring in the *Revolution* that women "do not want suffrage a thousandth part as keenly as they want a reform of the marriage and divorce laws."[85] She attacked the *Woman's Journal* for insisting "that the sum and substance of the woman question consisted in woman's demand for the ballot." Though Stone seldom directly responded to Stanton's salvos, the criticism of her journal drew a sharp response: "The statement of the *Revolution* is incorrect. It is untrue . . . [the *Woman's Journal*] finds space and opportunity to discuss every question, fact, and interest that concerns woman. Education, work, clothing, food, health, training of children, marriage—it has turned away from no fact of life, or problem of society, in which she has an interest."[86]

Stanton's preoccupation with the theoretical issue of marriage and divorce was reflected in a major speech delivered in New York at the celebration of the twentieth anniversary of the Worcester convention. Stone did not attend. Following Paulina Wright Davis's reading of her "History of the Woman Suffrage Movement," a partisan account that gave two sentences to the organization and work of the AWSA, Stanton spoke for more than three hours on the subject of divorce. "We are in the midst of a social revolution greater than any political or religious revolution that the world has ever seen," she said.[87]

Where Stanton had grown increasingly radical in her thinking on marriage, Stone had grown more conservative. Before marrying Blackwell, Stone had written a friend that she believed in divorce as a means of freeing a woman from "a loveless marriage" so that "a true love may grow up in the soul of the injured one from the full enjoyment of which no legal bond had a right to keep her." Or him? Apparently not, for now Stone wrote: "We believe in *marriage for life,* and deprecate all this loose, pestiferous talk in favor of *easy divorce.* Let it be observed that this plea for *free divorce* comes from the organ of the Union Woman Suffrage society, and is not the voice of the American Woman Suffrage Association, with Henry Ward Beecher at its head."[88] Stanton's theories, "legitimately carried out," would "abrogate marriage," Stone wrote. Betraying the depth of her feelings, she concluded, "and we have then the hideous thing known as 'free love.' Be not deceived—*free love means free lust.*"[89]

In Stanton's absence, Tilton shared editorial control of the *Revolution.* Rumors of his extramarital liaison with Victoria Woodhull were circulating in New York, and his editorials urging liberalized divorce caused an internal revolt in the Union Society, more recently known as "Mr. Tilton's Society." A group led by Isabella Beecher Hooker voted in November to restore the name "National" Woman Suffrage Association to the New York organization. Hooker also took charge of planning the January Washington convention, sending off a circular letter in November in which she promised prospective speakers and attendees that she would keep convention management "solely in my hands." Hooker went so far as to write Stanton and suggest she not attend "for the good of the movement."[90]

Hooker typified the "new" eastern bourgeois recruit to woman suffrage. The National welcomed her, just as Stone rejoiced over the entrance of such women into the American wing. They brought money, powerful friends, and political connections into the movement. Such women were generally less tolerant of the radical inclusiveness of early reformers; free divorce and free love were socially anathema to the increasingly nativist and exclusionary bourgeoisie. Alongside her personal revulsion to the idea of "free lust," Stone placed the practical exigency that free love and free divorce threatened the loss of what she liked to call the "sinews of war"—money.

The outraged press response to Stanton's divorce speeches intensified Stone's determination to keep the two associations separate. Just prior to the Cleveland convention, word reached her that Stanton, Anthony, and Tilton had been "stirring up some of our Western members who are ignorant of the facts" to join them in Cleveland in an attempted coup.[91] She and Blackwell urged friends to attend, and if that was not possible, to "write a letter . . . expressing your opinion that we should not merge . . . and that we should stick to the question of *Suffrage* and not complicate the cause with marriage, divorce & other outside questions."[92] At the convention, a reporter described the confusion of those who knew or cared little for the reasons for the schism:

Westerners were immediately flung into direst confusion by a reiteration of the battle cries. "Free divorce!" and "Spite and jealously!" Boston entrenches itself behind that one accusation of unworthy moral ideas, while New York attacks at random, professing not to understand what Boston can mean, since Mrs. H. B. Stanton, the chief promulgator of these immoral views, has permanently retired from connection with any society.[93]

Despite an attached rider affirming "That the ballot for women means stability for the marriage relation," Anthony's motion to unite failed by a vote of 112 to 47. At one point in the debate, Anthony accused Stone of "hounding" Mrs. Stanton. "Lucy Stone who wouldn't submit to the legal form of marriage—ought to be the last to say that Mrs. Stanton shouldn't preach that," said Anthony, a remark for which she later apologized. Resolutions were passed in favor of avoiding "side issues" and pledging the AWSA to the principle of "stability in the marriage relation." To answer those who charged the AWSA with favoring state work only, a resolution promising a renewed effort to enact a Sixteenth Amendment passed easily.[94]

Stone, disturbed by the forty-seven mostly western votes to merge the two societies, set off on a western speaking tour of her own. She met with only moderate success in her attempts to convince Westerners of the urgent need to remain separate, writing home:

I attended the Cuh. [Cuyahoga] Co. Soc. meeting here yesterday. Susan was there, & John Gage.. Susan told how she got money from Train, how I would not work with him, &c. &c. I stated the real ground of difference and urged that in any action they took they should make suffrage the main issue. . . . It was a small meeting. Not more than 100 present. I saw Judge Waite and his wife. They did not ask me to go with them. So I am at my cousins. . . . before next June, they will see the right thing to do. Harper's Weekly Nov. 26 has an article from Curtis which puts it clean and right. There will now be clear dividing lines and we shall go on better than ever.[95]

Before western audiences, Stone dressed plainly and spoke in homely familiar cadences. "She looked just like nineteen out of twenty people didn't think she would," wrote a local reporter, noting that in dress and appearance, she was "a farmer's wife–looking woman, very much resembling your aunt. . . . Her appearance made the audience her friends and her lecture most of them her admirers." He told how Stone warned the women present "not to be trapped into saying they didn't want to vote," advising, "If your husband says he don't want you to vote, ring it in his ears that you want to and shall. When he says good morning, tell him you want to vote; when he asks what you are going to have for dinner, tell him you want to vote; and whatever he asks from the time you rise up in the morning until you lie down at night, tell him you want to vote."[96]

Back in Boston by mid-December, Stone resumed work on the fundraising bazaar she had helped plan earlier that autumn. The woman suffrage bazaar was an enormous undertaking, occupying all three of Boston's major public auditoriums. Merchants, entertainers, craftsmen, and restaurateurs had donated time, goods, and services. There were daily theatrical and musical offerings, booths displaying crafts and various kinds of merchandise. Cakes containing gold rings and little china dolls were sold by the slice. At large concessions, women could buy "cooking-stoves, clothes-reels, bed-blankets, washing machines, wringers, pianos, sewing-machines of every variety, flowers, boxes of dried fish, soap, starch . . . there is no end of these money commodities." An art gallery displayed donated works, and one entire building had been "floored over and transformed into a large dining-room and restaurant." Hundreds of workers volunteered their time.[97]

Stone juggled moving preparations with supervision of the bazaar. The purchase of a home in Boston in the face of Blackwell's oft-expressed wish to live in New York or to move west marked a new departure for Stone. Aware that Harry was unhappy, she was nevertheless able to resist the ploys that had hitherto brought her around. He plunged into a prolonged bout of nervous depression. Stone wrote her Blackwell inlaws asking them to "unite in making the best of the purchase" to Harry, who "is not well, and is nervous, and could easily be discouraged about it. So please say all the good things you can about it." She asked George and Emily in particular to help in "making Harry satisfied with the place. . . . I feel anxious about it, because Harry is easily unsettled and he is not well enough now to bear worry."[98]

Pope's Hill, the Dorchester home Stone purchased for twenty thousand dollars, looked down on Boston Harbor to the north and westward to the Blue Hills of Milton. It had a seventeen-room house, barns, a carriage house, summer house, stables, orchards, shade trees, and gardens—its extensive grounds as close to Coy's Hill as proximity to a large city allowed. There, Stone would keep horses, cows, and chickens, grow vegetables and fruit, and cultivate an herb garden. "There was a good farmer spoiled when I went into reform," she told Alice. Stone would continue to live at Pope's Hill for the remainder of her life. Blackwell, despite his unsettled nature and his sporadic quests for fame and fortune, would also come to regard Pope's Hill, and Boston, as home.[99]

CHAPTER TEN

"Every Clean Soul"

"We *need* every clean soul to help us, now when such a flood of what is fatal to the peace, and purity of the family, is rolled in on our question."[1]

On the morning of January 11, 1871, Stone was in Worcester, Massachusetts, delivering the keynote address at a suffrage convention—far from Washington, D.C., where a new and devastating blow to woman suffrage was about to fall. If she had been feeling unusually optimistic in the new year, with Blackwell at home, a Beecher at the helm of the National society, and a profit of eight thousand dollars from the bazaar, her outlook would soon darken. In the coming year, woman suffrage, Stanton, Anthony, Tilton, and even the Reverend Henry Ward Beecher would be involved in a tangled web of scandal and intrigue that would have hecklers shouting "Free Love!" at suffrage gatherings for decades to come. The agent of this disaster, Victoria Woodhull, gave woman suffrage opponents their most effective and time-honored weapon—the "proof" that woman's rights was really a call for sexual license. With her free-love advocacy, Woodhull threatened more than the political structure Stone was building; she raised questions about female sexuality in general, questions that challenged Stone's own repressed sexuality. Stone masked her deeply ambivalent feelings by retreating into a neo-Calvinist sexual conservatism.

Though only thirty-three, Victoria Woodhull had already led a full and remarkable life. She had been variously a prostitute, mesmerist, a spiritualist claiming Demosthenes as her medium, quack healer, blackmailer, extortionist, stockbroker, journalist, and, at the time of her entrance into the woman suffrage campaign, a self-proclaimed candidate for president of the United States. At the same time she was dubbed "Mrs. Satan" in a Nast cartoon, and "Queen of the Prostitutes" in the daily papers, Isabella Beecher Hooker described her as a woman whose "motives are exalted and her life pure and her whole nature spiritual in an uncommon degree."[2]

Born to Buck and Roxanna Claflin and raised in squalor, at fifteen Victoria married a morphine-addicted quack doctor, Canning Woodhull, and quickly bore him two children. She and her sister Tennie (Tennessee) grew to be beautiful women, learning early on from their father how to exploit their beauty. Their entanglements with the law were many and varied. Before she was eighteen, Victoria had been charged along with other members of her family with running a bawdy house, with manslaughter, blackmail, adultery, and with numerous other crimes. The family avoided trial by staying one step ahead of the sheriff, moving on as necessary.[3]

Arriving in New York City in the late 1860s, Victoria and Tennie arranged a "magnetic healing session" with Cornelius Vanderbilt, after which he made possible their purchase of a stock brokerage firm on Wall Street and a newspaper, *Woodhull & Claflin's Weekly*. The Claflins' New York house was filled with some twenty-five relatives, among them Canning Woodhull, whom Victoria claimed to have divorced, and her new husband, Colonel James Blood. The Claflin tribe was a roisterous brawling bunch in and out of the city courts, regularly accusing one another of assault, attempted murder, theft, and various other crimes, a circumstance which did not deter a number of powerful men from calling on Woodhull and Tennie. Among these were two men who would influence Woodhull's political and social thinking; they were Congressman Benjamin Butler and Stephen Pearl Andrews, a radical social reformer and free-love advocate.[4]

Shortly after Woodhull's April announcement of her presidential candidacy, she had tried and failed to get the backing of the New York suffragists. Butler arranged for her to testify on behalf of woman suffrage before Congress the day the National convention was to begin in Washington. Woodhull appeared in a plain, dark dress, her curls tucked under a small "alpine hat," her manner of delivery delicate and reticent, "a perceptible tremor in her tones." Her argument—that under the Fourteenth Amendment, women were full citizens and thus entitled to vote—galvanized the suffragists who had gathered in the gallery to hear her speech. Hooker invited her to address the National convention that afternoon. Woodhull told the gathering of suffragists that she had been "assured" privately that her memorial "would be favorably reported, and that the heart of every man in Congress was in the movement." Her audience was understandably excited, and any reservations about Woodhull's motives were swept away by her announced intention to donate ten thousand dollars to the National Association. Stanton, who was not in Washington, wrote warning Anthony not to "have another Train affair with Mrs. Woodhull."[5]

Anthony's biographer, Ida H. Harper, described Woodhull's entrance into the woman suffrage campaign as having "precipitated a storm of criticism compared to which all those that had gone before were as a summer shower to a Missouri cyclone."[6] In the coming years, Stone would come close to despair as she surveyed the damage left in the storm's wake, but the extent of the disaster was not immediately apparent. Though the newspaper response to Woodhull's Washington appearance was immediate and outraged, the furor soon subsided. Higginson made brief mention in the *Woman's Journal* of those who would latch onto the growing strength of the suffrage movement to further their own aims—an obvious reference to Woodhull—but Stone ignored Woodhull in the months after the Washington appearance.

Back from her speaking tour at the end of January, Stone took over the paper from Blackwell, who left on the first of February bound for Santo Domingo, where he "has engaged to write . . . and has also, I believe, an eye to some private speculations there." Blackwell's "speculations" combined bona fide reform aspirations with an investment scheme for purchasing the rights to Samana Bay and, after its annexation, leasing the bay to the United States Navy. He and his fellow investors anticipated a twenty-five-fold return on their original capital.[7]

In Blackwell's absence, Stone attended to the paper and to the steady stream of visitors to her new house. She wrote on March 17: "My house is full. Mr. B's two sisters are here, also Antoinette Brown's two girls— and a young lady who is second cousin to me. Mr. Spofford, wife and child left a week ago . . . I am very busy as you must see.[8]

From Santo Domingo, Blackwell sent regular dispatches to the *Woman's Journal* describing the island and arguing for its immediate annexation. In his letters, Blackwell emphasized that "Only *colonization* by resident American landowners will ever develope [sic] this beautiful island and only the example of American *family life* will ever redeem the country from its present immorality."[9] It seems unlikely that Stone was unaware of Blackwell's financial interest in the venture. If she was untroubled by it, her old friend Charles Sumner was not. On his return in April, Blackwell went immediately to Washington to try to persuade Sumner to end his opposition in the Senate to the plan for annexation. When Sumner charged Blackwell with being guilty of "mental and moral obliquity" in connection with the annexation scheme, Blackwell responded somewhat disingenuously that "Neither Dr. Howe nor myself own a foot of land or a dollar's worth of pecuniary interest, present or prospective" in the matter of Dominican annexation."[10]

"Immorality" of a different sort was much on Stone's mind that spring. Though the Woodhull issue appeared to be fading, and despite Hooker's promise to stay clear of side issues, Stone remained wary. When Mary Livermore suggested that this might be a good time to reconsider union with the New York women, Stone urged caution. "I think it so much better, for us to keep clear of other organizations at least, till they prove, that their work is good," she wrote, urging a mutual friend to write Livermore to suggest "that it seems best to you, not to strike hands, with those people at Washington. They were our late enemies. We don't know that they are our friends . . . it is easier to stop a small leak than a great hole."[11]

Hooker's name appeared alone on the cautiously worded call promising to "confine" discussions at the May NWSA convention to the "Constitutional right of women to citizenship and suffrage." Stone published the call with the AWSA's in the *Woman's Journal*. Unbeknownst to either Hooker or Stone, the "small leak" was already on its way to becoming "a great hole." The extent of the damage would reveal itself slowly over the next two years.

Throughout April, Stone published the call to both American and National conventions. The tone of the paper that spring was upbeat; even the rapid growth of an Anti–Woman Suffrage organization failed to shake Stone's optimism. She described the opposition's growth as a tribute to the rapid spread of woman suffrage sentiment.[12] Looking back over the previous year's work, Stone had cause for satisfaction. Woman suffrage proposals were under legislative consideration in nearly every eastern, northern, and western state, and despite repeated defeats, they drew larger average votes each year. Women were enfranchised in both Utah and Wyoming. Over fifty new county societies and five new state societies had been organized in Massachusetts alone. Stone and Livermore had been accredited party delegates; the Sixteenth Amendment was reintroduced in Congress, and the bill to grant woman suffrage in the District of Columbia had made a good legislative showing. With paid subscriptions to the *Woman's Journal* nearing five thousand, and with the public memory of Train and the anti–Fifteenth Amendment campaign fast fading, Stone had reason to hope for continued progress.

Woodhull's attempt in the months following her January appearance to present her *Weekly* as "*the* Woman Suffrage paper of the country" was troubling, as was Stanton's public embrace of Woodhull following their meeting in New York. Still, Stanton was officially retired from woman suffrage work, and Anthony was away in the West. Stone continued to urge *Journal* readers to come to New York for the May meetings, trusting the Beecher sensibility to keep the "loose and pestiferous" at bay. What neither she nor Hooker knew was that through a slip of Stanton's tongue, Victoria Woodhull was in possession of a piece of gossip concerning

Theodore Tilton's wife Elizabeth and the Reverend Henry Ward Beecher, AWSA icon of respectability. As convention time neared, Woodhull pondered how best to make use of the weapon Stanton had unwittingly placed in her hands.[13]

Happily unaware of all this, Stone arrived in New York early in May. New York City buzzed with revelations of Tammany Hall corruption; Boss Tweed had just been sentenced to a year in jail. Alfred Beach's underground pneumatic tube whisked astonished passengers under Broadway's traffic-choked streets. Above ground, crowding and poverty had reached such epidemic proportions that in some sections of town, men were harnessed to pull carts and trolleys. Across the bridge in Brooklyn, immense crowds flocked to see P. T. Barnum's "Greatest Show on Earth," and on Sundays, thousands crowded into Plymouth Church to hear the Reverend Henry Ward Beecher preach.[14]

On the morning of May 10, Stone opened the AWSA meeting in Steinway Hall before a crowd of two thousand. Beside her on the platform sat the full panoply of reform greats. She enumerated the great gains of the past year in a speech punctuated by cheers, avoiding any mention of the rival association. The National Association had received an advertising boost from that day's *New York Tribune* with its bold headline—"Woman Suffrage and Free Love." Greeley expressed his outrage that "The people who 'work with and for' Mrs. Woodhull, new leader of the Woman Suffrage party, Woman Suffrage candidate for the Presidency and editor of *Woodhull & Claflin's Weekly,* are to meet in National convention tomorrow." He demanded an explanation from the New York suffragists.[15]

Greeley's headline eclipsed the news of the large and successful AWSA convention and heightened interest in the rival organization's proceedings. Despite her avowed resignation from woman suffrage work, Stanton had allowed Anthony to persuade her to attend. When some New York suffrage leaders refused to sit on the same platform with Woodhull, Stanton placed her between herself and Mott, but New York audiences proved less susceptible to Woodhull's charms. Gone were the tremulous voice and modest demeanor which had won her Washington listeners. Instead, Woodhull's peroration warned that if women did not get the vote in the next legislative session, "We mean treason! We are plotting Revolution! We will overthrow this bogus government."[16]

Following what immediately came to be known as "The Woodhull Convention," membership in the NWSA fell off so drastically that for the duration of 1871 and 1872, its leaders were able to hold "only parlor meetings." Members withdrew and formed separate suffrage organizations. Most of the New York women reorganized as the New York Central Woman Suffrage Association, an organization claiming over six hundred members. The Connecticut Woman Suffrage Association, led by Olympia Brown, severed its tie to the NWSA and declared itself an independent society resolving to work *"only* for the elective franchise." In Iowa, Pennsylvania, Maryland, and Washington, resolutions were passed disavowing any tie to the Woodhull organization.[17] The emotional response of women to Woodhull was astonishing. A letter to the *New York Tribune* from a "Mrs. G.C.M." summed up the feelings of many women: "I blush to think I am a woman. How long, in the name of common sense, are we to permit the vampires to suck our very heart's blood before we rise in our might and force the slimy things back where they belong? If every good and true woman would but come forward and give her verdict against such foul libels, it could not help but have a good effect. Why won't they do it?"[18]

Stone's hopes that Woodhull's name would disappear from the press faded as the following days' papers were filled with new Woodhull woes. Woodhull's mother filed charges against Colonel Blood, Woodhull's second husband, claiming that he had threatened to murder her, further titillating the public by testifying under oath that Victoria was never divorced from her first husband. Woodhull's angry response, a paid notice in the *New York World,* was defensive. "I advocate Free Love in its highest, purest sense," she wrote, promising to publish the names of those who "preach against free love openly, practise it secretly."[19] The next day, Woodhull summoned Tilton to her home and set in motion a chain of events which culminated in the longest-running and most famous trial of the nineteenth century, one that would link woman suffrage and free love for decades to come.[20]

Avoiding Woodhull's name, Stone acknowledged an awareness of the growing threat she posed in a *Journal* editorial, in which she observed that woman suffrage had reached "that stage of growth in the development of our ideas where two things become true":

First—Our enemies cease to attack our principles. But instead, they strive to create prejudice against the cause itself by exposing the weakness, folly or wickedness of individuals who, for any reason, have attached themselves to the movement.

Second—Unscrupulous persons, who have their own 'axes to grind' who are far more for other theories than for Woman Suffrage, attempt to forward these theories, and to ride into public favor by making use of the large sympathy which the justice and truth of our claim have won.

Stone advised readers "to waste no time in defense or attack of either of these classes of our real or practical enemies."[21] Her directive underscored her naïveté. Greeley's powerful animosity, the rise of sensationalism in the press, and Woodhull's own ambition would demand a response.

Greeley kept up his attacks on woman suffrage and free love throughout the summer and autumn. Occasionally, Stone reprinted Tilton's pro–
woman suffrage rejoinders from the *Golden Age,* but as that journal grew
more radical, the *Woman's Journal* became more censorious. Blackwell
accused his former friend of aligning himself with the "half-a-dozen restless men and women, perverted by the poisonous social malaria of a great
city," who sought to link woman's rights with their "wild and visionary"
theories.[22]

Stone let Blackwell address the subject in the paper, her own silence
both strategic and an indication of her profound unease and disgust when
presented with a woman who would insist upon her right to sexual grati-
fication. Nothing in Stone's experience had prepared her for a woman
who not only openly claimed to enjoy sex, but who justified the use of sex
and blackmail. Stone's battle for the right to say "no" to sex; her argument for abstinence as a form of birth control; her "revulsions of feeling"
about sex and insistence upon a celibate relationship in the early months
of her marriage suggest a denial of women's sexuality that went beyond
Victorian prudery. Whether abuse or trauma in her childhood contributed
to these feelings is necessarily conjecture.

Although she was approaching her fifty-third birthday, Stone regarded
sex with the black-and-white convictions of a young girl: restraint was
virtue; indulgence, vice. Retaining a schoolgirl's belief as well in the
inevitable triumph of virtue, Stone was confident of her ability to outlast
Woodhull. Meanwhile, the Anti-Woman Suffrage Committee pointed
gleefully at Woodhull as "proof" of the deleterious effects of the claim to
suffrage. Though Stanton, Anthony, Hooker, and the NWSA would all
repudiate Woodhull within the year, the damage had been done.[23]

Stone wrote naïvely to her friend Rebecca Janney, "The Woodhull &
Claflin tribe are a real curse, but they only make a temporary nuisance."[24]
Harriet Beecher Stowe wrote Higginson that "the Boston women have
only now to be quiet, patient, firm, and discreet and they may save the
cause."[25] They had not reckoned with the popular press, nor with the
public's delight in the "free-love and woman suffrage" debacle. Toward
summer's end, Greeley wrote in disgust that his "conception of the nature
and scope of the marriage relation" made his conversion to woman suffrage "a moral impossibility." Stone pleaded with Greeley in the *Woman's
Journal* to stop identifying the cause with a few outspoken adherents,
protesting that to do so "overlooks the fact that the great body of woman
suffrage *withdrew from all affiliation with these persons* two years ago,
on account of their connection of these views with suffrage." For Stone,
the wisdom of her separatist move was clear. As for her contention that
the majority of suffragists had withdrawn from any connection with the

New York association, by the end of 1871, fourteen of the fifteen state suffrage societies had voted to become auxiliaries to the AWSA.[26]

Stone's plea to newspapermen not to overlook the great majority went unheeded. Propriety, no matter how numerous or decorous its adherents, was not news, and Woodhull was. Later that summer, *Woodhull & Claflin's Weekly* outraged almost everyone with a poem describing Jesus having sex with Mary Magdalene in the Garden of Gethsemane while the apostles slept. One editor seized on the poem as an example of "the utter rottenness and daring impiety . . . of the Woman's Rights Movement." Again, letters protesting the innocence of the majority of suffragists were lost in outraged public sensibility.[27]

Having argued publicly and persistently that woman suffrage would purify politics, Stone was chagrined and frustrated. To aid in countering the publicity, she arranged through the Massachusetts branch of the AWSA to hire two more paid lecture agents/political organizers—Ada Bowles and Mary Eastman. Along with Margaret Campbell, they set up some twenty to thirty meetings each week in cities and towns throughout New England. The strength and power of this campaign was unprecedented. Had it not been followed by the wholesale retreat following the Beecher-Tilton trial, it might have entered the annals of political history as a model of political organization.[28]

"We intend to continue a system of suffrage meetings during the entire fall, winter, and spring," Stone wrote in September. She appeared at major organizing conventions, but much of her work that fall consisted of correspondence aimed at increasing attendance at the series of meetings preceding the November anniversary in Philadelphia and of the work of getting up the paper week after week.[29]

Putting out the *Journal* was a heavy chore. Stone likened it to caring for "a big baby which never grew up, and always had to be fed." Although Livermore's official withdrawal was not announced until December 1871, she was away lecturing for much of that fall. Blackwell agreed to take on more of the editorial writing, but it was Stone on whom the real work of the paper devolved. Her initials appeared only occasionally under a column, but the news that filled its pages and the causes it championed were hers. She wrote against subsistence wages for women, denounced the working conditions of sewing women, assailed those who paid inadequate wages to servant girls in the guise of "benevolence," and campaigned for pure food laws, for a national department of education, and for equal pay for women teachers.[30]

The *Journal* published short works of fiction by some of the most widely read authors of the time. Bret Harte, Elizabeth Stuart Phelps, Harriet Beecher Stowe, and Lydia Maria Child's stories appeared in the

Woman's Journal as a means of piquing reader interest. The paper also furnished a running legislative record of votes on suffrage proposals and printed the replies of legislative candidates to the woman suffrage canvass. Occasionally, it treated topical items, such as eyewitness accounts by midwestern correspondents of the great Chicago fire.[31]

In October, the *Journal* began publishing the call to the second AWSA anniversary convention. Stone's growing alarm and her personal repugnance can be read in the letters she sent to suffrage leaders begging them to make a special effort to attend the Philadelphia meeting. Her letter to clergyman-suffragist John K. Wildman shows her sense of urgency: "We *need* every clean soul to help us, now when such a flood of what is fatal to the peace, and purity of the family, is rolled in on our question . . . my one wish in regard to Mrs. Woodhull is, that [neither] she nor her ideas, may be so much as heard of at our meeting."[32]

Throughout the new crisis, Stone juggled domestic and official chores with perfectionist and punctilious care. Alice described her mother's insistence upon retaining control of every aspect of life at Pope's Hill. She supervised the care of the livestock, "dried all the herbs and put up all the fruits in their season. She made her own yeast, her own bread, her own dried beef, even her own soap." She also continued to welcome any and all members of the Stone and Blackwell clans, a hospitality her emotionally distant sisters-in-law did not always appreciate.[33]

Late in October, Stone left on a round of preconvention appearances that took her to various towns in New York and Rhode Island. She stopped in Boston only long enough to see to the *Journal* and to details of the upcoming bazaar before leaving for Philadelphia. Arriving there, Stone was dismayed to learn that Woodhull had hired distributors to give out tracts and copies of *Woodhull & Claflin's Weekly* outside the hall. Stone paid a group of small boys to collect and dispose of the unwanted literature.[34]

Inside the Philadelphia hall, delegates assembled from states as far away as California to hear the speeches and pass resolutions promising that enfranchising women would guarantee "equality in the home" and "greater purity, constancy and permanence in marriage." Greeley commented wryly that the Philadelphia meetings seemed "bent on a sort of purification within the suffrage ranks," an accurate assessment of the suffrage leaders' intentions.[35]

As the respectability pageant played itself out in Philadelphia, Woodhull was addressing an overflow crowd in New York on "The Principles of Social Freedom Involving the Question of Free Love, Marriage, Divorce, and Prostitution." A reluctant Tilton had been blackmailed into introducing her. After Woodhull's speech, a voice shouted from the rear, "Are you a free lover?"

"Yes! I am a free lover!" Woodhull responded. "I have an inalienable, constitutional, and natural right to love whom I may, to love as long or as short a period as I can, to change that love every day if I please!" Pandemonium broke out, and reporters rushed to file their stories. The riot that followed caused Steinway Hall's proprietors to refuse Woodhull the future use of the hall.[36]

The press pillorying that followed stung Woodhull into promising to reveal the "truth" about the "Free Lovers of Boston . . . and the Free Lusters . . . who affiliate with the Boston branch of the Suffrage movement."[37] Woodhull was in great demand in the weeks following her riotous meeting. Tilton's public appearance with Woodhull and a fulsome "biography" of her crediting him as author had the opposite effect on his career. Subscribers and patrons retreated from the *Golden Age*; his lecture engagements fell off, and he fell deeper into debt.[38]

In Pittsburgh, Stone and Blackwell learned of Woodhull's speech in a newspaper headlined: "Died of Free Love, November 25th In Steinway Hall the Woman Suffrage Movement."[39] Though the reports of its demise were premature, attendance was declining. To heighten interest, Stone spoke more often than she had in years. The grand finale to her lecture tour took place in Washington on December 8 and 9. There, Stone, Howe, Higginson, Livermore, and others argued the suffrage cause before an audience that included a number of powerful congressmen. Once again, Woodhull had arranged for the distribution of free-love tracts at the door and in the hall, prompting the Reverend James Freeman Clarke to make a public statement disclaiming any connection of the American Association to the offending tracts.[40]

On their way home, Stone and Blackwell stopped in New York, where a telegram awaited telling them that their house at Pope's Hill had burned the previous evening. "Sheer carelessness and an improper flue" had caused the fire, Blackwell wrote. He berated the servants "imbecility" in handling the fire—adding that Alice had flung silver, valuables, and other items from various windows and had forgotten to gather them all up again.[41]

A weary Stone suggested that they sell the land and what remained of the house and move closer to the offices of the *Woman's Journal* in Boston, but Blackwell had other plans. "I hesitated long and decided deliberately and somewhat reluctantly [to rebuild]," Blackwell wrote, ignoring Stone's wishes and treating both property (Stone's) and decision as if they were his alone. "Indeed, I can sell off the lower part of the lot if I wish and thus diminish the expense." While the rebuilding went on, the family moved into a smaller house on the property.[42]

In response to a letter from Nettie early in 1872 asking who actually was the editor of the *Journal,* Stone answered, "Harry! but he means to go to Santo Domingo next month, and then I shall edit it." Stone dreaded the prospect, having little confidence in her journalistic ability. However, she encouraged Blackwell in his plan to spend the rest of the winter in the Caribbean. Alice collaborated in the domestic double standard that saw her father as sadly overworked—"Papa looks so tired and worn that I think I should cry if I didn't feel so much like swearing"—and her mother as "getting to be just like Aunt Sarah, snarling all the time."[43]

Blackwell left again for Santo Domingo, leaving Stone to supervise plasterers, painters, carpenters, masons, and plumbers, as well as with the chore of selecting new furniture and household goods, running the paper, and managing the political and fund-raising campaign. Alice also required time and effort, as her diary for the month shows. Stone nursed Alice through a lengthy illness, took her to the city to shop for dress material, sat with her evenings to quiz her on her history lessons, and taught her how to sew linings into her dresses. If it occurred to Alice to question her father's leaving her mother to deal alone with the post-fire confusion, the newspaper, the family, and a frantic pace of public and private appearances, her diary does not mention it.[44] Stone's letters of the period betray no resentment.

As he prepared to sail from New York, Blackwell wrote, "I think of you as tired and worried and feel ashamed not to be helping you." Stone responded: "The Journal has gone on very well. I am so glad to find that I can do it. Now you shall never have the drudgery of it again. I never wanted you to, and always felt that it was too bad that my work should burden & chafe your shoulders, but I did not know how to prevent it. You shall be as free Harry darling, when you come home, as you have always needed to be."[45]

Not only was she willing to absolve Blackwell from any guilt over leaving, Stone was willing to take the blame for every troubling aspect of their relationship, writing,

When you are back, I want you to feel that you are not *bound* and *limited* by this place, and by us. You NEED change, variety, sunshine and birds. I have not always known it. But now that I DO know it, it shall not be my fault if you do not have all the freedom and variety you want. We will both of us, give you the warmest welcome when you choose to stay with us, and we will cheerfully second any of your plans that give you the larger sphere your nature needs. . . . so Harry darling, here is a kiss for you, and larger love than often falls to the lot of any man, either to have or to endure."[46]

Between the lines of this letter are all the insecurities and self-loathing that Stone had carried through the years. She saw herself as confining, narrow, dark—her love a thing to be endured. Endlessly bent upon build-ing a better Lucy Stone so as not to suffer his criticism and withdrawal, she had come to expect more and more of herself and less and less of Blackwell, and to see the job of keeping their marriage afloat as hers. At some deep level, Stone continued to see herself as the woman with a face that "kept off the sparks"—as the child unworthy of being petted and "trotted" on her father's knee, and as a woman scorned for one who was younger, prettier, more charming. Alice would say of her mother that she was "unduly lacking in self-esteem," and Stone's relationship with Blackwell bears this out.[47] Still, if it occurred to her in times of repose that her marriage was a disappointment, it was also true that she continued to love this mercurial and inconstant man.

As the May meetings approached, Stone sent out the usual barrage of imploring letters. She had learned from Blackwell in a letter written before his departure of Woodhull's plans to hold "a grand political convention & make a Presidential nomination" at the May NWSA meeting.[48] Anthony, who was traveling in the West, was "thunderstruck" to find her name signed to the call to the Woodhull nominating convention and wrote imploring Stanton not to proceed with such folly, but neither Stanton nor Hooker would be dissuaded. Both American and National associations convened on the same day that year, the AWSA meeting with self-conscious decorum in Apollo Hall, while across town, the NWSA drew a crowd to its proceedings in Steinway Hall.

Anthony had returned in time to quash the resolutions which would have led to Woodhull's nomination. When Woodhull attempted to speak anyhow, Anthony ordered the janitor to douse the gaslights. She too had come to regard Woodhull as disastrous, and that evening she noted in her diary: "A sad day for me; all came near to being lost. Our ship was so nearly stranded by leaving the helm to others, that we rescued it only by a hair's breadth."[49]

The New York suffragists' final disenchantment grew out of Woodhull's extortion campaign, a desperate attempt to keep her newspaper afloat that spring, by attempting to blackmail certain suffragists. She used dummy copies of the front page of her paper containing detailed allegations of sexual indiscretions, demanding five hundred dollars to keep her from printing. She tried this with many suffragists, among them Elizabeth Phelps, Laura Curtis Bullard, Lillie Devereaux Blake, and even Anthony herself.[50] Some of Woodhull's victims paid, believing that it was easier to destroy a reputation than it was to restore one, but their "contributions" were inadequate, and on June 22, 1872, the paper folded, and the doors to Woodhull's brokerage firm closed.[51]

Stone welcomed the news of Woodhull's departure, publishing a brief report in the *Journal* about the "unsuccessful attempt to displace Mrs. Stanton in the control of the convention." She hoped that now "they have got rid of the 'Free Love' incubus which has done incalculable harm to the cause of Woman Suffrage."[52] Both wings of the suffrage party considered the Woodhull chapter concluded. "A more stupendous fraud than Mrs. Woodhull never lived," Mary Livermore wrote a friend in the weeks after the convention, "Lying, blackmailing and Heaven only knows what else were charged upon her." She added that she hoped that with Woodhull gone, the differences keeping the two suffrage wings apart would disappear. "At any time, you may read of us all in convention together."[53]

Livermore's optimism was premature. In the weeks following Woodhull's departure, a surprising political development brought the two sides closer. National politics had taken a peculiar turn in 1872. The Republican party found itself sharply divided on a number of issues, among these allegations of widespread corruption in the Grant administration, and a group of reformers calling itself the Liberal Republicans broke ranks and formed a separate party, nominating Horace Greeley as presidential candidate. Rumors that the Democratic party would coalesce with the splinter group and endorse Greeley spurred mainstream Republicans to look for ways to consolidate remaining strength. The growing size of the woman suffrage movement and its public endorsement by such influential and wealthy Republicans as Curtis, Beecher, Higginson, and Phillips made courting it politically attractive.[54]

Blackwell had gone to the Philadelphia Republican convention early in June. On June 5, he wrote Stone that he had lobbied the various members and succeeded in getting Gerritt Smith to agree to help pass the woman suffrage plank. With Smith's backing, Blackwell succeeded at last in getting the Republicans to include a carefully worded and less-than-wholehearted promise of "respectful consideration" of the woman suffrage question as the fourteenth plank in its platform.[55] Anthony was also at the Republican convention, and Blackwell reported that she was "in a very reasonable mood." Blackwell enclosed a letter to Stone from Stanton that Anthony had given him, commenting how "glad of its kindly tone" he was.[56]

Stanton, obviously chastened by the experience with Woodhull, was conciliatory. She confessed to feeling more discouraged than at any time in their long fight, citing as the causes, "the nomination of Greeley, the impudence of Tilton, and the dissensions of our friends," avoiding any mention of Woodhull. She would continue to be defensive about Woodhull, writing that "All the agitation has helped in some way. The free love scare has made suffrage respectable."[57] She asked Stone to agree to let "bygones be bygones. Let all personalities be buried in the work that is before us."[58]

Soon after receiving her letter, Stone resumed printing Stanton's articles and furnishing reports of her speeches on the woman suffrage plank. Still, it was Blackwell and not Stone who carried on the summer's correspondence with Stanton and Anthony regarding plans for the upcoming presidential campaign.[59]

Returning from a brief vacation at Coy's Hill, Stone found a letter from Susan B. Anthony asking if the two associations could "cooperate and make a systematic campaign covering the whole ground" that autumn. Anthony asked if Stone "will be able to go into the campaign," adding in a lengthy postscript:

Lucy, who of us dreamed twenty years ago that we should live to see this recognition of our cause? I can hardly believe my senses. Verily the harvest is ripe, and God help *us* all now to go into the fields and reap the full grain in the ear.
Dear Lucy, Will you come to Rochester for the 17th. . . . it would *settle the question that we are all together as one grand woman* in this campaign.[60]

Stone, heavily involved in organizing mass rallies of the Republican women of Massachusetts, declined the invitation. Whether it was dislike, distrust, or the press of work that lay behind Stone's refusal is impossible to determine, but the result was the final alienation of Anthony. Certainly the political task Stone had set herself that fall was demanding. She hoped to display the potential for political power of women by orchestrating demonstrations involving half a million Republican women throughout New England.

On September 25, an audience of four thousand crowded into Boston's Tremont Temple, and that many more were turned away from the already overcrowded hall. Stone called the meeting to order with "unusual pleasure," rejoicing in the woman suffrage plank and saying that "new power, and stronger arms than ours today proffer us help." She likened her audience to "an army marching to victory," having "captured one stronghold after another," and went on to enumerate their gains. She drew a great laugh by telling how twenty years before, after one of her speeches, a young man wrote to ask if her speech had been written by Horace Greeley. Finally, she cheered the women on by noting that the force of the "political machinery" would "remove obstacles with far greater despatch" than they themselves could hope to do.[61] Stone's affiliation with Republicans drew scores of angry letters from *Journal* readers, many of whom had chosen to back Greeley and the Liberal Republicans and who now reminded Stone of her earlier insistence that the *"Woman's Journal* is not a party organ." In keeping with this policy, Stone regularly printed articles both for and against both candidates throughout the summer and fall.[62]

All but buried in the political news that September was a groundbreaking article by Stone headed "Wives and Money." In it, she regretted that wives were forced to *"ask"* their husbands for even the use of their own earnings after marriage. For those who had given up their careers and the chance to earn their own money, "custom everywhere, and the law in many places, puts all the money of the family in the hands of the husband," Stone wrote disapprovingly. She depicted the humiliation of forcing wives to beg for money, giving examples and concluding: "Sometime, the law will recognize the undoubted right of the wife to her full share of the money value which accrues to the marriage firm. . . . the great majority of married couples bear each their natural share of the family burden, care, and toil, and they should be alike independent in money matters."[63]

The right of a wife to shared money in "the marriage firm" was a revolutionary idea. In her own household, the tables were reversed. Blackwell hoped to raise twenty thousand dollars by borrowing and cashing in on what he termed the "securities and mortgages" which "Lucy and I have" to invest in the Santo Domingo project.[64] At the same time, Stone wrote that she was probably going to have to give up the *Woman's Journal* for lack of funds. Nettie wrote back immediately, pledging twenty-five dollars and advising Stone to "Beg or borrow but do push on through the year somehow." Stone worried aloud that they "were all coming to poverty," and Alice commented cheerfully in her diary that "I know how to empty slops, and if worst comes to worst, I can probably get a situation as a chambermaid."[65]

Stone and Blackwell apparently disagreed about whether the Santo Domingo investment was "theirs" or "his." When Harry contacted George about selling some of Stone's Montclair, New Jersey, properties, she wrote George for help in deterring him. Afterwards, she thanked George for his assistance in helping "Harry see what is the proper thing to do." Stone intended to hold her Montclair land, which paid a good rent and continued to appreciate in value. "I am so glad I have that nice little nest egg," she wrote to George. "You and I shall be the landlords of the family."[66]

Despite Stone's "poor fever," she employed a housekeeper and a "girl," and she continued to fill Pope's Hill with friends and guests. When Blackwell was not away, they paid calls and entertained, enjoying afternoon visits and dinner parties with the Garrisons, Howes, Welds, and Campbells and the many others in their wide circle of friends. Stone took Alice into Boston on shopping trips, and they went together to see the noted actress Charlotte Cushman perform. Alice reported afterward, "Mamma fairly shrieked out with laughter."[67]

The *Woman's Journal* too went along its usual course. If its existence was imperiled, its appearance was healthy. A good portion of its pages that autumn were filled with correspondence and articles about the impending election, including a number by Stanton. On November 2, at Stone's invitation, Stanton and her daughter Hattie drove out from Boston to spend the night at Pope's Hill. In her diary, Alice described Stanton, "a pleasant, short, excessively fat little old lady with white curls, and her daughter Hattie, who had come out in special compliment to me, and whom I was therefore expected to entertain."[68]

On the day of Stanton's arrival at Pope's Hill, *Woodhull & Claflin's Weekly* appeared again on the stands. Woodhull was able to resume its publication following a successful fund-raising trip to Boston, after which Boston papers reported receiving thirty letters from readers complaining that Woodhull had attempted to blackmail them. The November 2 issue of the *Weekly* was intended to convince those who had been reluctant to pay that Woodhull intended to make good on her threats. The paper contained two scandalous articles and a warning that "We have five hundred biographies of various persons in all circles of life, . . . the facts of which biographies are similar to those presented in this article."

The lead article concerned the Reverend Henry Ward Beecher, described as a man of "immense physical potency" whose "indomitable urgency" was strengthened by his "amative impulse," thereby leading him to conduct numerous extramarital affairs with his parishioners, including a long-running affair with Elizabeth Tilton. So sensational was the impact of the charge against Beecher, and so rapidly did the word spread, that the entire first printing of the *Weekly* sold out within minutes. Copies commanded up to forty dollars apiece, and newsboys and carriages waiting for a second edition created gridlock on lower Broad Street.[69] The paper also gave remarkably graphic details of the sexual misconduct of Luther Challis, a Brooklyn stockbroker. Woodhull was arrested under the newly enacted Comstock Law and thrown into the Ludlow Street jail. Challis's response was a libel suit, while Beecher tried to ride out the storm of publicity.[70]

Readers of the *Woman's Journal* found nary a mention of Woodhull in the week after the bombshell. Stone wrote instead of "Woman's Victory" in the presidential election. "The Women of America have won their first political battle" by taking "half a million votes from Horace Greeley" and delivering them to Grant and the Republicans, Stone wrote. Although her public tone was upbeat and congratulatory, private letters betray the worry that the allegations against Beecher had caused Stone and her fellow suffragists. Elizabeth Churchill wrote that she had succeeded in "landing" four clergymen to speak at an upcoming state convention "because their speeches and presence will go far to counteract the dreadful influence of the last Woodhull scrape."[71]

Stone was especially grateful that year for the American Association's plan of holding conventions in different regions of the country. St. Louis, the site of the convention, was far from New York City, where the Woodhull tempest raged with no promise of abatement. The *Journal* urged its readers to be present at the third anniversary convention on November 20 and 21. As she boarded the train in Boston bound for St. Louis, Stone could only hope that suffrage workers preparing to depart from various locations around the country could outface the humiliation of having its former president charged with gross sexual misconduct.

En route to the convention, Stone was stranded in a blizzard, which caused her to miss the opening ceremony. Arriving on the second day, she addressed the gathered delegates, reminding them of the many gains of the preceding year. Avoiding any mention of scandal or of the pounding woman suffrage was taking in the press, Stone asked the women in her audience to rejoice in the victory of the Republicans at the polls that month and to see each of the five hundred thousand votes cast for Grant as a vote for woman suffrage. The "final hour of victory could not be far away," she told the women with the silvery ring of conviction that had come to be her hallmark. Whether Republicans might also have believed in the political advantage of support for woman suffrage following the immense fall demonstrations and subsequent victory was made moot by the public outcry that followed revelation of the Beecher-Tilton scandal. There was little likelihood that any party would touch the hot potato of free love, and there was now no question but that woman suffrage and free love were connected in the public mind. One editorialist described the irrationality of the public response to the Woodhull alliance, regretting the injustice to "hundred of thousands of honest men and pure women earnestly in favor of the reform to say that they were following at the leadstring of the notorious female, Mrs. Woodhull and her gushing lover and eulogist, Theodore Tilton." Nonetheless, the writer put his finger squarely on the problem in his conclusion that despite the unreason of linking the majority of suffragists to free love, "five out of six people think so, and cannot be led to think anything else."[72] And, there was no escaping the fact that Beecher, the accused adulterer, had been president of the AWSA; while Tilton had led the Union society, and Victoria Woodhull called herself the "woman suffrage candidate" for president.[73]

All across the country, in the weeks following the Woodhull bombshell, woman suffragists struggled to keep the political question of suffrage afloat in the immense outpouring of public outrage that focused on woman's rights as the cause of the scandal. From Ohio, suffrage workers reported that "'free love' (whatever it may mean) is the most efficient agent employed to frighten people from our ranks." The Des Moines *Register* headlined its woman suffrage report "Halt in Progress of Woman

Suffrage." Indeed, throughout the country, support at the state and local level evaporated rapidly. Formerly friendly legislators advised woman suffragists that in the "current free-love storm" it would be best to table woman suffrage legislation. If it was irrational, the storm against the suffragists was also "continual."[74]

Stone was confronted by reports from suffrage agents of canceled appearances and lecture halls closed to woman suffrage. The publicity storm raged on and on, whipped to fury by the continuing revelations, charges, allegations, and snippets that Woodhull eagerly fed the waiting press from her cell in the Ludlow jail. In the meantime, in New York, woman suffrage's former friend and more recently its most powerful foe, Horace Greeley, died on November 29, 1872. The *Woman's Journal* paid him an eloquent tribute, praising him as "one of the noblest, most generous and humane of men" who was lamentably "betrayed into an antagonism" to woman suffrage by those who advocated "loose and immoral theories which would impair the sanctity and permanence of marriage."[75]

The "sanctity and permanence of marriage" had become one of the main themes of the *Woman's Journal,* as had the campaign to eradicate the "social evil." In its sharpened focus on issues of purity, chastity, and moral elevation, the *Journal* reflected the headlong rush of women into activities that set them apart from the goings-on in New York, and even from innocent parties to the scandal, among these Anthony. Olympia Brown told of making arrangements for a meeting of a woman's club, Sorosis, in the midst of the scandal: "Everything at this meeting was to be absolutely correct. Susan B. Anthony was not on the program, and a guard was stationed at the door lest Mrs. Woodhull, against whom popular prejudice was then at its height, should appear."[76]

More than a decade later, the editors of a prestigious journal, the *Nation,* directly attributed the subsequent rapid decline of suffrage sentiment to the scandal, writing that the movement for woman suffrage

received a severe blow from the figure cut by many of its leading supporters in the Tilton-Beecher scandal and by the adhesion of Victoria Woodhull and some other women of her kind. From this it can hardly be said ever to have recovered. Reformers who were at all squeamish about the company they kept began to fight shy of it, and it came to have in the eyes of the general public the air of being the first stage on the road to something in the nature of "free love." In fact if it were not for the greater respectability of the Associations in Massachusetts and the adoption of woman suffrage in some of the extreme western territories, the movement would have kept itself alive here with great difficulty.[77]

The defection even of formerly staunch supporters cut deeply into existing suffrage ranks as well as into the drive to recruit and organize new members. Proprietors would not rent their halls to suffragists, and even twenty years later, as suffragists posted notices of their meetings, it was not unusual to hear some man shout across the street to another, "Are you going to hear Woodhull tonight?" A Vermont suffragist insisted that the Woodhull matter "set the cause back twenty years," and that country people persisted in thinking as late as 1889 that women wanted suffrage "for free love." Decades would pass before another woman suffrage plank would find its way into a national political platform.[78]

There was no optimistic summary of progress in Stone's year-end message in the *Journal*. Despite her original elation over the Republican victory, and notwithstanding the suffrage legislation before nearly every state and the ever-wider circulation of the *Woman's Journal,* Stone now realized that no amount of counter-publicity could remove the connection in the public mind of free-loveism and woman suffrage. Sensing her depression, Nettie pressed her to come to New Jersey and spend Christmas with the family, but Stone was unwilling to leave the helm to others for even so short a visit. Stone's refuge was work.[79]

Antoinette Brown Blackwell, who had been in semiretirement as she raised her five daughters, was ready to return to public activity. She wrote asking Stone if she would agree to take her daughter Edith for six months, hoping to free herself and perhaps to distract and occupy Stone. Stone made Edith's wardrobe, enrolled her in school, helped with her lessons in the evenings, and taught her to sew.[80] Over the next two decades, Nettie's daughters moved in and out of the Pope's Hill house with easy regularity, an arrangement that appeared to please everyone. Stone loved having the children around her. Both she and Blackwell had a warmth that endeared them to their nieces and nephews. The children recalled their lengthy stays in Boston as treasured memories. Throughout her life, Kitty Barry, Elizabeth's ward, would refer to her adoptive mother as "Doctor," and to her Blackwell aunts as "Miss Ellen" and "Dr. Emily," but Lucy Stone was "Mamma" and Harry Blackwell was "Papa" to her, just as they were to Ellen's adopted daughter "Neenie." One of Stone's nieces told of the "motherly way and sweet voice" that encouraged them to unburden themselves to Aunt Lucy, who packed them "abundant lunches," told them stories by the hour, and made learning household tasks enjoyable. One of her nieces described how they "used to run races with the stockings, each taking one, and finishing at almost the same moment. Aunt Lucy so arranged it that she always came out just ahead, so that I always had something to strive for."[81]

When Ellen's ward proved too hard for Ellen to handle, she was packed off to Aunt Lucy, and Stone took over full care of the child, paying for her schooling. The house on Pope's Hill was generally filled to bursting with suffrage workers and family members, and Stone insisted upon having it so. Domestic help was difficult to find and keep, and her correspondence through the years was peppered with references to servant women coming and going, despite the fact that Stone treated the servants with the same kindness she showered on her family. Alice wrote an amusing account of a servant who regularly got drunk on her days off in Boston. On the return trip to Dorchester, the servant would loudly extol the virtues of Stone, praising her "outrageously." Alice confided to her cousin Kitty, "Now to be praised out of all reason by an abominably drunk woman on the steam cars you know isn't to one's credit."[82]

A neighbor, Florence Adkinson, wrote that "few knew how far-reaching" Lucy Stone's generosity was. "Flowers and fruits were sent from her garden, boxes of clothing went West, North, and south, a host of women who came to her in distress were helped to work or tided over hard places. She gave freely, and every gift was accompanied by thoughtful care and heart-warmth." Adkinson told of the many children, large and small, who "went from her presence strengthened, helped, and encouraged, to whom she was like a mother."[83]

Stone's gifts carried over as well into her work with the young suffrage workers, many of whom looked up to her as to a mother. In the trying years of the early 1870s, Stone needed all her inspirational skills to keep up the flagging spirits as suffragists reeled under the barrage of criticism that often took the form of attacks on their own moral probity.

Blackwell wrote the *Journal* state-of-the-movement editorial early in 1873. He referred to the previous year's "extremes, which threatened to identify our demand, in the public mind, with theories which seemed to us morbid, and practices which we regarded as immoral." Stone did not print notice of the upcoming January 1873 meeting in Washington of the NWSA, bringing an angry letter from Stanton begging her to "lay aside my 'personal feud with Susan' [and] 'give up my petty revenge' & c." Stone was "astonished" and indignant, writing Higginson: "Think of that from *her* to *me*." Only after the conclusion of the Washington convention, with nary a mention of Woodhull or free divorce, did Stone publish a full account of it in the *Woman's Journal*.[84]

Later that winter, in a speech before the Massachusetts society, Stone turned to the St. Louis proposal to regulate vice. She decried the statute, "which licenses prostitution and imposes pecuniary and other burdens upon fallen women, while it lets the fallen men go free."[85] The St. Louis acts regulating prostitution continued to draw Stone's fire throughout 1873. In February, she wrote: "Outside of the slave code, now happily obsolete, there is not to our knowledge anywhere a set of laws so odious, cruel, and vulgar." Stone protested that "Of those who commit this sin, the women alone, who are by far the smallest number of the guilty are required to have every name registered." She suggested that city officials publish the names of prostitutes' customers as a way of ending the trade. She also denounced the "weekly tax" that the women and not their male customers were forced to pay, but she saved her greatest outrage for the "most shameful of all" stipulation that "a medical examination is made by a *man-doctor* every week, and as much oftener as he pleases." This last phrase appears to go beyond Victorian delicacy to reveal Stone's deep distrust of male sexuality.[86]

Stone's anniversary address that spring was the most negative she had ever given. She had cause for worry. Membership was falling off at such a rate that the Massachusetts Woman Suffrage Association was forced to lower the number required for a quorum at business meetings. Attendance at the May NEWSA anniversary was down by more than a third. Other signs of attrition and strain could be read in the rapid movement of women into more socially acceptable forms of womanly activity. In 1873, women formed a number of new associations and clubs, many with membership lists that overlapped woman suffrage rolls. These new associations generally rejected attempts to include woman suffrage resolutions in their charters. Although many former leaders promised to continue support for woman suffrage, Lucretia Mott, Julia Ward Howe, and even Antoinette Brown Blackwell shifted the main focus of their attention to less controversial issues in 1873. Among the movements they helped found were the Women's Peace Movement, the Association for the Advancement of Women, and the Women's Temperance Crusade.[87]

Stone herself joined some of these organizations, signing the call to a New York "Woman's Congress," which was subsequently scheduled during the closing meetings of her own AWSA convention. Julia Ward Howe's reports from the Woman's Congress to the *Journal* display the anxious preoccupation with propriety that came to characterize post-scandal rhetoric. "The public may bless the true-hearted wives, mothers and maids whose eloquence was full of the spirit and sanctity of home," she wrote. Newspapers saw the society formed at the Congress, the Association for the Advancement of Women, as an attempt to "make a 'New Departure' from Woman Suffrage," a charge the *Journal* vigorously denied despite the new organization's vote to reject woman suffrage as one of its proposed aims.[88] That May, the AWSA did not meet in New York.

Despite the press of outside worries, life at Pope's Hill had a tranquil rhythm through the spring and summer of 1873. By midsummer, the Beecher-Tilton scandal seemed to be dying down, and in July, the *Woman's Journal* discreetly inserted a brief notice of Beecher's public denial of Woodhull's charges. Blackwell was at home more than usual, and on evenings when he and Stone had no other engagements, the family gathered in the gaslit parlor and listened to Blackwell read aloud from Eliot's *Middlemarch.* There were other homely pleasures that summer—fireworks viewed from the roof, carriage rides, trips to the seashore, and later that summer, shared sorrow as well when word reached them of the death of Sarah Stone Lawrence's daughter Anna. "Though they expected it, it was a sad blow for all of us," Stone wrote Nettie after the funeral.[89]

After a week's retreat to the White Mountains, Stone and Blackwell returned to take up the multiple chores of newspaper, organization, public speaking, and preparing and mailing the tracts and leaflets that continued to go out by the thousands. Despite the collapse of Wall Street in September and the failure of banks and brokerage firms in what came to be known as the Panic of 1873, Stone seemed less worried about finances than she had been the previous year.

That autumn, Stone was able to put aside the disquieting issue of woman's sexuality and do battle on the more comfortable ground of woman's education. An eminent Boston physician and faculty member of the Harvard Medical School, Dr. Edward Hammond Clarke, published *Sex in Education,* a "scientific" compilation of "case studies" illustrating the necessity for adapting woman's education to her more delicate nature. According to Clarke, women who tried to study ethics or metaphysics would suffer from menstrual irregularities; their energy would be drained from their ovaries so that they might become sterile, and they would be physically weakened and subject to brain fever. Clarke's book was immensely popular, going through nineteen reprintings.[90]

Stone happily commented on and rebutted the flood of correspondence sparked by Clarke's book. Both Higginson and Howe wrote lengthy rejoinders in the *Woman's Journal,* and Stone kept up a running commentary.[91] In early December, she directed her efforts at another "safe" issue, inviting "the women of New England who believe that 'TAXATION WITHOUT REPRESENTATION IS TYRANNY'" to begin making plans for a centennial celebration of the Boston Tea Party, a gala gathering in Faneuil Hall planned for December 15. Stone did the bulk of the correspondence and planning for the event, and she was gratified on the appointed day to look across the platform and see old friends, together again for the first time in many years. Frederick Douglass, William Lloyd Garrison, Wendell Phillips, Samuel May, Julia Ward Howe, Mary Livermore, Louisa May Alcott, Bronson Alcott, Elizabeth Peabody, Stephen Foster, and a number of others had answered her invitation. The hall was "packed solid with a dense mass of humanity—a vast audience representing all classes in life." Stone's speech at the celebration was stirring. She pleaded with the men of the country to understand that the wrong they continued to do to women was worse that that which spawned the original protest. "We have petitioned, we have remonstrated, and we have been spurned with contempt. . . . We have sent lecturers," she told them. "We have held conventions. We have scattered tracts by tens of thousands." She suggested that the thirty-four thousand women of Massachusetts who paid taxes "should form a long procession" behind Abby Kelley Foster and the sisters Grimké, "those three women whose high courage in defense of a great principle made it possible for me to speak here tonight. . . . Then I would summon the men, from Barnstable to Berkshire, and in single file they should march under the eyes of these women whom they tax without representation, to whom they give no jury trial of their peers, whom they claim the right to imprison, fine, and hang, while they allow them no voice in the law which may work such terrible results."

Stone went on to suggest that if at the time of the July 4, 1876, celebration, women continued to be "held politically below the pardoned rebels, below the enfranchised slaves, and on the same level as idiots, lunatics, and felons," they should join with her in a general boycott of the festivities. On the day of the centennial, Stone suggested that women everywhere should "draw down our curtains, and close our shutters." A few of the older women in each city and town should dress all in black and "stand in groups on the most prominent thoroughfares. They should hold black banners on which should be inscribed in blood-red letters, 'We are taxed, and we have no representation. We are governed without our consent. We . . . have no legal right to our children, nor power to sell our land, nor will our money.'"[92]

Alice was among the many thousands in the audience who cheered Stone's speech following its emotional conclusion. She wrote in her diary that her mother's speech on that occasion was "the most eloquent speech I ever heard from her." Later that month, Stone again remained behind in Boston while Harry and Alice traveled to New Jersey to spend Christmas with their Blackwell relations. During the course of her visit, Antoinette Blackwell took Alice to hear Susan B. Anthony lecture in New York. When Anthony came to call on Nettie in Somerville, Alice noted loyally in her diary: "I don't much like Miss A. She strikes me as being tall, sharp, dictatorial, conceited, pugnacious and selfish." Conscience drove her to add, "Also plucky, undoubtedly."[93]

A small notice in the last issue of the *Woman's Journal* for 1873 noted that two elderly women of Glastonbury, Connecticut, the Misses Julia and Abby Smith, had notified the town council that they would pay no more taxes on their farm and livestock until they were permitted to vote in the council's proceedings. Subsequently, the sisters' cows were seized for taxes and sold at auction, and the *Woman's Journal* discovered a fine new cause to champion and a pair of noble heroines. In the same issue as the first story of the Smith sisters' rebellion was the sad notice that on December 23, Sarah Grimké had died.[94]

Once again, the small band of aging crusaders gathered, this time to say good-bye to the abolitionist and pioneer orator who had won their collective admiration. Stone had maintained a warm friendship with Grimké through the years, and along with Garrison, Higginson, and Phillips, she was invited to speak at the funeral. Grimké was a "moral heroine," she said, praising the courage that had led the slaveholder's daughter to speak so fearlessly and write so bravely nearly forty years before. She told of reading the *Letters On the Equality of the Sexes* some thirty-five years before, and "the light they shed went far to dispel the darkness which those of this day know nothing of." In this last, Stone showed her identification with Grimké. Although she was fifty-five and Grimké had been eighty-one at the time of her death, there was the sense of shared experience between the two pioneers. They had been witnesses to the same historical moment, and now one of them was gone. With Grimké's passing, Stone came face to face with her own mortality.[95]

CHAPTER ELEVEN

"Will the Cause Be Ground to Powder?"

The "locomotive" young orator was now a dignified matron, her appearance suggesting the authority and mien of the senior stateswoman she had become. Stone's hair was streaked with gray, and rheumatism caused her joints to ache—a condition aggravated by the one hundred seventy pounds she carried on her small frame. The fervor and zeal of her youth had been pummeled and bruised by war and disunion, by disloyalty and depression. She had endured spiritual drought and physical isolation, childbirth and the death of loved ones, Blackwell's infidelity, their separations and reconciliations. Her idealism had been tempered by pragmatism, and while a reformer's passion continued to burn in her heart, Stone had learned to moderate its flame.

What had not changed was Stone's singularity of purpose, nor had she learned to relinquish control; insofar as she was able, Stone would order and control the world around her, confident in her ability to know what was best for the cause, for herself, and for Alice. Only with Blackwell had she learned to loosen the strings, accepting his imperfections and riding out the series of new crises that his business ventures continued to precipitate, lending him money, up to a point. Though she often claimed to have spent her last dollar, Stone had established her own portfolio of real estate, stocks, and bonds; and in hard times, various family members turned to her for support. Her sphere of financial responsibility broadened in the 1870s to include various nieces and nephews who looked to Aunt Lucy for emotional support as well. Alice would describe her mother as being "like the shelter of a great rock under which you felt a sense of safety and of strong protection."[1]

Stone's steadfastness proved both asset and liability, as all around her, American society altered at a dizzying pace. Immigrants poured into cities, flooding the labor market and bringing different customs and habits. Large concentrations of wealth from the rapidly industrialized economy lined the pockets of the new class of capitalists, while the poor endured crowded slums and inadequate wages. Stone's commitment to liberal principles was challenged by the realization that many of the downtrodden were as opposed to woman suffrage as were middle-class remonstrants.

Though she continued to oppose immigration quotas and to assail the living and working conditions of laboring-class women, when the opposition of immigrant groups and union leaders to woman suffrage became clear, Stone's private letters took on an increasingly nativist tone. The opposition of the downtrodden to woman suffrage puzzled and frustrated Stone. Her faith in the power of the ballot was absolute; she saw it as the solution to all society's ills. To her, the disfranchised were defenseless against every form of abuse, inside and outside the home. How anyone could spurn the suffrage remedy, least of all those whose family lives and marital relations were disrupted by grinding poverty, was beyond her understanding.[2]

Stone's spacious and well-ordered home was a model of bourgeois propriety, its care and maintainence both a drain on Stone's resources and a source of pride. Alice, now in her teens, continued to need looking after, but more and more, she provided companionship to her mother. Beneath a painfully shy exterior, Alice had become a young woman of independent opinions and prodigious intelligence. More Blackwell than Stone in appearance, she was nonetheless her mother's daughter in her capacity for work. After an initial period of rebellion, Alice had grown to share her mother's passion for suffrage. This would prove a social liability at times, and Alice confided to her journal that her peers found many of her views "peculiar." Coping with the twin burdens of her mother's fame and the minute attention Stone paid to every detail of her daughter's life might have fostered resentment or threatened a weaker personality, but Alice was constitutionally independent. The diary she kept through her adolescence reveals a refreshing, precocious, honest, and introspective young women interested in chronicling for posterity how it felt to grow up as the daughter of one of the most well-known and widely revered women in America.[3]

Although neither Stone nor Blackwell adhered to any organized religion, Alice experienced a rapturous conversion to Christianity at a revival meeting held by Robert Collyer, a friend of Stone from Oberlin. Afterward, the fifteen-year-old determined to have "a religious talk" with her mother. "'Set spinning and let go' is her theory," Alice wrote disapprovingly in her diary that night, adding, "I'd rather be blue Orthodox and believe in Hell than believe what she does." With sublime confidence, Alice added, "She'll have a pleasant surprise when she dies."[4]

Theology was not the only matter on which Alice and her mother differed. They experienced many of the cross-generational struggles typical of any family. Following a clothes-buying excursion into downtown Boston, Alice reported in her diary: "We mutually begged each other to put on our tombstones: 'Died of shopping with an unreasonable mother. Died of shopping with an impracticable daughter.'"[5]

Stone also advised Alice on matters social and sexual, advice that Alice copied down in some amazement in her diary. She told of hearing all about boys from her mother on the train into Boston—"all sorts of queer things, how if you show them any attention they immediately think that you want to marry them, and that they would like to marry you. How very inconvenient."[6]

After delivering the valedictory at her grammar school, Alice confided to her diary that she found the applause "very pleasant." Her parents also spoke, and Alice reported that her mother's "eloquent" speech held the audience spellbound, while her father's speech was "buncombe . . . pure Fourth of July buncombe."[7] Following her graduation, Alice enrolled at Chauncey Hall, an academically rigorous, formerly all-male private school in Boston where she proved herself a fine scholar.

The bond between mother and daughter was strong. Alice looked to her mother for approval, support, and security. Describing her parents years later, Alice depicted her mother as the moral authority of the household. "She seemed a very gentle person," Alice wrote, "but there was something underneath the gentleness and kindness like the firmness of a great rock." It was Stone who insisted that Alice make apology and reparation when she was in the wrong, causing Alice to reflect that her mother seemed "even more anxious that I should do right by everybody than that everybody should do right by me." If Alice looked to her mother for guidance, she looked to her father for fun, underscoring the difference that Stone herself felt all too keenly. She once told Alice that it was surprising that her father "should ever have married so grim a person" as herself.[8]

Alice adored her madcap father. He read aloud to her, devised special games, made up long imaginative stories, and planned outings and excursions to please her. She would later say of him that he "was not a disciplinarian, but he was the merriest and most delightful of comrades. All children adored him. He could spin fairy tales fully equal to 'Alice in Wonderland'. . . . He was a man of wide reading and large intelligence. To live with him was a liberal education."[9]

His nieces and nephews all responded to him with the same delight. Whatever his deficiencies as husband, provider, and helpmeet, he was dearly loved by every member of the extended Blackwell clan. One of

Kitty's favorite stories from her summer visits to Martha's Vineyard was of Uncle Harry refusing to abandon a jelly-making project when the local store ran out of jelly jars. Instead, he purchased a half dozen chamber pots and put up the jelly in these, much to the children's merriment.

A young visitor from Mount Holyoke College described her leave-taking after lunch at Pope's Hill. As Blackwell prepared to drive her and two schoolfriends to the station, he called out from the carriage: "Good-bye Mrs. Stone. Your husband has gone off with three ladies. You need not look for him soon."

"Good-bye Mr. Blackwell," Stone responded affably. "Your wife will expect you to tea."[10]

Along with his sense of gaiety and fun, Blackwell loved living close to the edge; he filled letters home with tales of narrowly avoided disasters, of trains missed and carriages overturned. "Papa was adventurous," Alice explained. "When we were out driving, if we came to a road marked Private Way, Dangerous Passing, it always impelled him to wish to turn in and explore it." A family friend recalled how when they had a train to catch or an appointment to make, Blackwell would insist that they had "oceans of time," while Stone would say sweetly, "I don't think so, dear," and she would leave without him.[11]

Still, while there was a lighthearted and merry side to Blackwell, the brooding ambition and recurrent depressions remained. That their marriage had gained a stronger footing was due in no small measure to Stone's recognition of the need to slake Blackwell's ambition and to stroke his ego. This meant lending him money and finding him a permanent niche in the suffrage movement. While his chief assets would continue to be his charm, wit, and contagious enthusiasm, the conventions of male–female relationships did not allow Blackwell to accept these as forming the coin of their relationship.

However she might labor to prove herself in the domestic sphere, Stone was essentially a professional woman and politician. Blackwell was the more ornamental partner, financially dependent, better at entertaining, merry with children. Were he not bedeviled by ambition, he might have been content to play the "wife" in their relationship. He needed a public role, however, and more and more he found it as political consultant to the suffragists. In this capacity, Blackwell achieved at last a measure of distinction and won the approbation he so desperately craved. In the rapidly shifting political ground of the mid-1870s, Blackwell's annual trips to Republican conventions to lobby and plead for inclusion of a woman suffrage plank gave him a place in the public eye and, following his modest success in the 1872 convention, won him the gratitude of suffragists.

Fourteen straight years of Republican control of the presidency and Congress had allowed cliques and corrupt factions to flourish. In the *Journal* office, Stone read of the growing scandals in the many newspapers she received as courtesy subscriptions. Reporters gleefully waded into the political morass; the circulation of their papers enjoying unprecedented growth as publishers redefined the purpose of the daily press. "Fraud in Bureau of Indian Affairs!" "Bribe-Taking in the Postal Service!" "Massive Kickbacks in War Department!" screamed the headlines as one sad and sordid saga of malfeasance and bribery in high places followed another.[12]

So long as the scandals did not touch on woman suffrage, Stone refrained from comment in her paper, pressing forward with political work and news of women as if there were no national uproar. Instead, the *Woman's Journal* reported in 1874 that Abby Kelley Foster had joined with the Smith sisters and other women in refusing to pay taxes. Foster's home was sold, and subsequently Stone and others staged a statewide Anti-Tax Convention, which drew thousands determined to repudiate taxation without representation. The *Journal* continued to agitate—for school committee representation, for changes in inheritance laws and tax laws, for changes in child custody laws, for municipal and presidential suffrage.[13]

Over a year had passed since Woodhull's November bombshell with its accusations against Beecher. The scandal gradually faded, and in January 1874, Stone relaxed her vigilance and printed a lengthy account of the NWSA's Washington convention. By summer she would regret the move as once again, woman suffrage and free love would be brought together in the headlines in a fresh outbreak of the Beecher-Tilton scandal. Beecher had weathered the initial storm and was again writing and drawing huge crowds of loyal followers to his Sunday sermons. Tilton, on the other hand, was a broken man, and in June 1874, he paid to publish a statement in the major New York dailies renewing his charge of adultery against Beecher.

Beecher voluntarily submitted to a full Congregational Church Investigating Committee. Testimony in the church trial made the front pages of city papers, and when the church committee exonerated Beecher, bold headlines proclaimed his innocence. In August, Tilton sued Beecher for $100,000 for the alienation of his wife's affections. This renewal of the Beecher-Tilton scandal dismayed Stone. Along with her political concern, Stone had great sympathy for Tilton's wife. During the 1860s, the two families had been good friends, and Stone regarded Elizabeth as a "most innocent" woman, "compelled to falsehood" by "five miserable years" of torment. In her friend's defense, Stone broke the *Woman's*

Journal policy of silence on the scandal, printing the full text of Elizabeth Tilton's denial of the allegations.[14]

As Woodhull's putative sources of the scandal, Susan B. Anthony and Elizabeth Cady Stanton found themselves besieged by reporters who camped on their doorsteps and followed them everywhere. Anthony refused comment, but Stanton gave a long interview to a reporter from the *Brooklyn Argus* in which she cheerfully confirmed that Anthony had told her the story, a statement that stunned and infuriated her old friend and caused a rift between them.[15]

Stanton's indiscretion infuriated Stone, still smarting from a suffrage setback in Michigan, which she laid at Stanton's feet. Stone was in Michigan campaigning for a Republican-sponsored woman suffrage bill before the state legislature. Stanton, in Michigan for a series of lyceum lectures on liberalized divorce, insisted on blasting the Republicans from the podium in her nightly lectures. Stone wrote Margaret Campbell in disgust, "It is a thousand pities that a great cause must be gibbeted by its friends." She accused Stanton of being "utterly indiscreet." Her letter ended, "Will *the cause* be ground to powder?"[16]

To the dismay of Stone and the other suffragists, the Beecher-Tilton trial lasted for over seven months—the longest-running trial in American history to that point, described by one historian as "the greatest national spectacle of the 1870s."[17] It was on July 2, 1875, that the verdict came in. Nine jurors voted for Beecher's acquittal, and three voted to convict, resulting in a mistrial.[18] Tilton was denied his award and shortly afterward moved to France; Beecher continued to preach and publish. Woodhull and Claflin came into a sum of money sufficiently large to permit them to reestablish themselves in England, where both eventually made highly advantageous marriages. The only lasting casualties of the Beecher-Tilton trial were Elizabeth Tilton and the cause of woman suffrage.

Stone bitterly laid the blame for the thinning of the ranks of suffragists and the difficulty of obtaining new recruits in the 1870s directly at the feet of Stanton and Anthony.[19] Inclined to filter all events through the lens of woman suffrage, Stone did not take into account that hers was not the only reform to lose momentum in the late 1870s. With the exception of the temperance crusade, reform in general was in decline. The nation seemed to have settled into a comfortable lassitude, its moral fervor blunted, its passion exhausted by the *sturm und drang* of the past two decades. The Gilded Age was rolling in on the heels of Reconstruction, and evangelists of reform found their message usurped and subverted by the purveyors of the Gospel of Wealth.[20]

Aware of the need to adapt her methods if woman suffrage were to survive, Stone conceived the idea of suffrage clubs. Woman suffrage increasingly drew its recruits from the expanding middle class. In the fluid social conditions of postwar America, social markers gained in importance in a confusion of manners and morals.[21] For middle-class women, the distinction between public and private spheres had grown sharper. Men carved out their fortunes in the public world—an arena marked by graft, corruption, a growing impersonality, and increasing labor violence. Women were charged with creating and sustaining the home as the locus of peace and purity and as a conspicuous marker of success. The size of a man's house, the splendor of his horses and carriage, the cut of his family's clothes, and the number of servants who freed his wife from the need to labor—all attested to a man's having arrived. Middle-class women, with increased leisure time on their hands, looked for suitable occupations. Stone's hope of adding the numbers and support of these women hinged on persuading them that suffrage activity was socially acceptable.[22]

Stone reasoned that if woman suffrage were to succeed with these women, the locus of activity would have to move from public to private sphere—from church halls, town auditoriums, and picnic groves into the parlors and ballrooms of America's growing bourgeoisie. The idea of organizing women into suffrage clubs resulted in the movement of growing numbers of middle-class women into suffrage activity. At the same time, suffrage clubs widened the distance between middle-class suffragists and the ranks of working-class women.

In the age of calling cards, dinner parties, and tea dances, women vied for the privilege of membership in clubs where they could boast of hobnobbing with socialites such as Julia Ward Howe. At evening sociables, well-briefed cadres of women lobbied legislators over coffee and cake. Newspaper reports of these gatherings often blurred the distinction between the political and the social, appearing with the news on the front page. A major New England daily, the *Boston Advertiser,* printed an account of a suffrage gathering on the front page under the headline, "Society and Suffrage." Its subhead read: "Reception to the Members of the Legislature at Mrs. Fenno Tudor's—A Brilliant Gathering—Converts Made Over Coffee and Cake." The reporter praised as "ingenious" the idea of bringing politicians and suffragists together socially, congratulating the women on their use of the occasion to dispel the belief that the "typical" woman suffragist is "an unhappy, uncomfortable sort of creature who is at perpetual loggerheads with the world in general and the masculine world in particular," one who "is loud of voice, ungracious and assertive in manner, scorns dress and other amenities of womanly life and makes herself an unpleasant feature in the social and domestic landscape."

"Judging from the company last night," the reporter concluded, "the *real* suffragist is elegant, cultivated and refined. She is a genial companion, happy in disposition, . . . a womanly woman, possessed of social graces as well as reformatory ideas." The report continued with a description of Tudor's Beacon Hill home, where

[E]very nook and corner of the brilliantly lighted rooms were filled. It was a pleasing scene; rare pictures looked down from the walls, soft lights in Venetian vases shone on baskets of beautiful flowers, while diamonds and other gems sparkled and reflected back the lights of the chandeliers; the pretty toilets of the ladies added color and life. . . . All the leading women of the movement were there, including Mrs. Julia Ward Howe, who held a court at the upper end. . . . Lucy Stone, too, was the centre of another circle.[23]

All members of both houses of the state legislature had been invited, and most had accepted, noted the reporter, going on to describe in elaborate detail the dresses of the various women present. The glimpse of Stone offered here is far removed from the young orator enduring the privations of the rural lecture circuit.

Still, though the atmosphere was vastly changed and the methods had been politicized, the message was much the same. The model club charter Stone provided charged members with the task of moving woman suffrage forward "by the systematic circulation of tracts and newspapers, by holding public meetings, and especially by helping to elect the friends of suffrage to the Legislature and to defeat its opponents." The effect of the formation of these clubs was a single-issue lobby with roots in every political district.[24]

"Organize! Organize!" Stone exhorted week by week in the *Woman's Journal*. She called for "political action in every town." In many cases, Stone's earlier efforts in setting up local educational organizations in the cities and towns she visited in the late sixties and early seventies provided the nuclei for suffrage club organization and expansion. The task of organization was also aided by the delegate structure of the AWSA with its districts following political lines.[25]

Stone's personal appearance schedule in the early days of organization was hectic. In one month in the early seventies, she made appearances at eleven political conventions, enrolled 1,087 members in political "clubs," and continued to speak at local gatherings. By the late seventies, each AWSA district had set up its own local political action group and was actively lobbying with the help of the Boston office, from which tracts, booklets, and other suffrage materials went out regularly. The organizational model Stone provided would be adopted by Carrie Chapman Catt in the final, successful march to an amendment in 1920.[26]

This concentration on local organization and increased state activity distinguished the American from its rival organization. The National

Woman Suffrage Association continued to focus on the Fourteenth Amendment avenue to suffrage. When in 1875, the final decision in Minor vs. Happersett ruled out the Constitutional remedy, the NWSA re-directed its efforts to passage of the Sixteenth Amendment.[27]

In the wake of the Beecher-Tilton trial, relations had again cooled between the two wings. When Anthony charged Stone with failing to support the Sixteenth Amendment, Stone dismissed the charge as nonsense, arguing that she had gone to Washington to aid in the original drafting of the amendment and had circulated petitions and urged its passage continuously.[28] However, while she fully supported the idea of the Sixteenth Amendment, she nonetheless cautioned *Journal* readers not to pin all their hopes on action at the federal level, reasoning that the ratification of the amendment was wholly dependent upon the political mood of the states. "In order to secure Congressional interference, State action must not be neglected or postponed," she warned.[29]

The *Woman's Journal* provided an ideal medium of communication for the continuing task of organization. It channeled and focused the strategies and methods of work, and it directed efforts in state legislatures, reporting regularly on the various meetings and the success of the suffrage clubs. While this confluence of the political and the social enriched the campaign chest and "forged the sinews of war," it widened the gap between middle-class suffragists and those whose share of the Gilded Age pie was inordinately small. Even without the barrier of class, strong opposition from labor organizations, from the Roman Catholic church, and from the powerful liquor interests deterred working-class and immigrant women from joining the woman suffrage cause. Stone was frustrated and stymied by the repeated rebuffs that met her overtures to women labor leaders despite the many articles championing the various causes of working women in the *Woman's Journal*. Her efforts on behalf of working women were sincere, and throughout her life, she never thought of herself as "gentry." However, she failed to understand the concerns of the new class of laboring women, and her frustration grew at what seemed to her their irrational and obdurate opposition to woman suffrage.

Stone failed also in her efforts to convince working women that the ballot would bring them the power to legislate better working conditions for themselves. In the difficult economic times of the mid-1870s, after the Panic of 1873, the increasingly "gentrified" woman suffrage movement widened the distance between most suffragists and working women. Preoccupied with etiquette books and advice on manners, dress, and social deportment, clubwomen had little in common with their overworked and underpaid working-class sisters.[30] The growing division between the two groups was all too evident at an 1874 AWSA meeting in New York's Cooper Union building. Stone had just begun to speak before a crowd of two thousand when she was interrupted by the entrance into the hall of a group of one hundred women. When a member of the audience raised her voice to welcome the "members of the Cooper Institute" (a women's improvement society that often met in the rooms above the auditorium), Dennis Griffin, a labor leader who had accompanied the group, announced that these were "not woman suffragists, but women suffering." He identified the new arrivals as parasol makers who had been attending a union meeting upstairs. They had been forced out of their employment unfairly, he explained, and they hoped to win sympathy for their cause from the large suffrage gathering.

Stone invited their spokeswoman to the podium, and as one of the young women made her way forward, Stone told the newcomers that if they were to become "woman suffragists," this would end their status as "women suffering," for "nothing could provide a better remedy for your oppressed condition than woman suffrage. If it is true that the ballot is worth 50 cents a day to every man in the nation, it would be worth just as much to every woman," she concluded. Her place at the podium was taken by a Miss Leonard, representative of the parasol makers.

Leonard began her speech tentatively, apologizing for her embarrassment and fright before such a large audience, but as she spoke, her voice gained strength. She explained at the outset that she represented "hundreds of women" who were "suffering not for the ballot, but for bread. I have never wanted the ballot," she told the assembled gathering of suffragists. "I believe it belongs to the men who have it. . . . Men are strong; they can get together and ask what they want; they can organize in large bodies, but the working women are the most oppressed race in the United States."[31] The young Miss Leonard was an articulate spokeswoman, and the views she expressed typified mainstream labor opposition to woman suffrage, a position that would remain unchanged until the early 1890s. Labor's growing strength and influence would prove a formidable obstacle in one state suffrage vote after another over the next twenty years.[32]

Although Stone continued to campaign for improved working conditions for working-class women, her relations with them took another turn for the worse in the mid-1870s, when protective labor laws for women were proposed. Stone angered women workers with her *Journal* editorials opposing protective legislation on the grounds that such special treatment would only erode women's chance of attaining equal pay. She warned women against accepting the "poorer substitute" of "special privileges" for the genuine article of "full equality in the workplace."[33]

As relations between labor and management deteriorated, Stone grew more troubled about union tactics. When the railroad strike of 1877 eventuated in President Rutherford B. Hayes's sending in federal troops, Stone blamed the workers for causing the violence. As a disfranchised woman who believed absolutely in the power of the ballot, she had no under-standing of why male workers did not "vote" to improve their lot.[34]

Though she had grown more conservative in some of her notions, Stone remained committed to a number of liberal and radical causes. She strongly opposed Chinese immigration quotas in the *Woman's Journal,* and she warned *Journal* readers of the growing tide of anti-Semitism. She campaigned vigorously for the rights of illegitimate children, and she consistently opposed capital punishment.[35] She also decried the alarming growth of Jim Crowism and the revival of "color lines" in the South. When separate but equal facilities were proposed, Stone denounced them as a direct violation of equal rights, quoting Sumner, who had insisted that "Separate is not equal . . . the substitute is invariably an inferior article," and reminding her readers that the same principle held for women.[36]

The *Journal's* subscription lists continued to grow, and by 1875, every state and thirty-nine foreign countries were represented there. Stone prided herself on the international scope of the paper. By means of international correspondence, she kept abreast of women's activities around the world. The *Journal* reported on the meeting of the International Association of Women in Geneva, Switzerland, and kept readers abreast of woman suffragists' gatherings in Paris, London, and Brussels. When Sweden altered its laws regarding women, or Germany passed new legislation, Stone called attention to it in the columns of the *Woman's Journal.* Articles appeared regularly heralding women's progress in places as far-flung as Russia and Turkey.

Throughout the early years of the newspaper's existence, Stone singlehandedly did the major work of getting up the paper week after week. She took on the tasks of corresponding with local, national, and international organizations, of soliciting manuscripts, of combing national and international newspapers for items of interest to women, of obtaining lists of patents granted so that the achievements of women could be noted, of transporting the paper to the printers (all of whom were female), and of seeing to its mailing. All of these paled, however, alongside the great job of raising money to "eke out expenses," an effort that largely devolved on Stone. To Margaret Campbell, Stone wrote wearily that

I walked miles to picture stores, crockery stores, grocery stores, book stores, to soap stores, to "special sales" going up flight after flight of stairs, only to find the men out, or not ready to advertise, and for all my day's toil, I did not get a cent. And when I came home at night to find the house cold, the fire nearly out in the furnace, and none on the hearth, &c. &c. it seemed as though the tired of a whole life came into my essence.[37]

Stone did agree to leave the paper long enough in the summer of 1876 to attend the Centennial Exhibition in Philadelphia. The event opened on

May 10, 1876, when President Ulysses S. Grant threw a switch activating a huge Corliss generating engine, causing the eight thousand machines on display to come to life in a throbbing hum that elicited gasps of amazement and shouts of approval from the huge crowd. A sign of the times, the centennial of the nation's political independence was heralded with a rhapsodic tribute to its material and industrial might.[38]

Although initially opposed to suffragist participation in the Centennial Exhibition, Stone, too shrewd a publicist to let such an opportunity go by, changed her mind. She prepared an exhibit showing the various historical attempts by women to protest taxation without representation and had it shipped to Philadelphia. Along with the exhibit, she planned a commemorative ceremony to coincide with the great July 4 celebration at the Centennial. Blackwell had gone to Cincinnati for the national Republican convention, from which he wrote home that he had succeeded in coaxing a "respectful consideration" woman suffrage plank into the party platform.[39]

In July 1876, Stone and Blackwell left for Philadelphia, where the AWSA held a centennial celebration of New Jersey's enfranchisement of women. Although the affair went off smoothly, Stone was disappointed at the lack of press attention. When, on the following day, Anthony led a group of women onto the speakers' platform during the official centennial celebration and presented the keynote speaker with a copy of the "Woman's Declaration of Rights," thereby disrupting the proceedings and capturing press headlines throughout the country, Stone admired the action, saying that it would "no doubt go down in the history books." To Campbell, she confided that she had "dreaded the effect of their presence in Philadelphia. But they seem to be on their good behavior."[40]

Stone and Blackwell remained at the Centennial Exhibition for over a week. If she was disappointed to find that her tax protest exhibit had been placed high up on a wall all but out of sight, the Exhibition itself was far from disappointing, with its dazzling array of inventions, new commercial products, and industrial machines—many festooned with bronze eagles and patriotic bunting and displayed amid bowers of flowers and ferns like priceless objets d'art. Stone and Blackwell were able to try the world's first telephone on display in the great hall; they watched a huge printing press "instantly" print a card of their devising, and they saw the first commercially produced typewriter demonstrated. When their weary feet had given out, they sat and sampled a delicious new nonalcoholic beverage its brewers hoped would appeal to the hard-drinking miners of Pennsylvania—root beer. Like the thousands of other daily visitors, Stone and Blackwell enjoyed the coming-out party of the Gilded Age.

Back in Boston later that month, Stone wrote Campbell that "nearly every body" had gone to the mountains or to the sea. The heat was oppressive, but Stone worried that were she to take a vacation, "the Journal would stop." At least part of her worry was over money, "shorter than usual." Like her father, Stone suffered from the "poor fever." Her letter to Campbell concluded, "We do not quite see how we are to get through the year. But I suppose we shall, some way."[41]

That same summer, Stone received a letter from Stanton stating her intention of writing a history of the woman suffrage movement and asking Stone for an account of her role in it. Stone's response was less than cordial: "In regard to the History of the Woman's Rights Movement, I do not think it *can* be written by any one who is alive today. Your 'wing' surely are not competent to write the history of 'our wing,' nor should we be of ours, even if we thought it best to take the time out while the war goes on; rations, recruits, and all are to get as we go."[42]

Pressed by Stanton in a second letter, Stone replied: "I have never kept a diary, or any record of my work, and so am unable to furnish you the required dates." Between the lines could be read Stone's continuing anger and suspicion. The bare-bones biography she included carried an implied rebuke in every line:

I made my first speech in the pulpit of my brother, in Gardner, Mass., in 1847. I commenced my regular public work for Anti slavery and Woman's Rights in 1848. I have continued it to the best of my ability ever since, except when the care of my child and the War prevented.

Stone asked Stanton not to attempt a biographical sketch of her, signing her letter, "Yours with ceaseless regret that any 'wing' of suffragists should attempt to write the history of the other."[43]

Anthony apparently persuaded Antoinette Brown Blackwell to intercede on Stanton's behalf. Stone reponded on July 20: "I utterly despise being written about Nettee. But Harry thinks I ought to give you dates and trust your good sense." She summarized her experience to date:

So I was born Aug. 13 1818. I went to Oberlin Aug. 1843 graduated 1847—married May 1 1855. There is nothing particular about me [word obliterated]. My father was a farmer—My mother made cheese. I helped, and worked hard—and played hard, and studied hard—At Oberlin I worked for 3 cts an hour and boarded myself—Had cents an hour for teaching—Earned my education as I went. Taught a Select School after I graduated in North Brookfield and paid a debt incurred in my education, then began to lecture.[44]

Stone's continuing wariness where Stanton and Anthony were concerned persisted, the gulf between them reflecting very basic differences. Stone admired Stanton's brilliance while finding her both disingenuous and damaging. With Anthony, the rift ran deeper. Following Stone's refusal of the olive branch Anthony offered in 1872, Anthony's dislike of Stone came close to being an obsession.[45] To Stone—rigidly controlled and righteous—such depths of pure emotion were incomprehensible. Unable to predict or control the behavior of either Stanton or Anthony, she continued to believe in the wisdom of maintaining a separate organization. Following a misunderstanding with another suffragist, Harriet Robinson, Stone delineated her philosophy of separate work, likening the woman suffragists' situation to that of workers constructing the recently completed five-mile-long Hoosac Tunnel:

They stood two in a place, on a scaffold up under the rocks, with a tallow candle in each hat to give its small light in the surrounding darkness.
One man held a chisel to the rock and the other struck it with all his might. Now and them came a cry of pain when the blow missed the rock and came down hard on the fellow workman. In the darkness they could not always see where their well-meant strikes would fall. But they never *meant* to hurt each other. I do not believe *we* mean to hurt, and there are miles of worse than solid rock yet to be chiseled out, and we must all help. So here is my hand on it, till we win the victory which surely waits for us.[46]

Now and then, Stone relaxed her vigilance slightly, as when in 1876, she lent *Woman's Journal* support to a petition for the Sixteenth Amendment that Stanton and Anthony were circulating. Although she was willing to lend organizational support, Stone made clear her wish to continue the separation.

Maintaining a separate organization was not always easy. Stone had grown increasingly weary. She was also more and more troubled by painful rheumatism, an affliction she attributed to "long cold rides on the cars" and "sleeping in cold beds in houses where there is no furnace."[47] Although she curtailed her long trips, she continued to appear at conventions and organizational meetings and to speak annually before state legislatures in Vermont, New Hampshire, and Maine.

In the meantime, Blackwell had begun to cast about for a new project. As he prepared to depart for Santo Domingo once again in 1877 in order to investigate the possibility of growing sugar beets there in the wake of the total collapse of the Samana Bay venture, which had cost Stone at least twenty thousand dollars, she appeared calm and indulgent, writing Nettie: "Harry has been for the last few days pottering with beet sugar,— Litmus paper,—bone black, lime, white of egg, and a mashed mass of beets ornament the kitchen at this moment. Did I tell you he is seriously thinking of going to Santo Domingo—and that we both really expect to go to Colorado to help there next Fall, when the question of Woman Suffrage is to be voted upon?"[48] The lack of censure shows the distance Stone had come in her relationship with Blackwell.

That autumn, Alice entered college at Boston University. At the same time, Stone also made arrangements for Antoinette and Sam's daughter

Edith to enter Swarthmore, agreeing to pay for her niece's education. Soon afterward, she and Blackwell departed for Colorado.[49]

Blackwell was captivated by the wild beauty of the Colorado mountains. Stone wrote home to Alice that her father had said he "would rather live here, earning two or three thousand a year, than to live in Boston earning nothing!" For her part, Stone wrote, "I agree with a woman who rode with us [who] said: 'I'd rather be hung than live here.'" She added, "Papa likes variety and change, and that is why he *thinks* he could stay here. The air is cool, and the sky is blue—there are finer views too than I ever saw elsewhere." She added, "But give me Pope's Hill."[50]

At fifty-nine, Stone missed the comforts of home. The young Lucy who had slept on the steamer deck crossing Lake Erie, who had sometimes slept three to a bed and waded miles through shoulder-high thistles in the Wisconsin wilderness, now wrote complaining that her lodgings had "no privy, no chamber vessel, no washbowl, but a nasty table at which we ate with miners, who put their knives into the butter, and who declared that if women voted, they (foreigners) would leave the country."[51] Whether it was the miners' table manners or their anti-suffrage views that most disgusted Stone is not altogether clear.

Back in Boston, she resumed writing and editing the *Journal*. More and more, Stone had come to value her work as journalist and publicist. When in late 1869, she had regretted having to trade what she regarded as her real talent—public speaking—for journalism, she had underestimated both her own talents and the changing dynamics of power. The power of the press to mold and affect public opinion and to facilitate political organization was more and more apparent to her. In 1874, Stone wrote Campbell of the publicity value of the *Woman's Journal*: "Our cause has a wider hearing today than it ever had. The women on the School Board—the Smith cows, Abby Foster's house—and last the Rum Crusade, all call attention to the woman question."[52]

In addition to using the pages of the *Journal* to transmit news of interest to women, Stone had become a press agent, regularly dispatching notices of meetings, reports of interest to women, and other miscellaneous information which she hoped might receive a wider reading to major papers in cities throughout the country. (When Alice came to work at the *Journal,* she expanded this function to a regular weekly press update dispatch, calling it *The Woman's Column.*) The paper linked suffragists on a personal level as well, as in the notice that read: "Will the Minnesota lady who lives on the eastern edge of the "Big Woods" . . . please send her name and address to Mrs. M. A. Dorsett, 1302 Commonwealth Avenue, Minneapolis?"[53]

Stone struggled to establish the *Journal* as distinct from other women's publications. She offered no fashion plates, published no household hints, and carried no recipes. In addition, men contributed editorially from the outset. The historical value of the *Woman's Journal* is incalculable. Writing of it in 1934, historian Inez Haynes Irwin apologized for sounding "rhapsodic" in writing that the *Journal* was "a burning cloud by day and a tower of flame by night. Just the names of its contributors . . . seem to list the liberal *Who's Who* of the period." Its broad humanitarian thrust was a tribute to the catholicity of Stone's and Blackwell's reform interests. The *Woman's Journal* protested what it termed the "murder" of Indians, accusing "profiteers" of fomenting trouble with Indians in order to usurp their lands. *Journal* editorials blasted the inhumane conditions in reform schools and protested the housing of the mentally ill in alms-houses. Again and again, it called attention to the grim working conditions and low wages of factory and sewing women and of domestic servants.[54]

The *Journal* continued to occupy Stone and Blackwell, too, when he was not involved in one of his business schemes. At home on Pope's Hill, the house continued to be filled with friends and family. Following their return from Colorado, their niece Florence came to live with them; the following year it was Agnes. The Blackwell family circle continued to grow with the marriage of George Blackwell to Stone's niece Emma in the autumn of 1875. Emma had been like a daughter to Lucy, and Alice referred to her cousin as "Mamma's baby—her first, I believe; [who] slept with her the first night of her life."[55] On her first introduction to the Blackwells, Emma encountered some of the same class prejudice Stone had endured. Stone's response to the Blackwells' attempts to gentrify Emma are telling. On their honeymoon trip to Europe, Emma and George stayed with Anna Blackwell in Paris, and Emma wrote of her new sister-in-law's attempts to add some "culture" to her by having her take French and music lessons. An indignant Stone fired back a letter instructing Emma to cease the lessons at once and travel instead to Italy and Switzerland.[56]

Stone continued to be sensitive to issues of class. In Gilded Age America, where social climbing was becoming a national pastime, Stone weeded her own garden, canned her own vegetables, made fruit preserves, and tended the animals and flowers—chores no gentleman's wife would consider doing herself. Alice recognized her mother's social shortcomings. In a letter to Kitty, she described Elizabeth Cady Stanton as "much more elegant and aristocratic" and "more used to society ways" than her mother.[57] If Stone was unpretentious, she was nonetheless aware of the value of having Julia Ward Howe and other socialites in the movement. She and Howe had become good friends, and in her public appearances,

Stone took to wearing a lace cap and shawl similar to those worn by Howe.

The Blackwell sisters never learned to overlook what they perceived as Stone's social disabilities. Keenly aware of class distinctions, they often despaired at the goings-on in their brothers' families. Following a visit with the Brown-Blackwells' oldest daughter, Emily lamented that she was *"so deplorably common,* narrow and undeveloped."[58] Their belief that Stone also was narrow and common did not stop them from sending one or another of their charges to live with her for extended periods. Emily and Ellen's wards came frequently, and just as Kitty and Florence had done years before, they came to call Lucy and Harry "Mama" and "Papa." Following yet another lengthy visit by one of her five daughters, Nettie wrote: "You see Lucy we do not hesitate to send you child after child on extemporized visits."[59]

The Blackwell family bond, despite advancing years and the geographical distance that separated them, had grown no less tight. From Anna and Marian in the south of France, from Elizabeth in England, from George and Emily and Ellen in New York, and from Lucy and Harry in Boston, advice on how to spend and invest money, raise children, and conduct private and public life was freely dispensed in voluminous letters. The tangled web of family finances is revealed in a letter from Sam to Elizabeth in which he writes, "Sometime ago I paid over to George for remittance to you the sum paid to me for you by Emily which I deposited in the U.S. Trust Co. together with the interest that it had earned there."[60]

In July of 1876, Emma gave birth to a boy, Howard Lane Blackwell. Stone wrote congratulating George on being the "man who had the good fortune to perpetuate the Blackwell name."[61] Emma's love for her aunt withstood the barrage of advice from Aunt Lucy about child-rearing, breast-feeding, and health and housekeeping matters. Despite George's impatience with woman's rights and Emma's own steadfast devotion to woman suffrage, their differences of opinion did not interfere with a deeply loving relationship.[62]

Stone and Blackwell too appeared to be growing closer with each passing year. They had reached the stage where each had come to accommodate the foibles and eccentricities of the other. For Blackwell, this meant putting up with Stone's dogmatism, perfectionism, and rigidity. For Stone, it meant being willing to indulge Blackwell financially and to allow him the latitude to pursue his "butterfly" interests. Following the final collapse of the Santo Domingo venture, Blackwell launched another bid for the fortune that had managed to elude him now for more than four decades. In 1878, he circulated a flyer inviting investment in a proposed beet sugar refinery in Portland, Maine. George wrote Elizabeth that "I hardly think it will prove a success," but Sam, Anna, and Stone all invested in the venture.[63] Blackwell got fifty thousand dollars each out of two other investors. When the venture ran into financial difficulties, Blackwell asked Stone if she would agree to a mortgage on the Pope's Hill house. She would not, and instead, she agreed to part with some of her precious Montclair, New Jersey, property.[64]

Blackwell entered the project with his usual enthusiasm, firing off a telegram to Stone in October: "BEET SUGAR MANUFACTURE A SUCCESS. SLAVERY IN CUBA IS DOOMED."[65] The venture would struggle along for nearly four years and eat up untold more dollars before collapsing entirely. In their approach to business, two more different people could not be imagined. Stone, with income from property and investments and with a firmly established paper running smoothly, permitted herself only brief vacations. Blackwell, on the other hand, had difficulty staying put. Less than a year into his new sugar beet venture, he sailed for Europe, ostensibly to purchase beet-processing machinery in Germany, though he planned lengthy visits to France and England to see family and to tour. He tried to convince Stone to come along, but she would not leave the *Journal,* paying for Alice to go instead. Before their departure from New York, Blackwell wrote, "I never intended to go to Europe without you and somehow I feel mean and grieved to leave you all alone in Boston with your (our) heavy load of cares, rheumatism and hot weather." He added, "I wish you *could* let old Bush take the WJ and go along with your cub and your husband to see the places and people over the water."[66]

From Europe, both Harry and Alice dispatched long and newsy accounts of their travels. Stone's self-imposed martyrdom was complete when the young woman who had come to help with the *Journal* broke her collarbone soon after arriving, and Stone wrote Nettie that she would have to cancel a short vacation. "I do not mean to be cheated out of my small holiday—since last August, I have not had a day of respite, and I have sore need of it," she wrote.[67]

On his return, Blackwell went to Maine to await delivery of the machines he had ordered, while Alice returned to college. She had gained an appreciation of her mother's labors, writing Kitty:

It is a heavy load for poor Mamma—the Journal every week, the general supervision of the suffrage cause in Massachusetts and the care of this big place indoors and out—planning what we are to have to eat three times a day, keeping an absentminded daughter clothed and in running order, seeing that the geraniums in the yard are covered up if the evening threatens frost, that the various fruits are picked at the right time and kept without spoiling etc. etc. ad infinitum. I should think she would go cracked; but she pursues the even tenor of her ways and shows no sign of breaking down.[68]

Far from slowing down, Stone found herself caught up in a new effort that fall. The October 1879 issue of the *North American Review* carried an anti–woman-suffrage polemic by the well-known historian and author Francis Parkman. Parkman called woman suffrage "the most reckless of all experiments," arguing that suffrage would develop "the defects of women and demolish their real power to build an ugly mockery instead. [sic] For the sake of womanhood, let us hope not."[69]

Stone's eight-page response in the November *Review* offered both a legal argument for the constitutionality of woman suffrage, and the standard social argument that woman suffrage would purify politics, to which Stone had added a new rhetorical twist: the suffragist as "true mother." Suffrage could not make women "defective" or unwomanly, she wrote, for "with women is the permanent factor of motherhood . . . her care is of the baby at her breast, of the child tugging at her finger, of her young sons and daughters. She longs to make smooth and safe ways for their feet. By a law which was not made by men and can not be abrogated, the mother is bound to her child by ties which neither distance, nor absence, nor time can change."[70]

Her first chance to demonstrate personally that voting would not defile women was thwarted that autumn by her refusal to relinquish her birth name. In May of 1879, the Massachusetts legislature passed a bill giving women a vote on school matters. Stone paid her property taxes as Lucy Stone, and according to the newspaper account, "armed with the receipted bill, she moved upon the Board of Registrars," where a young registrar, forgetting his specific instructions not to do so, permitted Stone to register in her own name. She read the newspaper account aloud to Alice, adding laughingly, "Talks as if I were a battalion or a regiment."[71]

Later, she wrote Blackwell: "I have crowed too soon about my registration. The registrar has sent me a note to say it is 'annulled' unless I write Blackwell after my name, which I shall never do." She added that Alice had gone to the polls and "voted for us all." (Ironically, for all his political activity, Blackwell did not become an American citizen until 1894 and was thus unable to vote.) Deciding on her next course of action, Stone wrote, "I rather think trial by newspaper is best." She drafted an appeal of the registrar's decision and sent multiple copies to Boston and New York papers:

I will say that my name is Lucy Stone, and nothing more. I have been called by it more than sixty years and there is no doubt whatever about it. If the use of a foot or cart-path for twenty years gives the right of way, surely the use of a name for three times twenty years should secure the right to its use. There is no law that requires a wife to take her husband's name.[72]

Despite broad press coverage and public sympathy, election officials were unmoved. If Stone felt any regret as other women cast their ballots, she kept them to herself. She was and would remain "Lucy Stone, (Only)," at whatever cost.

Stone was almost sixty-two, and the press of work began to take its toll on her health. The "care of the different societies, and of the Journal, and of the house," she wrote a friend, "so were upon even my strong health that when a hard cold came upon me, I could not throw it off, and *the accumulated tired* of years left me a prey to pneumonia."[73] Only when she began coughing up blood in January of 1880 did Stone reluctantly agree to go to Dr. Emily's clinic in New York, where her sister-in-law treated her with large doses of calomel, a harsh mercuric chloride purgative. Sarah disapproved of her sister's treatment, writing Emma that "poor Lucy will always suffer from those awful doses of calomel, but you need not say it to any of the Blackwells, not even George." She advised Emma to "steer clear of their treatments as far as you can."[74] When Stone's condition worsened, Emily consulted another physician who recommended Stone's immediate removal to a milder climate. By then, however, Stone was too ill to move. She faced the possibility that she might die, writing calmly to Alice that "while I am not at all afraid for myself, I should like to stay til you are older, and for the need Papa has of me." For the first week of March, Stone lay near death, but on March 10, she rallied. To Alice, she wrote that it had been "a serious question whether I should live. My strength and flesh went like dew."[75]

Alarmed, Alice took a leave of absence from Boston University and went with her mother to a "Health Home" in Wilmington, Delaware. There, Stone slowly gained strength. The time together brought mother and daughter closer. "[Alice] goes on with her lessons with praiseworthy persistence," she wrote Blackwell, "while her care of me is a miracle of thoughtfulness. She *is* a good child." As soon as she was able to resume corresponding, Stone caught up on suffrage news. "The New York law is almost worse than none. New Jersey and Iowa lost all they asked for, and I have not heard from Ohio where they were earnestly trying for school suffrage," she wrote Blackwell from Delaware.[76]

The press of his rapidly failing business had kept Blackwell in Maine throughout Stone's near-fatal illness. On April 12, he wrote from Portland that the beet-sugar business was likely to die, adding "Sic transit gloria Beet Sugar Industry!"[77] He wrote that as the Portland venture was a "limited company," he feared that when its indebtedness exceeded its limited liability, he would be personally liable for its debts. To prevent this, he wrote Stone of his intention of putting all of his property in her name and declaring bankruptcy. Troubled by the ethics of such a move, Stone wrote that while she wished "to enable you to turn about and manage to the best advantage for all concerned," she "would never do it with any view to not paying any just claim that the departure of your company from the terms of its 'limited liability' might create." She felt so strongly about it that she added, "If an honorable payment of what the beets may involve would take our home, we will sell my Montclair one and save the one on Pope's Hill."[78] Blackwell's siblings were also unhappy with their brother's plan, with Emily writing George that she was "very sorry" that Harry had to "resort to such meanness."[79] When Blackwell suggested that they rent out Pope's Hill for the income it would bring, Stone pleaded with him: "It seems to me much better that we should have the summer *together at home* where I long to get."[80] She got part of her wish. They were together in Boston to celebrate their silver wedding anniversary. Stone returned to work on the paper, and Blackwell went back to Maine, where the business continued to fall apart. The Brown-Blackwells were dependent upon the one hundred dollars per week that the company was paying Sam, and when the company went under, Stone searched for ways to help them out financially. She paid the $350 cost of Grace's schooling at Miss Andrews's as well as paying for Florence's elocution lessons and Edith's college tuition. She then offered Sam a job running the *Woman's Journal* during her convalescence, to which Harry objected that Sam

does not know the place, nor the people, nor the work. As a writer, I think he will prove prolix & dull—His letters to me from New Hampshire are wearisome and *prolix*. Sam is the best man in the world, but he is no longer young. I doubt whether he has the mental agility and adaptedness which the position would require. . . . I incline to the policy of giving my own time to it during the months of June, July, and August.[81]

Sam found other employment, and Stone recovered sufficiently to resume full charge of the paper. Blackwell remained in Maine hoping to salvage some portion of his now defunct refinery. "All I can do is pave the way for mean & mercenary men to follow & make fortunes from the path I have opened," he wrote.[82] His failure plunged him into a deep depression.

"I think all the Blackwells I know are more or less cracked," Alice wrote Kitty that May. Two weeks later, she wrote again, saying that her father was so "tired and blue . . . and is nervous and talks so queerly at times as to make me fear his head is affected."[83]

Blackwell was slow to snap out of his depression. In late August, Stone fell ill again, this time with a severe sore thoat. She went to recuperate at Sarah's home in Gardner, returning to Boston in time for Blackwell to attend the state Republican convention so as to petition (in vain) for the inclusion of a woman suffrage plank in the party platform. Stone wrote to cheer him:

I am very grateful to you for the constant effort, the patient faith and courage with which you do, single handed, year after year, try to secure political recognition for women. It is a shame you have no seconding. But among the pleasantest things we shall have to remember when we sit, an old couple, by our snug hearthstone, will be this very part you have taken in the interest of political justice for women. Distasteful and hard as it now seems, then, the end accomplished, it will look different.[84]

Whether Stone's words encouraged Blackwell is doubtful. What emerges in such exchanges, however, is the peculiar quid pro quo that had come to mark their relationship—her financial and moral support for his diverse business schemes in return for his efforts on behalf of woman suffrage. Beneath the surface coin of this exchange lay deeper and more complex needs, but it was clear that after twenty-five years, a deep and mutual love based upon a tolerant acceptance of one another's foibles had grown up between the righteous suffragist and the dilettante businessman.

CHAPTER TWELVE

"Another Year for Downright Work"

The fall and winter of 1880 to 1881 were cold and blustery. Stone, still weak from her late summer illness, was inundated by a steady flow of houseguests. Shortly after Stone's return from Gardner, Emily sent word from Martha's Vineyard that it was so cold that she would like to bring her entire party to stay at Pope's Hill until it was time for them to return to New York. In that same week, Bo wrote that he planned to visit, and Nettie sent word that Grace and Florence were on their way. All winter, guests poured in. Alice, worried about her mother's health, wrote Kitty that she wished the lot of visitors "at the bottom of the Red Sea." Stone was "tired and troubled," her exhaustion "the effect of years and years of work so much harder than falls to the lot of most women," Alice observed, adding, "But she has not the power of taking things easily." Stone's valuation of herself as ever-womanly deprived her of the power to refuse the endless requests from family, friends, and suffragists for hospitality, mothering, and emotional support.

More and more, this sense of herself as "motherly" and domestic had all but extinguished the spirit of the bloomer-clad young woman whose passions had proved contagious. Stone had become her own creation— the representation of propriety, decorum, and purity intended to counteract the suffrage scandals. In this guise, Stone could engage in "masculine" activity—politics, journalism, legislative lobbying, public speaking— without being accused of inciting women to sexual misconduct. The snowy lace fichu at her collar, the embroidered cap on her gray head, and the black silk dress she now wore for her public appearances dared her detractors to imagine an impropriety associated with such an image.

Living the image was exhausting. While Blackwell was some help when he was at home, in early 1881, he was in Maine in the last throes of the Maine Beet Sugar Company. In February and March, he made a last-ditch effort to attract new investors and set up a new manufactory in Schenectady, New York, an enterprise that Stone tried to discourage.

"Your advice to let it alone was good, but D.V. next year I will step out of it." His letter concluded, "God bless you both & forgive me for my folly." Later, Alice wrote: "Papa has been at home more than usual, but he feels defeated and humiliated & we don't know exactly how to cheer him up."[2]

While Stone was generally tolerant of Blackwell's need to pursue his "follies," she tried to persuade him not to jump into a new venture immediately. "Mother thinks her representations have led him to give up his idea of combining maple sugar with glucose; but if it isn't that it will probably be something else & possibly something worse," wrote Alice. When that attempt proved unpromising, Blackwell abandoned it too and lapsed into a deep depression. Alice wrote that he was again feeling "blue," adding, "I think the trouble with him now is mental more than physical . . . he declared that there was nothing that was worth doing except for a diversion." Her mother and father were a strange pair—he who proclaimed to find no activity worth doing except as diversion, and she who found no diversion worth doing except as it pertained to suffrage.[3]

Blackwell's depressions were Stone's concern, too. Just as she felt herself responsible for almost every aspect of home and suffrage work, Stone also took on the task of cheering Harry. Following the harvest of the crop of sorghum Blackwell planted on the grounds of Pope's Hill, she spent long evenings taking turns with him at the hand-cranked centrifuge with which he hoped to extract sugar from sorghum mash. With no illusions about the profitability of the enterprise, Stone recognized its psychological value, writing Alice, "Papa is taking genuine comfort out of it, and that is worth a great deal."[4]

As Stone gradually regained physical strength, she stepped up her political efforts. The January 1, 1881, *Woman's Journal* began with a homely imperative: "Today opens another year for downright work." The previous year she had begun a lobbying campaign to introduce woman suffrage referenda at New England town meetings. "Next year," Stone wrote, "with more time and preparation, we shall have this effective instrumentality as a powerful ally." That spring, she toured New England town meetings, setting up lobbying organizations all along the way.[5]

All forms of partial suffrage were "effective instrumentalities" to Stone. She believed that full enfranchisement would come through women's proving themselves in local referenda, municipal suffrage, school suffrage, and presidential suffrage. She continued to believe that a Sixteenth Amendment could not be ratified unless public opinion changed. Still, she urged readers to circulate petitions in support of the federal amendment, defending herself against the charge of opposition to it by writing in the *Journal* that the AWSA "has always favored it as a possible future instrumentality." Although historians have often undervalued the work of the American wing in the years of the division, most frequently citing the differences over the Sixteenth Amendment, it is interesting to note that in 1882, for example, AWSA was responsible for sending the congressional committee in Washington more than two-thirds of all the petitions received favoring the Sixteenth Amendment.[6]

Organizationally, Stanton and Anthony's NWSA was all but moribund in 1882, its national membership lists showing about one hundred members. Its chief work had come to be the planning and execution of the large and well-attended annual Washington meetings designed to rally support around the Sixteenth Amendment. In 1880, at Stanton's urging, Anthony had given up organizing in order to work on the first volume of the *History of Woman Suffrage*.[7] Once that work was behind her, Anthony returned to suffrage activity, with unfortunate consequences for Stone. One of Anthony's first actions upon returning to political activity was to plan a New England–wide campaign to win AWSA affiliates over to her own organization. She enlisted the help of a disaffected former Stone ally, Harriet Robinson, and the two likened the campaign to a battle, using the terms "battleground" and "territory." In a long series of letters, Anthony gave Robinson detailed instructions on how to win individual AWSA leaders over to the NWSA, including "a little stratagem" for "winning over Mrs. Garrison from Lucy's camp." Secrecy and strategy were important, Anthony wrote, advising Robinson to "keep *cool*—keep quiet—as military men say—'lay low—and work on'—*move* on to the taking of the fort."[8]

In May 1881, Anthony arranged a NWSA convention in Boston during anniversary week. Whatever her private misgivings, Stone heralded Anthony's meeting in the *Journal*, praising "the distinguished women who have been at the head of that association for many years, Mrs. Stanton, Miss Anthony, Mrs. Joslyn Gage . . . [who] were sure to attract interest and draw an audience." She quoted from speeches praising Anthony for her ceaseless efforts on behalf of women. The NWSA resolutions passed at the convention eschewing reliance upon "the popular vote of the ignorant masses" to grant suffrage state by state drew a response from Blackwell, who quoted the resolutions as indicative of the continuing need for separate work.[9]

Stone's arguments regarding the need to remain apart were less convincing to suffragists who no longer saw the reason for maintaining two distinct organizations. Harriet Sewall, poet and activist, wrote Robinson chiding her for her part in the attempted takeover of AWSA auxiliaries. "I love and honor Mrs. Stone," Sewall wrote, "and I think her sex can never show enough gratitude toward her. The only weakness I have seen in her is her inveterate dislike of Mrs. Stanton, but if she had no weakness, I am afraid she would be taken away to live with the angels."[10]

The first volume of the *History of Woman Suffrage* appeared as the conventions were taking place. Stone's attempt at an evenhanded review in the *Journal* recommended it as a "large, interesting, and handsome" volume "illustrated with portraits of several Suffragists. . . . Much of it is compiled from existing reports, some from recollections of the authors." She noted that "much is autobiography." Stone objected to its timing, she told readers, both "because it is premature" and because "the editors of this book are not in a position to write fairly of the work of a large class of Suffragists, from whose methods of work during the last dozen years, their own have widely differed."[11]

Had Stone cooperated by furnishing the "chapter say of ten pages" which Stanton had requested, it is unlikely to have made much difference in a volume consisting of 878 pages. The suffrage and property act petitions Stone had begun circulating in 1850, the legislative campaigns, the scores of conventions organized and speeches delivered, the printing and circulating of hundreds of thousands of tracts, the worldwide fame of the pioneer suffragist—all were reduced in the "history" to a scattering of speeches and the text of Stone and Blackwell's marriage protest.[12]

Alice believed that her mother had a genuine aversion to publicity; even to friends and family, Stone never expressed any anger or resentment at her own exclusion from her rivals' book. She had neither time nor inclination to memorialize her work. Early summer was in any case a busy time for her. Close on the heels of the May anniversaries came Alice's graduation from Boston University on June 1, 1881. Alice took her place alongside her mother at the paper, apparently never seriously considering either marriage or a career outside woman suffrage. Blackwell continued to hope that she would marry, but like so many educated young women of her generation, Alice remained single.[13]

Stone did attempt to broaden her daughter's circle of friends and interests by asking a friend, Isabel Barrows, to "try to draw [Alice] out into wider and more varied interest." The Barrows were well-traveled, sophisticated people, and they invited Alice to become a regular part of their summer group trips to a camp in Canada. From this association grew Alice's lifelong interest in a variety of causes, among them the Armenian question.[14]

With Alice working alongside her, Stone was willing to leave the paper and go with Blackwell to Martha's Vineyard for a short vacation in August. In her absence, Alice printed what must have seemed to her an innocuous article by Frances Dana Gage endorsing "marriages of convenience" for those "well past middle age" who would mutually benefit by the arrangement.[15]

One week later, Stone expressed her "very sincere regret" that during "the temporary release of the editor of this paper from her post," an "article which seemed to convey approval of such marriages" had been printed. In a revealing conflation of herself with her paper, Stone wrote that "the *Woman's Journal* holds another view. It does not in the least approve or accept as marriage, anything short of that great baptism of affection which blends two hearts in one." Stone believed that "the marriage bond entitles two human beings to assume the responsibility of a relation out of which other lives may come. . . . In joy and in sorrow, in sickness and health, in prosperity and adversity, they share the good, increasing it by sharing, and they divide the losses and the evil of life by bearing them together." To this, Blackwell added his own comments, writing that when two young people marry, "if they are resolved to make the best of themselves and of each other, they can and will grow nearer together as the years go by . . . and hope springs freshly from the ashes of every disappointment."[16] Between their two statements lay the nexus of beliefs that had held them together through their own disappointments.

Alice's letters to her aunts and cousins describe her parents' deep affection for one another. She told of looking into her mother's room one morning and finding

that Papa had come across from his room and was having a cuddle. I called them lazy things, and Papa fired off all sorts of jokes at me. Their two heads did look so funny, Papa's full of sleepiness and with the eyes shut, but the mouth opening to let out extraordinary puns and Momma's as round and rosy as an apple, with the eyes twinkling and the corners of the mouth curling up. I wanted to bring my camera and photograph them on the spot.[17]

Following Stone's return from the Vineyard, Alice departed for a holiday at a camp in Maine, from whence she sent her mother birthday greetings. Stone thanked her, saying that on her birthday, she had thought of "my own poor old Mother who welcomed me with sorrow 'because the life of a woman is so hard.'" Although she herself enjoyed comforts her mother had never known, Stone's life in many ways was as strenuous, and she had grown to dread the extended speaking trips that she continued to make.[18]

In September, Stone again left the newspaper in Alice's care and set off on a five-state speaking tour. She spoke on successive nights in Syracuse, Rochester, and Buffalo, where the ninth Woman's Congress was taking place. From Buffalo, she and Blackwell spoke at various cities and towns in Ohio and Kentucky, arriving in late October in Louisville where the AWSA was to hold its anniversary meeting on October 25 and 26—the first national convention to take place south of the Ohio River. Delegates came from as far as California, and newspapers reported crowds at the final sessions in excess of fifteen hundred people.[19]

Stone's opening speech summarized the year's progress—suffrage amendments pending in Indiana, Nebraska, and Oregon; twelve states already enjoying school suffrage; changes in the laws, and partial suffrage, in England and Scotland; and women working alongside men in professions hitherto closed to them. She urged her audience to continue to organize and to lobby vigorously for municipal and presidential suffrage as well as for the constitutional amendment.[20]

Alice, nominally in charge of newspaper and house, was deluged with advice and directions from her mother. From stops all along the way, Stone sent off long missives filled with careful directions and minute details about the care of Pope's Hill, the mailing of suffrage tracts, and the composition of the paper. She advised Alice on what to put in the *Journal,* reminded her to pay the coal bill and to collect the milk money, directed her to buy herself a new hat—"I do not think the last year fall hats will do"—to switch to her winter clothes, and where to find them—"cloak in one of the back hall trunks, dresses in the cedar closet." She added, "You must not forget that your blue dress (silk and cashmere) is proper for this time of year. The sage green was to be mended, and the pieces were in the pocket." Even Alice's conversation did not escape Stone's direction. Shy Alice dreaded socializing, and as she prepared to make a round of visits, her mother advised her that "with the Moores you can talk about all the Blackwells, and Mrs. Nina Moore. And with Mrs. Knox Goodrich, suffrage will be a topic. . . . She is not a woman of much education and has no pretence, so you need not be afraid of her." Once, Stone added in a postscript: "It is a wonderful mother instinct that *longs to brood* its young even when they are grown up."[21]

Back in Boston in November after a return trip that included seven speaking stops in Indiana, numerous stops in Illinois, and then the slow railroad journey back to Boston, Stone barely had time to change clothes before leaving for the Rhode Island Woman Suffrage Association anniversary. That winter, to her usual round of activities Stone added the task of raising funds for an all-out campaign to get out the vote for the upcoming suffrage amendment in Nebraska.[22]

As Stone worked on the Nebraska campaign, Anthony and Stanton were hard at work on the second volume of the *History of Woman Suffrage,* covering the period following the Civil War. Faced with the problem of how to treat the schism and the formation of the American Association, Anthony wrote Robinson that "A bright idea has struck us— & that is—as the American W.S.A. is really a *Mass. Society* that you do it up in you. Mass chapter—*then we shan't have to touch it* at all." She

added, "Whittle the American down to its legitimate alpha and omega."
In another letter, Anthony directed Robinson to "prove that no *national*
work is ever done by the American."[23]

When Stanton's daughter Harriet came home from England to assist
her mother in readying the second volume for the printers, she was dismayed to find that "this history of the suffrage movement did not include
a line on the birth and activities of the American Woman Suffrage Association." She pointed out that "they had given out to the public that the
book was to be a history of the suffrage movement and not merely of the
National Woman Suffrage Association." Stanton and Anthony refused to
have anything to do with the addition but permitted Harriet to write a
chapter on the AWSA. In her autobiography, Harriet Stanton Blatch described the "dog's life" she led in "compiling the 60,000 words" in the
short time her mother had allotted to the project.[24]

Stanton and Anthony's "history" drew some sharp criticism. E. L.
Godkin, partisan to neither "wing" of suffragists, commented in the *Nation* on its treatment of the schism:

The causes of this split are neither clearly nor ingenuously set forth in this 'History,'
which has been compiled by the faction known as the National Women Suffrage
Association. Its early connection and cooperation with a notorious charlatan of the
male sex and an equally notorious blackmailing adventuress are but faintly suggested;
and the real character of its policy, begun in 1867, of offering its support to any party
ready to cajole it with empty phrases, may easily escape the ordinary reader.[25]

As the second volume of the *History* made its appearance, Stone was
involved in her usual round of summer activities. She traveled, made
speeches, superintended the suffrage festival, put up jars of peaches and
plums, tended her kitchen garden, and ordered summer covers for the
parlor furniture. Late that summer, Alice took over the paper while her
mother at last took an extended vacation, traveling first to Nantucket,
then to Martha's Vineyard, and finally to Gardner for a visit with Sarah.
From Gardner, Stone sent a charming letter to Emma and George's son
Howard, advising him on the control of his temper. He must "make a fist
and count to 100" when he wished to strike out, she told him, just as she
had done at his age. She wrote of her delight in the roses, the bluebells,
the larkspur. She told of finding birds' nests in the rushes and bringing
dishes of milk to the kittens in the barn, where "they put their little noses
right in and drink it all."[26]

Stone largely ignored the second volume of the *History*, despite advice
from friends who urged her to make a public correction of the record in
the interest of posterity. She refused, believing that "the truth is always
sure to appear at last" and that any public discussion would only "put
weapons in the hands of the enemy." A *Woman's Journal* editorial en-

couraged women's political clubs to purchase both volumes of the *History* to add to their suffrage libraries.[27] The private struggle behind the public display of equanimity is apparent in the three drafts of a letter written in 1882. Stone might again have been the small child perched on a rock, instructing herself in the control of her temper. She was responding to a letter from John Hooker, Isabella Beecher Hooker's husband, chiding her for continuing to let "hatred and envy" divide the associations. Her first draft began, "I know there has been and still is an effort. . . ." This she crossed out and began again: "I know it has been so loudly asserted that 'envy and jealousy and a desire of leadership' animated the American Association and that many many people believe this and all the more because we have not taken any pains to deny it. . . ." This too is crossed out, and the third and final draft begins: "We felt unspeakable regret and sorrow for the action of the National in 1869 and for several years after. We had many consultations into which I do not think a personal feeling entered. . . . Believe me, it was never personal enmity that actuated us in this matter."[28]

In her own mind, Stone was able to draw a clear line between personal enmity and political aversion. Writing to Alice from Nebraska in September 1882, where she was conducting an intensive effort on behalf of the suffrage amendment, Stone told her that "our friends are trying to get a plank in [the state Republican] platform . . . and if Susan Anthony does not crowd herself in or meddle, we have great hope. . . ." However, when it became apparent that Anthony's campaign through Nebraska was drawing large audiences and raising much-needed campaign funds, Stone revised her opinion, and the *Woman's Journal* reported favorably on Anthony's meetings, giving summaries and excerpts of speeches and commending her good work.[29]

In conjunction with the Nebraska campaign, Stone had arranged to hold an AWSA convention in Omaha. She invited Anthony to share the platform and to address the audience.[30] Despite the efforts of both wings, the Nebraska campaign was doomed. Stone wrote Alice that "there is not a ghost of a chance to carry the amendment, and that too on account of the Germans, Bohemians, and Irish and Scandinavians who will all vote against it."[31]

The political analysis of the Nebraska defeat that appeared in the *Nation* concurred with Stone's assessment, concluding that the woman suffrage amendment lost because "the colored people as a class, the foreign-born, the liquor-dealers and their 'interest', . . . had all voted against it." The writer suggested that "long memories of the attempt of the organization directed by Mrs. Stanton and Miss Anthony to block negro suffrage in Kansas in 1867" might have contributed to black opposition to the measure.[32]

Stone and Blackwell had scheduled speaking stops all along the return route. When the exhausted pair slept through their stop at Cleveland and woke to learn that the next planned stop was not until Erie, Pennsylvania, they begged the conductor to persuade the engineer to stop the train and let them off in Painesville, Ohio. He would only agree to stop two miles from the station. Thus it was that at two o'clock in the morning, they found themselves walking along a deserted stretch of railroad tracks somewhere east of Cleveland. In a letter to the *Journal*, Stone described how carrying their valises soon grew too strenuous for Blackwell, and he directed her to "wait with the satchels while I go on and see what I can find." The letter offers a rare picture of the sixty-four-year-old suffragist, alone with her valises along an empty stretch of railroad track, yet able to wring pleasure from the moment: "So I stopped. The cocks crowed in the neighboring yards. The comet blazed in the East. The aurora borealis flickered and faded away in the North. The moon and stars, clear, cold, and unsympathetic looked down upon me standing there on the frost-covered ground, between two iron rails that ran backward and forward as far as the eye could see, glittering with frost under the moonlight."[33]

Stone was growing too old for these adventures, and when she could, she avoided longer trips. There was plenty to do close to home that year. The growing success of women's political groups in lobbying for partial suffrage sparked a strong countereffort by the anti-suffragists. They established a headquarters in Boston with the intention of canvassing every town in the state. Stone often published reports of anti-suffrage activities, continuing to insist that increased opposition was a tribute to the growing strength of woman suffrage, and that anti-suffrage activity would only draw a greater hearing to it.[34]

If she believed this, Stone underestimated her opponents. Middle-class women, or "Remonstrants," as anti-suffrage women came to be known, rallied under a "pro-family" anti-suffrage banner. Magazine articles, novels, ladies' magazines, engravings, and advertisements all celebrated the Gilded Age's *belle idéal*—a domestic and dependent beauty whose home was her castle. In fiction, political cartoons, and editorials, woman suffragists were lampooned as unwomanly, "third-sex" creatures doomed to spinsterhood.[35]

Strong opposition came as well from Catholic periodicals. Priests warned Catholic women of the "dangerous consequences" woman suffrage posed to the sanctity of the family.[36] Against the weight of hierarchical disapproval, Stone found her eloquence unavailing, her tracts discarded unread. Still, the greater the opposition, the harder Stone worked. Overwork contributed to a severe cold that winter. Alice wrote Kitty that "[Mother] doesn't want to speak or stir. She lay in a large chair in the library and took flaxseed tea, and had herself all done up with pepper poultices." In the evening, Blackwell and Maggie (the hired girl) "undertook to give Mamma a rum sweat." Blackwell put too much alcohol into the dish, and the sheets Stone was wrapped in caught fire. "Mother started up in wrath and indignation between Papa and Maggie, and fled from them as naked as she was born." Alice concluded that "The scorching or the excitement, or something did Mamma good." At breakfast the following morning, Alice reported that her mother laughed with the others over Blackwell's puns, jests, and his observation that her "rate of speed" on her naked run "was about a mile in two minutes."[37]

Stone was back on the hustings later that month, coordinating a last-minute lobbying effort to get a woman suffrage bill passed in the Massachusetts legislature. She sent a letter to each of the state legislators querying him on his position on the proposed amendment, enclosing a self-addressed and stamped postcard. Their responses enabled Stone to target doubtful members for further lobbying and to compile a list of opponents for future campaign reference.[38]

Later that spring, when a mortgage he held came due, Blackwell repaid Stone three thousand dollars of the money she had advanced him for the Maine Beet Sugar Company. She used part of the money to pay for her niece Grace's ocean passage home from England. She also offered to send Blackwell and Alice on a trip to California. Once again, Alice wrote Kitty that "Poor Papa is tired and worn."[39]

Alice returned in time to take over the *Journal* so that her mother could attend Oberlin's fiftieth anniversary celebration. Just before her departure, Stone wrote Sarah that she had learned that many of her old friends were to be there. "Nettie says, 'Let us go and all grow young again,'" she wrote.[40] Blackwell agreed to accompany her but commented wryly to Alice that he anticipated being the "worst bored man at Oberlin" and that "a whole week of contact with people who believe in hell and also mention the devil will, I fear, be too much of these good things for a person of impaired spiritual digestion like myself."[41]

En route, Stone and Blackwell stayed at a friend's house in Ohio. Stone described the house in a letter to Alice as "the most magnificent house I was ever in. . . . The cook has the gas in jets *in the stove,* and only turns it on as much as she pleases."[42] The meetings she and Blackwell held all along the way were large and successful, and at Oberlin, Lucy and Antoinette eagerly renewed old acquaintances, reminisced, and toured the much-altered campus. Paved roads and tall buildings stood in place of the primitive structures of earlier years. Stone was the only woman among the honored speakers at the Fourth of July ceremony marking the semicentennial of the college. The *Cleveland Leader* printed the full text of her speech enumerating women's progress on its front page the following day. She made only passing mention of the college's having denied her practice in rhetoric and the right to read her graduation essay, saying cheerfully that "time has altered all this and settled it right."

Stone used the occasion of her speech to review the gains in education for women over the past fifty years, saying that from their modest beginnings at Oberlin, opportunities had grown so that women of the day could "behold more than half the colleges of the land wide open to women." As a result, Stone told them, "In ten thousand homes all around us are educated mothers who bring to the grave duty of rearing sons and daughters well stored and well disciplined minds, and here is the center of our national safety." To the "great questions which involve human interests" the addition of "the feminine thought, the feminine judgment and view" are added, to the betterment of society."[43]

Returning to Boston, Stone resumed editing, traveling, speaking, writing, cooking, canning, corresponding, and attending lectures at the local woman's club. "The talk on Darwin at the club was *very* interesting," she wrote Alice. Blackwell was once again involved in a sugar enterprise, and "he assures me he has 'found a process that will be valuable.'"[44] Stone's letters to Alice were full of the homely occurrences of life at Pope's Hill. She told how she and Maggie had been "putting up tomatoes" with frequent interruptions, as it was ironing day. As they labored in the steamy mess, Blackwell drove up in the carriage with an unexpected lady visitor. When he pointedly reminded Stone that the lady visitor "had had no dinner and must have some," Stone suggested that he show the visitor the view from the rooftop. She quickly "cut off a piece of beef . . . broiled it, warmed some cold potatoes, cooked some tomatoes, made a cup of tea, and, all hot and sweating, presented it with pears for dessert. Then I took her to the station. . . ." If Stone resented such incursions, there is no hint of it in the letter.[45]

Through that fall and winter, various Blackwell nieces and relations were in and out of Pope's Hill. There was jubilation when the news came in November that Washington Territory had voted to strike the word "male" from all election laws. "The young, progressive West leads the way, where, sooner or later, the East will have to follow," Stone wrote.[46]

The December 2, 1883, issue of the *Journal* carried the news of the death of Sojourner Truth at the age of one hundred ten. Stone wrote a deeply moving obituary for the freed slave woman who had become a legend in her time, quoting from Sojourner's famous "Ain't I a Woman?" speech in an elegiac tribute that concluded: "We shall not look upon her like again."[47]

A second loss, this one nearer to home, occurred just two months later in early February 1884. Picking up the morning paper, Stone read of the sudden death the previous day of Wendell Phillips. Alice said later that it was "the only time that I ever heard my mother literally 'lift up her voice and weep,' sobbing and crying out loud, like a little girl." Invited to deliver a eulogy at his memorial service, Stone praised in Phillips that which she no doubt valued above all in herself: "He took ever the side that seemed to him the right side, and fully expected to see it prove itself to be so."[48]

Stone herself was none too well that spring. In addition to the painful rheumatism and the recurring problems with her throat, she confided in a letter to her dear friend Margaret Campbell: "I have a heart trouble. . . . Dr. Emily says . . . there is a weakness in the muscles that should send the blood onward. . . . I have too a trouble with my kidneys." She briefly considered taking a two-month winter vacation in the South to soothe her joints and try to ward off the anticipated severe cold that had come to plague her winters. Instead, she remained in Boston, laboring through the spring at editing the paper, circulating the pamphlets, and lobbying the Massachusetts legislature to secure passage of a bill favorable to women and the defeat of another inimical to their interests. She prepared and circulated a petition calling for the recognition of the validity of contracts drawn up between husbands and wives, and she organized another legislative effort aimed at securing police matrons so that arrested females might be in the care of women.[49]

In July, Stone made out a new will leaving the bulk of her estate to Alice. She made provision for Blackwell, allowing him the use of the Pope's Hill house during his lifetime. In a letter explaining the will to Alice, Stone cautioned her to make out a letter stipulating what she (Alice) would like done with the money in the event that Blackwell should survive them both. Alice should write the letter so that it "would be binding as a will upon Papa if he survives us," Stone wrote. She advised Alice to keep her money in real estate. "Bonds or stocks are always liable to be stolen . . . but land stands." While Stone's holdings were primarily in land, she also enumerated four thousand dollars' worth of stocks and another four thousand in railroad bonds in her will. Stone advised Alice not to "get entangled with the prefers. of Geo. [Blackwell]," as she believed that it was "better not to have business relations with one's own family. Have your property clear by yourself."[50]

That summer, Stone's longtime housekeeper, Mary Flynn, quit to move closer to her "sweetheart" in the city. Flynn departed reluctantly, later praising Stone effusively. "I couldn't tell you her goodness!" Flynn said. "She didn't treat me like a servant, she treated me like a daughter," adding that "If I was sick, she sat up with me herself." Stone "urged me to go to night school, and when I wouldn't, she taught me herself." Because Stone believed in higher wages for domestic work, Flynn reported that she was paid "the very highest wages." She later reminisced about one Fourth of July when "Mr. and Mrs. Blackwell were going away. Just before leaving the house, she came into the kitchen and said: 'We may be in for dinner, Mary. I have provided everything, lamb, green peas, new potatoes and ice cream, so have it ready about one o'clock.'" Flynn continued, "Of course I was mad, for I wanted to go out with my friends. I had dinner ready at the time she told me and was looking down the road in the direction of the railroad station when I saw my brother, his wife and four children coming up the road. Mrs. Stone had invited them out from the city to spend the day with me and had provided the dinner as a surprise."

Flynn insisted that Stone "was always sunny tempered. I never saw her in a temper. She frequently suffered from headaches. During those attacks, I used to brush her hair." Flynn told how as she was leaving to go to confession, Stone would teasingly say to her: "Come in here, Mary, I'll figure them up for you." Her employer was "constantly helping the colored people and the poor of all races," Flynn said, adding that "If Miss Alice isn't rich, they must have given away her fortune."[51]

Perhaps the most touching story about the loyalty of Stone's household help concerned a German immigrant, Mary Lapp, who had worked for Stone in the 1860s. As Lapp lay dying in a sanatarium outside Dorchester, she pleaded with the nurse to try to find a woman named Lucy Stone for whom she had worked in New Jersey many years before. She said that if the nurse could just assure her that the woman's two daughters could get to Mrs. Stone, she would know that they would be well cared for. When the nurse told the woman that she of course knew of Lucy Stone and that she lived nearby in Dorchester, Lapp was visibly relieved. Following Lapp's death, Stone took in one of the children, Beth Hagar, and raised her, arranging for the adoption of the other.[52]

Despite her reputation as a generous employer, following Flynn's departure, Stone could find no one to help with the cooking or cleaning of the seventeen-room house. She wrote Alice that Blackwell had promised to "go to the Swedish engagement office Saturday, but he forgot it and went instead to Governor Claflins." Feeling the burden of household responsibilities, Stone wrote that summer that "a wife is like a horse harnessed in, with the whip behind, and she has to *draw*"[53]

Stone's argument that women would purify politics was put to the test in 1884 in a presidential election that caused a rift between herself and Higginson. Voters were asked to choose between James G. Blaine, a political spoilsman and lackluster Republican senator from Maine whose close ties to the scandal-ridden Grant administration made him anathema to many fellow Republicans; and Grover Cleveland, a reform Democrat credited with purging Buffalo of political corruption, but who was charged with having fathered an illegitimate son.[54]

Higginson joined a splinter group of Reform Republicans, "Mugwumps," who voted to support Cleveland. Stone, to whom apparently no amount of political chicanery could compare to a single sexual transgression, chose to back Blaine. The innate horror with which she had come to regard sexual improprieties came to the surface in the Cleveland–Blaine campaign. She saw Cleveland as a threat to the purity and safety of the home. She and Higginson locked horns over the issue in a series of *Woman's Journal* editorials. Higginson urged readers to overlook Cleveland's "single sin," while Stone exhorted Republican leaders "to search for the truth of the charges against him. If, by the testimony of credible witnesses, it is clear that he is a man of dissolute life, as is affirmed," she wrote, "then he should be dropped at once."[55]

Following a family council (which included Emily), Stone and Blackwell made the decision to print letters offering "evidence" of Cleveland's debauchery on the front pages of the *Woman's Journal*. One letter told of seeing Cleveland and his "veiled paramour freely exposed in their nightclothes and seen by several reputable witnesses." Anyone willing to overlook "such an offence," wrote Stone, "shows a shocking state of morals. . . . It is clear that women are needed in politics."[56]

Higginson's lead editorial the following week expressed his regret that the *Woman's Journal* had chosen to involve itself at all in the election, as both candidates had declared themselves in favor of woman suffrage. Prior to printing Higginson's editorial, Stone sent him a note asking him to consider withdrawing it, but he insisted that she print it "as is" or he would "as soon be dropped altogether."[57]

In the same issue with Higginson's editorial, Stone printed her own plea to readers to reject Cleveland on grounds that nothing less than the survival of the family was at stake, and that "all precious things" would be placed "in gravest peril" if Cleveland were to be elected. Higginson's attempts to reason with the strong tide of emotion behind such rhetoric were useless. Nonetheless, he wrote in the *Journal*, "There are many to whom it seems almost wicked to compare in importance any amount of lying or stealing with a single sexual transgression; and there are many to whom it seems almost wicked to compare any amount of sexual transgression with a single well-proved instance of lying and stealing. To adjust the balance between these two extremes has been no easy thing."[58]

Higginson's reasoned appeal was wasted on Stone, who saw no "extremes." After the election, Higginson tendered his resignation from the paper, assuring Stone that "we will always be friends." Stone responded warmly that "No difference that has occurred makes the least difference in my feeling toward you. No one will give you more cordial good wishes than I." Privately, she expressed irritation at Higginson's final editorial, in which he made reference to thirty years of attempting to "educate women up to the franchise." Then too, Higginson's salary of six hundred dollars per year had strained *Journal* resources.[59]

Articles by Higginson continued to appear in the *Woman's Journal*, and relations between him and Stone remained friendly, but the close bond of affection and esteem that had brought Higginson from Worcester to the farmhouse on Coy's Hill some thirty years before to officiate at his friend's unconventional wedding ceremony was weakened. Politics had made polite comrades where before there had been good friends.

The Blaine-Cleveland matter generated the most mail the *Journal* had ever received. Many of the letters requested cancellation of the writers' subscriptions. In a letter to her friend Cornelia Hussey written shortly after Cleveland's victory, Stone reported that some of the letters were so "bitter" and "personal" that "we quietly put them in the wastebasket." Despite the loss of subscribers, Stone characteristically did not question her position. Her letter to Hussey ended indignantly: "Think of it, a male prostitute in the White House, and no woman a voter!"[60]

More and more Stone came to cast woman suffrage as an antidote to masculine corruption. Men were weak, sexually corruptible, susceptible to graft, and, under the influence of drink, brutes as well. Boss Tweed, Tammany Hall, drunkenness, wife-beating, prostitution—all would be brought under control by the benign influence of the female vote. In urging municipal suffrage, she told audiences: "The evils that threaten our city government will involve us all. The only power that can give permanent safety is the vote of women." It was not surprising that powerful and moneyed liquor interests saw woman suffrage as threatening, particularly as the women grew more sophisticated in their political tactics. When the various state legislatures convened in January 1885, Stone instructed readers to adopt a two-part approach. "Personally speak to the member, and petition him from his neighbors," she told them. Though results were slow and often discouraging, women nonetheless were showing themselves to be a force in politics.[61]

That year, the NWSA began to draw closer to the American association in its goals and strategies. At the seventeenth annual Washington NWSA convention, delegates adopted a plan to "secure full suffrage by statute from State legislatures; also to secure full suffrage in all elections by statute in the respective territories" and to establish a "permanent business headquarters." In another major departure, the business committee report announced its intention to present a plan for a delegate structure to be voted on at the next meeting.[62] The rival associations were moving closer.

Later that spring, word came at last that the money Stone and Anthony had been left in the will of Eliza Eddy was available to them. The wording of Eddy's will, drawn up by Wendell Phillips, offers an interesting insight into Eddy's and Phillips's assessment of Stone and Blackwell's financial relations. Half the bequest was to go to Susan B. Anthony, "and the other portion I leave to Lucy Stone, wife of H. B. Blackwell, as her own absolute and separate property, free from any control of him."[63]

Hoping to let bygones be bygones, Stone wrote Anthony a cordial note inviting her to spend the day at Pope's Hill when she came to Boston to collect her share of the Eddy fund. "I gave her a time table, and told her I would meet her at any train, if she would let me know—Instead she sent a hateful note, that made me feel the last plank between us had broken."[64] Stone and Anthony each received more than twenty-four thousand dollars from the Eddy estate. Stone used the income from the Eddy fund to seed legislative campaigns and to start up a woman suffrage news service, while Anthony bought out the publishing rights of the first two volumes of the *History of Woman Suffrage* and paid to have a thousand copies donated to libraries across the country.[65]

Too busy that summer to go with Blackwell and Alice to Martha's Vineyard, Stone wrote of returning from a convention in Rhode Island and catching sight of the sea at Nantucket as she rode by on the railroad, "and the well remembered sight of the breakers, white crested and pea green, made me long for a quiet sit with only the breakers. But I can't knock about. . . ."[66] Along with the newspaper and the news service, the ordering, printing, and distribution of suffrage tracts and pamphlets had become a big business. In 1886 alone, Stone reported mailing off almost a quarter of a million pamphlets to twenty-four different states and territories. In early September, she was off again—to Iowa and Indiana, to Ohio, to Michigan, to Minneapolis (site of that year's October AWSA convention), with a stopover in Albany to address the legislature and to speak at the annual New York State Woman Suffrage Association meeting there. Blackwell accompanied her, and Stone wrote Alice that "when he isn't speaking, he is off trying to organize people to raise sorghum."[67]

Later that winter, Stone was nearly crippled by a harsh bout with rheumatism, and in January, a severe cold prevented her from making several scheduled convention appearances. She recovered slowly through the spring and summer, and by autumn was able to resume work. Dr. Emily advised against her travels, but Alice wrote her dissent:

The little change and outing does her good every year. Also it's cheering to have big audiences rise up *en mass* and applaud greatly when you come in, and to have women whom you don't know come and embrace you with tears and bring up their children to shake hands and impress it upon the youngsters that they are to remember the hand-shake and tell their children about it & c. & c. as they have been doing to her out west. Part of the affection even overflows upon me. . . . One comes into an inheritance of affection as of money, which one has done nothing to earn; it is very pleasant, yet makes one feel a little astonished.[68]

Relations between the two wings of suffragists thawed slightly. That autumn, Anthony wrote requesting the donation of a large quantity of pamphlets to be given out at an NWSA booth at the New Orleans fair. Stone complied. Stanton sent along a cordial note to Antoinette Brown Blackwell, saying "she did wish I could get you to meet with her and Susan and me once more, to have it seem like the old days. . . ."[69]

Stone responded, "As to meeting with Mrs. Stanton, it is out of the question with me. She sent a letter to Mr. Shattuck of this city which he read to a little group, of which I was one, in which she said I was 'the biggest liar and hypocrite she had ever seen.' After that, you will see that I cannot with any self respect meet her with a pretence of good fellowship." Stone added, "For yourself, of course, such a letter about me need make no difference—Mrs. Stanton is as bright and witty as ever and Susan just as egoistical."[70]

If she continued to cherish hard feelings toward both women, Stone had grown friendlier toward their efforts. Following the NWSA convention in February 1886, she wrote Alice: "The Washington Convention seems to have been very good indeed. It is a great comfort to feel that it helped rather than hindered."[71] At the NWSA convention, the members voted to cooperate with the AWSA in a joint effort to lobby congress for equal suffrage in the territories. They had approved the delegate basis, and subsequent events moved the two societies closer.

For much of 1886, Stone enjoyed better health than any obese sixty-eight-year-old woman with rheumatism, heart trouble, and kidney problems could expect. Still, she had grown keenly aware of the passing of time, and that summer, she invited a group of the surviving antislavery and woman's rights activists out to Pope's Hill for a grand reunion. A picture taken that day shows the group seated around the porch. There are Abby Kelley Foster, Samuel May, Harriet and Samuel Sewall, as well as the four sons of William Lloyd Garrison: William, Jr., Francis, Wendell, and George. Elizabeth Buffum Chace and Sarah Southwick are there as well. A portly Stone clad in a dark dress and lace cap looks away from the camera with a slight smile on her face. Absent are those who were already lost to death—Sarah Grimké, Stephen Foster, William Lloyd Garrison, Wendell Phillips. The circle grew smaller year by year.

That autumn, Stone wrote Margaret Campbell, "I long for younger hands and for personal relief from the work."[72] Despite her words, it took life-threatening illness to convince Stone to turn the task over to younger hands, even temporarily. Emma and George invited Stone to come to Thomasville, Georgia, where they had gone for the winter, assuring her that the mild climate would help her recuperate. Concerned for her health, they enlisted Blackwell's aid in trying to persuade her to make the trip. He wrote George of his frustration in trying to "get Lucy out of her present woman suffrage rut, which grieves me inexpressibly." He added that he did not know if she would agree to travel to Georgia, for, as he concluded cheerfully, "like Lincoln, I have no influence with this Administration."[73]

Stone's health worsened in February 1887, but only when Dr. Emily warned her that the illness might prove fatal if she did not get to a warmer climate did she finally agree to leave the paper in Alice and Harry's hands and travel to Georgia. In Thomasville, she was gravely ill, and she wrote Blackwell a valedictory letter thanking him "for the abundant and unselfish work you have done for women." Knowing how much he disliked the routine of the paper, she cheered him by writing that "in the long hereafter, the world will be better for it." Turning to practical matters, she told where to find her will, asking that he "respect its conditions." Her letter ended with a note of apology and love: "I wish there were rest and leisure for you to do the things you like best and in any event and for always my heart is warm to *you*, dear darling Harry."[74]

Blackwell wrote to cheer her with a description of his newest attempts to make sugar from molasses and of his campaign for a suffrage amendment in Rhode Island. In Georgia, Stone recovered slowly, feeling more and more guilty about being away from the work of the paper, writing to Alice, "I think how the short Eds. and the long Eds. gnaw at you, and however tired, they hold you with relentless grip! But it is . . . well worth weariness and fatigue. Nevertheless I do not want my sole daughter to be drawn to death in it, nor the man whose name I do not take hurried to death by it."[75]

When she was well enough, Stone ventured out with Emma. More inclined to society ways, Emma persuaded Stone to accompany her on a round of "fashionable calls," which Stone described in a letter to Alice. Alice teased her by return mail: "It seems funny to think of you making fashionable calls. I hope you don't find it too great a bore."[76] Much more to Stone's taste was a day spent in a school for black children. She was appalled at the dry, rote methods employed by the two Yankee women ("Excellent women, but so unfit for the place!") who drilled their students in what she characterized a "most melancholy showing" filled with warnings about "G-A-W-D" in which the students showed no interest. However, as Stone began to speak to them of matters relating to their own history and experience, "The whole school lighted up with interest, eager, and all alive, showing how far removed they were from the dull, stupid set they appeared to be before the ghastly solemn face of their too pious teachers. . . . I told them the things to do them good, stir their pride, their hopes, their ambitions to be as good as the best, and their wide-open eyes told how well they understood."[77]

Stone wrote often from Georgia, and Alice responded with a long series of chatty letters. Besides assisting in the editing of the *Woman's Journal*, Alice was busy with the *Woman's Column*, now a weekly dispatch financed by some of the proceeds of the Eddy fund. Offering a brief synopsis of suffrage news, it went out to more than a thousand newspapers that spring. (Within three years, it would reach more than seventeen thousand subscribers.)[78]

From Boston, Alice wrote in early April that she was deeply hurt to learn that Anthony had won over Alice's good friend, Rachel Foster, and proposed to set up a rival woman suffrage news service with her. Foster had convinced the Pennsylvania association to drop its subscription to Alice's *Woman's Column* and subscribe instead to the rival newsletter. Stone's response was fierce and protective: "Penn. is an ass, the very foolishest ass," she wrote. "We won't help them an atom." Her first fury spent, Stone went on to try to imbue in Alice her own attitude toward the underhanded tactics of her opponents:

You will be glad of any real help any of them give to the cause, even the worst of them, if you put the cause FIRST OF ALL. . . . Its success and prosperity have always been more to me, than any personal feeling, and any damage to IT far more than any personal ill will, or misunderstanding of myself, so I could always rejoice in good work no matter who did it. Try to look at it in this way dear, and let Rachel Foster's little trick go out of sight in the hope of the good to the cause in Penn. I am glad you wrote me about it, and I hope you will always tell me when anything hurts or troubles you. What are mothers for if they can't take children up when they need comfort?[79]

When Alice balked at the suggestion that the time had come for the two associations to unite, her mother wrote: "They are now doing very good work as an association, and APPARENTLY there is no reason why we should not unite." Reunion was not far off, and throughout the summer and autumn of 1887, plans proceeded for uniting the two societies. A week-long celebration of the fortieth anniversary of the Seneca Falls meeting of 1848 was being planned for the following year, and Stone wrote that "we might propose to make it a Jubilee Anniversary and union of the two national societies." Stone still did not fully trust to the political discretion of the rival society, writing that she hoped for a loose organization in which "each should be responsible for its own work, but all *meeting* upon occasion, and working together as friendly societies, escaping in this way, any indiscretions which the National Branch might run into."[80]

Stone used the money from the sale of another piece of Montclair property to send Alice to Europe in the summer of 1887. This time, Blackwell did not go. Instead, he remained in Boston working with Stone. Together, they held a series of Working-Girls' Club meetings in the parlor at Pope's Hill. They also ran a successful campaign to include a woman suffrage plank in the Prohibition party platform. That autumn, Kansas again placed a woman suffrage referendum on the ballot, and Blackwell went to Kansas to campaign. Anthony was also in Kansas, and she and Blackwell shared a lecture platform. At the conclusion of her speech, she offered the audience a reduced annual subscription rate of one dollar per year if they would subscribe to the *Woman's Tribune*, turning to look at Harry as she made this announcement and saying, "You see, Mr. Blackwell, we mean to *cut under* the Woman's Journal."[81]

If Anthony's unabated antagonism gave her pause, Stone nonetheless went ahead with preparations for the eventual merger. At the October anniversary meeting of the AWSA, she presented a proposal that stated that, as differences between the two associations "have since been largely removed by the adoption of common principles and methods," the delegates vote to appoint "Mrs. Lucy Stone . . . to confer with Miss Susan B. Anthony . . . and if it seems desirable . . . appoint a committee to meet a similar committee appointed by the National to consider a satisfactory basis of union." The proposal was approved handily, and Anthony agreed to the meeting. On December 21, 1887, she and Rachel Foster met with Stone and Alice at Number 3 Park Street in Boston and agreed upon a committee. The members of the National committee were May Wright Sewall, Rachel Foster, Clara Colby, Olympia Brown, Laura Johns, and Harriet Shattuck. In addition to Blackwell, the members of the American committee were William Dudley Foulke, Julia Ward Howe, Hannah Tracy Cutler, Mary Thomas, Margaret Campbell, and Anna Howard Shaw.[82]

While the negotiating committee was meeting, Anthony completed final arrangements for an international celebration of the fortieth anniversary of the Seneca Falls convention of 1848. Until that time, no particular symbolic significance had been accorded to the small meeting in upstate New York, occurring as it did almost simultaneously with similar meetings in Ohio and well after Stone had already begun to draw large crowds to her lectures on woman suffrage. Anthony may have viewed the selection of an anniversary to mark the beginning of national suffrage work as another piece of territory to be gained. For years, suffragists had celebrated the Worcester convention as marking the first national suffrage work. Anthony had managed to draw delegates from England, Scotland, Germany, Finland, Norway, Sweden, and France to the gala celebration in Washington, D.C., beginning on March 26, 1888. Stone and Blackwell were invited to speak on Pioneer Day, the day set aside to pay tribute to the early suffragists.

Anthony's speech was conciliatory, beginning with the acknowledgment that it was Stone who first had drawn her to work for woman's rights. Both Julia Ward Howe and Frances Willard told how they too had been won over by Stone. The next day's *Washington Post* carried a lengthy account of the tributes to Stone, identifying her companion as "Mr. Blackwell, or as he is better known, the husband of Lucy Stone."[83]

Because the final plan for unity had to be approved by each association at its annual meeting, negotiations for the union went on for almost two years. It was February 1890 before the first full meeting of the National American Woman Suffrage Association, as the new association was to be called, took place. At that meeting, Anthony would deliver a parthian shot at Stone. One of the first conditions Stone had insisted upon at the initial 1887 meeting was that in the spirit of good will and as a demonstration of neutrality, none of the three principals involved in the original schism—Stanton, Stone, or Anthony—would attempt to take the presidency of the united organization.[84] However, as convention time neared, Anthony began a letter writing campaign urging all national members to "be on hand at our next annual Washington convention to stand firm as a rock for perfect freedom *in the union* and for Mrs. Stanton as President of it."[85]

When the time came to depart for Washington, Stone was too sick to accompany Alice and Blackwell. She suffered from a flare-up of heart problems and respiratory ailment. Though she held out hope that she would improve sufficiently to attend the final joint meetings, sending along her best cashmere skirt with Blackwell and directing him to hang it so that the wrinkles would be out by the time she arrived, her health did not improve. She would not have been happy sharing the platform with Anthony as "in a voice vibrating with emotion" she urged the audience: "Don't vote for any human being but Mrs. Stanton." Stanton was elected, and Anthony became vice president. Stone was unanimously elected chairman of the executive committee, a vote she regarded as "complimentary."[86]

At seventy-two, Stone was slowing down, and her agreement to merge the two associations grew from her realization that she could no longer single-handedly keep her national association afloat. Alice had neither the time nor the inclination to head the movement. Although intellectually Stone knew that the time for unification had come, emotionally it was a blow. Stone was what she did; her work was her *raison d'être*. Who was she if she did not work? Stone would struggle with the question in the few short years that remained to her.[87]

CHAPTER THIRTEEN

"Make the World Better"

The union of the two suffrage wings seemed to take from Stone the sense of mission that had driven her so relentlessly through the past two decades. As she waited for word from Blackwell and Alice in Washington in February 1890, she wrote that her heart and respiratory problems left her "choking and breathless." Just back from the funeral of her brother Bowman, Stone was at low ebb emotionally as well. Even before the news reached her that Stanton had been elected to the presidency and Anthony to the vice presidency of the new joint association, Stone was all too aware of the historical implications of having either Stanton or Anthony take the helm. At the conclusion of merger negotiations, she had written Nettie that Anthony "so much wished to be President herself! To bring her to the top at last would be such a vindication, she cannot bear to forego it." Both women understood that Stanton's presidency was in name only; soon after the election, Stanton sailed for England, where she remained for almost two years, leaving Anthony at the helm of the new joint organization.[1]

However often Stone told herself that the work was all, and that personal glory should play no part in the great work of woman suffrage, she had believed throughout the long years of her silence that sooner or later the "better doings" of her wing would become clear to all. With her rivals "vindicated" and in charge of the vast organization she had largely built, Stone tasted defeat, writing to Alice and Harry that she sympathized with them for having to endure "the humiliation which will be poured upon our side—only for the cause we would not bear it." She added that the *Herald* and the *Globe* had each carried an account of Anthony's birthday celebration, and on the following day, had carried "further reports of Susan's birthday, and her red velvet gown, and the letters from various persons sent as special despatches. . . ." One of the special dispatches was Stone's own warmly worded letter of congratulation.[2]

Stone's insistence that for her part, envy had never played a role in the division was probably true; nevertheless, her letters to Harry, Alice, and Nettie that February came near to sounding envious. Anthony's ascendancy struck at Stone's sense of the moral order of the world; she had been unswerving in her belief that hers was the higher road. Perhaps she could sense as well the ebbing of the tide of history. Still, Stone would continue to refuse any public correction of the record. When later that spring Stanton's "Reminiscences" giving an ingenious and disingenuous treatment of Train and Woodhull appeared in serial form in the *Woman's Tribune,* Stone ignored the account. Over her objections, Blackwell printed a long correction in the *Woman's Journal* in which he used verbatim quotes from Stanton's *Revolution* editorials to point to the inaccuracies in her history of the era.[3]

Still, however chagrined she was in private, Stone was determined to present a public show of magnanimity in a series of conciliatory moves. In addition to the birthday telegram, she published a long and flattering account of Anthony's birthday celebration in the *Woman's Journal.* Immediately after the close of the convention, she wired Anthony permission to add her name as guarantor of payment of any outstanding convention debts.[4]

The private toll exacted by the public display can be read in the harsh tone that crept into her letters. When Alice wrote describing the funeral of Stone's friend Miriam Cole and quoting from Mr. Cole's eulogy of his wife, Stone fumed in disgust at his "hypocrisy," declaring that it was he who had "refused [his wife] the things she most wanted" and made her work so hard that "her discouraged soul weakened her body, and *now* he marvels at the Providence that did it, and at her acceptance of the 'dispensation of suffering' & c. The old Skunk! The Buzzards ought to get him."[5]

Describing a talkative admirer who shared her train compartment on a trip from New York to Boston, Stone told how she "groaned in spirit" at the prospect of having to converse, and "escaped" by taking a nap. When the press heralded the arrival in Boston of the spiritualist and theosophist Madame Blavatsky, Stone wrote Sarah that the woman "is a great fraud and humbug. She is too fat to walk. She lays on a lounge all day and smokes, rolling up her cigarettes herself."[6]

One of Stone's lifelong dreams had been to visit the Swiss Alps. When Alice asked her why she did not now take a trip to Switzerland, Stone responded with premonitory finality: "Oh, why don't I do so many things! It is too late. I shall never do it now." She cheered herself by adding, "But I have done what I wanted to do. I have helped the women."[7]

That summer, a recurrence of heart problems and trouble with her throat kept her from traveling to South Dakota to labor on behalf of the woman suffrage referendum then before the voters. Blackwell set off in July to join Susan B. Anthony in the campaign there, stopping en route in Washington, D.C., where he tried to obtain letters of endorsement from Republican congressmen. Arriving in South Dakota just in time to see his hopes for Republican party endorsement of a woman suffrage plank go down in defeat, he wrote Stone: "We have made the best fight we could before the Platform Committee and have failed."[8]

Without Republican party endorsement, the South Dakota referendum had no hope of passage. Stone, slow to recover from this fresh siege of heart problems and suffering badly from arthritis, wrote asking Blackwell if he would cancel the rest of his tour and return to Boston to help her. She did not think that she could get out the *Woman's Journal* alone, she wrote.[9] Blackwell wrote back that "I think I had better carry out the programme, which will detain me only 11 days longer." The eleven days would stretch to nearly two months as he continued to add new speaking engagements. It is a sad commentary on Stone's continuing lack of self-esteem, and her inability to think of herself as deserving of better treatment, that she did not appear to begrudge Blackwell either his refusal or his moment of glory. Though his letters home described the referendum's passage as "doomed" and "hopeless," he was exuberant. "I *am making* good speeches," he wrote in one letter; in another he reported: "I had most of the evening to myself and made a good speech well received." The climate was "heavenly," the air "fresh, dry, elastic, and balmy." He urged Stone to turn the care of the paper over to Alice and Mrs. Adkinson and join him. "I will take the best care of you," he promised.[10]

Stone responded dolefully that Alice was "nerve-worn, and looks pale and tired . . . so I hope you won't stay the whole month, all the more as we cannot carry S. Dakota no matter how many stay. Besides, here are the houses to rent and sell. . . ." The houses to which she referred were a number of small homes Blackwell had arranged to have built on the perimeter of Stone's property. She wrote again on September 14: "I do not write about Dakota matters much. Of course Susan will be glad to keep you, and you are doing good. The papers give you much praise." She again urged him to return, reminding him that he was under no obligation to stay. Blackwell responded airily that he hoped she would not "think me indifferent to returning home when I say that I wish I could spend next month in this State."[11]

Stone was paying all of Blackwell's expenses; still, she did not refuse him when he sent for extra funds in order to extend his stay. She did take issue with him by mail over a magazine article he had prepared that fall arguing that giving the vote to educated southern women would "diminish the power of semi-barbarous illiteracy." A number of southern legislatures were looking for ways to curtail the voting rights of blacks, and Blackwell's article was intended to convince them that enfranchising "educated and propertied women" would obviate the need to disfranchise anyone. Although Stone agreed to print his article, she did not endorse it, and a note of impatience crept into her next letter to Alice. "Papa wrote without my knowledge to Laura Clay and offered to go and speak to the K[entucky] convention." From South Dakota, Blackwell went forward with his southern strategy, directing Stone by letter to "follow up the Mississippi propaganda *at once,* mailing to *each* member of the Constitutional Convention at Jackson a copy of The Elective Franchise leaflets in an envelope." Whether Stone mailed the leaflets or not is unknown. Still, though she disliked the strategy, Stone was no more likely to interfere in Blackwell's politics than in his business schemes.[12]

As usual, Pope's Hill was bursting at the seams with assorted visitors that autumn and winter. Despite her protestations to the family that she was no longer able to take on the care of her teenaged nieces, all the Blackwells continued to regard Stone as the refuge of last resort. When Emily wrote that she "was at [my] wits' end" to know what to do with her rambunctious ward Cornelia, she asked Stone if she would agree to take the girl for two years. Emily appealed to Stone's sense of fairness—after all, she wrote, Lucy had done as much for Sam and Nettie's daughters. Stone already had two teenagers on hand; the Brown-Blackwells' Ethel, and Beth Hagar, the fourteen-year-old daughter of her former servant, were with her that year. Not surprisingly, Stone agreed to take Cornelia; she was conditioned to take good care of everyone except herself.[13]

Despite her unstinting generosity to her Blackwell in-laws—with both time and money—Stone failed to win either their approval or affection. Though it was she who regularly gave or lent money, the Blackwells invariably thanked Harry. Not one of the Blackwells ever acknowledged the extent to which Stone underwrote their brother's many unfortunate business ventures, nor did they mention the many other ways Stone helped all of them out financially. Stone's money went to help support Ellen and Marian, paid the tuition of Sam and Nettie's children, provided annuities for Ellen and Anna, and furnished large loans to George and more modest sums to Emily.[14]

In crediting Harry with what at some level they must have known was Stone's generosity, the Blackwell siblings display the dependence upon illusion that to some extent characterizes all family relationships, but that in their case was particularly marked. In their private letters to one another, they often lamented Harry's fiscal unreliability, his mental instability, his imprudence, his inability to persevere, his injudicious behavior, his lack of principle, and his lack of business sense, not to mention his marital infidelity. At the same time, most of the Blackwells collaborated in the myth that it was Blackwell's heavy commitment to suffrage work that prevented his business success.

Stone was certainly aware of their disapproval of her; Blackwell's insistence on sharing their letters made sure of that. If it hurt her, she kept it to herself. Instead, she colluded with them, doing her part to maintain the same illusions about Harry's behavior, helping to create the myth that but for woman suffrage, he would have been a rich man. Thanking him for his commitment to woman suffrage, she wrote that "Few men would have done it, leaving business, friends, pleasure for it."[15]

Stone's generosity extended to her own family as well. She paid for the college education of her niece Emma and contributed regularly to the support of her brother Frank. She also routinely sent off money and goods to Nebraska to Frank's son, Luther, and to his wife, Kate. Kate Stone wrote often thanking her "Aunt Lucy" for the crates and barrels of clothes, blankets, and shoes. Along with her thanks came updated shoe and clothing sizes for her five children along with hints that school would be starting soon and last year's things were "all outgrown."[16]

The same sense of generosity prompted Stone to receive with unflagging hospitality the army of impromptu visitors who showed up on her doorstep, although she complained privately to Emma that such visits "cut sadly into my day's work." Only with Emma did Stone feel free to express her impatience with some of Blackwell's more expensive and speculative business ventures. She wrote Emma in disgust that he had purchased "more marsh land which must be drained or filled. It is all to be left to Alice, who has no business capacity, left as the other marsh is, covered with mortgages. I am very sorry about it."[17]

That autumn, Stone and Brown Blackwell laid plans for a grand celebration of the fortieth anniversary of the "first *national* woman's rights meeting" (emphasis theirs). The occasion was timed to coincide with the January convention of the Massachusetts association. By drawing public attention to the first large-scale organized suffrage effort, they may have hoped to compete with Anthony's attempt to forward Seneca Falls. While the anniversary celebration was a success, there was little general interest in the historical skirmish over "firsts."[18]

Brown Blackwell was generally unconcerned about the place of her work in history, but she too had begun to feel the tide of history slipping away. She was determined that their meetings in the little house outside

Oberlin should be crowned a woman's rights "first," and with this in mind, she addressed the first biennial meeting of the Federation of Women's Clubs on the topic of the historic "first."[19]

If such quiet rumblings continued to percolate underground, on the surface all appeared harmonious. Stone used the *Woman's Journal* to spearhead a fund-raising drive to pay for a bust of Anthony to be exhibited at the Chicago World's Fair. In May 1891, she hosted a reception at Number 3 Park Street for Anthony, Anna Howard Shaw, and Annie Besant, a visiting English suffragist. By standing beside Anthony in the receiving line, Stone hoped to put to rest any extant rumors about their continuing hostility. In September 1891, Stone wrote Anthony a cordial letter regretting her inability to stop in Rochester for a visit on the way back to Boston from a Chicago visit, praising her for her constant labor on behalf of women. For her part, Anthony clung tightly both to the reins of the new association and to her anger. When in 1891, Stanton wrote Anthony that she would not be returning to America for the second united convention and wished her name withdrawn as candidate for the presidency, Anthony fired off a twenty-two-page letter, pleading with Stanton not to retire until it was "quite certain" that Anthony herself and "not Lucy" was sure to be elected to take her place.[20]

Stone's election was unlikely. Though nominally in charge of the executive committee, she was only peripherally involved in the NAWSA. Freed from the organizational work of the AWSA, she turned her interest to other organizations, speaking before Grange meetings, labor societies, working girls clubs, and college settlements. She continued to hold educational meetings of the Working-Girls' Club in her parlor, reporting proudly that the yearly attendance of their local club had reached six thousand. She had taken an active role in the New England Woman's Press Association, the Association of Collegiate Alumnae (now known as the American Association of University Women), the New England Women's Club, and the Massachusetts Woman Suffrage Association. From her office at the *Woman's Journal*, Stone carried on a correspondence with hundreds of women, directing them in the fundamentals of organizing, lobbying, and raising funds. In 1891, she was one of the founding members and a moving force behind the Women's Industrial and Educational Union.[21]

Still, this cumulative activity was not the same as holding the reins of a national organization. As busy as she continued to be, Stone missed the sense of purpose that had driven her in past decades. What pleasure she took came in evenings spent listening to Blackwell read aloud, and in the deep joy and almost childlike awe with which she approached the beauty of the natural world. For her seventy-third birthday that summer, George and Emma gave her a microscope, and Stone wrote in delight that she found it "a wonder and a joy." She added that the "pollen of the hollyhock, to the naked eye only dust, under the glass is piled up balls like so many shot."[22]

Alice had begun to press for permission to record some of her mother's reminiscences. Stone had little patience with the project, although occasionally she agreed to sit down and discuss the early years of suffrage work. In discussing her early work, Stone could survey the changes in her own thinking. When she came across an article advocating that women should share in the breadwinning in families, she told Alice: "I do believe that a woman's truest place is in a home, with a husband, and with children, and with large freedom—pecuniary freedom, personal freedom, and the right to vote." She went on to explain, "She bears the children, and her hands are full." Almost as an afterthought and mindful perhaps of her own experience, she added, "But if the bread-winning falls to her, she must be equal to it."[23]

She had been equal to it. Pope's Hill and the portfolio of stocks, bonds, and real estate she had managed to hold on to stood as comfortable testimony to her breadwinning ability. Little by little, Stone added improvements to the house—electricity, a telephone, central heat. Still, though the pages of the *Woman's Journal* were filled with advertisements for ready-made goods and laborsaving devices—"Gold Dust Washing Powder," "The Stevens Dish Washer (the only perfect Dish Washing Machine Ever Invented)," "Rising Sun Stove Polish," "Castilian Cream Spot Remover," Franco-American canned goods, and condensed milk, Stone held to her old ways. She kept a cow for the family's milk, baked her own bread, and made her own soap. Her pantry shelves were lined with row upon row of home-canned cherries, blackberries, tomatoes, peaches, plums, and pears. She tended to geraniums and new litters of kittens, to fabric selection and furniture purchases. Her letters to family were comminglings of the domestic and the political, filled with descriptions of homely chores and legislative lobbying. In a single letter, she would write about her garden, her canning, a trip to Chicago to assist in the planning for the 1893 World's Fair, and a speech before the legislature. Upon learning that there was to be no exhibit on the "Political Status of Women" at the Fair, Stone dispatched a spate of letters with plans for correcting the omission.[24]

Along with much of middle-class America, Stone had grown more nativist as immigrants continued to pour into the country. Although she continued to oppose immigration quotas, writing in 1891 that "The Grievance is not that the foreign-born are let in, but that the native-born women are shut out," Stone's prejudices were apparent. She had come to draw clear lines between the "right" sort of woman, and the other kind. In a letter to Anthony written on her return from Chicago, Stone described those who were planning for the Women's Department as "fine-looking noble women." The head of the committee, Mrs. Potter Palmer, she described as "so beautiful and so gracious. So tactful, so rich and so clearly a suffragist that she will win for our cause by her very personality." This contrasted with Stone's attitude toward the largely immigrant women involved in the Homestead Strike. She wrote privately to her friend Judith Smith: "When I saw what 'furies' the women made of themselves at the time of the Pinkerton slaughter, it seems to me we must claim that women who are to vote must have been at least 21 years in the country first. In that time they may, free from old world ideas, have learned some self-control."[25]

Fifty years earlier, woman suffrage was closely linked to the radical movements of its time—abolitionism, utopianism, labor reform; but in the 1890s, this was no longer true. Although organized labor would move away from its earlier opposition in the 1890s and would endorse woman suffrage, laboring women were unlikely to feel at home in the middle-class enclave of woman suffragists. Mary Livermore spoke to their gentrified concerns in añ article in the September 1891 issue of the *North American Review* in which she credited fifty years of work for women's enfranchisement with changing "the whole social system. . . . The agitation of the woman suffrage question for half a century has made possible that large work of women today in education, philanthropy, reform and cooperative work." Livermore continued: "There are upwards of sixty cooperative societies of women, of national scope, engaged in the philanthropies of the country." Among the various reforms undertaken by these amalgamated groups were protective agencies, working girls' guilds, women's industrial and educational unions, industrial schools, kindergartens, and day nurseries.[26]

An occurrence at the Executive Committee preceding the 1891 NAWSA convention in Washington underscored the rising social status of woman suffrage. Stone and the others at the meeting were surprised by an invitation from the White House from Mrs. Lavinia Scott Harrison to be her guests that afternoon at tea. The women adjourned the meeting in order to attend. For Stone and the other early suffragists, afternoon tea at the White House with the wife of the President of the United States was far removed from the early days of suffrage when they had been pelted by rotting fruit and doused by firehoses.[27]

Stone described the distance traveled in another of her homely farm metaphors later that summer:

I felt my heart in my throat for gladness at the great changes that have come to women. The contrast between the time when I was young and eager for opportunities and there were none to this day when so much is gained, and I was glad I had lived to help. I used often to think that we girls (in my time) were like the cows we saw, which were in barren pastures but which could look over where abundant grass and waving growing grain grew beyond their reach, and now the bars are down and open. Thank god![28]

There was a valedictory note to Stone's letter. At the NAWSA meeting that year, Stone twice submitted her resignation as Executive Committee chairman, and twice the membership voted not to accept it—an honorific gesture, for Stone's participation was peripheral. She remained active in local work, however, and that autumn, she was heavily involved with preparations for the massive Massachusetts Woman Suffrage Association's fund-raising fair scheduled for the second week in December. In the weeks leading up to the event, the *Woman's Journal* helped to generate excitement by describing the various booths and attractions. The list of vendors offers a window into middle-class domestic life. Manufacturers of ice-cream freezers and one-minute coffeepots, of rubber aprons, and Knox gelatin, and a host of other makers of newfangled products had all agreed to donate a percentage of the profits on goods sold at the fair to the MWSA. When fair week arrived, thousands of visitors poured into the hall. They were entertained by a Ladies' Orchestra and by the Mendelssohn's Ladies' Quartette. Throughout Boston's cavernous Horticulture Hall, the yellow suffrage ribbons bedecked exhibitors' tables. In the lower hall, there were demonstrations of the many laborsaving devices and products of the day—the electric washboard, gas stove, and strawberry huller, condensed milk and bottled lemonade—as well as regular demonstrations of new cooking techniques.

There were attractions for children as well. Among the "multiplicity of delights" were "peregrinating turtles, hopping birds, wriggling serpents," and chief among the amusements a "tall antique clock, with yellow drapery up which mice were running, while other mice perched on the face of the dial. When a nickel was dropped in, the clock struck one, the mouse ran down, and a Christmas present to the value of five cents was deposited at the bottom." Each auxiliary society had its own table or booth, and women wearing yellow ribbons distributed suffrage tracts and leaflets along with tens of thousands of complimentary copies of the *Woman's Journal.*[29]

Following the close of the fair, Stone and Blackwell were at home together, enjoying a brief hiatus between the fund-raiser and the January conventions. One morning, as they sat at the breakfast table listening to the winter wind blow outside, Stone commented to Alice that the sound brought to mind her own family hearth at Coy's Hill, and she described how she and her siblings had sat before the great hearth and heard the wind howl outside while they listened to the men's tales of Indians and bears and wolves. The preindustrial atmosphere of her childhood home was a very long way from the large, centrally heated home with its bathtubs, telephone, and gaslights in which she sat reminiscing. Still, these changes were no more dramatic than the legal, political, and educational changes in the status of women that Stone had helped to bring about. Hannah Stone, isolated, intimidated, uneducated, unable to own property, incapable of earning a living wage, subject by law to corporal "discipline" by her husband, was worlds removed from her daughter Lucy.[30]

Early in January, Carrie Lane Chapman came to supper with the family, and Stone regaled her with stories of the pioneer suffragists. Chapman was a frequent visitor that winter. She and her husband had moved to Boston for the winter largely to afford Carrie the opportunity to meet frequently with Stone, who had become her political mentor. For her part, Stone had been impressed by her first meeting in Iowa a few years before with the bright and ambitious young woman, telling friends that one day Chapman "was going to be heard from by all of them." Chapman wished to learn all that she could from the woman whose speaking and lobbying techniques and fund-raising campaigns she so admired. Twenty years later, Carrie Chapman Catt would use the political expertise gained that winter to lead the final victorious lobbying campaign that resulted in the long-awaited woman suffrage amendment.[31]

Catt accompanied Stone and Blackwell to Washington in January for the 1892 NAWSA convention. All three suffrage leaders—Stanton, Stone, and Anthony—missed the opening session, having been called to an unexpected suffrage hearing before the House Judiciary Committee. Stone began by saying that she felt her talk that morning was "cheapened" by the knowledge that her listeners did "not care so much for us as if we had votes." She went on to remind them of women's need to have a say in making the laws that governed "who shall own the property, and what rights the woman shall have . . . whether she shall buy or sell or will or deed." She argued for doing away with coverture by giving women full contractual rights within the marriage. Absent such rights, she pointed out, "if the wife loan the husband her money . . . in case the husband fails in business, she can not get her money." Where before she had been certain that women would purify politics, she had tempered her rhetoric, saying "it has been said that women are more economical, peaceful and lawabiding than men. . . . But whether this be so or not, it is right that every class should be heard in behalf of its own interest." Stone's speech that morning was overshadowed by Stanton's brilliant address, the great "Solitude of Self" speech, which Stone printed in its entirety in the *Woman's Journal*, leaving out even a summary of her own address to the committee.[32] At the NAWSA convention, Anthony was at long last elected to the presidency, while Stone and Stanton became honorary presidents.[33]

Back in Massachusetts that spring, Stone led a drive to win passage of presidential and municipal suffrage in the state legislature. She sent off letters and tracts and collected and forwarded petitions. Addressing the legislature in February and again in March, Stone argued eloquently for partial suffrage. When her rheumatism permitted, Stone held a Monday suffrage open house in the parlors at Number 3 Park Street.[34]

In April, Brown Blackwell tried once again to interest Stone in clarifying the historical record, writing, "You never put your best foot forward." Stone had no time for history; her schedule was crowded "with committees and a convention"—this despite a bout with rheumatism that caused her to write that she had "never been so miserable. . . . More pain, keen, like a hard digging of a knife into my joints. It is three Mondays since I have been at the office." To Emma and George, she complained that "I can't get about much." She had also begun to experience digestive difficulties, and she was too ill to travel to Washington for the NAWSA meeting early in 1893. She sent a letter instead, and its ring of valediction indicates that Stone was aware that time was running out for her. The audience listened in silence to Stone's message:

Wherever woman suffragists are gathered together in the name of equal rights, there am I always in spirit with them. Although absent, my personal glad greeting goes to every one . . . to the strong, brave, younger workers who have come to lighten the load and complete the victory. We may surely rejoice now when there are so many gains won and conceded, and when favorable indications are on every hand. The way before us is shorter than that behind; but the work still calls for patient perseverance and ceaseless endeavor. The end is not yet in sight, but it can not be far away.[35]

In February, she invited Frank and Sarah to Pope's Hill to see Anne Whitney's bust of her before it was shipped to Chicago, where it was to be displayed in the Women's Building. She had at first refused to sit for the bust. Only when the fund-raising committee convinced her that the money collected for the bust could not go for suffrage did she agree to the project. Although Stone would not have admitted it, her invitation to Frank and Sarah was acknowledgment of the pride and pleasure she took in it. It was a fine likeness, and today it sits in the main reading room of the Boston Public Library.[36]

Stone's physical decline was apparent that spring. She was steadily losing weight, and she complained of feeling tired all the time. In late April, Blackwell left for Kentucky to attend the National Convention of Republican Clubs, and the letter she wrote him while he was away shows her awareness that she had entered upon her final illness. On May 1, she wrote:

Dear Harry

This is our 38th wedding day. After this *always,* I shall like to have my rents, interest, & c. put in my bank. It is the *right* way. I shall be just as willing as heretofore to help you out upon occasion. But all my property will be simpler in the final settlement if it appears according to the facts.

I have never liked the having it put in your bank but as I have said, you did so much for women that I had allowed it. But now we will let it go into my bank.

Yours always affectionately
Lucy Stone[37]

The terms of Stone's will provided Blackwell a generous income and the use of Pope's Hill for his lifetime—conditional upon his returning to the estate securities and land he had borrowed on. In this provision, Stone revealed her understanding of Blackwell's fiscal irresponsibility and attempted to provide for Alice, who showed little practical inclination. Although in life, she had been patient and generous with the butterfly in him, she would not jeopardize Alice's future livelihood nor the continuation of the work for suffrage by affording Blackwell unlimited access to her money. Alice was the chief beneficiary of what Stone had parlayed into a sizable estate. Because the Eddy fund and numerous smaller bequests had been given to her personally to use as she saw fit, she entrusted the money to Alice's care with careful instructions as to how it was to be used. She recommended that Alice consult William Bowditch, a good friend and shrewd businessman, for advice in financial matters.[38]

Frail and weak, Stone was nonetheless determined to travel to Chicago in mid-May as a delegate to the World's Congress of Representative Women being held in conjunction with the World's Fair. There, during the week of May 15 to May 22, distinguished women from twenty-seven countries presided over eighty-one different meetings. The meetings took place in various rooms in the Art Palace. Police and newspapers reported the total attendance at the week-long Congress as upward of 150,000.[39]

Blackwell was to have been home from Kentucky before Stone and Alice left, but when the day for their departure arrived, there was no sign of him. Unbenownst to them, he had gone off on a two-day excursion to Mammoth Cave. Alice and Stone set off without him. He later wrote that he had confused the dates and arrived home two days after they had gone.[40] On the day Stone was scheduled to speak, women crowded the corridors hours in advance in hopes of seeing this most famous and beloved pioneer. Lillie Devereux Blake described catching sight of her in the corridor that day—"a small figure, somewhat bent, touchingly slow and feeble of motion."[41] Despite her frailty, the speech she delivered, "The Progress of Fifty Years," showed that Stone had lost none of her power. Although the silvery voice had lost its great reach, it had not lost its capacity to move the hearts of listeners.

For the last time, Stone addressed a crowd. In a lyrical speech, carefully cadenced, her timing honed by half a century of experience, Stone took the emotional pulse of her audience and then gathered them in—her voice a silken cord that wrapped itself around the homely metaphors and down-to-earth wisdom that were her stock in trade. In her speech that day, Stone traced the path of the American woman's rights movement, paying tribute one by one to the "peerless women" who had gone before. "The young women of today do not and can never know at what price their right to free speech and to speak at all in public has been earned," she told the hushed audience. She mentioned the pathbreaking work of the Grimké sisters and Abby Kelley Foster, and though she might well have mentioned her own early work, she did not.

She went on to describe the ever widening spheres of vocational opportunity for women. "The idea that [women's] sphere was at home, and only at home, was like a band of steel on society. . . . The taking care of the house and children, and the family sewing, and teaching the little summer school at a dollar per week, could not supply the needs nor fill the aspirations of women."

She described how "every departure from these conceded things was met with the cry, 'You want to . . . take women out of their sphere.'" Women were told that to demand equality was "to fly in the face of Providence, to unsex yourself,—in short, to be monstrous women, women who, while they orated in public, wanted men to rock the cradle and wash the dishes. We pleaded that whatever was fit to be done at all might with propriety be done by anybody who did it well. . . . We endeavored to create that wholesome discontent in women that would compel them to reach out after far better things."

Her stocktaking continued: She contrasted the legal status of women in her own childhood, when "the law gave no right to a married woman to any legal existence at all" to that of the present day, with its vast improvements in married women's property and personal rights. She enumerated the gains in political power as well: in twenty states school suffrage for women, municipal suffrage in Kansas, full suffrage in Wyoming, excellent prospects for suffrage in Colorado. In closing, Stone summed up the gains that educational improvements, increased legal rights, and free speech had wrought. As she pronounced each item, the women applauded long and loud:

As a result we have women's clubs, the Woman's Congress, women's educational and industrial unions, the moral education societies, the Woman's Relief corps, police matrons, the Woman's Christian Temperance Union, colleges for women, and co-educational colleges and the Harvard Annex, medical schools and medical societies open to women, women's hospitals, women in the pulpit, women as a power in the press, authors, women artists, women's beneficent societies and Helping Hand societies, women school supervisors, and factory inspectors and prison inspectors, women on state boards of charity, the International Council of Women, the Woman's National Council, and last, but not least, the Board of Lady Managers.

Stone concluded: "By what toil and fatigue and patience and strife and the beautiful law of growth has all this been wrought? These things have not come of themselves. They could not have occurred except as the great movement for women has brought them out and about. They are part of the eternal order, and they have come to stay." There was not a woman there who did not know how deep was the debt she owed to Lucy Stone. Her speech ended with a heartfelt plea for each woman in the audience to carry on—to labor unceasingly until that future day when every woman would possess "equal and full justice in all things."[42]

Physically spent, Stone slowly made her way back to her seat on the platform as wave after wave of applause rang through the hall. Alice looked on beaming and proud, happily unaware that she had heard her mother's final speech and that the silvery voice had performed its magic for the last time.

Stone summoned up what energy she could for two more weeks of meetings and conferences. She attended a reception at the home of the Women's Congress director, Mrs. Potter Palmer; met with Abigail Duniway and Carrie Lane Chapman to draw up a plan of work and to arrange funds for the Colorado campaign; and sat in on two days of meetings about the upcoming Kansas drive for woman suffrage. On Sunday, May 28, she and Alice returned to Pope's Hill.

By the time of her return, Stone's stomach problems had worsened considerably. Nevertheless, she continued to correspond with the western suffragists and to prepare editorials for the *Woman's Journal*. Only to Sarah did she confide that the persistent vomiting from which she now suffered left her so physically weak that "I feel as if I had been put through a wringer. . . . I was never this way before." She added matter-of-factly, "I think it may be the final breaking up."[43]

Stone wrote again on July 31 to say that Dr. Emily had been to see her and had pronounced her "rundown," prescribing iron pills and pepsin. "I lose flesh and strength," she reported. As Blackwell and Alice were due to leave on August 1 for the Chicago World's Fair, where Blackwell had agreed to take Stone's place as a speaker, Stone looked about for a place for herself for the duration of their absence. As she faced what she had come to realize was her final illness, Stone longed for a last visit to the familiar and beautiful surroundings of Coy's Hill. Her childhood home had been purchased by a family named Day, and Stone had written Mrs. Day asking if she would agree to board her for the first two weeks in

August. Apparently, Mrs. Day was unable to take her, and Emma and George drove her instead to Gardner to stay with Sarah while Blackwell and Alice set off for Chicago.[44]

Stone left for Gardner with twenty dollars, but she was embarrassed soon after arriving to find that Blackwell was two years behind on the interest he owed Sarah and Henry Lawrence on money he had borrowed from them. She gave Sarah the twenty dollars as partial payment, explaining crossly in her next letter to Blackwell: "That is how I am penniless and I have had to buy medicine on Sarah's credit or with her money." Sarah's house "seems to be the harbor for forlorn people who need shelter," she wrote, describing her deteriorating physical condition to him in graphic detail, apologizing for sending him such a "sickish" letter, and concluding, "I think my working days are over."[45]

Either in denial of the seriousness of Stone's illness or honestly unaware of how weak and spent she was, Blackwell wrote on his return that he was willing to meet her at the railroad station, "or if you prefer, to come to Gardner for you." Although she was wasted by disease and vomiting continuously, on her return to Pope's Hill, Stone insisted that Alice travel as usual to her camp with the Barrowses, and she wrote asking Emma if she would come to stay. George resented the request and asked Emma why Alice could not stay at home and nurse her mother. Emma responded by pleading with George to rent out their house for the next few months and take a house near Pope's Hill so that she might nurse her aunt in her last illness. When George objected, she wrote, "I long to do everything possible for Aunt Lucy, who has done so much for me. She has given me schooling and education in so many other ways—as well as all sorts of pleasures from the time I could walk."[46]

George continued to criticize Alice for not contributing to the care of her mother, but Emma had a more sympathetic understanding of her cousin's shortcomings, and she chided George for judging Alice too harshly. "She loves her mother and wants to help her, but feels inadequate—she *isn't* heartless or indifferent," she wrote. Apparently George blamed Alice's inability to care for her mother on woman's rights. To George, Alice's college education, public speaking engagements, and career in journalism had unsuited her for proper womanly duties. Emma countered, "Aunt Lucy has all these [powers], and has been a most faithful home-maker, and women with none of them have been miserable homemakers." Emma defended Alice as having an "absolutely different temperament."[47]

While Emma and George debated who should care for Stone, Blackwell consulted other doctors. Stone was diagnosed as having stomach cancer, and the prognosis was poor. Medical texts of the time describe stomach cancer as inoperable and incurable. Treatment was palliative rather than curative. Doctors recommended gastric lavage and the administration of alkalies for the relief of the pain, which medical texts described as "atrocious" in many cases.[48]

Emma wrote George with a trace of annoyance that Beth Hagar and Miss Hayes, a sister-in-law of the Barrowses, continued to stay on at Pope's Hill despite Stone's illness. "They don't seem to realize that they are unwelcome," she wrote, although it is doubtful that Stone herself would have considered them so.[49] By mid-September, it was clear that the family needed a full-time nurse for Stone, but they had difficulty in finding one. Stone's good friend Ada Watson had offered to come, but family difficulties delayed her arrival until the first of October.

In the meantime, Emma cared for her aunt. Alice tried to learn to help but was bumbling and inept at nursing chores. Instead, she sat at her mother's bedside and took dictation for *Journal* editorials and notes for carrying on the suffrage campaigns when Stone was strong enough to speak. Stone's bed was moved into the parlor, with screens placed around it to offer her some privacy. Whenever she could, she had the family move her onto the veranda so that she could enjoy the beauty of the outdoors. She commented to Alice that she had never before noticed "how much beauty there was in the two elm trees in front of the house." To Emma, she spoke of the great enjoyment she had derived throughout her life from the natural world. "I fully expect to find the next world just as good as this one," she told her. Evenings, when she was up to it, Stone sat by the hearth fire, sometimes conversing, more often silent. When she was no longer strong enough to sit up, she gazed out the window. "I have had a pile of good from the clouds," she said one morning.[50]

In late September, over Alice's protest that she was too weak, Stone summoned the strength to write two letters herself. The first was to Mrs. John R. Hanna, a Denver suffrage leader, recommending that Hanna make the acquaintance of Carrie Lane Chapman, a "refined, educated, noble woman, with single-hearted interest in the enfranchisement of her sex."[51] The second letter was to her brother Frank, to tell him that she was dying. Worried that without her help, he would have difficulty supporting his family, she advised him to take out a mortgage on his farm so that he and Harriet could continue to live there. She concluded: "You have been a dearly beloved brother, and I have always had profound respect for your integrity, your honesty, your love of truth. Everyone knew your word was as good as your bond. . . . I have no fear or dread of the life beyond, and some time, somewhere, I hope to meet you there."[52]

One by one, friends came to say good-bye. While Stone permitted Emma and Alice to screen her callers, she insisted on seeing many of her old friends. Sometimes those who called were able to keep up their spirits in Stone's presence; at other times they broke down and cried. Emma described for George how Mrs. Barrows had maintained a "brave, bright face" in Lucy's room and then had "come down stairs and cried with Alice." Emma described her own tears to George: "When Auntie and I were alone together and she began to speak to me about going away, I told her that I did not want to make her feel bad, but she must let me cry a little—and so I put my head on her shoulder—she was sitting in the rocking chair, and she said I need not try to—but she spoke so quickly, and bravely, so calm and trustful herself that I was comforted."[53]

During one of her doctor's visits, Stone asked him how soon she might expect the end. He patted her hand comfortingly and murmured something about remaining serene. Surprised, she said to him: "There is nothing to be unserene about." Stone's theism included belief in an afterlife, and she consoled her friends and family with the thought that they would meet again. Emily reported that Stone was facing death "brightly and calmly," and indeed, she sounded more worried about the effect of Stone's death on Harry. "It will be a breaking up for him, for he has identified himself with Lucy in a wonderful way."[54]

William Bowditch and his wife came to say farewell. Stone told him how much it had meant to her to have the help of a prominent man like himself. She spoke of her own humble social origins and the scorn that Wendell Phillips had endured in the early years for hiring "a country girl" whom "nobody knew" to speak for the antislavery cause, when as one critic pointed out, he could have had the famous orator Edward Everett. She told the Bowditches how grateful she had felt when Julia Ward Howe, "with all she stood for," joined the movement. Alice reported that as her mother spoke, "Mr. Bowditch cried so he could hardly talk to her, and kissed her hand repeatedly, and came away. He told me he was ashamed to have 'made such a botch of it,' but he remembered her as a young girl at anti-slavery conventions, and he had known her all his life."[55]

As Stone entered the last two weeks of her life, friends continued to come in a steady stream: Cora Bennison, Adeline Howland, Sarah Henshaw, Mary Fifield. Blackwell had written to Julia Ward Howe, and she too came to say good-bye. The two of them spoke for some time. When Howe told her that she had heard a rumor that Stanton was also dying, Stone speculated on how "odd" it would be if Stanton were the first person she saw on the other side.[56]

Ada Watson arrived at last to relieve Emma, who returned to her family in New Jersey. Stone missed Emma, and on September 25, Alice wrote that her mother worried that Emma would not return, saying "She wishes most to have you [Emma] at the end." Ada and Alice were able to care for Stone's "material needs," Alice wrote, "but she wants you because she loves you."[57]

On the days when she was strong enough to talk, Stone gave Alice detailed instructions on the use she wished made of the different suffrage legacies, and on the details of the house, even suggesting a menu for the gathering that would follow her funeral. She also instructed Alice to take care of her nephew Luther's children and to provide for their education if she could. She instructed Blackwell to send a hundred dollars to Carrie Lane Chapman in Colorado, and she dictated her last *Journal* editorial just twelve days before her death.[58]

When it was clear that Stone had not much longer to live, Alice pleaded with Emma to come. Her mother was "miserable," she wrote, and each day Stone asked hopefully, "Do you expect Emma today?" Stone's physical discomfort had increased, and behind the brave show in front of friends, the pain and the agony of gastric lavage had become intolerable. Alice wrote Emma, "Mamma keeps expressing the wish to take ether or something that would painlessly end her life. She is pretty miserable. When Aunt Emily was here, I told her that if Mama *should* get into distress and want it done, I mean to do it for her."[59]

Blackwell was inconsolable in the face of his impending loss. To his sister Anna, he wrote on October 10, "It is my sorrowful task to tell you that my dear wife Lucy Stone, who has been my best friend & comfort for more than 38 years is almost surely about to leave me. She is very weak, suffering so much." To Julia Ward Howe, he wrote, "Dear Mrs. Howe, what shall I do without her?"[60]

He was the last to leave her bedside each night and the first to return each morning. His efforts to do something to alleviate Stone's suffering in her last days were "piteous," wrote Emma. She described his frenzied and foolish attempt just days before Stone died to find her something that might stay on her stomach:

Saturday evening it occurred to him that frozen watermelon might take the place of the innutritious ice. He would not take the horse, said he would bring it in his arms— it would not probably be over forty pounds, and he could bring a hundred for *her*. So he took the electric cars for Neponset, where they had no melons, thence into Boston, and home at 10:30 from his fruitless melon quest—when it was as near absolute certainty as anything could be that if he had had it before her she would not have touched it.[61]

On October 14, Emma reported that Stone "cannot keep even ice water on her stomach . . . it is a strange and solemn thing to see one known and loved so long, slowly withdrawing into silence and shadow." Though Stone could no longer sit up and was too weak to say more than a sentence, she was still "willing to have old friends take a last goodbye."

Samuel May came, and Emma reported that "Mrs. Ruffin and Mrs. Sparrows, two colored women, came last evening to bring resolutions of appreciation from their club. Dr. Ripley of Minneapolis came yesterday. . . . Aunt Lucy pressed her hand."[62]

Flowers poured into the house. Pink and white roses arrived by the dozens, along with pansies, maidenhair fern, nasturtiums, and lilies of the valley. Mr. Carter, the elderly man who years before had sold them their house on Pope's Hill, arrived at the house bearing a great bouquet. Handing the flowers to Alice, he told her, "If they bring one smile to your mother's face, it is all I want."[63]

On Wednesday, October 18, Emma wrote George that "We can see the strength slowly waning. . . . she still speaks, but with difficulty." That evening, Stone signaled Alice that she wished to say something. Alice leaned down and heard her mother whisper faintly: "Make the world better." Stone soon lapsed into unconsciousness, and at twenty minutes to eleven, Lucy Stone breathed her last. Emma wrote to her mother only minutes later: "She has left us. . . . I am glad for her that it is finished, but it leaves the others here bitterly bereft."[64]

Epilogue

Alice and her father saw to it that the news of Stone's death went out over the wire service almost immediately. Amid the expressions of sadness and regret that greeted the news in towns and cities throughout the world stood a lone diary entry: "Lucy Stone died this eve'g at her home—Dorchester, Mass. aged 75—I can but wonder if the Spirit now sees things as it did 25 years ago!!"[1]

Blackwell, for his part, was bereft. The bridge was at last broken, and the "unsuitable" match that had linked the single-minded reformer to the mercurial gadfly was ended. Family members reported that Harry was inconsolable. Emily wrote to Elizabeth: "Poor Harry is almost morbid in his regret for Lucy. It takes the form of self reproach for shortcomings and neglects. He loses sight of the fact that with all her good qualities, she was in many respects difficult and trying and quietly domineering, and that all their married life was full of trial, which was largely due to her peculiarities."[2]

If his sisters faulted Stone, Blackwell blamed himself, telling them that it would have been better for Stone if she had never married him. The Blackwells rallied around him with the protective myopia that pervaded their family relationship. On the way home from the funeral, Sam said to Emily, "Well, there is one thing, Harry can think of his 40 years of married life without any shade of self reproach, for certainly he has been a most exceptionally good husband."[3]

Emily wrote to console him that winter: "Few men would have modified their whole life to suit their wife's needs and wishes as you did. . . . I sincerely hope the morbidly painful feeling you were suffering from has yielded to a different view of the matter and a truer one." Blackwell was not to be consoled, and in the months following Stone's death, Alice often came upon him sitting alone in her mother's darkened room, suffering the "bitterest of depressions."[4]

Because Stone had clearly stipulated that she wished to be cremated,

Blackwell's depression was commingled with dread as he awaited completion of Massachusetts's first crematorium, so that he could comply with her wishes. Alice wrote that her father "looks forward toward the whole matter of cremation with dread and a sort of horror." When word reached him that the crematorium was ready, he, Frank Garrison, and Alice rode out with the body on December 30. The process of cremation took twenty-four hours.[5]

New Year's Eve brought a blizzard, but Blackwell insisted upon going out by sleigh to retrieve Stone's ashes. Writing to Sarah and Henry Lawrence on his return to Pope's Hill, he concluded: "It seemed appropriate that our Lucy the pioneer in woman's rights should have thus become a pioneer in Boston of cremation—thus in death as in life seeking to make the world better."[6]

The generous income Stone had settled on Blackwell gave him the means to realize the dreams of his youth, and at last he became a philanthropic gentleman of leisure. Perhaps driven by remorse, over the sixteen remaining years of his life, Blackwell devoted himself wholeheartedly to woman suffrage. In his "Reminiscences," he reflected that he had only persuaded Stone to marry him by promising that he would devote himself to the cause of women. "Therefore, am I not under an honorable obligation to devote every energy of mind and body to make that promise good," he asked rhetorically. His later efforts on behalf of woman suffrage earned him a place in the *National Cyclopedia of American Biography*.[7]

Alice developed into a skilled journalist and polemicist, remaining at the helm of the *Woman's Journal* until 1917 when it briefly became the *Woman Citizen* before resuming its original title. Throughout the years, until her death at age ninety-two in 1950, Alice's name could be found heading the list of supporters of one liberal cause after another. She assisted in the formation of the League of Woman Voters, translated Armenian poetry into English, wrote a biography of Catherine Breshkovsky, and in 1930, completed the biography of her mother begun soon after her death.

In the three decades that followed Stone's death—what might roughly be regarded as the span of memory of those who had known her either personally or by hearsay—Stone's fame continued to grow. A dormitory at Columbia University was named for her, as were public schools, scholarships, parks, and the chapel at Forest Hills cemetery in Boston. Pope's Hill, with its acres of fruit trees, its vegetable and flower gardens, and its ocean views, became the "Lucy Stone Home," a place where the poor women of Boston could come for the day with their children for fresh air and healthy food.

Women made pilgrimages to Coy's Hill annually to celebrate the anniversary of Lucy Stone's birth. Ten years after her death, four hundred people gathered atop Coy's Hill for a memorial service. In 1915, a thousand people made a pilgrimage to her birthplace. A Lucy Stone League was formed, and for decades, women who wished to retain their own names in marriage were known as "Lucy Stoners."[8]

The *Woman's Journal* continued publication until 1931. To this day, it stands as the most complete archival source for the work done by nineteenth-century women to secure legal and political rights. Its volumes complement the *History of Woman Suffrage*, just as the life of its editor rounds out the picture of the three great women whose efforts on behalf of their sisters were undeniably heroic. The work goes on.

Notes

Long citations for works not listed in the Bibliography are in the Notes; short citations are given from the first citation for works in Bibliography.

ABBREVIATIONS USED IN NOTES

AAS	American Antiquarian Society	IBH	Isabella Beecher Hooker
AASC	Antislavery Collections, Boston Public Library	KBB	Kitty Barry Blackwell
		LC	Library of Congress
ABB	Antoinette Brown Blackwell	LS	Lucy Stone
AKF	Abigail Kelley Foster	MAL	Mary Ashton Livermore
ASB	Alice Stone Blackwell	MB	Marian Blackwell
ASC	Antislavery Collections, American Antiquarian Society	MC	Margaret Campbell
		MH	Mary Higginson
AWSA	American Woman Suffrage Association	NAWSA	National American Woman Suffrage Association
BFP	Blackwell Family Collection, Schlesinger Library	NWSA	National Woman Suffrage Association
BLC	Blackwell Family Collection, Library of Congress	OB	Olympia Brown
		RS	Robinson-Shattuck Collection, Schlesinger Library
BPL	Boston Public Library		
EB	Elizabeth Blackwell	SB	Samuel Blackwell
ECS	Elizabeth Cady Stanton	SBA	Susan B. Anthony
Elb	Ellen Blackwell	SCB	Samuel Charles Blackwell
ELB	Emma Lawrence Blackwell	SF	Stephen Foster
EmB	Emily Blackwell	SL	Schlesinger Library
FS	Francis Stone	SM	Samuel May
FS, Jr.	Francis Stone, Jr.	SSC	Sophia Smith Collection, Smith College
GWB	George Washington Blackwell		
HBB	Henry Browne Blackwell	SSL	Sarah Stone Lawrence
HEHL	Henry E. Huntington Library	TWH	Thomas Wentworth Higginson
HLB	Hannah Lane Blackwell	WBS	William Bowman Stone
HR	Harriet Robinson	WJ	*Woman's Journal*
HS	Hannah Stone	WLG	William Lloyd Garrison
HWS	*History of Woman Suffrage*		

Introduction

1. P. T. Barnum to Dr. Trall [Stone's lecture agent in 1854], February 11, 1854; April 27, 1854, NAWSA Collection, LC.
2. Harriet Sewall to HR, February 26, 1882, RS.

CHAPTER ONE
"EXTRA! EXTRA!
Lucy Stone Is Dead!"

1. HBB to Anna Blackwell, October 10, 1893, BLC.
2. Quote in Stanton, *History of Woman Suffrage* (hereafter *HWS*) IV:712.
3. *Boston Globe,* October 19, 1893. According to Emily Blackwell, Alice and Harry Blackwell dispatched a press release within an hour of Stone's death (Hays, *Extraordinary Blackwells,* 268).
4. All headlines from October 19, 1893, except New York *Sun,* October 20, 1893.
5. BLC, Ctrs. 87–89 contain numerous accounts of buildings, scholarships, dormitories, etc. named for Lucy Stone.
6. Funeral details in *Boston Daily Globe,* October 22, 1893; *WJ,* October 28, 1893.
7. Charles Gordon Ames (1828–1912) was a Unitarian clergyman, social reformer, editor, literary biographer, and poet. Quote in *WJ,* October 28, 1893.
8. *Ibid.*
9. Press tributes reprinted in *WJ,* November 4, 18, 1893.
10. *New York Tribune,* September 28, 1930. Higginson quote in *WJ,* October 28, 1893. Thomas Wentworth Higginson (1823–1911) was a novelist, biographer, poet, critic, clergyman, abolitionist, and commander of the first black regiment in the Union Army in the Civil War. He officiated at Stone's wedding in 1855.
11. LS quoted by MAL in *WJ,* October 28, 1893.
12. H. L. Mencken in *American Mercury* 21 (December 1930):508.

CHAPTER TWO
"I Am Sorry It Is a Girl.
A Woman's Lot Is So Hard."

1. ASB, *Lucy Stone,* 3.
2. Sarah Stickney Ellis, *The Daughter of England* (London: Fisher, Son & Co., 1842), 73. Though Ellis is English, her quotation sums up female experience in early nineteenth-century America as well.
3. *Reminiscences of Lucy Stone by her daughter Alice Stone Blackwell,* BLC, 9; hereafter cited as LS, *Rem.* Copies of this and other family reminiscences are in both BLC and BFP. When duplicates exist, I cite the BLC copy. Information on early nineteenth-century farm women's chores in Conkin, *Prophets,* 6–7.
4. Bartlett, *Stone Genealogy,* 42–43. The Cambridge Petition was a citizens' protest against the establishment of a Royal Commission; witch-hunt in Bartlett, 46–47.
5. Bartlett, *Stone Genealogy,* 48.
6. Middlesex County Probate Records, No. 21596. *Vital Records of Leicester, Massachusetts to the Year 1849* (Worcester, Mass.: Franklin P. Rice, 1903). Woods's story in BLC.

7. FS enlisted at the age of fourteen in the same 1755 Crown Point expedition that claimed the life of his father, Jonathan Stone. *Vital Records of Leicester, Mass.* (Worcester: Franklin P. Rice, 1903). "Brains" in Bartlett, *Stone Genealogy*, 238–240; Temple, *History*, 245, 746.

8. Worcester County Probate Record No. 56594. LS, *Rem.*, 7.

9. Joseph P. Kett, "Growing Up in Rural New England, 1800–1840," in *Anonymous Americans: Explorations in Nineteenth-Century Social History*, ed. Tamara K. Hareven (Englewood Cliffs, N.J.: Prentice-Hall, 1971), 3. FS to LS, [date illegible], 1861, BLC.

10. Eric Wolf, *Peasants* (Englewood Cliffs, N.J.: Prentice-Hall, 1966), 2; and Joel Halpern and John Brode, "Peasant Society: Economic Changes and Revolutionary Transformations," *Biennial Review of Anthropology, 1967* (Stanford, Calif.: Stanford University Press, 1967), 58. Colonial New England class structure also in Peter Dobkin Hall's *Organization;* in Greven, *Four Generations;* and in Main, *Social Structure.* "Country girl" in LS, *Rem.*, 20; "heredity" in HBB, Autobiographical Papers, BLC, 115.

11. Copy of "Disappointment" speech in BLC.

CHAPTER THREE
"As Light as Thistle Down"

1. LS, *Rem.*, 22. Descriptions of Coy's Hill in Temple, *History*, 2, 13, 15, 52; and in "Picturesque Drives Over Coy's Hill," a typescript in the Warren, Massachusetts, Public Library.

2. Temple, *History*, 448, 52, 29. LS, *Rem.*, 23; and "Picturesque Drives."

3. LS, *Rem.*, 6; ASB, *Lucy Stone*, 9.

4. Anecdote from reminiscences of Aunt Ann of Belleville, BLC, Ctr. 90.

5. LS, *Rem.*, 1.

6. *Ibid.*, 10.

7. "Poverty-stricken" in LS to HBB, July 22, 1864 in BLC; domestic details in BLC, Ctr. 82; LS, *Rem.*, 22.

8. LS, *Rem.*, 1.

9. *Ibid.*, 9, 12.

10. Reminiscence of Aunt Ann, BLC, Ctr. 90.

11. LS, *Rem.*, 12; ASB's early version of her mother's reminiscences in BLC, Ctr. 87.

12. *Ibid.*

13. LS, *Rem.*, 7.

14. *Ibid.*, 7, 8.

15. LS, *Rem.*, 11. Stone's father and his cronies abuse of alcohol was not unusual. Russel Nye described a "drinking problem of national proportions" in early nineteenth-century America. Nye, *Society*, 48. See Jack H. Mendelson and Nancy K. Mello, *Alcohol, Use and Abuse in America* (Boston: Little, Brown, 1985), 18–36.

16. LS, *Rem.*, 8.

17. SSL, *Rem.*, BLC, Ctr. 87.

18. Among the adult traits Stone shared with sexually abused children were her need to feel in control, her rejection of sexuality, low self-esteem, rigid behavior patterns, and her later expressions of disgust at men and their vices—attitudes that seem excessive even by Victorian standards. See Christopher Bagley and Kathleen King, *Child Sexual Abuse: The Search for Healing* (London and New York: Tavistock/Routledge, 1990), 119–130. Stone also displayed traits common to adult children of alcoholics. See Barbara Wood, *Children of Alcoholism* (New York: New York University Press, 1987).

19. LS, *Rem.*, 7.

20. *Ibid.*, 11.

21. Reminiscence of Aunt Ann, BLC, Ctr. 90; LS, *Rem.*, 5.

22. LS, *Rem.*, 22, 23.

23. *Ibid.*, 19.

24. *Ibid.*, 3. Though corporal punishment in the schools was common, Stone's recollection of the particular force of the blow seems to mark it as unusual.

25. Emily Pierce to LS, January 2, 1847, BLC. Pierce was a childhood friend of Stone's.

26. BLC, Ctr. 90; According to Alice Stone Blackwell, Hannah did permit one "storybook" in the house which she believed to be both "true and instructive." ASB, *Lucy Stone*, 17; LS, *Rem.*, 3. For reading habits in rural New England, see William Gilmore, *Reading Becomes a Necessity of Life: Material and Cultural Life in Rural New England, 1780–1835* (Knoxville: University of Tennessee Press), 1989.

27. LS, *Rem.*, 10.

28. Freeman H. Hubbard, *Encyclopedia of North American Railroading: 150 Years of Railroading in the United States and Canada* (New York: McGraw-Hill, 1981), 152.

29. LS, *Rem.*, 3.

30. Temple, *History*, 269. See Thomas Dublin, *Women At Work*, for the impact on the women themselves and on the community. Alice Hyneman Rhine, in "Women in Industry," *Woman's Work*, ed. Meyer, 281–283, makes a distinction between the transitory experience of the young women of the 1830s and 1840s who entered the mills to "help lift a mortgage from the family farm, or to assist some son or brother in obtaining an otherwise impossible university education" or to "secure independence, or household and dress adornments" and the oppressive experiences of women who worked in the factories and sweatshops later in the century. See also Gerda Lerner, "The Lady and the Mill Girl: Changes in the Status of Women in the Age of Jackson," *Mid-Continent American Studies Journal* 10(1969):5–15; Cott, *Bonds*, chapter on "Work."

31. Frances Wright D'Arusmont (1795–1852) was a pioneer woman orator whose social reforms included improved working conditions, the abolition of slavery, woman's rights, equal education for all, and various other social and political programs.

32. Quote in Waterman, *Frances Wright*, 179.

33. Wright's speech in *Free Inquirer*, April 29, 1829.

34. LS, *Rem.*, 14.

35. Handwritten reminiscence of LS by HBB, BLC, Ctr. 90.

36. LS, *Rem.*, 11–12.

37. *Ibid.*, 11.

38. *Ibid.*

39. *Ibid.* Stone's typification of her father's behavior as Puritan is belied by numerous examples of kind and loving fathers of the period. A Massachusetts contemporary, Josephine Amelia Perkins, described her father as "kind and affectionate" in Stein's *Fragments of Autobiography*, 6; Elizabeth Cady Stanton described her father as "kind to us all" in Griffith, *Own Right*, 6. Stone's future father-in-law was described by his daughters as gentle and loving.

40. TWH to MH, NAWSA Collection, LC.

41. *Genesis* 3:16; anecdote in HBB's handwritten reminiscence of Lucy Stone's childhood in BLC, Ctr. 86. Stone refers to the "sadness" this text caused her as a child in a speech at the 1852 Woman's Rights Convention in Syracuse. *Proceedings*, 70.

42. LS, *Rem.*, 10.

43. ASB, *Lucy Stone*, 21–22.

44. The threat of "spinsterhood" abounds in poems, stories, and newspaper and magazine articles from the late eighteenth and early nineteenth centuries. The options for single women are summarized in Helene Roberts, "Marriage, Redundancy, or Sin," in Vicinus, ed., *Suffer and Be Still*, 276.

45. HBB handwritten reminiscence of LS in BLC, Ctr. 90.

46. *Ibid.*, 3.

47. "Bears, wolves" in LS, *Rem.*, 7; other topics recur in the Stone siblings' letters to one another in the 1830s.

48. Mary Lyon, pioneer Massachusetts educator and founder of Mount Holyoke, was in Brookfield in 1831 or 1832 to raise funds for her proposed woman's seminary. Green, *Mary Lyon*, 88.

49. ASB, *Lucy Stone*, 20.

50. Summer schools often were taught by women; winter schools, attended by older, more boisterous scholars whose labor was needed on the farm summers, traditionally were taught by men. The men earned four to five times as much as the women for teaching. For a first-person account, see Burton, *District School;* Fennelly, *Town Schooling,* and Kaestle, *Pillars.* Rhoda's advice in HBB's handwritten reminiscence, BLC, Ctr. 90.

51. Eliza Stone to FS, Jr., Sept 20, 1836, BLC.

52. LS, *Rem.,* 4; LS to FS Jr., [pencil dated] 1836, BLC.

53. LS, *Rem.,* 5.

54. *Ibid.,* 4.

55. *Liberator,* January 7, 1832.

56. Elizabeth Margaret Chandler was an antislavery author, poet, and editor of the "Ladies Repository" column of the *Genius of Universal Emancipation;* Frances Maria Stewart was the first American-born woman to speak publicly. In 1832, Stewart, a black woman, gave a series of four lectures to a young women's club in Boston; the text of her lectures appeared in the *Liberator,* April 28, 1832–May 7, 1833. Maria Weston Chapman was an antislavery writer, a founding member of the Boston Female Anti-Slavery Society, and a delegate to the World's Anti-Slavery Convention of 1840. Lydia Maria Child was an author, reformer, and feminist theorist who was the most well-known of the abolitionist writers. I am indebted to Carolyn Karcher for sharing her fascinating biography-in-progress of Child with me. Child's influence in the antislavery movement has been underestimated, and certainly her writing had an influence upon Stone.

57. Quotes in Lerner, *Grimké,* 145–154.

58. LS address at funeral of Abby Kelley Foster [Abby Kelley married fellow abolitionist Stephen Foster in 1843] in *WJ,* September 24, 1887.

59. Lerner, *Grimké,* 195.

60. Stanton, *HWS,* I:81.

61. LS, *Rem.,* 18.

62. Lerner, *Grimké,* 192.

63. LS, *Rem.,* 9.

64. *Ibid.,* 18.

65. LS to FS, Jr., December 1, 1837, Unproc., SL.

66. Green, *Mary Lyon,* 185.

67. *Ibid.,* 184, 201.

68. LS, *Rem.,* 21.

69. *Ibid.,* 8.

70. LS to FS, Jr., August 31, 1838, BLC.

71. *Ibid.*

72. From a typescript of SSL reminiscences of LS dictated to ASB, August 16, 1898, BLC.

73. *Ibid.* SSL remembered it as the "Quackenboag" Seminary, which may have been the name of the school in early years. SSL and LS attended Quaboag and Wilbraham for more than one term. The Warren school listing Sarah and Lucy Stone as pupils and over which J. Pearl presided is the Quaboag Seminary. See *Annual Catalogue of the Officers and Students of the Quaboag Seminary, Warren Mass. for the Year Ending 21st November, 1843* (West Brookfield, Mass.: Merriam and Cooke, 1843), 2, 10.

74. LS to WBS, June 18, 1840, BLC. Although there were other reasons for the 1840 schism in the American Anti-Slavery Society, the immediate cause was the naming of Abby Kelley to the executive board. Stewart, *Holy Warriors,* 74–96.

75. LS to WBS, June 18, 1840, BLC.

76. Lucy Stone's name and the curriculum are in the Quaboag Seminary *Annual Catalogue* in both 1842 and 1843. Oberlin College accepted women as early as 1833, but they were not allowed in the degree-granting program until 1837. In 1841, Oberlin awarded the first Bachelor of Arts degrees to three women: Mary Hosford, Elizabeth Smith Prall, and Mary Caroline Rudd.

77. From "Mrs. Mary Ann Bishop Blair," a typescript in the Warren, Massachusetts, Public Library.

78. Williams, *Appleton's,* 183.

CHAPTER FOUR
"This Is Not a World
to Sit Down and Whimper In"

1. Williams, *Appleton's*, 183. LS to FS and HS, August 30, 1843, BLC.

2. Williams, *Appleton's*, 183; reminiscence in folder labeled "Education," BLC. LS to FS and HS, August 30, 1843, in BLC; ASB, *Lucy Stone*, 45.

3. "Education" folder, BLC.

4. Williams, *Appleton's*, 183–184; LS, *Rem.*, 3.

5. LS, *Rem.*, 3–4; LS to FS and HS, August 30, 1843, BLC.

6. LS, *Rem.*, 4; LS to HS and FS, August 30, 1843, BLC.

7. LS to FS and HS, September 11, 1843, BLC.

8. Newspapers cost only one-fourth the cost of letter mail. See Arthur Summerfield, *U.S. Mail: The Story of the United States Postal Service* (New York: Holt, Rinehart, 1960), 45.

9. In keeping with Oberlin's policy that "older steadier women must room with young ones to keep them straight," Stone had a succession of young roommates. In 1845, Stone reported that her "flirty" young roommate had been expelled. "I had dreadful times with her," she wrote. LS to FS, Jr., April 15, 1845; May 12, 1845, BLC.

10. Not long after its opening, Oberlin welcomed a large contingent of black and white anti-slavery students and faculty who had left the Lane Seminary in Cincinnati, Ohio, because of their strong antislavery views. One of the Lane refugees, Asa Mahan, became president of Oberlin in 1835, a position he held through Stone's years at the college. "Hotbed" quote in Brandt, *Town*, 117; "given" in Ginzberg, "Women in an Evangelical Community," 86.

11. James Harris Fairchild (1817–1902) taught mathematics, philosophy, and theology at Oberlin while Stone was a student. Later he became Oberlin's president. Fairchild's speech in *Oberlin Quarterly Review* 4(1849):236–254; 345–357.

12. Among Stone's classmates and friends were: Sallie Holley, (1818–1893), an abolitionist and woman's rights lecturer; Robert Kedzie (1823–1902), a surgeon in the Civil War; Sarah Pellet (1824–1898), a childhood friend of Stone's from North Brookfield and later a fellow lecturer on temperance and woman's rights; Lettice Smith (1823–1911), who completed the theological course at Oberlin with Antoinette Brown and later taught at Antioch College; Edward Henry, a classmate and admirer of Stone's; Hannah Tracy (1815–1896), a young widow who became a physician, woman's rights lecturer, and writer.

13. Quotes from James P. McKinney letter to *WJ*, June 14, 1902.

14. LS to HS and FS, September 11, 1843, in BLC. For a discussion of factionalism in the antislavery movement, see Friedman, *Gregarious Saints;* Stewart, *Holy Warriors*.

15. LS to FS and HS, August 30, 1843, BLC. Charles Grandison Finney (1792–1875) was one of the leading evangelists of the Second Great Awakening. Arthur and Lewis Tappan, wealthy New York abolitionists, brought him to Oberlin in 1835.

16. ASB, *Lucy Stone*, 50, 51.

17. Diet in LS to FS and HS, August 30, 1843, BLC; "pellets" in *Plain Speaker* No. 2, BLC. This was the newspaper Stone put out while she was at Oberlin. Sylvester Graham was a popular lecturer and diet reformer of the early nineteenth century. (I am grateful to my editor, Adaya Henis, for pointing out that Graham crackers were believed to be "anaphrodisiacs.")

18. ASB, *Lucy Stone*, 49.

19. LS to SSL, March 13, 1846, BLC.

20. *Ibid.*

21. LS to FS, Jr., May 12, 1845, BLC; Cazden, *Antoinette Brown Blackwell*, 25. Stone withdrew fifty-five books in her time at Oberlin. O'Connor, *Pioneer Women Orators*, 69. Description of Stone in classmate James McKinney, letter to *WJ*, June 14, 1902.

22. LS to FS and HS, August 16, 1846, BLC.

23. FS to LS, January 11, 1845, in BLC. This is not in Francis Stone's handwriting, and either the writer or the copyist doubtless corrected the letter for spelling and grammar.

24. FS to LS, December 15, 1845, BLC; LS to SSL, March 13, 1846, BLC.

25. HS to LS, September 28, 1845; January 11, 1845, BLC.

26. LS to FS, Jr., May 12, 1845; February 15, 1846, BLC.

27. Although Stone remembered printing more issues of *The Plain Speaker*, only "No. 2" survives. The major article in this issue deals with the elitist nature of academies and colleges, protesting that a more widespread system of higher education was called for.

28. LS to Adolphus Sturge, [1845], BLC. I am grateful to Alex Tyrell and to Peter Sturge for identifying Adolphus Sturge, a Cleveland businessman and reformer, as nephew to the well-known English abolitionists, Joseph and Charles Sturge. Article in "Speeches" folder, BLC; WBS to LS, February 17, 1846, BLC.

29. SSL to LS, June 7, 1846, Unproc., SL.

30. LS to SSL, March 13, 1846, BLC.

31. LS to SSL, March 16, 1846, BLC. Robert Washington to LS, May 27, 1846, BLC. Washington's letter is written in pencil in a large, childlike script. The letter contains multiple misspellings and repeated words and phrases. There is no mention of a Robert Washington in the Oberlin College records of that time. As Washington was a name frequently assumed by former slaves, it seems likely that he is the same "Robert" she had described in earlier letters.

32. LS to FS and HS, February 3, 1846, BLC.

33. ASB, *Lucy Stone*, 52.

34. From a typescript of Antoinette Brown Blackwell's memoirs (partial) compiled by Sarah (Mrs. Claude) Gilson, 54, SL.

35. *Ibid.*

36. LS to FS, Jr., February 15, 1846, BLC; ABB, reminiscence of Oberlin years in *WJ*, February 10, 1894.

37. ABB, *Rem.*, to ASB, BLC. Present-day scholarly interest in nineteenth-century friendships such as that of Stone and Brown, e.g. Smith-Rosenberg's "Female World," points to the possibility of a romantic or sexual element in the intensely close friendships that women formed in the late nineteenth century. I am reluctant to impose such a post-Freudian and presentist interpretation on Brown and Stone's friendship.

38. The correspondence of Brown Blackwell and Stone is in Lasser and Merrill, *Friends and Sisters;* "admiration" in Gilson, 82; ABB to LS, March 28, 1848, BFP. Stone's letters to ABB for this period are lost, but ABB quotes from Stone's letter in her response, ABB to LS, [Winter] 1847, quoted in Gilson, 118.

39. ASB, *Lucy Stone*, 61–62. The Ladies' Board, comprising faculty wives and the principal, had the task of overseeing the academic progress and moral development of the female students.

40. Its full title was the "Young Ladies Association of Oberlin Collegiate Institute for the Promotion of Literature and Religion"; quote in ASB, *Lucy Stone*, 61.

41. "Remarks of the Critic" in the association's minutes give duties of "Critic." Material on the formation of the debating club in a letter from ABB to LS, September 22, 1848, and in the *Minutes of the Young Ladies Association of Oberlin Collegiate Institute for the Promotion of Literature and Religion, 1846–1850*, Oberlin College Archives. The topic of Stone's debate was "Is it the duty of Christians in the United States to go to foreign countries while there are three millions of heathens in our own country?" Copy of speech in BLC.

42. LS to FS and HS, August 16, 1846, BLC.

43. *Ibid.*

44. James McKinney letter to *WJ*, June 14, 1902.

45. *Ibid.*

46. AKF to LS, 1846, AAS; LS to WBS, February 15, 1846, BLC.

47. LS to SF, March 25, 1846, ASC.

48. LS to SSL, March 13, 1846, BLC.

49. HS to LS, December 15, 1845, BLC.

50. LS to FS and HS, February 3, 1846, BLC.

51. FS to LS, January 10, 1847, BLC; HS to LS, January 11 , 1846, Frank and Harriet Stone's baby daughter did not live long, dying before her first birthday.

52. SSL to LS, June 7, 1846, Unproc., SL.

53. LS to SSL, March 31, 1845, BLC.
54. SSL to LS, August 19, 1845; November 14, 1846, BLC.
55. LS to SSL, September 14, 1845, BLC.
56. LS to SF and AKF, March 25, 1846 in AKF Collection, AAS.
57. LS to FS and HS, August 16, 1846, BLC.
58. ABB reminiscence in *WJ*, February 10, 1894.
59. Stone's letters to her siblings are lost, but their responses make clear her arguments.
60. SSL to LS, November 28, 1846, BLC.
61. FS, Jr., to LS, June 6, 1847, BLC.
62. Luther Stone to LS, December 2, 1846, BLC.
63. SSL to LS, November 14, 1846, BLC.
64. LS to SSL, January 8, 1847, BLC.
65. SSL to LS, March 28, 1847, in BLC.
66. FS to LS, January 10, 1847, in BLC.
67. *Ibid.*
68. FS, Jr., to LS, [Spring] 1847, BLC.
69. LS to HS, March 14, 1847, BLC.
70. *Ibid.*
71. WBS to LS, June 13, 1847, BLC.
72. "Speeches" folder, BLC; O'Connor, *Pioneer Women Orators*, 71.
73. LS to HS, March 14, 1847, BLC.
74. LS to FS and HS, [Spring], 1847, in BLC.
75. *Ibid.*
76. LS to FS and HS, July 4, 1847, BLC.
77. *Ibid.*
78. WLG to HG, August 28, 1847, in *Garrison Letters*, III:212–213.

CHAPTER FIVE
*"Whether We Like It or Not,
Little Woman, God Made You an Orator"*

1. Information on Mexican War in Frederick Merk's *Manifest Destiny and Mission in American History* (New York: Knopf, 1963).
2. Immigration in Marcus Hansen's *The Atlantic Migration* (Cambridge: Harvard University Press, 1940); labor unrest in the 1840s in Dublin, *Women At Work*.
3. Stone's letter is lost, but ABB quotes Stone in her September 22, 1847, reply, BFP.
4. *Ibid.*
5. Lee Chambers-Schiller, in *Liberty, A Better Husband* (New Haven: Yale University Press, 1984), uses the term "cult" to describe the embrace of "single blessedness," a term then in use, by certain mid-nineteenth-century women. Chambers-Schiller maintains that "Only in singlehood might a woman retain her independence and develop her individuality" (51). The leader of New York's Female Guardian Society wrote that among the "more pernicious" errors of the times were "those which represent love and marriage not only as essential to the happiness of our sex but in reality the only end and aim of our existence" (quote in Degler, *At Odds*, 161).
6. Speech titled "The Condition of Woman," BLC, Ctr. 85.
7. The "unsexed woman" threat was used often by opponents of woman's rights. See Cott, *Bonds of Womanhood* and *Root of Bitterness;* Kelly, *Private Woman*. Stone's early speeches can be thought of as dialogic, hence the emphasis on the "womanliness" and marriageability of educated women.
8. LS, *Rem.*, BLC.
9. LS to WBS, June 9, 1848, BLC.
10. *Ibid.*

11. The physical peril of early antislavery speakers is well documented. For "vulgarity" see Berg, *Remembered Gate;* Wright's reputation in Flexner, *Century,* 27.

12. ABB to LS, June 28, 1848, BLC.

13. *Liberator,* April 16, 1852.

14. "Golden age" in O'Connor, *Pioneer Women Orators,* 122; Emerson quoted in Higginson, *Cheerful Yesterdays,* 327.

15. Quote in "Education" folder, BLC; lengthy applause that preceded her speeches in almost all newspaper accounts; see, e.g., *National Anti-Slavery Standard,* September 10, 1853.

16. Hardware merchant quoted in MAL, *Rem.,* BLC, Ctr. 87.

17. Higginson, *American Orators,* 86.

18. Speech of November 5, 1848, to Ladies' Anti-Slavery Society at Salem, BLC; *Liberator,* May 27, 1853; *National Anti-Slavery Standard,* September 10, 1853.

19. *Liberator* of October 6, 1848, lists Stone as a featured speaker—the only female—along with Garrison, Higginson, and Phillips at an upcoming convention.

20. Francis Jackson (1789–1861), a wealthy Boston merchant and antislavery activist; Charles Fox Hovey (1807–1859), a prosperous Boston businessman and contributor to reform causes; and Elizabeth Peabody (1804–1894) a prominent Boston reformer, all became strong supporters of the woman suffrage cause.

21. Sedgwick quoted in Kelly, *Private Woman,* 320.

22. LS letters to SM quoted in ASB, *Lucy Stone,* 77–80.

23. Stone's response in ASB, *Lucy Stone,* 89.

24. Biographical notes of LS compiled by HBB in BLC, Ctr. 86.

25. The full story of woman's rights activity in the 1840s has yet to be told. Stone's account in 1840 of her local literary society's vote to send women to Congress, the Ohio activism she described in her letters, the group described by Antoinette Brown in her 1846–1847 letters to LS, Lucretia Mott's lending library of woman's rights books and pamphlets—all point to the need to do further research into this decade. A concise summary of the 1840 split in the antislavery ranks is in Griffith, *Own Right,* 32.

26. Cromwell, *Lucretia Mott,* 28–29.

27. *Seneca County Courier,* July 14, 1848, in a reprint in the Seneca Falls Historical Society.

28. While the first eight resolutions proposed at the Seneca Falls convention were passed handily, the ninth, the woman suffrage resolution, proved far more controversial. Even Lucretia Mott and Stanton's own husband objected to its inclusion, but Stanton was adamant. Only after Frederick Douglass had spoken eloquently in its favor did it pass by a small majority. Stanton, *HWS,* I:804–810.

29. ECS to Amy Post, September 9, 1848, HEHL.

30. ABB to LS, tentatively dated December 1848, although internal evidence indicates that it was probably written in early November 1848, BLC.

31. The sixteen sons and daughters of Jesse and Mary Hutchinson were gifted musicians. They were also entertainers, teetotalers, and devout abolitionists. From the 1830s to the late nineteenth century, they traveled throughout the country, drawing large crowds to their musical evenings. Branch, *Sentimental Years,* 179–180.

32. ASB, *Lucy Stone,* 92.

33. LS, *Rem.,* 13.

34. Theodore Parker (1810–1860) was a Unitarian clergyman and orator active in antislavery and reform circles.

35. Newspaper clipping, BLC, Ctr. 87.

36. LS, *Rem.,* BLC, Ctr. 85.

37. *Liberator,* July 14, 1848.

38. Nellie Blessing Eyster, "An Evening With Lucy Stone," BLC, Ctr. 87.

39. Newspaper clipping of a speech made at Mechanic's Hall in 1856, BLC, Ctr. 87.

40. ASB, *Lucy Stone,* 80.

41. *Liberator* report quoted in ASB, *Lucy Stone,* 76.

42. ASB, *Lucy Stone,* 80.

43. *Ibid.*

44. LS quoted in *National Anti-Slavery Standard,* September 10, 1853.
45. Copy of LS speech at New England Anti-Slavery Convention, BLC, Ctr. 85.
46. *Ibid.*
47. ASB, *Lucy Stone,* 92–93.
48. *New York Tribune* clipping, [pencil dated 1852], BLC.
49. LS to ABB, August 1849, BLC.
50. LS, *Rem.,* 5.
51. LS to ABB, August 1849, BLC.
52. *Ibid.*
53. ASB, *Lucy Stone,* 92–93.
54. LS to ABB, August 1849, BLC.
55. *Liberator,* May 17, 1850; June 7, 1850. Paulina Wright Davis (1813–1876) was an abolitionist and woman's rights activist who had made her living as a lecturer on physiology following the death of her first husband. Harriet Hunt (1805–1875) was a physician, social reformer, lecturer, and suffragist.
56. ASB, *Lucy Stone,* 97.
57. LS to ABB, June 9, 1850, BLC. Jane Elizabeth Hitchcock Jones (1813–1896) was an Ohio abolitionist and antislavery speaker.
58. LS to SM, July 25, 1850, BLC.
59. *Ibid.*
60. LS to SM, October 13, 1850, BLC.
61. *New York Daily Tribune* account of the first National Woman's Rights convention, October 25, 1850.
62. *1850 Proceedings,* 13.
63. *New York Daily Tribune,* October 26, 1850
64. The *New York Daily Tribune* reports that Stone's remark was followed by "great applause."
65. *New York Herald,* October 28, 1850.
66. *Westminster Review,* July 1851, 311.
67. SBA's attribution made in 1890 at the fortieth anniversary of the first national woman's rights convention.
68. ABB to LS, [late February 1850], BFP.
69. Mississippi had passed an earlier Married Woman's Property Act, but it had been much less effective than New York's. See Peggy A. Rabkin, *Fathers to Daughters: The Legal Foundations of Female Emancipation* (Westport, Conn.: Greenwood, 1980).
70. ABB to LS: "I thought you seemed a little [sad] by your writing" in December 30, 1850, BLC.
71. Deacon L. Sampson to LS, June 16, 1851; LS to Deacon Sampson, June 21, 1851, BLC.
72. *Una* 3(April 1855): 59.
73. The People's College received its original charter from the New York state legislature in 1853. It was not built until 1859, however, by which time it had become an all-male agricultural institution. See *People's College* [no author given] (New York: Wynkoop, Hallenbeck & Thomas, 1859).
74. LS to SBA, quoted in Harper, *Susan B. Anthony,* I:116.
75. Notes of Aunt Ann, BLC, Ctr. 90.
76. ASB, *Lucy Stone,* 104.
77. Quote in Hays, *Morning Star,* 94–95.
78. LS to SBA in Harper, *Susan B. Anthony,* I:116.
79. ASB, *Lucy Stone,* 104–112.
80. LS to SBA, quoted in Harper, *Susan B. Anthony,* I:116.
81. Hays, *Morning Star,* 96.
82. ABB to LS, August 16, 1853, BLC.
83. Harper, *Susan B. Anthony,* I:88–89.
84. *New York Tribune,* April 28, 1853; May 15, 1853.

85. Harper, *Susan B. Anthony*, I:94–95.

86. ABB to LS, January 24, 1853, BLC.

87. *New York Tribune*, April 28, 1853; May 15, 1853.

88. The petition was circulated by Abigail May Alcott (1800–1877), an antislavery activist and woman's rights advocate, who was also sister of Samuel May, wife of transcendentalist Bronson Alcott, and mother of author Louisa May Alcott.

89. *Liberator*, May 22, 1853. The committee later voted that it was "inexpedient" to act upon the woman's rights petition and tabled the motion.

90. HBB to Theodore Parker, [May] 1853, Unproc., SL.

91. EmB Diary 1850–1858, BFP.

92. HBB to EmB, June 3, 1850, Unproc., SL.

93. HBB to EmB, September 29, 1850, Unproc. SL.

94. HBB to EmB, August 23, 1850, Unproc., SL.

95. HBB to SCB, June 2, 1853, BLC.

96. HBB, *Rem.*, 115, BLC. *EmB Diary* in BFP. HBB's proposal may be inferred by references made to it in his and Stone's letters exchanged immediately after their first meeting.

97. EmB to HBB, November 5, 1848, Unproc., SL. Reference to Blackwell's "mesmerizing" Stone in her July 27, 1853, letter to him in BLC.

98. Material on the Blackwell family background and emigration to America in Hays, *Extraordinary Blackwells*, 3–40; Hannah's recollection in BLC, Ctr. 94. In a diary entry dated June 19, 1842, SCB noted that his mother told him of her father's infidelity as well as his conviction for forgery prior to his deportation. SCB Diary, BFP.

99. Anna Blackwell, *Rem.*, BLC.

100. Anna Blackwell, *Rem.;* and Hays, *Extraordinary Blackwells*, 15; murder in letter from SB to MB, February 10, 1833, Unproc., SL.

101. Reference to the amount of Blackwell's losses and to the sale of the business is made in a letter to Samuel Guppy of November 1, 1832, Unproc., SL.

102. SB to W. Ludlow, owner of a Cincinnati refinery, December 8, 1837, Unproc., SL.

103. SB to Francis Short, Esq., September 1, 1837, Unproc., SL.

104. Letters between Guppy and Blackwell in Unproc., SL, give details of the partnership.

105. Sam Guppy to SB, July 20, 1836, Unproc., SL.

106. Sam Guppy to SB, August 13, 1836, Unproc., SL.

107. W. Ludlow to SB, December 8, 1837, Unproc., SL.

108. Hays, *Extraordinary Blackwells*, 37.

109. HBB to Anna Blackwell and HLB, February 8, 1840, BLC.

110. Hays, *Extraordinary Blackwells*, 51.

111. HBB's journal entries of February 13, 1846; January 28, 1846; April 28, 1845, in HBB Diary, BLC, Ctr. 66.

112. HBB Diary, April 30, 1845; January 31, 1846, BLC.

113. HBB Diary, October 6, 1846, BLC.

114. SCB Diary, January, 1848, Unproc., SL.

115. SCB Diary, April 9, 1848, Unproc., SL.

116. EB to Anna Blackwell, May 20, 1848, Unproc., SL.

117. Kenyon Blackwell to SCB, undated but clearly written just after Kenyon's arrival in New York in December, 1848, Unproc., SL.

118. HBB to W. W. Wright, a friend from Kemper College days, August 3, 1848, BLC.

119. EmB to HBB, November 5, 1848, Unproc., SL.

120. EmB to HBB, December 17, 1848, Unproc., SL.

121. *Ibid.*

122. SCB to HBB, December 19, 1848, BLC.

123. HBB to Dennis Harris, July 5, 1849, Unproc., SL.

124. HBB to EmB, September 29, 1850; December 7, 1852; EmB to HBB, December 5, 1852—and land deeds dating to 1848, all in Unproc., SL.

125. HBB to Theodore Parker, [May] 1853, Unproc., SL.

CHAPTER SIX
"Putting Lucy Stone to Death"

1. The best source of information on Stone's career in this period is the *Liberator*. TWH quote in *New York Daily Tribune*, October 20, 1854.
2. The *Tribune* referred to the World Temperance Convention as "the Orthodox, White, Male, Adult, Saints' Convention." When Brown attempted to speak, men shouted insults, stamped their feet, and pounded canes on the floor; fights broke out. *New York Daily Tribune*, September 2, 1853.
3. Stanton, *HWS* I:554–556; *New York Daily Tribune*, September 7, 1853; ASB, *Lucy Stone*, 121.
4. Stanton, *HWS* I:576.
5. LS to SBA, March 22, 1853, BLC.
6. LS to ECS, [Spring, 1853] BLC.
7. LS to HBB, September 24, 1853, BLC.
8. HBB to LS, May 2, 1854, BLC; LS to HS, [November], 1853, BLC.
9. HBB speech and newspaper report in *1853 Proceedings*, 42–56.
10. *Liberator*, December 20, 1853.
11. Quote in LS, *Rem.*, 17.
12. *Frederick Douglass Paper*, February 17, 1854. This paper was a predecessor of Douglass's *North Star*.
13. A partial record of Stone's 1853 earnings in LS, *Rem.*, 16; also in letters to HBB of November 26, 1853; November 27, 1853; January 1854, in BLC; quote in LS to TWH, July 15, 1854, in Thomas Wentworth Higginson Papers, BPL.
14. References to James Mott's brother's investments for Stone are in James Mott to LS, March 15, 1854, BLC. HBB wrote at the time of their marriage that Stone had $6000 in cash as well. HBB to EmB, March 3, 1855, Unproc., SL.
15. LS to HBB, November 26, 1853, BLC; HBB to LS, January 3, 1854, BLC.
16. Family letters place Harry in Wisconsin buying land for speculative purposes in the same period. See ElB to HBB, September 17, 1853, BLC; HBB to GWB, December 24, 1853, Unproc., SL.
17. Railroad information in Fishlow, *American Railroads;* for story of western migration, see Billington, *Western Frontier*.
18. "The Wisconsin Emigrant" is in Douglas Miller, *Then Was the Future: The North in the Age of Jackson, 1815–1850* (New York: Knopf, 1973), 6–9.
19. Stone and Blackwell's correspondence through the winter of 1853–1854 is filled with the complex details of her loans, his plans, etc. Quotes in HBB to LS, January 22, 1854, BLC. Blackwell gives his story of the land-buying expeditions in his *Rem.*, 150–51, BLC.
20. The figure of two thousand dollars was obtained by adding the amounts mentioned by Stone in her letters of November through February in the winter of 1853–1854. The sum may have been larger.
21. HBB to LS, January 22, 1854, BLC.
22. HBB, *Rem.*, 150–151, BLC.
23. Sarah Mapps Douglass (1806–1882) was an educator and member of a prosperous Philadelphia black Quaker family.
24. LS to Lydia Mott, March 5, 1854, BLC.
25. *Ibid.*
26. LS to HBB December 30, 1853, BLC. Charles Burleigh (1810–1878) was a Garrisonian abolitionist, lawyer, woman's rights reformer, and close personal friend of LS.
27. LS to HBB. Tremont House, [January, 1854], BLC.
28. HBB to LS, December 22, 1854, BLC.
29. Alcott quoted by HBB in letter to LS, January 22, 1854, BLC.
30. HBB's courtship letters are voluminous. An abridged collection appears in Wheeler, *Loving Warriors;* the bulk of the courtship letters are in BLC.

31. James Mott to LS, June 29, 1853, BLC.

32. EB to HBB transcribed exactly in a letter written by LS to SSL, November 6, 1853, BLC.

33. HBB to SSL, April 21, 1854, BLC. HBB's reference to an earlier meeting, which he also mentions in HBB to LS, March 18, 1855, in BLC, is not corroborated by Stone. His first mention of Stone in his letters to his siblings is after seeing her at the Massachusetts legislative hearing.

34. LS to HBB, April 25, 1854, BLC.

35. HBB to LS, May 2, 1854; May 5, 1854, BLC.

36. Even natural means such as rhythm were doomed, given the mistaken "scientific" notion that ovulation directly preceded the menses. Avoiding pregnancy meant total abstinence, an impracticable solution; or coitus interruptus, considered unnatural and/or unreliable. See Gordon, *Woman's Body*, 21; and her essay on "Voluntary Motherhood" in *Clio's Consciousness Raised*, 54–71.

37. Wright, *Marriage and Parentage*, 243, 246.

38. HBB to LS, April 25, 1854, BLC.

39. LS to WLG, May 19, 1854, BLC.

40. LS to HBB, April 25, 1854, BLC.

41. LS to HBB, July 23, [1854], BLC.

42. Letter quoted in Wheeler, *Loving Warriors*, 88.

43. EB to HBB, December 27, 1854, BLC.

44. EB to HBB, September 17, 1853, BLC.

45. EmB to EB, June 20, 1854, BFP.

46. HBB to LS, June 18, 1854, BLC.

47. *Ibid.*

48. LS to HBB, July 23, 1854, BLC.

49. HBB to LS, September 1, 1854, BLC.

50. *Ibid.*

51. LS to HBB, October 8, 1854, BLC.

52. EB to EmB, September 15, 1854, BLC.

53. HBB to LS, September 27, 1854, BLC.

54. LS to HBB, October 8, 1854, BLC.

55. LS to HBB, October 10, 1854, BLC.

56. LS to HBB, September 3, 1854; October 22, 1854, BLC.

57. LS to HBB, October 10, 1854, BLC.

58. LS to HBB, November 5, 1854, BLC.

59. HBB to LS, December 22, 1854, BLC.

60. "Lucy Stone that was" quoted in HBB to LS, December 22, 1854; HBB to LS, December 10, 1854, BLC.

61. HBB to LS, December 23, 1854, BLC.

62. LS to HBB, December 25, 1854, BLC.

63. EmB to EB January 2–5, 1855, BLC.

64. Mention of Anna Blackwell's letter and HBB's explanation in HBB to LS, January 3, [1855], BLC; Stone's response in LS to HBB, January 18, 1855, BLC.

65. EB to EmB, January 23, 1855, BLC; SCB quote in this letter.

66. HBB to LS, January 22, 1854, BLC.

67. LS to HBB, January 18, 1855, BLC.

68. HBB to LS, December 22, 1854; HBB to LS, March 18, 1855; April 2, 1855, BLC; LS to HBB January 18, 30, 1855; February 19, 1855, BLC.

69. Stone's confidences to Sarah regarding her "sufferings and fear" in HBB to LS, March 18, 1855, in BLC; "vulgar" in EB to HBB, February 22, 1855, BLC.

70. HBB to LS, March 18, 1855, BLC.

71. LS to HBB, March 29, 1855, BLC.

72. LS to ABB, March 29, 1855, BLC.

73. HBB to LS, April 2, 1855, BLC.

74. HBB to LS, May 5, 1854, BLC; HBB to LS, January 3, 1855, BLC; LS to HBB, April 8, 1855, BLC.

75.   HBB to LS, March 18, 1855, BLC.

76.   HBB to LS, April 13, 1855, BLC.

77.   HBB to LS, April 20, 1855, BLC.

78.   EB to HBB, April 6, 1855, Unproc., SL.

79.   TWH to MH, in Higginson, *Letters and Journals,* 59.

80.   Boston *Post* parody copied in BLC, Ctr. 82.

81.   Higginson, *Letters and Journals,* 59.

82.   *Ibid.*

83.   *Ibid.* "Ashes of roses" is a light grayish-red color tinged with violet, a traditional bride's dress color in 1855.

84.   The text of the Marriage Protest in *Liberator,* May 4, 1855.

85.   HBB to EmB, May 9, 1855, Unproc., SL.

86.   Higginson, *Letters and Journals,* 59.

87.   LS to HS, January 8, 1856, BLC; HBB to Ainsworth Spofford, May 1, 1855, BLC.

88.   LS to HS, May 10, 1855; May 26, 1855, BLC.

89.   ElB to EmB, May 6, 1855, Unproc., SL.

90.   *Union* quoted in LS to SBA, May 29, 1855, in Harper, *Susan B. Anthony,* I:130.

91.   EmB to "Family," June 1855, Unproc., SL.

92.   LS to SBA, May 30, 1855, BLC.

93.   HBB to LS, August 29, 1855, BLC.

94.   HBB to LS, [Walnut Hills, summer 1855]; HBB to LS, September 12, 1855, BLC.

95.   EB to HBB, September 5, 1855, Unproc., SL.

96.   SBA to her family, September 27, 1855, quoted in Stanton, *HWS,* I:256–257.

97.   "Disappointment" speech in Stanton, *HWS,* I:165–167. The reference to a "crossed" ninepence is to a sum gained fraudulently, a nineteenth-century idiom.

98.   HBB to GWB, October 19, 1855, Unproc., SL.

99.   LS to S. Kinnicutt, [1856], in Antislavery Collection, BPL.

100. HBB to LS, [Walnut Hill, summer 1855]; August 29, 1855; September 12, 1855; October 13, 1855; in BLC.

101. LS to SBA, November 2, 1855, in BLC.

102. LS to SBA, November 8, 1855, in BLC.

103. LS to HBB, January 25, 1856, BLC.

104. LS to HBB, January 30, 1856, BLC.

105. LS to HBB, February 3, 1856, BLC.

106. HBB to LS, January 16, 1856; February 7, 1856, BLC.

107. John Pierpont (1785–1866) was an influential Unitarian clergyman, poet, reformer, and grandfather of J. P. Morgan.

108. LS to HBB, January 25, 1856, BLC.

109. LS to HBB, February 3, 1856, BLC.

110. HLB to GWB, February 25, 1856, Unproc., SL.

111. Accounts of the Margaret Garner trial in LS to Anna Parson, May 11, 1856, BLC; LS, *Rem.,* 17–18; *Lily,* February 15, 1856.

112. *Lily,* February 15, 1856.

113. HBB to LS, February 7, 1856, BLC.

114. LS describes the transfer of funds in her letter to HS, March 25, 1856 in BLC; LS to WBS, March 19, 1856, BLC.

115. HBB to LS, March 26, 1856, BLC.

116. HBB, Handwritten "Autobiography" in BLC, Ctr. 72, 13.

117. HBB to LS, April 1, 1856, BLC.

118. LS to HBB, May 9, 1856, BLC.

119. HBB to LS, May 18, 1856, BLC.

120. HBB to LS, May 12, 1856, BLC.

CHAPTER SEVEN
"Rock the Cradle Lucy/
And Keep the Baby Warm!"

The title of this chapter is taken from a popular 1850s song.
1. LS to WBS, June 7, 1856, BLC.
2. HBB to SCB, June 20, 1856, BLC.
3. LS to HS, July 1, 1856, BLC; ASB, *Lucy Stone*, 161.
4. LS to HS, July 1, 1856, BLC.
5. LS to WBS, June 7, 1856, BLC.
6. Anecdote in BLC, Ctr. 86, in clipping about the 1915 dedication in Viroqua of a plaque to mark the spot where LS spoke.
7. LS to "Friends at Home," July 29, 1856, BLC.
8. LS to HS, July 1, 1856, BLC.
9. LS to HBB, April 26, 1856, BLC.
10. There are voluminous records of HBB's and GWB's complicated land transactions in Unproc., SL. In one letter to George, which Harry marked and underlined *'Destroy this letter'*, Blackwell told of using part of Worthington's $25,000 "for arrangement of our affair with Mr. Tucker"; HBB to GWB, [internal evidence dates it in late May 1856], Unproc., SL.
11. George wrote Edward Howells that the defective titles should surprise no one since "the fact that there was some shadow of a doubt as to the title of these lands was the reason for selling at so trifling a price." GWB to E. B. Howells, April 11, 1862, Unproc., SL. For more details of these complex transactions, see HBB to GWB, May 23, 1856, Unproc., SL; HBB discusses further summer 1856 land purchases in HBB to HLB, June 21, 1856, BLC.
12. LS to SBA, July 1, 1856, BLC.
13. LS to SBA, September 7, 1856, BLC; LS to SBA, September 21, 1856, BLC.
14. Quote in Harper, *Susan B. Anthony*, I:146.
15. LS to SBA, July 30, 1856, BLC.
16. LS to ABB, [Summer 1856], BLC.
17. LS to SBA, August 23, 1856; September 21, 1856, BLC.
18. LS to SBA, October 22, 1856, BLC.
19. *1856 Proceedings*, 6.
20. *1856 Proceedings*, 15–16.
21. HBB to GWB, [undated, but late 1856 from internal evidence], Unproc., SL.
22. Among the many requests was an invitation from the famous novelist and reformer Horatio Alger to give a series of lectures in New York in December. Stone accepted. LS to Horatio Alger, October 24, 1856, BLC. Blackwell borrowed the $5000 from William Green, the wealthy father-in-law of his friend Augustus Moore. He convinced Moore to invest with him. HBB to GWB, November 12, 1856; December 5, 1856, Unproc., SL.
23. LS to HBB, January 5, 1857, BLC.
24. LS to HBB, January 18, 1857, BLC.
25. LS to HBB, January 4, 1857, BLC.
26. LS to HBB, March 4, 1857, BLC.
27. LS to Henrietta Crosby Ingersoll, June 17, 1857, in Henrietta Crosby Ingersoll Collection, LC. The Boston *Traveller* reported that Representatives Hall was "crammed to the ceiling" to hear Stone's speech. Clipping in BLC, Ctr. 87.
28. LS to HBB, March 4, 1857, BLC.
29. HBB to LS, February 11, 1857, BLC.
30. LS to Henrietta Crosby Ingersoll, June 17, 1857, Henrietta Crosby Ingersoll Collection, LC.
31. HBB to GWB, May 9, 1857, Unproc., SL.
32. HBB to GWB, June 8, 1857, Unproc., SL.

33.   LS to WBS, [Summer 1857], BLC.
34.   HBB to Augustus O. Moore, June 20, 1857, BLC.
35.   HBB to GWB, August 23, 1857, Unproc., SL.
36.   LS to SBA, July 24, 1857, BLC.
37.   LS to SBA, July 20, 1857, BLC.
38.   HBB to LS, September 8, 1857, BLC.
39.   HBB to GWB, September 16, 1857, Unproc., SL.
40.   *Ibid.*
41.   Full text of Stone's letter in *Orange Journal,* January 18, 1857.
42.   *New York Tribune,* January 18, 26, 1858. Although Stone was unaware of it at the time, most of the articles were bid on and purchased by a neighbor, Rowland Johnson, who returned them that same evening.
43.   ASB, *Lucy Stone,* 196.
44.   LS to HS, February 10, 1858, BLC.
45.   HBB to LS, March 12, 1858, BLC.
46.   HBB to LS, March 3, 1858, BLC. The emphasis is his.
47.   *Ibid.*
48.   Rose Terry, "Eben Jackson," in *Atlantic* 1(1):524.
49.   LS to HBB, May 21, 1858, BLC.
50.   LS to HBB, March 8, 1858, BLC.
51.   HBB to LS, March 24, 1858, BLC.
52.   HBB to GWB, April 5, 1858, Unproc., SL.
53.   LS to HBB, April 3, 1858, BLC.
54.   HBB to LS, [undated, but internal evidence puts it at April 1], 1858, BLC.
55.   LS to HBB, April 25, 1858, BLC.
56.   Quote in Henry Whittemore, *The Founders and Builders of the Oranges* (Newark, N.J.: L. J. Hardham, 1896), 272. Abigail Hutchinson Patton (1829–1892) was known as Abby throughout her life. She was the only female member of the famous Hutchinson Family quartet. After her 1849 marriage to Ludlow Patton, she retired from public life, returning only infrequently to sing at woman's rights and antislavery conventions.
57.   LS to SBA, April 1, 1858, BLC.
58.   LS to HBB, April 25, 1858, BLC.
59.   *Ibid.*
60.   HBB to GWB, April 28, 1858, Unproc., SL.
61.   HBB to LS, May 7, 1858, BLC.
62.   LS to HBB, May 9, 1858, BLC. Stone was troubled by severe boils throughout this period, as her letters to HBB show.
63.   HBB to LS, May 9, 1858, BLC.
64.   EB to HBB, April 11, 1858, BLC.
65.   EmB to GWB, June 4, 1858; HBB to GWB, September 6, 1858, Unproc., SL; HBB to LS, March 25, 1858, BLC.
66.   LS to HBB, May 26, 1858, BLC.
67.   LS to HBB, June 13, 1858, BLC.
68.   HBB to LS, June 1, 1858, BLC; LS to HBB, June 2, 1858, BLC.
69.   HBB to LS, June 28, 1858, BLC.
70.   HBB to GWB, September 6, 1858, Unproc., SL.
71.   When Moses Crowell, the recipient of the deeds, went to Wisconsin to sell the lands in the early 1860s, he found his ownership of the lands challenged by others claiming valid title. A lengthy correspondence and numerous threats of legal action finally resulted in a settlement by HBB and GWB. Details in a series of letters exchanged between GWB and HBB and Moses Crowell and his lawyer, Edw. Howells, Esq., between November 1861 and September 1863, when the matter was finally settled with money Stone provided. Letters in Unproc., SL.
72.   Cazden, *Antoinette Brown Blackwell,* 120–122.
73.   HBB to GWB, October 1, 1858, Unproc., SL.
74.   EmB to EB, October 1, 1858, Unproc., SL.

75. LS to HS, December 5, 1858, BLC.
76. HBB to HB, December 18, 1858, BLC.
77. LS to HS, December 5, 1858, BLC.
78. HBB, Autobiographical papers, BLC, Ctr. 67.
79. LS to ABB, February 20, 1859, BFP.
80. See "Mothers of Civilization" in Ryan, *Womanhood,* 137–192; Kelley, ed., *Woman's Being.*
81. LS to HS, June 14, 1859, BLC.
82. ABB to LS, July 22, 1859; August 22, 1859, BLC.
83. Stephen Douglas (1813–1861), a Democratic U.S. senator (Illinois, 1847–1861), introduced the Compromise of 1850 and the Kansas-Nebraska Act. The story of the hoax appeared in the October 1859 issues of the *Liberator.*
84. WLG to S. G. Howe, November 12, 1855, in Garrison, *Letters,* IV: 359.
85. *Liberator,* October 1859.
86. Frederick Douglass's article on Stone is reprinted in Foner, *Frederick Douglass,* 74–76.
87. LS to HS, December 18, 1859, BLC.
88. At this point, the leaders of the women's movement celebrated the 1850 Worcester convention as marking the beginning of organized woman suffrage activity.
89. Robert Dale Owen (1801–1877) was a utopian reformer, state legislator, Indiana congressman, and advocate of increased property rights for women as well as liberalized divorce laws in Indiana. Quote in Horace Greeley, *Recollections of a Busy Life* (New York: J. B. Ford, 1868), 574.
90. Ernestine Rose (1810–1892) was a Polish-born woman's rights advocate who was quoted as declaring herself "for free love on principle." The "Friends of Freethought" Convention at which Rose had spoken took place in June 1858, and though free love was advocated at some of the talks at that convention, Rose denied any association with the Free Lovers.
91. SBA to LS, March 23, 1860, BLC.
92. *1860 Proceedings,* 65–66.
93. *1860 Proceedings,* 65–66; Griffith, *Own Right,* 104.
94. *1860 Proceedings,* 86.
95. *New York Tribune,* May 21, 1860.
96. LS to HBB, September 14, 1860, BLC.
97. SCB to HB, December 27, 1869, Unproc., SL.
98. LS to HBB, January 31, 1861, BLC. A description of the mob activity can be found in Harper, *Susan B. Anthony,* I:207–212.
99. The decision to cancel the antislavery meetings is in WLG to Oliver Johnson, April 19, 1861, in Garrison, *Letters,* V:17. The women's decision was apparently a tacit agreement, as I did not come across any exchange of letters on the subject.
100. HBB to GWB, July 29, 1861, Unproc., SL.
101. WBS to LS, December 9, 1861, BLC.
102. Ainsworth Spofford to HBB, May 2, 1862, BLC.
103. HBB to GWB, July 29, 1862, BLC. As for how George was to sell the device, HBB wrote: "The only way to get over red tape obstacles will probably be to approach Gen. Halleck, or Sec'y Stanton, or old Uncle Abe *direct.*" He recommended that George should "step out with Uncle Abe in the back garden and perforate an incredible mass of wood" as a means of ensuring the weapon's adoption.
104. HBB writes of Stone's "severe headache" to GWB, May 29, 1862, Unproc., SL.
105. SCB tells of Stone's caring for Marian and Hannah in letter to GWB, June 18, 1862, Unproc., SL.
106. EB to GWB, August 14, 1862, Unproc., SL.
107. EB to GWB, August 23, 1862, Unproc., SL.
108. EB to GWB, September 10, 1862, Unproc., SL; HBB to GWB, November 16, 1862, Unproc., SL. George was drafted after being dismissed from his Washington position.
109. HBB to GWB, November 16, 1862, Unproc., SL.
110. LS to FS, December 1, 1862; December 31, 1862, BLC.

111. Stanton, *HWS*, II:51–65 describes the founding and work of the Woman's National Loyal League, including the text of Stone's speech. Eleanor Flexner calls this organization the "National Woman's Loyal League" in *Century of Struggle*, 111.

112. Receipts to Ellen in BLC show that Stone paid $22.50 per week to her for "taking care of Alice" while she lectured.

113. LS to Charles Burleigh, December 12, 1864, BLC.

114. Blackwell's account book for 1864 in BLC.

115. J. Kenyon Blackwell to HBB and SCB, March 4, 1864, BLC. This letter was in response to Harry Blackwell's somewhat disingenuous letter of the previous month in which he had insisted that "We have never at any time since you loaned us the money, up to othe present *been able* to repay you." HBB to J. Kenyon Blackwell, February 11, 1864, BLC.

116. LS to HBB, June 14, 1864, BLC.

117. LS to SBA, July 12, 1864, BLC.

118. LS to HBB, July 22, 1864, BLC.

119. LS to HBB, July 31, 1864, BLC.

120. LS to HBB, June 14, 1864, BLC.

121. LS to HBB, June 21, 1864, BLC.

122. LS to HBB, August 9, 1864, BLC.

123. . LS to HBB, September 4, 1864, BLC.

124. LS to HBB, September 20, 1864, BLC.

125. LS to HBB, October 4, 1864, BLC.

126. LS to HBB, October 23, 1864, BLC.

127. HBB to GWB, October 16, 1864, Unproc., SL.

128. LS to HBB, December 4, 1864, BLC.

129. LS to HBB, December 17, 1864, BLC.

130. LS to HBB, December 22, 1864, BLC.

131. Wheeler, *Loving Warriors*, 212.

CHAPTER EIGHT
Kansas: The Rift Widens

1. LS had rented out their Montclair home, writing HBB: "We won't go back there to live & be worried again." June 21, 1864, BLC.

2. HBB to LS, March 22, 1865, BLC. I have not located the spring 1865 letters of SBA and LS, but reference to the correspondence is in SBA, *Diary*, LC. Information on the growing split between antislavery leaders and suffragists in DuBois, *Feminism and Suffrage*. Phillips's speech in *New York Times*, May 10, 1865.

3. LS to HBB, November 12 and 19, 1865, BLC.

4. Stanton, *HWS*, II:90–112.

5. Support for black suffrage in the North was highly doubtful. In a series of late 1860s' referenda, only two states, Iowa and Minnesota, voted in favor of black suffrage. Gillette, *Right to Vote*, 25–27.

6. McPherson, "Abolitionism," 41. ASB, *Lucy Stone*, 201–202.

7. Railroad scheme in Brink, *Hutchinsons*, 239.

8. Land buying in HBB to GWB, April 23, 1866, Unproc., SL; *1866 Proceedings*. HBB wrote Stone from New York on the day following the convention that it "evidently went off well." HBB to LS, May 12, 1866, BLC.

9. HBB to LS, May 7, 1866; May 12, 1866, BLC.

10. McPherson, "Abolitionism," 42; Harper, *Susan B. Anthony*, I:263.

11. Douglass quoted in Harper, *Susan B. Anthony*, I:261–264.

12. LS to AKF, January 24, 1867, BLC.

13.   Ann Smith to Gerrit Smith, January 20, 1867, describes the train incident. Letter in Harlow, *Gerrit Smith*, 471. General suffrage activity in Stanton, *HWS*, II:172–182.

14.   *Woman Suffrage in New Jersey: An Address Delivered by Lucy Stone at a Hearing Before the New Jersey Legislature, March 6th, 1867* (Boston: C. H. Simonds, [no date]).

15.   Berwanger in *West and Reconstruction* analyzes the political situation in Kansas (164–175), as does Bright, *Kansas*, 208. Samuel Newitt Wood, a Republican legislator and friend of woman suffrage, had voted against black suffrage each year since 1862. See Samuel Wood to LS, November 24, 1855, NAWSA Collection, LC. Berwanger believes that Wood's intention in adding the woman suffrage referendum was to defeat black suffrage (165–166). Additional information on Wood and the Kansas campaign is in McKenna, "With the Help of God and Lucy Stone."

16.   Charles Robinson (1818–1894), former governor of Kansas, was related to Stone. Bowman Stone successively married three of Charles Robinson's sisters: he married Phebe Robinson in 1842; after her death, he married Samantha Robinson in 1852; following her death, he married Martha Robinson in 1885. Bartlett, *Stone Genealogy*, 594.

17.   HBB to ECS, April 5, 1867, BLC.

18.   HBB to ECS, April 21, 1867, BLC.

19.   LS to SBA, April 10, 1867, quoted in Stanton, *HWS*, II:235.

20.   The fees went to Wood at Impartial Suffrage headquarters for financing printing, advertising, and touring expenses. Quote in HBB to ECS and SBA, April 21, 1867, BLC.

21.   LS to SBA, May 1, 1867, BLC.

22.   LS to SBA, May 9, 1867, BLC.

23.   *1867 Proceedings;* Wilder, *Annals*, 456.

24.   LS to SBA, May 1, 1867, BLC.

25.   Starrett, "Reminiscence" in Stanton, *HWS*, II:251.

26.   LS, *Rem.*, 4; *New York Tribune*, May 29, 1867.

27.   Curtis quoted in Stanton, *HWS*, II:287.

28.   Information on Mary Greeley's mental instability in Seitz, *Greeley*, 333–334.

29.   Griffith, *Own Right*, 127; quote from Stanton, *HWS*, II:269.

30.   HBB to LS, October 25, 1867, in BLC. According to Blackwell, "Wood became discouraged, went home early in August and has not done anything since. . . . He was out of money. The mail to Cottonwood was *robbed* and he never got any letters till a few days ago *for six weeks.* The campaign was left to run itself."

31.   Brown quote and account of growing racial divisiveness in Berwanger, *West and Reconstruction*, 171–173.

32.   EB to GWB, September 17, 1867, Unproc., SL; EB to HBB, October 22, 1867, BLC.

33.   HBB, "Reminiscence of Lucy Stone," BLC, Ctr. 86. That ASB resented the rival for her mother's affections seems clear. In her biography of her mother, Alice makes no mention of Annie Gleason, writing instead that "All [Stone's] wealth of deep maternal tenderness was poured out upon her one little daughter." ASB, *Lucy Stone*, 203.

34.   LS to HBB, October 13, 1867, BLC.

35.   HBB to LS, October 25, 1867, BLC.

36.   Kathleen Barry, in *Susan B. Anthony*, writes that Harry Blackwell and Sam Wood hatched a "secret plan" that spring to bring Train into the campaign (180). Barry's citation is to a "report" by IBH to Susan Howard on January 2, 1870, based on notes taken by IBH at a "confidential meeting." Barry's text places the meeting in December 1870 (180), an obvious error. The "notes" IBH scribbled after her meeting with Blackwell read, "Late 66 [should read 1867] Anthony and Stanton went. Wood invited Train for woman suffrage. . . . " Blackwell's name does not appear in IBH "notes." Train himself published a letter signed by Wood, Stanton, and Anthony, and dated October 2, 1867, inviting him to Kansas in *Great Epigram Campaign*. Neither Stanton nor Anthony in any public or private reminiscence or letter makes mention of Blackwell in connection with the invitation to Train. Blackwell, however, does mention to Stone that he is "in negotiations with Democrats" in HBB to LS, October 25, 1867, BLC.

37.   LS to WLG, March 6, 1868, AASC.

38.   Train, *Epigram*, 47. In later years, Stanton referred to Train as "a reform 'squatter.'" Stanton, *Eighty Years*, 214; Stanton once told Stone that she had believed that the Irish would elect

Train to the presidency, and that she and Anthony would be named to his cabinet. ASB to Mary Hunter, August 13, 1938, BLC.

39. Quote in Train, *Epigram*, 60–61.

40. *Ibid.*, 16.

41. *Ibid.*, 58.

42. ECS letter quoted in Harper, *Susan B. Anthony*, I:293.

43. ASB, *Lucy Stone*, 209; Gillette, *Right to Vote*, 32–33.

44. Quote in Hays, *Morning Star*, 197; HBB to LS, October 29, 1867, BLC.

45. Harper, *Susan B. Anthony*, I:290. Stanton and Anthony agreed to Train's terms for the newspaper: i.e., that Train and David Melliss (Democratic editor of the *New York World*) would finance and provide what editorial material they wished to the newspaper, and Anthony and Stanton could have what space they wanted for their woman's rights ideas. Harper, *Susan B. Anthony*, I:293.

46. Election results from Wilder, *Annals of Kansas*, 463:

For striking out "White" in the list of voter qualifications (pro–black suffrage) =   10,483
Against striking out the word "White" =   19,421
For striking out "Male" (pro–woman suffrage) =   9,070
Against striking out "Male" (anti–woman suff.) =   19,857

Later, the *Revolution* credited Train with having won 9,000 votes for women. Charles Robinson offers a clear rebuttal of this in a letter to OB, December 22, 1867, OB Collection, SL.

47. Emporia *News*, November 15, 1857. Kansas reflected a national trend of Republican losses that fall, resulting in a shift toward the center at the cost of both black and woman suffrage (Gillette, *Right to Vote*, 31–40).

48. LS to OB, December 22, 1867; Charles Robinson to OB, December 1867, in OB Collection, SL.

49. WLG to Alfred Love, December 18, 1867, in AASC.

50. Anthony acknowledged receiving "scores of letters" from the leading advocates of suffrage. The "old associates" boycotted her meetings and begged her to repudiate Train. Harper, *Susan B. Anthony*, I:294.

51. Stone's account of this meeting, containing the quote from Anthony, is in a letter to Matilda Joslyn Gage, editor of the *National Citizen*. NAWSA Collection, BLC, Ctr. 38.

52. LS to OB, January 6, 1868, in OB Collection, SL.

53. SBA *Diary*, January 1, 1868; LC.

54. *Revolution*, January 8, 1868.

55. *New York Times*, January 12, 1868.

56. WLG to SBA, January 4, 1868, in WLG, *Letters*, VI:29.

57. *Revolution*, January 29, 1868.

58. ECS to OB, January 1868, in OB Collection, SL.

59. *Revolution*, December 24, 1868; January 14, 1869; January 21, 1869.

60. LS to HBB, April 1868, BLC.

61. LS to HBB, April 11, 1868, BLC.

62. Stanton, *HWS*, II:310–312.

63. Harper, *Susan B. Anthony*, I:304; Stanton, *HWS*, II:341.

64. Harper, *Susan B. Anthony*, I:305–306.

65. SBA to OB, July 20, 1868 in OB Collection, SL.

66. Alice did not get along with Annie, the apparent reason for Annie's placement at the home of Mary Ann Blair. SCB to HBB, August 19, 1868.

67. The Newark *Daily Advertiser* account of Stone's attempt to vote is reprinted in Stanton, *HWS*, II:478; Quote in HBB, Notebooks, BLC.

68. Details of the N.E.W.S.A. convention in *Revolution*, November 12, 1868. November of 1868 marked the entry into the woman suffrage ranks of Julia Ward Howe (1819–1910), a socially prominent, highly respected Boston Brahmin famous for having written the "Battle Hymn of the Republic." Stone would tell her daughter "It was so much to [me] when Mrs. Howe with all she stood for joined the movement. . . . it was like the shadow of a great rock in a weary land" (LS, *Rem.*, 20).

69. LS to ASB, December 14, 1868, BLC.

70. LS to ASB, November 30, [1868], BLC.
71. LS to ASB, December 20, 1868, BLC.
72. HBB to Seth Rogers, November 6, 1868, BLC.
73. Sumner quoted in LS to Mrs. Field, March 24, 1869, BLC. This is probably Anna C. Field, a fellow suffragist. George Washington Julian (1817–1899) was an Indiana congressman and longtime friend of woman suffrage.
74. *Revolution*, January 14, 1868.
75. Stanton, *HWS*,II:358. Although some women's historians maintain that SBA and ECS called the January 19–20, 1869, convention in Washington to lobby for a Sixteenth Amendment, ECS opposed a federal suffrage resolution put forward by George T. Downing, speaking forcefully and at length in favor of a resolution opposing the Fifteenth Amendment on the grounds that it would create "antagonism between the Negro and the woman, and must result, especially in the Southern States, where violence is the law of life, in greater injustice and oppression toward women." SBA introduced a separate resolution calling for suffrage based upon "loyalty and *intelligence* [emphasis hers]." See convention report in *The Woman's Advocate*, I:173–174. DuBois in "Outgrowing the Compact" argues ably for the importance of the women's role in the political debate surrounding Reconstruction. However, in her valorization of ECS and SBA, she overlooks the confusion which existed at this particular moment in women's history.
76. Julian describes his efforts on behalf of a woman suffrage amendment in George W. Julian, *Political Recollections, 1840 to 1879* (Westport, Conn.: Jansen, McClurg, 1884), 324.
77. ECS to Parker Pillsbury quoted in Stanton, *HWS*, II:372; DuBois details the *Revolution's* anti–Fifteenth Amendment campaign in *Feminism*, 173–177.
78. Postscript in *HWS*, II:372; new office announcement in *Revolution*, April 22, 1869. The benefactor was Elizabeth Phelps, a wealthy New York reformer, not to be confused with Elizabeth Stuart Phelps, the well-known novelist.
79. MB to HBB, February 28, 1869, Unproc., SL.
80. SCB to HBB, March 6, 1869, BLC.
81. EmB to HBB, April 7, 1869, BLC.
82. ElB to HBB, June 7, 1869, BLC.
83. LS to SM, April 9, 1869, BLC.
84. *Revolution*, April 29, 1869; May 6, 1869.

CHAPTER NINE
"Out of the Terrible Pit"

1. *New York Times*, May 11, 1869; Brooklyn *Daily Union*, May 15, 1869.
2. Reference to Blackwell's role in the negotiations in *Revolution* account of convention, May 20, 1869.
3. *New York Tribune*, May 13, 1869.
4. *Proceedings, American Anti-Slavery Society*, New York, May 11, 1869.
5. Foster's quotes and all subsequent quotes are from the 1869 A.E.R.A. reports in Stanton, *HWS*, II: 382–392; *New York Times*, May 12, 13, and 14, 1869; *New York Tribune*, May 13, 14, and 15, 1869; Brooklyn *Daily Union*, May 15, 1869; and *Revolution*, May 20, 1869, unless otherwise noted. I have been unable to locate any official 1869 *Proceedings* of the A.E.R.A. convention.
6. Brooklyn *Daily Union*, May 15, 1869; *New York Times*, May 15, 1869.
7. Stanton, *HWS*, II:383.
8. *Ibid.*, 383–384.
9. *Ibid.*, 391–392.
10. *Ibid.*, 320. Listing the "long-time friends against them" Stanton gave the names of "Charles Sumner and Henry Wilson in the Senate, William Lloyd Garrison and Gerrit Smith in reform, Horace Greeley and most of the Liberals in the press," and the "majority" of woman

suffragists. Although later accounts by Stanton and Anthony ascribed the split to different causes (see Stanton, *HWS*, II:400), there was no such confusion at the time of the formation of the new organization. Both the *Revolution* (May 20, 1869) and the *Woman's Advocate* (May 29, 1869) as well as many other newspaper accounts made clear that it was the issue of support for or opposition to the Fifteenth Amendment that precipitated the formation of the New York association. The first resolution adopted by the new organization was "Oppose the Fifteenth Amendment." *Advocate* (June 19, 1869).

11. Hannah Tracy Cutler, Stone's Oberlin friend who was then serving as president of the Ohio delegation to the A.E.R.A., provided Stone with a typewritten account of the events which led up to the formation of the National Association including the meetings at which all parties had agreed to correspond extensively prior to organizing a national society. Cutler typescript is in BLC. Livermore reminded SBA of the prior agreement in a letter quoted in Harper, *Susan B. Anthony*, I:328.

12. Cutler Typescript, 6, BLC.

13. Details of the Saturday night meeting at the Woman's Bureau are sketchy. The *Revolution* reported that "a meeting was called at the Woman's Bureau which resulted in reorganization under the name of the National Woman Suffrage Association." Males were excluded from membership, as there had been "so much trouble with men in the Equal Rights Society that it was thought best to keep the absolute control henceforth in the hands of women." *Revolution*, May 13, 1869; *New York Times*, May 17, 1869.

14. *Revolution*, May 20, 1869.

15. Among those antagonized was Aaron Powell, editor of the *Anti-Slavery Standard* and longtime supporter of woman suffrage. Powell accused the national organization of refusing to recognize the intent of the "negro-hating, copperhead journals such as the New York *World*" who only championed woman suffrage to defeat the Fifteenth Amendment. *Woman's Advocate* 1 (April 1869):225.

16. Circular in BLC; LS to ECS, October 19, 1869, BLC.

17. LS to Elizabeth Buffum Chace, July 11, 1869, NAWSA Collection, LC.

18. Elizabeth Buffum Chace to LS, August 17, 1869, NAWSA Collection, LC.

19. LS to Margaret Whipple, August 16, 1869, in BLC. Isabella Beecher Hooker was half-sister to the famous clergyman Henry Ward Beecher; to the novelist Harriet Beecher Stowe; and to the well-known educator Catherine Beecher.

20. LS to Charles Sanborn, August 18, 1869; LS to Lucy Larcom, August 20, 1869, in Alma Lutz Collection, SL.

21. LS to Elizabeth Buffum Chace, July 11, 1869, NAWSA Collection, LC.

22. *Revolution*, June 8, July 9, July 23, and October 15, 1869.

23. EB to EmB, August 20, 1869; MB to EB, September 1, 1869; EmB to EB, October 11, 1869, Unproc., SL.

24. EmB to EB, December 1869; EmB to EB, March 15, 1870, in Unproc., SL.

25. Newspaper quoted in *Woman's Advocate* 1(February 1869):173.

26. In researching the history of Roseville, I found only one prominent family of the late 1860s whose last name began with the letter "P." In addition, the Pattons were Roseville neighbors and close family friends in the early sixties. Abby Patton, like Stone, was a well-known public figure as a member of the singing Hutchinsons. Unlike Stone, at the wish of her husband, Abby had retired from public life after marriage, resuming her singing career only sporadically. With her charm and social graces and her leaning toward poetry, she was more suited to Blackwell than the serious, reform-minded Stone. In 1891, in a privately published book of poetry and reminiscence, Abby Patton wrote of a great and secret love whose name was "known only by God" (*A Handful of Pebbles*, 23). In 1864 and 1865, Stone and Abby Patton were good friends, exchanging books and letters, yet not a single letter from Abby remains in the Blackwell archives, nor does Stone mention her in her numerous reminiscences. Blackwell was intimately associated with the Pattons, following them to Florida in the spring of 1869. Sam's stiff and formal letter regarding this trip indicates family disapproval. While it seems unlikely that Blackwell would have openly pursued his business partner's wife, the business association ceases in the summer of 1869 at about the time the family begins to deplore his "running after Mrs. P. at Roseville," and Blackwell was certainly an impulsive and romantic man. One other possibility is Rebecca Palmer, the widow at whose home Blackwell

boarded off and on throughout the 1860s. However, there is no evidence that she was ever at Roseville.

Soon after ASB died in March 1950, Edna Stantial, her literary executor, wrote to Howard Lane Blackwell that just before Alice died, she directed Stantial in destroying "certain letters and papers that might prove embarrassing to 'the family.'" One can only speculate that letters to and from the Pattons, missing completely, were among those destroyed. See Edna Stantial to Howard Lane Blackwell, [no date, but written soon after ASB's death], Unproc., SL.

27.　EB to EmB, August 20, 1869, Unproc., SL.

28.　EmB to EB, September 14, 1869, Unproc., SL.

29.　An account of a typical skirmish in the western tour of September 1869 is in *Revolution*, September 9, 16, and 23, 1869. Details of the western tour are in Merk, "Massachusetts," 4.

30.　LS to ABB, October 31, 1869, BLC.

31.　*Ibid.*

32.　EmB to EB, October 11, 1869, Unproc., SL.

33.　EmB to EB, October 27, 1869, Unproc., SL.

34.　LS to ECS, October 19, 1869, BLC.

35.　*Revolution*, October 28, 1869.

36.　LS to ABB, October 31, 1869, BLC.

37.　HBB to LS, November 1, 1869, BLC.

38.　Stanton, *HWS*, II:763–764. The AWSA convention and Lois Merk's dissertation should clarify the confusion which persists among women's history writers about the differences between the two organizations. The most commonly held theory is that the division was on the issue of state versus federal action. The AWSA consistently pledged itself to work on state, federal, and local levels. The radical-versus-conservative theorists are also puzzling. On sexual matters, Stanton and Anthony were more radical; on social issues, Stone tended to be more liberal.

39.　*New York World*, November 27, 1869; Cleveland *Plain Dealer*, November 25, 1869.

40.　SBA to OB, [October] 1869, OB Collection, SL.

41.　Henry Ward Beecher (1813–1887) was pastor of Plymouth Congregation Church in Brooklyn. A prominent social reformer, he edited the *Christian Union* and was a frequent contributor to the *Independent*. His chief claim to fame was as an orator and preacher; his Sunday sermons drew thousands to Brooklyn's Plymouth Church.

42.　SBA quoted in *New York Tribune*, November 25, 1869.

43.　*New York Tribune*, November 25, 1869. Soon after the close of the Cleveland convention, Anthony entered the Dansville Sanitarium for a rest cure. The *Revolution* would limp along for less than a year before folding, leaving Anthony with a $10,000 debt which she would work valiantly to repay. Harper, *Susan B. Anthony*, I:335.

44.　*New York Tribune*, November 25, 1869.

45.　*New York Times*, November 25, 1869.

46.　LS to ASB, December 9, 1869, BLC.

47.　*Ibid.*

48.　EmB to EB, [undated, but internal evidence indicates that it was probably early December 1869], Unproc., SL.

49.　EmB to EB, December 20, 1869, Unproc., SL.

50.　Papers relating to the formation of the joint stock company are in NAWSA Collection, LC, and in Unproc., SL.

51.　LS to Charles Mumford, April 17, 1870, in Alma Lutz Collection, SL.

52.　LS to ASB, February 26, 1870, BLC.

53.　GWB to EB, February 18, 1870, Unproc., SL. This family collaboration in the myth of Blackwell's prosperity persists throughout his lifetime, though family letters make clear that they were all too aware of his numerous financial scrapes and failures.

54.　GWB to EB, February 18, 1870, Unproc., SL.

55.　EmB to EB, March 15, 1870, Unproc., SL.

56.　HBB to GWB, March 9, 1870, Unproc., SL.

57.　EmB to EB, March 15, 1870, Unproc., SL.

58.　KBB to EB, March 28, 1870, Unproc., SL.

59.   The NWSA constitution is in Stanton, *HWS*, II:401. The text of the "Union" constitution in *WJ*, April 9, 1870.

60.   Mott quoted in Cromwell, *Lucretia Mott*, 192.

61.   Tilton quoted in Stone's account of the reconciliation attempt in NAWSA Collection, LC.

62.   *WJ*, April 9, 1870.

63.   *Revolution*, May 14, 1870. Tilton claimed broad support for his Union Society, publishing the names of supporters in the *Independent*. Many of those named wrote public disclaimers, insisting that their names were used without their knowledge or consent and denying any connection to the Union Society.

64.   *New York Herald*, April 9, 1870.

65.   EmB to EB, April 13, 1870, Unproc., SL.

66.   LS to EmB, April 15, 1870, Unproc., SL. The business letter from Harry Blackwell was postmarked P.O. Box 299, New York City—the address that Blackwell returned to during each of their separations.

67.   *WJ*, April 9, 1870.

68.   *Revolution*, December 23, 1869.

69.   *WJ*, April 30, 1870.

70.   *Ibid.*, May 7, 1870.

71.   AWSA convention proceedings and speeches in *WJ*, May 21, 28, and June 4, 1870.

72.   *Nation* quoted in *WJ*, June 11, 1870; ECS in *Revolution*, May 19, 1870.

73.   Cutler Typescript, 9.

74.   ECS to Martha Wright, quoted in Griffith, *Own Right*, 145.

75.   *Revolution*, May 19, 1870.

76.   Details of the McFarland-Richardson case are in *New York Times*, November 25, 1869; May 11, 12, 15, and 18, 1870. Abby McFarland had purportedly obtained a "quickie" Indiana divorce, but its validity in New York was questionable. Stanton's statement in *New York Times*, May 18, 1870.

77.   Harper, *Susan B. Anthony*, I: 353; *New York Times*, May 18, 1870; editorials quoted in *WJ*, June 4, 1870.

78.   *WJ*, September 3, 1870.

79.   ASB to KBB, September 1870, quoted in Hays, *Morning Star*, 215.

80.   LS to MB, September 15, 1870, BLC.

81.   *WJ*, September 17, 1870; September 24, 1870; October 8, 1870.

82.   LS quoted in *WJ*, October 8, 1870.

83.   *WJ*, October 22, 1870.

84.   Lori Ginzberg offers an excellent historical analysis of the shift from moral suasion to politics in *Women and the Work of Benevolence*.

85.   ECS editorial quoted in *WJ*, October 15, 1870.

86.   *Revolution*, September 29, 1870; *Woman's Journal*, October 22, 1870.

87.   Davis, *History*, 24, 56.

88.   LS to Anna Parsons, July 8, 1853 in BLC; *WJ*, October 22, 1870.

89.   Although the editorial is unsigned, Stone's distinctive prose style and idiosyncratic punctuation mark it as her work. *WJ*, November 5, 1870.

90.   Convention call and SBA to ECS quoted in Harper, *Susan B. Anthony*, I:373–374. ECS told of her chagrin at Isabella Hooker's suggestion in letter to Martha Wright quoted in Griffith, *Own Right*, 147. Woodhull testified later that she did indeed have an affair with Tilton at the time. See *Trial*, I:554.

91.   LS to John K. Wildman, November 7, 1871, BLC; Harriet Beecher Stowe to TWH, May 24, 1871, AASC.

92.   HBB to James Freeman Clarke, November 17, 1870, BLC.

93.   *New York Tribune* report, November 26, 1870.

94.   Phonographic report of convention in *WJ*, December 3, 1870.

95.   LS to HBB, November 27, 1870, BLC. Curtis's article in *Harper's Weekly*, November 26, 1870.

96. *Register* report in Noun, *Strong*, 159–160. Noun places the visit in 1871, but a letter from LS to ASB describing the visit is dated Des Moines, December 1, 1870, in BLC.

97. *WJ*, December 31, 1870.

98. LS to GWB, December 16, 1870, Unproc., SL.

99. ASB, *Lucy Stone*, 232–233.

CHAPTER TEN
"Every Clean Soul"

1. LS to John K. Wildman, November 7, 1871, in BLC.

2. Anthony also publicly supported Woodhull, declaring at the January convention: "I will take by the hand every prostitute I can find . . . . [Victoria Woodhull] was not dragged to the front; she came to Washington from Wall Street with a powerful argument and with lots of cash behind her, and I bet you cash is a big thing with Congress" (NAWSA Collection, LC). Letter quoted in Griffith, *Own Rights*, 146. Linda Gordon in *Woman's Body*, 95–104, sees Woodhull's free love advocacy as one of the "closest successors to the perfectionist reform groups of the first half of the century" (96). Despite Woodhull's evident courage in saying in public what others would not, her use of sex for blackmail and extortion, and in particular her use of her newspaper to extort money seem to me to undermine her credibility as a serious social reformer.

3. Information on Woodhull in Arling, *Siren*, 1–15.

4. Details in Arling, *Siren*, 47–49; and in *New York Herald*, November 10, 1872. Benjamin Butler (1818–1893) was a lawyer, Union officer, and politician, serving as a Republican congressman from 1866 to 1875. Stephen Pearl Andrews was a reformer and social theorist, a proponent of world unitary government, and author of "The Science of Society," a highly regarded reform treatise, in addition to being an Owenite and free-love theorist who testified under oath that he wrote Woodhull's editorials. *Trial*, III:400.

5. Washington *Daily Patriot* quoted in Harper, *Susan B. Anthony*, I:376; convention in Stanton, *HWS*, II:464; ECS to SBA, January 31, 1871, in Griffith, *Own Right*, 148.

6. Harper, *Susan B. Anthony*, I:377.

7. ASB to KBB, February 1, 1871, BLC. The Santo Domingo story is long and complex. Like so many reform activities, it held the promise of combining moral reform ("rescuing" the country from invasion by British-ruled Haiti) with the promise of great profits. Samuel Gridley Howe led the 1871 fact-finding excursion, and Blackwell found work as a correspondent for a magazine, *Hearth and Home*, and accompanied them, already interested in an investment scheme there, as George Blackwell's earlier letter indicates. Howe was drawn into the investment scheme by Blackwell, convinced that his stock in the Samana Bay Company soon would worth "twenty-five times its purchase price" (Howe, "My Experiences in Santo Domingo," 12). Howe's biographer researched the entire incident carefully and concluded that it was a "colossal swindle," in which Howe served as the "respectable front behind whom scoundrels could hide" (Schwartz, *Samuel Gridley Howe*, 316). It is possible that Blackwell was unaware of the "sordid story of the negotiations and private advantage" later exposed in a Senate report on the proposed annexation treaty (Senate Executive Committee Document, 41st Session, No. 17, 98–102).

8. LS to MC, March 17, 1871, BLC.

9. HBB to LS, April 1, 1872, BLC.

10. Blackwell quotes Sumner's charge of "moral obliquity" in his letter of response (HBB to Charles Sumner, November 20, 1871, BLC). Here Blackwell seems guilty of hairsplitting; though plans for the investment scheme had been underway for over two years, the final capitalization of the Samana Bay Company was still in progress when he wrote, and his own interest was certainly more than "prospective" at that point. On February 18, 1870, George Blackwell had written Elizabeth that Harry had a "fancy to preempt half St. Domingo, round about the Bay of Samana . . . ." in Unproc., SL.

11. LS to Rebecca Janney, March 19, 1871, BLC.

12.   *WJ*, February 4, 1871, March 11, March 18, and March 25, 1871.

13.   Stephen Pearl Andrews testified during the Beecher-Tilton trial that Stanton called on Woodhull on May 3 or 4, 1871, and at that time confided the rumor about Elizabeth Tilton and Henry Ward Beecher (*Trial*, III:396).

14.   Background material in David Wallechinsky and Irving Wallace, *The People's Almanac* (Garden City, New York: Doubleday, 1975), 190–191.

15.   *New York Tribune*, May 10, 1871.

16.   *WJ*, May 20, 1871; Harper, *Susan B. Anthony*, I:383.

17.   Blake and Wallace, *Champion*, 91; Brown, *Acquaintances*, 91. Noun in *Strong*, 177–197, offers an excellent analysis of the organizational disintegration in Iowa resulting from the Woodhull alliance.

18.   *New York Tribune*, May 13, 1871.

19.   *New York World*, May 22, 1871. *Woodhull & Claflin's Weekly*, May 20, 1871. On the witness stand, Colonel Blood himself testified that he was "unsure" as to whether he and Woodhull were married or not—all gleefully reported in the dailies.

20.   *Trial*, I:412.

21.   *WJ*, May 20, 1871.

22.   *WJ*, August 19, 1871; September 2, 1871; December 9, 1871. Israel Kugler summarizes the Greeley-Tilton 1871 newspaper debate in *From Ladies to Women: The Organized Struggle for Woman's Rights in the Reconstruction Era* (New York: Greenwood Press, 1987), 92–94. Greeley's animus toward Woodhull was exacerbated by her charge in the *Weekly* that he was the cause of his wife's mental illness (Arling, *Siren*, 114).

23.   Anthony was the first to become disillusioned with Woodhull, separating herself soon after the May 1871 convention. Stanton and Hooker remained loyal through the following year, when Woodhull's egregious public behavior and private blackmail attempts finally caused them to break with her. See SBA to Martha Coffin Wright, May 30, 1871, in SSC. Anti-Suffragists' accusations in *WJ*, March 11, 18, and 25, 1871.

24.   LS to Rebecca Janney, July 3, 1871, BLC. Janney chaired the Executive Committee of the Ohio Woman Suffrage Association.

25.   Harriet Beecher Stowe to TWH, May 24, 1871, AASC.

26.   Greeley quoted in *WJ*, August 19, 1871; ASB, *Lucy Stone*, 226.

27.   New York *Examiner and Chronicle* quoted in *WJ*, September 23, 1871.

28.   Merk describes this unprecedented campaign in chapter 10 of "Massachusetts in the Woman Suffrage Movement," noting "the unfortunate impact" of the Beecher-Tilton trial (102).

29.   *WJ*, September 30, 1871. ASB to KBB, February 5, 1871, BLC; LS to MC, March 17, 1871, BLC.

30.   ASB, *Lucy Stone*, 238; *WJ*, June 10, 1871; August 19, 1871; October 21, 1871; October 14, 1871; and November 4, 1871.

31.   *WJ*, October 7, 14, 21, and 28, 1871; November 4, 1871.

32.   LS to John K. Wildman, November 7, 1871, BLC.

33.   ASB, *Lucy Stone*, 233. When Stone invited Marian to spend the winter, Marian declined, writing George, "It is impossible for me to feel at home in Lucy's house. I cannot even spend a month there with any comfort. That home can never be anything to me." MB to GB, October 24, 1871, Unproc., SL.

34.   NAWSA Collection, LC.

35.   Press comments reported in *WJ*, December 9, 1871; Greeley in *New York Tribune*, November 22, 1871.

36.   Arling, *Siren*, 135; *Trial*, II:900.

37.   *Woodhull & Claflin's Weekly* quotes from November 1871 are in NAWSA Collection, LC.

38.   Seitz, *Decade*, 209.

39.   The meeting actually took place on November 20. Lancaster *Gazette*, November 25, 1871.

40.   *WJ*, December 23, 1871.

41.   *WJ*, December 16, 1871; HBB to EB, December 31, 1871, BLC.

42. HBB to GWB, February 10, 1872, Unproc., SL.

43. LS to GWB, February 9, 1872, Unproc., SL; ASB Diary, February 11, 1872, BLC.

44. ASB Diary, February 14, 25, 1872; March 5, 1872, BLC.

45. HBB to LS, March 20, 1872, BLC; LS to HBB, April 11, 1872, BLC.

46. LS to HBB, April 11, 1872, BLC.

47. ASB, *Lucy Stone*, 264.

48. HBB to LS, March 20, 1872, BLC.

49. SBA to ECS, March 13, 1872; SBA to ECS and Isabella Beecher Hooker; and SBA Diary quoted in Harper, *Susan B. Anthony*, I:413–415. The day after the NWSA convention, Woodhull formed the Equal Rights Party, which nominated her as presidential candidate.

50. Elizabeth Phelps was a wealthy New York suffragist, not to be confused with Elizabeth Stuart Phelps, the writer. Lillie Devereaux Blake (1833–1913) was a well-known fiction writer and woman's rights activist. Laura Curtis Bullard made a fortune selling a patent medicine, bought the *Revolution* when it failed, and actively supported woman's rights. Accounts of the blackmail scheme (which in one case included a threat on the recipient's life if she did not pay up) are in Arling, *Siren*, 164–165; in NAWSA Collection, Reel 58; in Blake and Wallace, *Champion*, 90. See also SBA to IBH, June 19 and 24, 1872, in IBH Collection, Stowe-Day Library. Woodhull defended her use of blackmail, writing that for women, blackmail was the "only method of righting themselves" and a way to "avenge the oppressions of [their] sex" (*Woodhull & Claflin's Weekly*, April 6, 1872).

51. Arling, *Siren*, 165–168.

52. *WJ*, May 18, 1872; MAL letter quoted in Noun, *Strong*, 221.

53. MAL letter to Elizabeth Boynton Harbert quoted in Noun, *Strong*, 221.

54. Risjord, *America*, 491–492. The Democrats did endorse Greeley at their July convention.

55. *WJ*, June 15, 1872; Stanton, *HWS*, II: 517–520.

56. HBB to LS, June 5, 1872, BLC.

57. ECS to HBB, September 15, 1872, NAWSA Collection, LC.

58. ECS to LS, May 31, 1872, NAWSA Collection, LC.

59. *WJ*, September 7, 1872; October 26, 1872.

60. SBA to LS, September 4, 1872, NAWSA Collection, LC.

61. LS quoted in *WJ*, September 28, 1872.

62. *WJ*, June 29, 1872; September 14, 21, and 28, 1872.

63. *WJ*, September 7, 1872.

64. HBB to GWB, September 15, 1872, Unproc., SL.

65. ABB to LS, September 6, 1872, BLC; ASB Diary, June 22, 1872.

66. LS to GWB, December 7, 1872, Unproc., SL.

67. ASB Diary, October 12, 1872, BLC.

68. ASB Diary, November 2, 1872, BLC.

69. Arling, *Siren*, 176.

70. *Woodhull & Claflin's Weekly*, November 2, 1872; details of arrest and trial and Challis case in *New York Herald*, November 3, 5, 6, 8, 10, 11, and 19, 1872.

71. *WJ*, November 9, 1872; Elizabeth Churchill to LS, November 8, 1872, BLC.

72. The "eulogist" reference was doubtless to the "biography" that Woodhull had blackmailed Tilton into printing in the *Golden Age* that autumn (*Trial*, I:414, 473). The details of the biography were so far-fetched that *Harper's Weekly* wrote of it: "If apples are wormy this year, and grapes mildew, and ducks' eggs addle, and bladed corn be lodged, it may all be ascribed to the unhallowed influence of Mr. Tilton's life of Victoria Woodhull" (quote in Arling, *Siren*, 120). *Register* quote in Noun, *Strong*, 200.

73. *WJ*, November 30, 1872.

74. Report of Ohio convention in *WJ*, November 25, 1872; Noun, *Strong*, 199. Lillie Devereaux Blake describes the damaging effects of the "continual publicity" associating woman suffrage and free love in Blake and Wallace, *Champion*, 91.

75. *WJ*, December 28, 1872; December 7, 1872.

76. *WJ*, January 25, 1873; February 15, 1873; and March 1, 1873; Brown, *Acquaintances*, 53.

77. *Nation*, February 19, 1885.

78. Margaret Campbell wrote from Maine in December 1872 that proprietors had refused her the use of their hall "believing that the whole thing is *'free love'* in disguise." MC to *WJ*, December 28, 1872; NAWSA Collection, LC; ASB to Mary Hunter, August 12, 1838, BLC; Vermont woman quoted in ASB to LS, June 12, 1889, in NAWSA Collection, LC.

79. ABB to LS, December 1, 1872, BLC.

80. ABB to LS, February 17, 1873, BLC.

81. ASB, *Lucy Stone*, 234.

82. ASB to KBB, July 7, 1873, BLC.

83. Adkinson quoted in ASB, *Lucy Stone*, 235.

84. LS to TWH, January 3, 1873, AASC; *WJ*, January 25, 1873.

85. *WJ*, February 1, 1873.

86. *WJ*, February 15, 1873.

87. Attendance figures in *WJ*, June 1, 1872; May 31, 1873; Howe in Clifford, *Mine Eyes,* 184–188; growing power of temperance in "Separate Paths: Suffragists and the Women's Temperance Crusade," *Signs* 10(Spring 1985): 460–476.

88. *WJ*, October 25, 1873; November 22, 1873.

89. LS to ABB, July 12, 1873; *WJ*, July 12, 1873.

90. Edward Hammond Clarke, *Sex in Education, or, a Fair Chance for Girls* (Boston: James P. Osgood, 1873), 12, 22, 83–91, 126.

91. From December 1873 through May 1874, there are letters on Clarke's book in most issues of the *Woman's Journal*. In 1874, Howe gathered a number of essays in *Sex and Education, A Reply to Dr. E. H. Clarke's Sex in Education* (Boston: Roberts Brothers, 1874).

92. *WJ*, December 20, 1873.

93. ASB Diary, December 15, 1873; December 31, 1873, BLC.

94. *WJ*, December 27, 1873.

95. *WJ*, January 3, 1874.

CHAPTER ELEVEN
"Will the Cause Be Ground to Powder?"

1. From 1910 tribute to LS made by ELB, BLC, Ctr. 86.

2. Alice Kessler-Harris offers a good analysis of the causes for the opposition of working women to woman suffrage in *Out to Work*. The *WJ* consistently opposed immigration quotas. Examples of Stone's nativism in LS to ASB, September 21, 1877; September 24, 1882, BLC. See also DuBois, "The Radicalism of the Woman Suffrage Movement," *Feminist Studies* 3(Fall 1975): 63–71.

3. Marlene Merrill's annotated edition of Alice Stone Blackwell's diary, *Growing Up in Boston's Gilded Age,* offers a thoughtful and sensitive analysis of Alice in the introduction.

4. ASB appended a note to ABB's *Memoirs* describing her mother as a "theist." BLC. Quote from ASB Diary, August 26, 1872, BLC.

5. ASB Diary, June 27, 1872, BLC.

6. *Ibid.*, June 14, 1873, BLC.

7. *Ibid.*, June 27, 1872, BLC.

8. KBB, *Rem.*, BLC, Ctr. 79; ASB, *Rem.*, BLC, Ctr. 86.

9. ASB, *Lucy Stone*, 203–204.

10. Sadie Pritchett, "Reminiscence of Lucy Stone," *WJ*, August 18, 1894.

11. ASB Diary, July 27, 1873, BLC; ELB, *Rem.*, BLC; Hattie Turner, *Rem.*, BLC, Ctr. 86.

12. Scandals of Grant administration in Seitz, *Decade*, 260–291; Mott, *Journalism*, 411–415.

13. *WJ*, January 31, 1874; February 14, 21, 28, 1874; March 14, 1874; June 20, 1874; September 12, 1874.

14. *WJ*, September 26, 1874; August 1, 1874; May 8, 1875.

15. Harper, *Susan B. Anthony*, I:461–462; Griffith, *Own Right*, 158–159.

16. LS to MC, June 13, 1874, BLC.

17. Information on trial and quote in Waller, *Reverend Beecher*, 7–11. Stone wrote Anna Field, a wealthy and influential friend, asking if she could find some literary occupation for Elizabeth Tilton, who would need to support herself and her children. LS to Anna Field, September 8, 1874, BLC.

18. The tangle of lies, misstatements, and garbled testimony has never been sorted out fully; debate over the guilt or innocence of Henry Ward Beecher continues. The three-volume verbatim transcript of the trial contains thousands of pages of testimony, much of it contradictory.

19. See Stone's account of the schism and the effects of the Beecher-Tilton trial dated February 4, 1882, in NAWSA Collection, Ctr. 38, BLC.

20. For analyses of the shifts taking place in American society and culture in this period, see Sproat, *Liberal Reformers;* Alan Trachtenberg, *The Incorporation of America: Culture & Society in the Gilded Age* (New York: Hill and Wang, 1982); Clark, *Henry Ward Beecher.*

21. Stow Persons, *The Decline of American Gentility* (New York: Columbia University Press, 1973), 80–93. Material on the suffrage movement from 1870 to 1890 is sparse. A recent work, Sally Roesch Wagner, *A Time of Protest,* is informative on specific protests but offers no overview of the period. See also Grimes, *Puritan Ethic,* 78–98.

22. Persons, *Decline,* 88. Kelley, *Private Woman,* 331–335; Merk, "Massachusetts, " 102–116. Even Sorosis, careful to keep suffrage from its list of aims, came under fire for bringing women into the masculine, political world. A *Harper's Weekly* cartoon of the time showed "nervous husbands caring for their babies" while wives busied themselves with club activities (Blair, *Clubwoman,* 25). Some organizations, such as the Women's Industrial and Educational Union (1877), attempted to cross class lines. See Croly, *History of Woman's Club Movement.*

23. *Boston Advertiser,* February 17, 1881.

24. Merk, "Massachusetts," 102–130, offers an excellent analysis of the organization and work of the Suffrage Clubs and Leagues.

25. *WJ,* May 10, 1873.

26. Merk, "Massachusetts," 129; Hays, *Morning Star,* 267.

27. *Minor v. Happersett* decision in Kerber and Mathews, *Women's America,* 479. The NWSA curtailed its support for the Sixteenth Amendment during the legal appeal, feeling that it would weaken the constitutional argument.

28. The *WJ* masthead proclaimed its support for a federal amendment from the first issue on. See *WJ,* December 9, 1871, November 30, 1872; December 16, 1876; July 22, 1882.

29. See Merk, "Massachusetts," 77–78, for a discussion of AWSA on the Sixteenth Amendment. *WJ,* December 18, 1876.

30. *WJ,* April 12, 1884; June 30, 1877. See Nancy Schrom Dye, "Creating A Feminist Alliance: Sisterhood and Class Conflict in the New York Women's Trade Union League," *Feminist Studies* 2(1975); Robin Jacoby, "The Women's Trade Union League and American Feminism," *Feminist Studies* 3(Fall 1975). For Catholic opposition, see James Kenneally's "Catholicism and Woman Suffrage," 43–57. Kenneally discusses the various cultural and political issues that divided the Catholic Church and woman suffragists in the last three decades of the nineteenth century, arguing that not only ideological conservatism, but a number of other factors—among them nativism, temperance, the school issue, and the growing labor movement—accounted for Catholic opposition to woman suffrage.

31. Quotes from a phonographic report of the convention in *WJ,* October 18, 1873.

32. Kenneally, "Women and the Trade Unions," 42–55; Kessler-Harris, *Out to Work.*

33. *WJ,* May 27, 1876.

34. Many union leaders also opposed strikes as being synonymous with violence and anarchy. The first nationwide labor organization, the National Labor Union, refused to sanction strikes. For a more comprehensive study of the early unions and strikes, see Gutman, *Work, Culture, and Society.*

35. *WJ,* July 30, 1870; July 26, 1873; July 21, 1877; September 22, 1877; August 10, 1872.

36. *WJ,* August 10, 1872; July 21, 1877; September 22, 1877.

37. LS to MC, April 12, 1877, BLC.

38.   See Samuel Burr, *Four Thousand Years of the World's Progress* (Hartford: L. Stebbins, 1878); and *The Stranger's Illustrated Pocket Guide to Philadelphia* (Philadelphia: J. Lippincott, 1876).

39.   HBB to LS, June 16, 1876, BLC.

40.   LS to MC, July 19, 1876, BLC; *WJ*, July 15, 1876.

41.   LS to MC, July 19, 1876, BLC.

42.   LS to ECS, August 3, 1876, BLC.

43.   LS to ECS, August 30, 1876, BLC.

44.   LS to ABB, July 20, 1876, BLC.

45.   Anthony's diary entries and letters are peppered with furious references to Stone written in large spiky letters.

46.   LS to HR, January 27, 1876, RS; *Woman's Journal*, December 8, 1877. Stone's letter was intended to placate Robinson after a slight disagreement.

47.   LS to ELB, undated, but internal evidence points to May 1876, Unproc., SL.

48.   LS to ABB, January 21, 1876 [7?], in BLC. [Dated 1876, but internal evidence indicates that the letter probably was written in January of 1877.]

49.   LS to ABB, July 15, 1877, BLC.

50.   LS to ASB, September 21, 1877, BLC.

51.   *Ibid.*

52.   LS to MC, March 30, 1874, BLC.

53.   Merk, "Massachusetts," 195.

54.   Irwin quoted in Hays, *Morning Star,* 217. On working conditions for women, see *WJ,* January 30, 1875; May 1, 1875; July 10, 1875.

55.   ASB to KBB, December 21, 1879, BFP. On learning that her brother George was to marry Emma, Elizabeth wrote that she was glad to learn that Emma resembled their own mother: "I recognize the likeness and rejoice that she is without certain Stone and Lawrence peculiarities which would not have suited you." EB to GWB, [1875?] Unproc., SL.

56.   Quote in Hays, *Blackwells,* 195.

57.   ASB to KBB, December 24, 1882, BLC.

58.   EmB to EB, August 13, 1881, in BLC; EB to GWB, [1875?], Unproc., SL.

59.   ABB to LS July 5, 1880, BLC.

60.   SCB to EB, August 10, 1870, Unproc., SL.

61.   LS to GWB, July 22, 1876, Unproc., SL. Although both Elizabeth and Ellen took in male foundlings, neither the males nor their female counterparts were given the Blackwell name. Marian wrote to Ellen that she was "merely speaking the sentiment of most, if not all of us, when I say that I should much prefer that they had another name, and I think if that matter were settled, there would be a much more cordial feeling towards them." MB to ElB, November 1, 1875, Unproc., SL. Kitty Barry only added the name Blackwell when she came to live with ASB long after the death of EB.

62.   On the birth of their second son in 1879, LS advised the new parents: "Teach them gentle ways" (LS to GWB, October 9, 1979, BLC); and on breast-feeding: "breasts you know must be kept well drawn" (LS to SSL, September 29, 1879, BLC).

63.   GBB to EB, June 30, 1878, BFP.

64.   ASB to KBB, April 27, 1879, BFP.

65.   HBB telegram to LS, October 28, 1878, BLC.

66.   HBB to LS, July 8, 1879, BLC. Solon Wanton Bush (1819–1898) was a minister and occasional editor of the *Journal* in Stone's and Blackwell's absence.

67.   LS to ABB, August 25, 1879, BLC.

68.   ASB to KBB, September 28, 1879, BLC.

69.   Francis Parkman, *North American Review,* 129 (October 1879): 321.

70.   LS, *North American Review,* 129 (November 1879): 431–432.

71.   ASB to KBB, November 30, 1979, BLC.

72.   LS to HBB, November 26, 1879, BLC; LS to HBB, December 12, 1879, BLC. Letter in Stannard, *Mrs. Man,* 108–109. ASB comments in her "Reminiscence" of her father (BLC, Ctr. 72) that he did not become a U.S. citizen until August 26, 1896.

73.   LS to MC, March 16, 1880, BLC.

74. SSL to ELB, March 29, 1880, Unproc., SL.
75. LS to ASB, March 6, 1880; March 10, 1880, BLC.
76. LS to HBB, April 6, 1880, BLC.
77. HBB to LS, April 12, 1880, BLC.
78. LS to HBB, April 1, 1880, BLC.
79. EmB to GB, July 12, 1880, Unproc., SL.
80. LS to HBB, April 9, 1880, BLC.
81. ABB to LS, July 5, 1880; HBB to LS, August 16, 1880; BFP. See LS accounts for 1880, BLC.
82. HBB to LS, May 12, 1880, BLC.
83. HBB to LS, April 21, 1880, BLC.
84. LS to HBB, September 16, 1880, BLC.

CHAPTER TWELVE
"Another Year For Downright Work"

1. ASB to KBB, September 5, 1880; May 1, 1881, BLC.
2. HBB to LS, March 6, 1881; ASB to KBB, May 1, 1881, BLC.
3. ASB to KBB, May 1, 1881, BLC.
4. LS to ASB, December 24, 1884, BLC.
5. *WJ*, January 1, 1881; March 19, 1881.
6. *WJ*, August 22, 1882. In the mid-seventies, Stone's support of the Sixteenth Amendment slackened following two Supreme Court decisions. The first of these, *Minor v. Happersett*, responded to women's Fourteenth Amendment claim to the ballot by insisting that suffrage was a matter for the "States in which they reside" to decide, passing "appropriate State legislation" if they wished to "clothe" women with the right of suffrage (decision quoted in *WJ*, June 4, 1881). The second case, *Myra Bradwell v. Illinois*, reaffirmed this decision, ruling that the Fourteenth Amendment "did not add to the privileges and immunities of a citizen . . . . No new voters were necessarily made by it." The court ruled that "The Constitution of the United States does not confer the right of suffrage upon anyone" (in Catt, *Woman Suffrage*, 96). Stone's belief that a Sixteenth Amendment was constitutionally dubious did not prevent her lukewarm support of it in the late 1870s, but she intensified her efforts for partial suffrage and state constitutional amendments in keeping with the holdings of the Supreme Court.
7. Membership figures from NWSA *Report* for 1882, 148. SBA had worked in 1880 to raise funds for a rival newspaper, the *National Citizen and Ballot-Box*, which folded in 1881. Chicago *Tribune*, April 30, 1881.
8. Robinson, an able speaker, writer, and suffragist, had tangled with Stone earlier over a political issue. The Anthony-Robinson correspondence about organizing New England covers the years 1879–1882, in RS. Quotes in SBA to HR, June 12, 1880, [some question as to whether this is actually 1881].
9. *WJ*, June 4, 1881.
10. Harriet Sewall to HR, February 26, 1882, RS. Harriet Winslow Sewall (1819–1889), wife of abolitionist Samuel Sewall, was a poet, abolitionist, philanthropist, and suffragist.
11. *WJ*, June 11, 1881. Ironically, the frontispiece of *HWS* bore the inscription : "The world belongs to those who *take* it."
12. ECS wrote Harriet Robinson on October 26, 1880: "I now think we will confine ourselves to the work of the National Association," explaining that Robinson would have thirty-five pages to summarize her book, *Massachusetts in the Woman Suffrage Movement*. She suggested that Robinson "merely" say "that in your work & the Woman's Journal all the facts of history, relationship to the American association & the various New England Assoc. are fully recorded and will be preserved for the future historian." Letter in RS.

13.   ASB, *Lucy Stone*, 263. In never marrying, Alice was like nearly 50 percent of the women who graduated from college in the 1880s. See Helen Lefkowitz Horowitz, *Alma Mater: Design and Experience in the Women's Colleges from Their Nineteenth-Century Beginnings to the 1930s* (Boston: Beacon Press, 1984), 279–281. ASB tells of disappointing her father in his hope that she would marry in ASB to LS, June 15, 1886, Unproc., SL. Hays, *Morning Star,* suggests that ASB had a brief romance with a young Armenian she had met through the Barrowses. In 1896, on his way to study at the Sorbonne, he fell sick and died (300).

14.   ASB, *Lucy Stone,* 272. The Barrowses, described by Alice as "widely travelled and cosmopolitan," coedited the *Christian Register*. Isabel Barrows also served as secretary of the National Conference of Charities and Correction.

15.   *WJ*, August 13, 1881.

16.   *WJ*, August 20, 1881.

17.   ASB to EmB, November 28, 1886, Unproc., SL.

18.   LS to ASB, August 19, 1881, BLC.

19.   *WJ*, November 5, 1881.

20.   *WJ*, October 29, 1881.

21.   LS to ASB, July 15, 1882; September 24, 1882; August 24, 1883; April 28, 1883; May 3, 1883, all in BLC.

22.   SBA mentions LS's fund-raising campaign for Nebraska in SBA to HR, December 18, 1881, RS.

23.   SBA to HR, December 18, 1881; February 10, 1882, RS.

24.   SBA to HR, February 10, 1882, RS; Blatch, *Challenging Years,* 61, 62.

25.   *Nation*, October 12, 1882.

26.   LS to Howard Lane Blackwell, [August], 1882, Unproc., SL.

27.   LS to Rebecca Janney, February 28, 1871; January 13, 1882; ASB, *Lucy Stone,* 227; *WJ,* June 6, 1882.

28.   LS to John Hooker, April 16, 1883 in BLC. John Hooker (1806–1901), an activist and reformer, was the husband of woman's rights activist Isabella Beecher Hooker.

29.   LS to ASB, September 21, 1882, in BLC; *WJ,* October 14, 1882.

30.   *WJ*, September 23, 1872.

31.   LS to ASB, September 24, 1882, BLC.

32.   *Nation*, November 16, 1882.

33.   Trip account in *WJ*, November 4, 1882.

34.   *WJ*, April 12, 1884. A good account of the growth of organized anti-suffrage work is in Merk, "Massachusetts," chapter 18. Merk points out that Boston was the hub from which nationwide anti-suffrage activity radiated.

35.   John Crowley, "W. D. Howells: The Ever-Womanly," *American Novelists Revisited: Essays in Feminist Criticism,* ed. Fritz Fleischmann (Boston: G. K. Hall, 1982), 171–188. See also "The Lady and Woman's Rights" in Persons, *Decline,* 80–94.

36.   Archbishop John Williams of the Boston Archdiocese warned women not to take part in politics. Catholic bishops in Baltimore, Cincinnati, Colorado, and Milwaukee issued similar warnings. See Kenneally, "Catholicism and Woman Suffrage."

37.   ASB to KBB, January 28, 1883, BLC.

38.   Merk, "Massachusetts," 35.

39.   Stone's accounts show irregular deposits by Blackwell against the Maine Beet Sugar Company over many years—sometimes $300, other times $400. Stone's accounts in BLC, Ctrs. 69–70. ASB to KBB, March 25, 1883, BFP.

40.   LS to SSB May 29, 1883, Unproc., SL.

41.   HBB to ASB, June 24, 1883, BLC.

42.   LS to ASB June 22, 1883, BLC.

43.   A typescript of the Oberlin speech is in BLC.

44.   LS to ASB, August 26, 1883, BLC.

45.   LS to ASB, August 22, 1883, BLC.

46.   *WJ*, November 24, 1882.

47. *WJ*, December 2, 1883.

48. ASB, *Lucy Stone*, 262; memorial tribute in *WJ*, March 8, 1884.

49. Letters in Hays, *Morning Star*, 279. Stone petitioned for the defeat of House Bill 352 (which sought to deny married women the ability to dispose of their own separate estates) and for passage of House Bill 192 (which gave a woman deserted by her husband the right to dispose of any property which had been gained by her after the desertion without her husband's written consent). Reports on these campaigns are found in Stone's annual speech to the New England Woman Suffrage Association at the 1884 May anniversary meeting in *WJ*, May 31, 1884.

50. Will dated July 21, 1884, BLC; LS to ASB, July 21, 1884, BLC.

51. Mary Flynn Head, Typescript of a 1914 interview, BLC.

52. ASB, *Lucy Stone*, 256–257.

53. LS to ASB, July 15, [1884], July 29, 1884, BLC.

54. Risjord, *America*, 499.

55. *WJ*, October 4, 1884; August 9, 1884.

56. LS to ASB, July 31, 1884, BLC; *WJ*, October 11, 1884; October 4, 1884.

57. Quote in LS to ASB, August 31, 1884, BLC.

58. *WJ*, November 1, 1884.

59. LS to TWH, December 18, 1884; LS to ASB, December 28, 1884, BLC.

60. LS to Cornelia Hussey, November 28, 1884, BLC.

61. Quote in *WJ*, February 14, 1885; *WJ*, January 10, 1885.

62. Report on the seventeenth NWSA convention in *WJ*, January 24, 1885.

63. Text of Eddy will in *WJ*, May 2, 1885.

64. LS to ABB, January 10, 1886, BLC.

65. Harper, *Susan B. Anthony*, II:600, 614. Stone's accounts show that she used the Eddy fund to provide up to $1000 for various state legislative campaigns as well as to pay for the printing of leaflets and for funding the *Woman's Column*. BLC, Ctr. 70.

66. LS to ASB, August 3, 1885, BLC.

67. LS to ASB, October 29, 1885, BLC, pamphlets in Merk, "Massachusetts," 195–198.

68. ASB to EmB, Nov 14, 1886, Unproc., SL.

69. ABB to LS, January 6, 1886, BFP.

70. LS to ABB, January 10, 1886, BLC.

71. LS to ABB, February 28, 1886, BLC.

72. Quote in Hays, *Morning Star*, 282.

73. HBB to GWB, February 13, 1887, Unproc., SL.

74. LS to HBB, February 20, 1887, BLC.

75. LS to ASB, March 31, 1887, BLC.

76. ASB to LS, March 27, 1887, BLC.

77. LS to ASB, [first page missing, but probably April 1887], BLC.

78. *WJ*, November 12, 1887; ASB, *Lucy Stone*, 242.

79. LS to ASB, April 12, 1887, BLC.

80. LS to ASB, April 12, 1887, BLC.

81. HBB to LS, October 14, 1887, in BLC; HBB to ASB, September 10, 1887, BLC. The *Woman's Journal* cost $2.50 per year.

82. Merk, "Massachusetts," 238; Stanton, *HWS*, IV:426.

83. *Washington Post*, April 1, 1888.

84. The best available account of the negotiations is in Merk, "Massachusetts," 237–251.

85. SBA's letter cautioned recipients to tell no one of her plan and expressed the hope that Stanton's election would occasion a "revolt" by AWSA affiliates. Then, "If any *won't* stand it—let *them secede again*—then will come the odium to them that *won't work with the majority*" (SBA to OB, March 11, 1889, in OB Papers, SL).

86. Harper, *Susan B. Anthony*, II:631–632; LS to HBB, February 18, 1890, BLC.

87. LS to HBB, February 16, 1890, BLC.

CHAPTER THIRTEEN
"Make the World Better"

1. LS to ABB, [Dorchester, Winter 1888], BLC. Bowman Stone died on February 4, 1890.
2. LS to HBB and ASB, February 17, 1890, BLC; congratulatory letter in Harper, *Susan B. Anthony*, II:668.
3. *WJ*, May 24, 1890.
4. *WJ*, February 22, 1890; Stone's telegram in Harper, *Susan B. Anthony*, II:676.
5. LS to ASB, March 1889, BLC.
6. LS to SSL, September 6, 1891 in Unproc., SL. Helena Blavatsky (1820–1891) was a Russian immigrant and well-known spiritualist who founded the Theosophical Society. LS to SSL, May 7, 1891, Unproc., SL.
7. ASB, *Lucy Stone*, 270–271.
8. HBB to LS, August 27, 1890, BLC.
9. LS to HBB, September 11, 1890, BLC. The prospects for the South Dakota woman suffrage referendum had worsened when the state Republican party split. "I fear for a house divided against itself," Stone wrote (LS to HBB, July 19, 1990, BLC). With liquor interests arrayed against suffrage, with Republicans splintered, and with the woman suffragists battling one another in public and in private, the amendment went down to defeat in November by a vote of 45,862 to 22,072. Catt and Schuler, *Woman Suffrage*, 116; Harper, *Susan B. Anthony*, II:694–695.
10. HBB to LS, August 18, 22, 23, 24, 26, 27, and 30, 1890, BLC.
11. LS to HBB, September 1, 1890, BLC; HBB to LS, September 22, 1890, BLC.
12. HBB to LS, [September] 1990, BLC; *WJ*, September 27, 1990; LS to ASB, October 24, 1990, BLC.
13. EmB quoted in LS to HBB, August 20, 1890, BLC.
14. LS accounts for 1890 show EmB repaying her $700 (LS believed Emily owed $1400); GWB made irregular payments to LS of $600 and $700 on money he had borrowed. LS sent support payments to Marian, Anna, and Ellen. LS accounts in BLC, Ctr. 70.
15. EmB to EB, August 15, 1894, BLC; EB to GWB, August 27, 1883, Unproc., SL; LS to HBB, February 20, 1887, BLC; the family's praise of Harry for his financial support in numerous letters, among these EmB to GWB, January 14, 1884, Unproc., SL.
16. LS to ASB, August 6, 1891; ELB to GWB, September 6, 1893; LS to ASB, August 6, 1891; Kate Stone to LS, June 20, 1892; all in Unproc., SL.
17. LS to ELB, [Summer] 1891, Unproc., SL.
18. LS to ABB, September 18, [1890], BLC. *WJ*, May 30, 1891.
19. ABB to LS, April 20, 1892, BFP; ABB's address to the Federation of Women's Clubs was made on May 11, 1892.
20. *WJ*, May 2, 1891; LS to SBA, September 6, 1891, BLC; Anthony's letter quoted in Griffith, *Own Right*, 203.
21. Stone's interests in this period in ASB, *Lucy Stone*, 264–265; in reports in the *Woman's Journal*, as well as in the wide-ranging correspondence she carried on in later life. *WJ*, May 2, 1891, reported that nearly every state now had Working Girls' Clubs, reporting Boston attendance figures and noting that the Brooklyn Working Girls' Club alone had 15,000 members, while the New York club had 2,400.
22. LS to ASB, August 21, 1891, BLC.
23. LS, *Rem.*, 22.
24. *WJ* ads from 1891. An analysis of the transformation in women's work in the home is in Ruth Schwartz Cowan, *More Work for Mother* (New York: Basic Books, 1983). Letter writing campaign in LS to ASB, August 6, 1891, Unproc., SL.
25. *WJ*, June 13, 1891. LS to SBA, September 6, 1891, BLC; LS to Judith Smith, July 22, 1892. The "furies" to whom LS referred were women who joined their striking husbands in the July

6, 1892, armed attack on Pinkerton guards during the Homestead strike. Nine strikers and seven Pinkertons died in the attack.

26. *North American Review,* September 1891.

27. For gentrification of the woman suffrage movement, see Morgan, Buechler, Kugler, Kraditor. Gutman, *Work,* analyzes the link between reform and politics. For the roots of change, see Hewitt, *Women's Activism;* Ginzberg, *Women.*

28. LS to ASB, August 14, 1892, BLC.

29. *WJ,* December 5, 12, and 19, 1891.

30. LS, *Rem.,* 5–6.

31. Peck, *Carrie Chapman Catt,* 42; 66–67.

32. Stanton's speech in *WJ,* January 23, 1892. Stone's House Judiciary speech, though omitted from the *WJ,* is in Stanton, *HWS* IV:191–193.

33. Convention report in *WJ,* January 23, 1892.

34. The *WJ* of 1892 carries regular reports of Stone's legislative activities along with the standing invitation to the Monday open house.

35. ABB to LS, April 20, 1892, Unproc., SL; LS to Judith Smith, July 22, 1892, BLC; LS to GWB, August 29, 1892, in Unproc., SL. LS letter to 1893 NAWSA convention in Harper, *Susan B. Anthony,* II: 738–739.

36. ASB, *Lucy Stone,* 273–274; LS to FS, Jr., February 11, 1893, BLC.

37. LS to HBB, May 1, 1893, BLC.

38. LS to ASB, July 21, 1884, BLC. Will of LS in BLC, Ctr 87. The terms of the will show the extent of LS holdings. William Ingersoll Bowditch (1819–1909) was a Harvard-educated lawyer and good friend who had worked with Stone in both the antislavery movement and in the woman suffrage movement and authored one of Stone's favorite woman suffrage pamphlets, *Taxation of Women in Massachusetts* (Cambridge, Massachusetts, 1875).

39. Harper, *Susan B. Anthony,* II:746; Eagle, *Congress of Women.*

40. HBB to LS, May 15, 1893, BLC.

41. Blake quoted in Wheeler, *Loving Warriors,* 345.

42. Text of LS speech in Eagle, *Congress of Women,* 58–61.

43. LS to SSL, July 14, 1893, Unproc., SL.

44. LS to SSL, July 31, 1893, Unproc., SL.

45. LS to HBB, August 15, 1893, BLC.

46. HBB to LS, August 30, 1993, BLC; ELB to GWB, September 6, 1893, Unproc., SL.

47. ELB to GWB, September 8, 1893, Unproc., SL.

48. Among the doctors the Blackwell consulted were Drs. Gage and Fifield, two well-known Boston surgeons. Information on contemporary medical treatment in Albert Mathieu, *Treatment of the Diseases of the Stomach and the Intestines* (New York: William Wood & Co., 1894), 246–247.

49. ELB to GWB, Sept. 3, 1893, Unproc., SL.

50. ASB, *Lucy Stone,* 277; ELB to SSL, [early September 1893], Unproc., SL.

51. Letter of September 19, 1893, quoted in LS, *Rem.,* 15.

52. LS to FS, Jr., September 20, 1893, BLC.

53. ELB to GWB, September 28, 1893, Unproc., SL.

54. ASB to ELB, Sept 25, 1893; EB to GWB, Oct. 1, 1893, Unproc., SL.

55. LS, *Rem.,* 20.

56. *Ibid.,* 22.

57. ASB to ELB, September 25, 1893; October 11, 1893, Unproc., SL.

58. ASB, *Lucy Stone,* 280–281.

59. ASB to ELB, October 10, 1893; October 11, 1893, Unproc., SL.

60. HBB to Anna Blackwell, October 10, 1893, BLC; HBB to Julia Ward Howe, September 24, 1893, BLC.

61. ELB to GWB, October 16, 1893, Unproc., SL.

62. ELB to SSL, October 16, 1893, BLC; ELB to GWB, October 14, 1893, Unproc., SL.

63. ELB to SSL, October 17, 1893, Unproc., SL.

64. ELB to GWB, October 18, 1893; ELB to SSL, October 18, 1893, Unproc., SL.

Epilogue

1. SBA Diary entry, October 18, 1893, BLC.
2. EmB to EB, August 15, 1894, Uproc., SL; EmB to HBB, December 1893, BLC.
3. SCB quoted in EmB to HBB, December 1893, BLC. Margo Horn has written about the interdependency of the Blackwell siblings relationship to one another in "Family Ties."
4. EmB to HBB [December] 1893, BLC; ASB, *Lucy Stone*, 287; ASB to SSL, December 27, 1893, Uproc., SL.
5. HBB to EmB, December 31, 1893, BLC; ASB to SSL, December 27, 1893, Unproc., SL.
6. HBB to SSL and HL, December 31, 1893, Unproc., SL.
7. *National Cyclopedia of American Biography*, 20:294.
8. Newspaper accounts of pilgrimages, Lucy Stone League, various tributes, in BLC.

Bibliography

MANUSCRIPT COLLECTIONS

American Antiquarian Society (AAS)
 Antislavery Collections (ASC)
 Abigail Kelley Foster Collection
 Wendell Phillips Collection
Boston Public Library (BPL)
 Antislavery Collections (AASC)
 Maria Weston Chapman Collection
 Kate Field Collection
 Galatea Collection
 Thomas Wentworth Higginson Papers
Brown University
 Woman's Rights Collection
Library of Congress (LC)
 Susan B. Anthony Collection
 Mary Ann Bickerdyke Collection
 Blackwell Family Collection(BLC)
 Frederick Douglass Collection

Henrietta Crosby Ingersoll Collection
National American Woman Suffrage
 Association (NAWSA) Collection
 Wendell Phillips Collection
 Reid Family Collection
 Elizabeth Cady Stanton Collection
Schlesinger Library (SL)
 Blackwell Family Papers (BFP)
 Unprocessed Papers (Unproc.)
 Olympia Brown Collection
 Alma Lutz Collection
 Robinson-Shattuck Collection
Smith College
 Sophia Smith Collection
Stowe-Day Library, Hartford, Connecticut
 Isabella Beecher Hooker Collection

REPORTS, PROCEEDINGS, TRACTS

Proceedings of the Woman's Rights Convention Held at Worcester, October 23 and 24, 1850. Boston: Prentiss and Sawyer, 1851.

Proceedings of the Second Woman's Rights Convention of October 15, 16, 1851 in Galatea Collection, BPL.

Proceedings of the Third National Woman's Rights Convention. Syracuse: J. E. Masters, 1852.

Proceedings of the Fourth National Woman's Rights Convention. New York: Fowlers and Wells, 1853.

Proceedings of the Seventh National Woman's Rights Convention. New York: Edward O. Jenkins, 1856.

Proceedings of the Ninth National Woman's Rights Convention. Rochester: A. Strong and Co., 1859.

Proceedings of the Tenth National Woman's Rights Convention. Boston: Yerrinton and Garrison, 1860.

Proceedings of the Eleventh National Woman's Rights Convention. New York : Robert Johnston, 1866.

Proceedings of the First Anniversary of the American Equal Rights Association. New York: Robert Johnston, 1867.

Stone, Lucy. *Woman Suffrage in New Jersey.* Boston: C. H. Simonds, 1867 [?].

Theodore Tilton Against Henry Ward Beecher, in the City Court of Brooklyn. 3 vols. Verbatim Trial Report. New York: McDivitt, Campbell and Co., 1875.

Woman's Rights Tracts in Galatea Collection, BPL.

NEWSPAPERS AND PERIODICALS

Anti-Slavery Standard
Boston Daily Globe
Boston Herald
Boston Pilot
Brooklyn Daily Argus
Brooklyn Daily Eagle
Golden Age
Independent
Ladies Literary Cabinet
Ladies Literary Museum
Liberator
Lily
New England Palladium
New York *Sun*

New York Times
New York Tribune
New York World
North American Review
North Star
Revolution
Thomas's Worcester Spy
The Una
Washington Union
Woman's Advocate
Woman's Journal
Woman's Tribune
Woodhull & Claflin's Weekly

BOOKS AND ARTICLES

Abbott, Lyman. *Henry Ward Beecher.* Hartford: American Publishing, 1887.

Adams, Charles F. "Some Phases of Sexual Morality and Church Discipline in New England," Massachusetts Historical Society *Proceedings,* Second Series, 6(1891):477–516.

Anthony, Katharine Susan. *Susan B. Anthony: Her Personal History and Her Era.* Garden City, N.Y.: Doubleday & Co., 1954.

Arling, Emanie Sachs. *The Terrible Siren: Victoria Woodhull.* New York: Harper & Brothers, 1928.

Bacon, Margaret Hope. *Mothers of Feminism: The Story of Quaker Women in America.* San Francisco: Harper & Row, 1986.

———. *I Speak for My Slave Sister: The Life of Abby Kelley Foster.* New York: Thomas Y. Crowell, 1974.

———. *Valiant Friend: The Life of Lucretia Mott.* New York: Walker and Co., 1980.

Ballantine, W. G. *Oberlin Jubilee: 1833–1883.* Oberlin: E. J. Goodrich, 1883.

Banner, Lois W., and Mary S. Hartman, eds. *Clio's Consciousness Raised: New Perspectives on the History of Women.* New York: Octagon Books, 1976.

———. *Elizabeth Cady Stanton: A Radical for Woman's Rights.* Boston: Little, Brown, 1980.

———. *Women in Modern America: A Brief History.* San Diego: Harcourt Brace, 1984.

Barry, Kathleen. *Susan B. Anthony: A Biography of a Singular Feminist.* New York: New York University Press, 1988.

Bartlett, J. Gardner. *Gregory Stone Genealogy.* Cambridge, Mass.: Murray Printing Company, 1918.

Bell, Clark. *Speech to the Jury in the Proceeding Before Chief Justice Charles P. Daly and a Jury Upon the Inquiry as to the Sanity or Insanity of George Francis Train.* New York: Russell Bros., 1873.

Berg, Barbara J. *The Remembered Gate: Origins of American Feminism*. New York: Oxford University Press, 1978.

Berwanger, Eugene. *The Frontier Against Slavery: Western Anti-Negro Prejudice and the Slavery Extension Controversy*. Urbana: University of Illinois Press, 1967.

———. *The West and Reconstruction*. Urbana: University of Illinois Press, 1981.

Billington, Ray. *The Far Western Frontier, 1830–1860*. New York: Harper, 1956.

Blackwell, Alice Stone. *Lucy Stone: Pioneer of Woman's Rights*. Boston: Little, Brown, 1930.

Blackwell, Elizabeth. *Essays on Medical Sociology*. London: Ernest Bell, 1902.

Blair, Karen J. *The Clubwoman as Feminist: True Womanhood Redefined, 1868–1914*. New York: Holmes and Meier, 1980.

Blake, Katherine Devereaux, and Mary Louise Wallace. *Champion of Woman: The Life of Lillie Deveraux Blake*. New York: Fleming H. Revell Co., 1943.

Blatch, Harriet Stanton. *Challenging Years: The Memoirs of Harriet Stanton Blatch*. New York: G. P. Putnam's Sons, 1940.

Bleyer, Willard Grosvenor. *Main Currents in the History of American Journalism*. New York: Da Capo, 1973.

Bloomer, Dexter C. *Life and Writings of Amelia Bloomer*. Boston: Arena Publishing Co., 1895.

Bolton, Sarah Knowles. *Famous Leaders Among Women*. New York, Boston: T. Y. Crowell, 1895.

Boorstin, Daniel. *The Democratic Experience*. New York: Vintage Books, 1974.

Boydston, Jeanne, Mary Kelley, and Anne Margolis. *The Limits of Sisterhood: The Beecher Sisters on Women's Rights and Woman's Sphere*. Chapel Hill: University of North Carolina Press, 1988.

Branch, Edward Douglas. *The Sentimental Years: 1835–1860*. New York: D. Appleton-Century Co., 1934.

Brandt, Nat. *The Town That Started the Civil War*. Syracuse: Syracuse University Press, 1990.

Brigance, William Norwood., ed. *A History and Criticism of American Public Address*. New York: McGraw-Hill, 1943.

Bright, John D., ed. *Kansas: The First Century*. New York: Lewis Historical Publishing Co., Vol. I, 1956.

Brink, Carol Ryrie. *Harps in the Wind: The Story of the Singing Hutchinsons*. New York: Macmillan, 1947.

Brown, Olympia. *Acquaintances Old and New Among Reformers*. Milwaukee: S. E. Tate, 1911.

Brown, Richard D. *Modernization*. New York: Hill & Wang, 1976.

Brownlee, W. Elliot, and Mary M. Brownlee. *Women in the American Economy: A Documentary History, 1675–1929*. New Haven: Yale University Press, 1976.

Buechler, Steven M. *The Transformation of the Woman Suffrage Movement: The Case of Illinois, 1850–1920*. New Brunswick: Rutgers University Press, 1986.

Buhle, Mari Jo, and Paul Buhle. *The Concise History of Woman Suffrage*. Urbana: University of Illinois Press, 1978.

Burnett, Constance. *Five for Freedom*. New York: Greenwood, 1968.

Burton, Warren. *The District School As It Was*. Boston: T. R. Marvin, 1852.

Carnegie, Andrew. *The Gospel of Wealth*. London: C. F. Hagen, 1889.

Carroll, Berenice A., ed. *Liberating Women's History: Theoretical and Critical Essays*. Urbana: University of Illinois Press, 1976.

Carter, James G. *Letters on the Free Schools of New England*. Boston: Summings, Hilliard & Co., 1824.

Catt, Carrie Chapman, and Nettie Rogers Shuler. *Woman Suffrage and Politics: The Inner Story of the Suffrage Movement*. Seattle: University of Washington Press, 1926.

Cazden, Elizabeth. *Antoinette Brown Blackwell: A Biography*. Old Westbury, N.Y.: The Feminist Press, 1983.

Clark, Clifford Edward. *Henry Ward Beecher: Spokesman for a Middle Class America*. Urbana: University of Illinois Press, 1978.

Clarke, Mary Stetson. *Bloomers and Ballots: Elizabeth Cady Stanton and Woman's Rights*. New York: Viking, 1972.

———, ed. *Women's Rights in the United States*. New York: Grossman, 1974.

Clifford, Deborah Pickman. *Mine Eyes Have Seen the Glory: A Biography of Julia Ward Howe.* Boston: Little, Brown, 1979.

Colley, Winifred. *The New Womanhood.* New York: Broadway Publishing, 1904.

Conkin, Paul. *Prophets of Prosperity: America's First Political Economists.* Bloomington: Indiana University Press, 1980.

Conrad, Susan Phinney. *Perish the Thought: Intellectual Women in Romantic America.* New York: Oxford University Press, 1976.

Cott, Nancy. *The Bonds of Womanhood.* New Haven: Yale University Press, 1977.

————. *A Heritage of Her Own.* New York: Simon and Schuster, 1979.

————. *Root of Bitterness.* Boston: Northeastern University Press, 1986.

Crawford, Mary Caroline. *Romantic Days in Old Boston: The Story of the City and of Its People During the Nineteenth Century.* Boston: Little, Brown, 1910.

Croly, Jane. *The History of the Woman's Club Movement in America.* New York: Henry Allen, 1898.

Cromwell, Otelia. *Lucretia Mott.* New York: Russell & Russell, 1971.

Dall, Caroline Wells. *The College, The Market, and The Court, Or Woman's Relation to Education, Labor and Law.* New York: Arno, 1972. (Reprint of 1867 edition.)

Davis, Pauline Wright. *A History of the National Woman's Rights Movement for Twenty Years.* New York: Journeymen's Printer's Cooperative Association, 1971.

Degler, Carl N. *At Odds: Women and the Family in America from the Revolution to the Present.* New York: Oxford University Press, 1980.

DePauw, Linda Grant, with Conover Hunt and Miriam Schnier. *Remember the Ladies: Women in America, 1750–1815.* New York: Viking, 1976.

Doctor Youman's Illustrated Marriage Guide and Confidential Medical Adviser: A Practical Treatise on the Uses and Abuses of the Generative Functions. Williamsburgh, N.Y.: J. Fletcher & Co., 1876.

Dorr, Rheta. *Susan B. Anthony, the Woman Who Changed the Mind of a Nation.* New York: AMS Press, 1970.

Douglas, Ann. *The Feminization of American Culture.* New York: Knopf, 1977.

Dublin, Thomas. *Women at Work: The Transformation of Work and Community in Lowell, Massachusetts, 1826–1860.* New York: Columbia University Press, 1979.

DuBois, Ellen Carol. *Feminism and Suffrage: The Emergence of an Independent Woman's Movement in America, 1848–1869.* Ithaca: Cornell University Press, 1978.

————, ed. *Elizabeth Cady Stanton, Susan B. Anthony: Correspondence, Writings, Speeches.* New York: Schocken Books, 1981.

————. "Outgrowing the Compact of the Fathers: Equal Rights, Woman Suffrage, and the United States Constitution, 1820–1878," *Journal of American History* 74(December 1987):836–862.

Eagle, Mary K., ed. *The Congress of Women.* New York: Arno, 1974. (Reprint of 1893 edition.)

Earle, Alice Morse. *Child Life in Colonial Days.* Detroit: Gale Research Company, 1982. (Reprint of 1899 edition.)

Elsmere, Jane Shaffer. *Henry Ward Beecher.* Indianapolis: Indiana Historical Society, 1973.

Eminent Women of the Age. Hartford: S. M. Betts & Co., 1868.

Epstein, Barbara L. *The Politics of Domesticity: Women, Evangelism, and Temperance in Nineteenth Century America.* Middletown, Conn.: Wesleyan University Press, 1981.

Faber, Doris. *Petticoat Politics: How American Women Won the Right to Vote.* New York: Lothrop, Lee and Shephard, 1967.

Farmer, Lydia. *What America Owes to Women.* Chicago: C. W. Moulton, 1893.

Fennelly, Catherine. *Town Schooling in Early New England: 1790–1840.* Old Sturbridge Village Booklet Series. Meriden, Conn.: Meriden Gravure Co., 1962.

Fishlow, Albert. *American Railroads and the Transformation of the Ante-Bellum Economy.* Cambridge: Harvard University Press, 1965.

Fletcher, Robert Samuel. *A History of Oberlin College.* 2 vols. Chicago: R. R. Donnelly & Sons, 1943.

Flexner, Eleanor. *Century of Struggle: The Woman's Rights Movement in the United States.* Cambridge, Mass.: Harvard University Press, 1959; revised 1979.

Foner, Phillip, ed. *Frederick Douglass on Women's Rights*. Westport, Conn.: Greenwood Press, 1976.

Foulke, William Dudley. *A Hoosier Autobiography*. New York: Oxford University Press, 1922.

Friedman, Lawrence J. *Gregarious Saints: Self and Community in American Abolitionism, 1830–1870*. Cambridge: Cambridge University Press, 1982.

Fuller, Paul. *Laura Clay and the Woman's Rights Movement*. Lexington: University Press of Kentucky, 1975.

Garrison, William Lloyd. *Letters*. 6 vols., ed. by Walter Merrill. Cambridge: Belknap Press of Harvard, 1971–1981.

Gay, Peter. *The Bourgeois Experience: Victoria to Freud. Vol. II: The Tender Passion*. New York: Oxford University Press, 1986.

Gillette, William. *The Right to Vote: Politics and the Passage of the Fifteenth Amendment*. Baltimore: Johns Hopkins University Press, 1965.

––––––. *Retreat from Reconstruction 1869–1879*. Baton Rouge: Louisiana State University Press, 1979.

Ginzberg, Lori D. *Women and the Work of Benevolence: Morality, Politics, and Class in the Nineteenth-Century United States*. New Haven: Yale University Press, 1990.

––––––. "Women in an Evangelical Community: Oberlin 1835–1850," *Ohio History* 89(Winter 1980):78–88.

Gordon, Ann D., and Mari Jo Buhle. "Sex and Class in Colonial and Nineteenth Century America," *Liberating Women's History*, ed. Berenice Carroll. Urbana: University of Illinois Press, 1976.

Gordon, Linda. "Voluntary Motherhood: The Beginnings of Feminist Birth Control Ideas in the United States," *Feminist Studies* 1(Winter–Spring 1973):5–22.

––––––. *Woman's Body, Woman's Right*. New York: Grossman Publishers, 1976.

Graham, Abbie. *Ladies in Revolt*. New York: The Womans Press, 1934.

Green, Elizabeth Alden. *Mary Lyon and Mount Holyoke: Opening the Gates*. Hanover, N.H.: University Press of New England, 1979.

Greven, Philip J., Jr. *Four Generations: Population, Land and Family in Colonial Andover, Massachusetts*. Ithaca: Cornell University Press, 1970.

Griffith, Elisabeth. *In Her Own Right: The Life of Elizabeth Cady Stanton*. New York: Oxford University Press, 1984.

Grimes, Alan P. *The Puritan Ethic and Woman Suffrage*. New York: Oxford University Press, 1967.

Grimké, Sarah Moore. *Letters on the Equality of the Sexes and the Condition of Woman*. Boston: I. Knapp, 1838.

Gutman, Herbert. *Work, Culture, and Society in Industrializing America*. New York: Knopf, 1976.

Hall, Florence Howe, ed. *Julia Ward Howe and the Woman Suffrage Movement*. New York: Arno, 1969.

Hall, Peter Dobkin. *The Organization of American Culture, 1700–1900*. New York: New York University Press, 1982.

Hanaford, Phebe. *Daughters of America*. Boston: B. B. Russell, 1883.

Harper, Ida Husted. *A Brief History of the Movement for Woman Suffrage in the United States*. New York: National Woman Suffrage Publishing Co., 1919.

––––––. *Life and Work of Susan B. Anthony*. 3 vols. New York: Arno, 1969.

Hays, Elinor Rice. *Those Extraordinary Blackwells: The Story of a Journey to a Better World*. New York: Harcourt, Brace, 1967.

––––––. *Morning Star: A Biography of Lucy Stone, 1818–1893*. New York: Harcourt, Brace & World, 1961.

Heath, Effie Margaret. *The Story of Lucy Stone: Pioneer*. London: Allenson & Co., 1935.

Hersh, Blanche Gassman. *The Slavery of Sex: Feminist Abolitionists in America*. Urbana: University of Illinois Press, 1978.

Hewitt, Nancy. *Woman's Activism and Social Change: Rochester, New York, 1822–1872*. Ithaca: Cornell University Press, 1984.

Hibben, Paxton. *Henry Ward Beecher: An American Portrait*. New York: Readers' Club Press, 1942.

Higginson, Thomas Wentworth. *American Orators and Oratory*. Cleveland: Imperial Press, 1901.

————. *Cheerful Yesterdays.* New York: Arno, 1968. Reprint of 1899 edition.

————, ed. *Woman's Almanac for 1858.* Worcester, Mass.: Z. Baker, 1858.

————. *Letters and Journals of Thomas Wentworth Higginson, 1846–1906.* Boston: Houghton Mifflin, 1921.

Hill, Mary A. *Charlotte Perkins Gilman: The Making of a Radical Feminist 1860–1896.* Philadelphia: Temple University Press, 1980.

History of Worcester County, Massachusetts, Embracing A Comprehensive History of the County From Its First Settlement to the Present Time. Boston: C. F. Jewett, 1879.

Horn, Margo. "Family Ties: The Blackwells, A Study in the Dynamics of Family Life in Nineteenth-Century America." Ph.D. dissertation, Tufts University, 1980.

Hosford, Frances Juliette. *Father Shipherd's Magna Charta: A Century of Coeducation in Oberlin College.* Boston: Marshall Jones Company, 1937.

Howe, Julia Ward. *Reminiscences 1819–1899.* New York: Negro Universities Press, 1969.

Hutchinson, John Wallace. *Story of the Hutchinsons.* New York: Da Capo Press, 1977.

Hyman, Harold Melvin, ed. *The Radical Republicans and Reconstruction, 1861–1870.* Indianapolis: Bobbs-Merrill, 1967.

Irwin, Inez Hayes. *Angels and Amazons.* New York: Arno, 1974.

Kaestle, Carl F. *Pillars of the Republic: Common Schools and American Society, 1780–1860.* New York: Hill and Wang, 1983.

Kelley, Mary. *Private Woman, Public Stage: Literary Domesticity in Nineteenth Century America.* New York: Oxford University Press, 1984.

Kenneally, James J. "Catholicism and Woman Suffrage," *Catholic Historical Review* 53(April 1967):43–57.

————. "Women and the Trade Unions, 1870–1920: The Quandary of the Reformer," *Labor History* 14(1973):42–55.

Kennedy, David M. *Birth Control in America.* New Haven: Yale University Press, 1970.

Kerber, Linda K. *Women of the Republic: Intellect and Ideology in Revolutionary America.* Chapel Hill: University of North Carolina Press, 1980.

Kerber, Linda K., and Jane DeHart Mathews, eds. *Women's America: Refocusing the Past.* Rev. ed. New York: Oxford University Press, 1987.

Kessler-Harris, Alice. *Out to Work: A History of Wage-Earning Women in the United States.* New York: Oxford University Press, 1982.

Kingsbury, George W. *History of Dakota Territory.* Chicago: S. J. Clarke, 1915.

Kisner, Arlene, ed. *Woodhull & Claflin's Weekly: The Lives and Writings of Notorious Victoria Woodhull and Her Sister Tennessee Claflin.* Washington, N.J.: Time Change Press, 1972.

Kraditor, Aileen. *The Ideas of the Woman Suffrage Movement, 1890–1920.* New York: W. W. Norton, 1981.

————. *Means and Ends in American Abolitionism: Garrison and His Critics on Strategy and Tactics, 1834–1850.* New York: Pantheon Books, 1969.

Kugler, Israel. *From Ladies to Women: The Organized Struggle for Woman's Rights in the Reconstruction Era.* New York: Greenwood Press, 1987.

Langford, Laura. *The Woman's Story, As Told By Twenty American Women.* New York: J. B. Alden, 1889.

Lasser, Carol, and Marlene Merrill, eds. *Friends and Sisters: Letters Between Lucy Stone and Antoinette Brown Blackwell, 1846–1893.* Urbana: University of Illinois Press, 1987.

Lerner, Gerda. *The Creation of Patriarchy.* New York: Oxford University Press, 1986.

————. *The Grimké Sisters From South Carolina.* Boston: Houghton Mifflin, 1967.

————. *The Majority Finds Its Past.* New York: Oxford University Press, 1979.

————. *Women and History.* New York: Oxford University Press, 1986.

Lewis, Helen Matthews. *The Woman Movement and the Negro Movement—Parallel Struggles for Rights.* Charlottesville: University of Virginia Press, 1949.

Livermore, Mary A. "Cooperative Womanhood in the State," *North American Review* (September 1891):283–295.

Lutz, Alma. *Created Equal.* New York: Octagon Books, 1974.

Main, Jackson Turner. *The Social Structure of Revolutionary America*. Princeton: Princeton University Press, 1965.

Marbury, M. Marion. *Vicky: A Biography of Victoria Woodhull*. New York: Funk and Wagnalls, 1967.

Martin, Theodora Penny. *The Sound of Our Own Voices: Women's Study Clubs, 1860–1910*. Boston: Beacon Press, 1987.

Martineau, Harriet. *Society in America*. 3 vols. London: Saunders and Otley, 1837.

McKenna, Jeanne. "With the Help of God and Lucy Stone," *Kansas Historical Quarterly* 36(Spring 1970):13–26.

McNall, Sally Allen. *Who Is In the House? A Psychological Study of Two Centuries of Women's Fiction in America, 1795 to the Present*. New York: Elsevier, 1981.

McPherson, James. "Abolitionism, Woman Suffrage, and the Negro, 1865–1869," *Mid America* (January 1965):40–47.

Melder, Keith. *Beginnings of Sisterhood: The American Woman's Rights Movement 1800–1850*. New York: Schocken Books, 1977.

Merk, Lois Bannister. "Massachusetts and the Woman Suffrage Movement." Ph.D. dissertation, Harvard University, 1961.

Merrill, Marlene Deahl. *Growing Up in Boston's Gilded Age*. New Haven: Yale University Press, 1990.

Meyer, Annie Nathan. *Woman's Work in America*. New York: Arno, 1972. (Reprint of 1891 edition.)

Minot, George Richards. *The History of the Insurrections in Massachusetts in 1786 and of the Rebellion Consequent Thereon*. New York: Da Capo, 1971. (An unabridged reprint of the first edition published in Worcester, Massachusetts, in 1788.)

Mitchell, Juliet, and Ann Oakley, eds. *The Rights and Wrongs of Women*. Hamondsworth, N.Y.: Penguin, 1976.

Modelski, Andrew. *Railroad Maps of America: The First Hundred Years*. Washington, D.C.: Library of Congress, 1984.

Montgomery, David. *Beyond Equality: Labor and the Radical Republicans, 1862–1872*. Urbana: University of Illinois Press, 1981.

Morgan, David. *Suffragists and Democrats: The Politics of Woman Suffrage in America*. East Lansing: Michigan State University Press, 1972.

Morison, Samuel Eliot, with Henry Steele Commager and William E. Leuchtenburg. *The Growth of the American Republic*. 7th ed. 2 vols. New York: Oxford University Press, 1980.

Morris, Celia. *Fanny Wright: Rebel in America*. Cambridge, Mass.: Harvard University Press, 1984.

Mott, Frank Luther. *American Journalism*. Rev. ed. New York: Macmillan, 1950.

Nash, Gary B. *Race, Class, and Politics: Essays on American Colonial and Revolutionary Society*. Urbana: University of Illinois Press, 1986.

Nevins, Allan, ed. *American Social History As Recorded by British Travellers*. New York: Henry Holt & Co., 1923.

Nichols, Carole. *Votes and More For Women: Suffrage and After in Connecticut*. New York: Institute for Research in History. Haworth Press, 1983.

Norton, Mary Beth. *Liberty's Daughters: The Revolutionay Experience of American Women, 1750–1800*. Boston: Little Brown, 1980.

Noun, Louise R. *Strong-Minded Women: The Emergence of the Woman-Suffrage Movement in Iowa*. Iowa Heritage Collection Edition. Ames: Iowa State University Press, 1986.

Nutt, Charles. *History of Worcester and Its People*. New York: Lewis Historical Publishing Co., 1919.

Nye, Russell Blaine. *Society and Culture in America: 1830–1860*. New York: Harper & Row, 1974.

O'Connor, Lillian. *Pioneer Woman Orators: Rhetoric in the Ante-Bellum Movement*. New York: Vantage Press, 1952.

Oliver, Robert T. *History of Public Speaking in America*. Boston: Allyn & Bacon, 1965.

O'Neill, William L. *Everyone Was Brave: A History of Feminism in America*. Chicago: Quadrangle Books, 1969.

Ostrogorski, Moisei. *The Rights of Women: A Comparative Study in History and Legislation*. Philadelphia: Porcupine Press, 1980. (Reprint of the 1893 edition.)

Park, Maud Wood. *Lucy Stone: A Chronical Play.* Boston: Walter Baker Co., 1938.

Parton, James. *The Life of Horace Greeley.* New York: Arno, 1970.

Peck, Mary Gray. *Carrie Chapman Catt.* New York: H. W. Wilson, 1944.

Pivar, David J. *Purity Crusade: Sexual Morality and Social Control, 1868–1900.* Westport, Conn.: Greenwood Press, 1973.

Porter, Kirk. *A History of Suffrage in the United States.* New York: Greenwood Press, 1969.

Riegel, Robert. *American Feminists.* Lawrence: University of Kansas Press, 1963.

Risjord, Norman K. *A History of the United States.* Englewood Cliffs, N.J.: Prentice-Hall, 1985.

Robinson, Harriet Jane. *Massachusetts in the Woman Suffrage Movement.* Boston: Roberts Bros., 1881; rev. 1883.

Roche, Regina. *The Children of the Abbey: A Tale.* Dublin: P. Wogan, 1809.

Rosenberg, Rosalind. *Beyond Separate Spheres: The Intellectual Roots of Modern Feminism.* New Haven: Yale University Press, 1984.

————. "In Search of Women's Nature, 1850–1920," *Feminist Studies* 3(Fall 1975):141–154.

Ryan, Mary P. *Womanhood in America.* New York: New Viewpoints, 1975.

Schwartz, Harold. *Samuel Gridley Howe, Social Reformer, 1801–1876.* Cambridge: Harvard University Press, 1956.

Scott, Anne Firor. *Making the Invisible Woman Visible.* Urbana: University of Illinois Press, 1984.

Scott, Anne Firor, and Andrew M. Scott. *One Half the People.* Philadelphia: Lippincott, 1975.

Seitz, Don Carlos. *The Dreadful Decade.* New York: Greenwood Press, 1968.

————. *Horace Greeley, Founder of the New York Tribune.* Indianapolis: Bobbs-Merrill, 1926.

————. *Uncommon Americans: Pencil Portraits of Men and Women Who Have Broken the Rules.* Indianapolis: Bobbs-Merrill, 1926.

Severance, Caroline M. *The Mother of Clubs,* ed. Ella Giles Ruddy. Los Angeles: Baumgardt Publishing, 1906.

Shaplen, Robert. *Free Love and Heavenly Sinners: The Story of the Great Henry Ward Beecher Scandal.* New York: Knopf, 1954.

Sinclair, Andrew. *The Better Half: the Emancipation of the American Woman.* Westport, Conn.: Greenwood Press, 1981.

Sklar, Kathryn Kish. *Catharine Beecher.* New Haven: Yale University Press, 1973.

Smith, Daniel S. "Family Limitation, Sexual Control, and Domestic Feminism in Victorian America," *A Heritage of Her Own,* ed. Nancy Cott and Elizabeth Pleck. New York: Simon and Schuster, 1979.

Smith, Helen Krebs. *The Presumptuous Dreamers: a Sociological History of the Life and Times of Abigail Scott Duniway, 1834–1915.* Lake Oswego, Oreg.: Smith, Smith and Smith, 1974.

Smith, Julia E. *Abby Smith and Her Cows.* New York: Arno, 1972.

Smith, Wilda M. "A Half Century of Struggle: Gaining Woman Suffrage in Kansas," *Kansas History* 4(Summer 1981):74–95.

Smith-Rosenberg, Carroll. "The Hysterical Woman: Sex Roles and Role Conflict in 19th Century America," *Social Research* 39 (Winter 1976):652–678.

————. "The Female World of Love and Ritual: Relations Between Women in Nineteenth Century America," *Signs* 1(1975):1–29.

Sochen, June. *The New Woman: Feminism in Greenwich Village, 1910–1920.* New York: Quadrangle Books, 1972.

Spender, Dale, ed. *Feminist Theorists: Three Centuries of Key Women Thinkers.* New York: Pantheon Books, 1983.

Sprague, Henry H. *Women Under the Law of Massachusetts: Their Rights, Privileges, and Disabilities.* 2nd ed. Boston: Little Brown, 1903.

Sproat, John G. *The Best Men: Liberal Reformers in the Gilded Age.* New York: Oxford University Press, 1968.

Squire, Belle. *The Woman Movement in America.* Chicago: A. C. McClurg, 1911.

Stampp, Kenneth M. *The Era of Reconstruction, 1865–1877.* New York: Knopf, 1965.

————. *America in 1857: A Nation on the Brink.* New York: Oxford University Press, 1990.

Stannard, Una. *Mrs. Man.* San Francisco: Germainbooks, 1977.

Stanton, Elizabeth Cady. *Address of Elizabeth Cady Stanton on the Divorce Bill*. Albany: Weed, Parsons and Co., 1861.

————. *Eighty Years and More*. New York: European Publishing Co., 1898.

Stanton, Elizabeth Cady, with Susan B. Anthony, Matilda Joslyn Gage, Ida Husted Harper, and others. *History of Woman Suffrage*. 6 vols. New York: Fowler and Wells, 1881–1922.

Stein, Leon, ed. *Fragments of Autobiography*. New York: Arno, 1974. A reprint of autobiographical pieces by women published between 1832 and 1938.

Stewart, James Brewer. *Holy Warriors: The Abolitionists and American Slavery*. New York: Hill & Wang, 1976.

Stuart, Granville. *Forty Years on the Frontier As Seen in the Journals and Reminiscences of Granville Stuart*. Cleveland, Ohio: Arthur Clark Co., 1925.

Suhl, Yuri. *Eloquent Crusader: Ernestine Rose*. New York: Julian Messner, 1970.

Swisshelm, Jane Grey. *Half a Century*. Chicago: Jansen, McClure and Company, 1880.

Szatmary, David P. *Shays' Rebellion: The Making of an Agrarian Insurrection*. Amherst: University of Massachusetts Press, 1980.

Temple, Josiah Howard. *History of North Brookfield, Massachusetts*. Boston: Rand, Avery, 1887.

Thornton, Willis. *The Nine Lives of Citizen Train*. New York: Greenberg, 1948.

Train, George Francis. *The Great Epigram Campaign of Kansas*. Leavenworth: Prescott and Hume, 1867.

————. *My Life in Many States and in Foreign Lands, Dictated in My Seventy-Fourth Year*. New York: D. Appleton, 1902.

————. *Union Speeches Delivered in England During the Present American War*. Philadelphia: T. B. Peterson & Bros., 1862.

Tyler, Alice Felt. *Freedom's Ferment: Phases of American Social History to 1860*. Freeport, N.Y.: Books for Libraries Press, 1970.

Wagner, Sally Roesch. *A Time of Protest: Suffragists Challenge the Republic, 1870–1887*. Sacramento: Spectrum Publications, 1987.

Waller, Altina. *Reverend Beecher and Mrs. Tilton: Sex and Class in Victorian America*. Amherst: University of Massachusetts Press, 1982.

Walters, Ronald G., ed. *American Reformers, 1815–1860*. New York: Hill & Wang, 1978.

Ward, Elizabeth Stuart Phelps. *Our Famous Women*. Hartford: A. D. Worthington, 1884.

Waterman, William Randall. *Frances Wright*. New York: AMS Press, 1967.

Welter, Barbara, ed. *The Woman Question in American History*. Hinsdale: Dryden Press, 1973.

Wheeler, Leslie. *Loving Warriors*. New York: Dial Press, 1981.

Wilder, Daniel Webster. *The Annals of Kansas*. Topeka: G. W. Martin, 1875.

Willard, Frances. *A Woman of the Century*. Buffalo: C. W. Moulton, 1893.

Williams, Wellington. *Appleton's Northern and Eastern Traveller's Guide*. New York: D. Appleton, 1850.

Wilson, Don W. *Governor Charles Robinson of Kansas*. Lawrence: University of Kansas Press, 1975.

Wood, Margaret L. *Memorial of Samuel N. Wood*. Kansas: Hudson-Kimberly Publishing, 1892.

Wright, Henry Clarke. *Marriage and Parentage: Or, The Reproductive Element in Man, As A Means to His Elevation and Happiness*. Boston: Bela Marsh, 1855.

Yellin, Jean Fagan. *Women & Sisters: The Antislavery Feminists in American Culture*. New Haven: Yale University Press, 1989.

Index